5/2015

D0824727

Mathematics in Middle and Secondary School

A Problem Solving Approach

Mathematics in Middle and Secondary School

A Problem Solving Approach

Alexander Karp
Teachers College, Columbia University

Nicholas Wasserman
Teachers College, Columbia University

INFORMATION AGE PUBLISHING, INC.
Charlotte, NC • www.infoagepub.com

Library of Congress Cataloging-in-Publication Data

A CIP record for this book is available from the Library of Congress
http://www.loc.gov

ISBN: 978-1-62396-812-0 (Paperback)
      978-1-62396-813-7 (Hardcover)
      978-1-62396-814-4 (ebook)

Printed in the United States of America

CONTENTS

PART IV   309

PART V   381

FOREWORD

Even in the late nineteenth century the great German mathematician and mathematics educator Felix Klein pointed out the rift between university study and the demands of school education, what he dubbed a *double discontinuity*. When university students learn something very different and disconnected from what is taught in schools, graduates who become teachers are puzzled by the fact that they have had to learn so many things that appear useless in the teaching of mathematics to schoolchildren. Novice teachers find it hard, without external help, to make the connection between what they have studied in mathematics and what they are told in pedagogical courses. They struggle to overcome difficulties specific to mathematics education, failing to ensure, among other things, that the true spirit of mathematical investigation penetrates the study of even the most traditional topics of school mathematics.

Reflecting on teacher education, Lee Shulman came up with a useful concept he termed, "pedagogical content knowledge." By this he meant the knowledge of "the most useful [for purposes of teaching] forms of representation of those ideas, the most powerful analogies, illustrations, examples, explanations, and demonstrations—in a word, the ways of representing and formulating the subject that make it comprehensible to others" (Shulman, 1986, p. 9). Pedagogical content knowledge also implies the knowledge of what topics children find interesting, or difficult, as well as the knowledge of typical student misconceptions within a particular discipline.

Mathematics in Middle and Secondary School, pages ix–xii
Copyright © 2015 by Information Age Publishing
All rights of reproduction in any form reserved.

Today the importance of imparting "pedagogical content knowledge" to future teachers is widely recognized. Let us mention, for instance, the work of Deborah Ball and Hyman Bass in further conceptualizing pedagogical content knowledge and subject matter knowledge specific for mathematics teaching (i.e., the *Mathematical Knowledge for Teaching framework*, Ball, Thames, & Phelps, 2008); or Liping Ma's 1999 influential book, in which the profound importance of "studying teaching materials intensively," of gaining experience of working in school mathematics, and of searching for different ways of communicating a particular topic to students, is especially highlighted.

It seems in fact that one should perhaps be talking not only and not so much about pedagogical content *knowledge* but also about pedagogical content *skills*. Teachers should not just be familiar with a series of examples of representations and problems, but should also be able to tell which of these would be most effective in their own concrete lessons. They should not only know in principle what students might find difficult or interesting, but they should also be able to apply this knowledge in selecting the most appropriate student assignments. In a teacher, the purely mathematical knowledge and skills must be transformed into pedagogical mathematical skills. Teachers are not simply skilled in solving mathematical problems; they are also able to organize the solution of problems in class so that students can acquire these same skills themselves. Mathematical knowledge in its own right is not automatically transformed into the skill of understanding how students themselves reason and how this reasoning can be used in the organization of fruitful mathematical activity. The purpose of teacher education is to help in the acquisition of the necessary pedagogical content knowledge and skills.

Without foundation courses in mathematics and general pedagogy this cannot be achieved, but in our view, they alone are insufficient. It is not enough for the future teacher to master a dozen or so courses in mathematics and then a few more devoted to general issues of education. Equally, it is not enough to rely on a single, one-semester-long, course in methods of mathematics instruction. Such a course is essentially an introduction for future mathematics teachers to the specific demands of their profession and it merely suggests in a general way the overall framework within which they are expected to work. What is needed in addition to all this are special methods courses that would help teachers acquire pedagogical content knowledge and skills. It is for the sake, and on the basis, of this kind of course that this book has been written.

Such a course entails the active involvement of teacher learners in studying mathematics, but mathematics of a special kind and examined from a distinct vantage point. The aim of such a course is to show that even those parts of the school course that at first glance appear to be purely routine, can, in fact, be approached in an investigative way, transforming their assimilation by schoolchildren from meaningless rote learning to activities that demand exploration and creativity. Such a course must contain a very large number of examples that one can then use in one's own lessons. However, even more important, in our view, is for teacher learners to gain the experience of reflecting upon and independently searching for suitable classroom tasks and assignments themselves. In doing so, future teachers will learn how to structure *mathematical* material as a way of solving the *pedagogical* problems that they encounter.

For us, the most fundamental form of mathematical activity is *problem solving*. Following the National Council of Teachers of Mathematics we consider problem solving as a "major means of doing mathematics." Consequently, our key aims are: to introduce future teachers to contemporary research into problem solving and to familiarize them with a number of outstanding mathematical problems. Such problems can indeed be far harder than those that teachers will be able to give their students in regular lessons. Some of the problems examined in this book were set in mathematical Olympiads and other competitions of the highest level. Nevertheless, we believe that the experience of reflecting on such problems will be of great use to future teachers—not just because it will help them work with students who are especially interested in mathematics, but, more importantly, because it will make them realize the depth and richness of the regular school course by perceiving it as a field of true exploration.

In contemporary literature on mathematics education much attention is devoted to problem posing as *the* means of heightening the students' active participation and of engaging them in the process of mathematical creativity (see the works of John Mason and Anne Watson, and Lyn English, to mention just a few). We therefore find it very important to show future teachers how to pose and construct problems themselves; and to provide suggestions on how to design lessons on the basis of problem posing and problem solving. We also discuss in detail what aspects of mathematics seem to cause schoolchildren the greatest difficulties.

A substantial part of the book is devoted to lesson planning. We find it important not simply to give teachers a few models of well-designed lessons (or, indeed, some examples of poor lesson planning). It is vital to help novice teachers in the *independent* construction of lessons, showing them what sorts of issues need careful reflection, and thereby taking them through the entire process of lesson planning. Here, we rely on our extensive experience in running seminars for student teachers.

The book, as we envisage it, can be used in a variety of ways since pedagogical content knowledge and skills can be formed in studying a whole range of different courses. It can be used for the course in methods of teaching mathematics—targeting students who have already completed the first introductory course in teaching methods. In addition to this, specific use can be made of different parts of this book. Thus, the first part of the book is introductory and to a certain degree reiterates some of the main principles that are usually given in the first course in methods of mathematical instruction. This part of the book can therefore be used as supplemental material for such a course or can be recommended for independent revision at more advanced levels. The book can also serve as a textbook for a course in "Problem Solving," relying especially on Chapters 3–6 and on materials (above all the problems themselves) from the remaining chapters. A course "Teaching Algebra" can be based on Chapters 6–10, while a course "Teaching Geometry" can make good use of Chapters 6 and 11–12. In particular, the book should be of help as a manual in seminars for student teachers.

PART I

This part is introductory. Its purpose is to present key concepts that will be developed and discussed throughout the book. It also introduces commonly used terminology.

CHAPTER 1

CHAPTER 1

CHALLENGES AND ISSUES IN MATHEMATICS EDUCATION

The aim of the chapter is to introduce briefly the principal challenges that a novice teacher of mathematics faces in the classroom, and to outline the methods and principles recommended by the current science and practice of mathematics education.

The chapter discusses:

- The goals and objectives of teaching mathematics.
- The Principles and Standards for School Mathematics (PSSM), as outlined by the National Council of Teachers of Mathematics (NCTM).
- The Common Core Standards for Mathematical Practice (SMP).
- Lesson studies and their significance.
- Some characteristics of lessons and the learning process.
- The qualities that an effective teacher of mathematics needs to possess.

Mathematics in Middle and Secondary School, pages 3–28
Copyright © 2015 by Information Age Publishing

WHY TEACH MATHEMATICS?

A few years ago one of the authors had the opportunity to attend a very impressive conference on mathematics education. Interesting papers were presented; detailed statistics were cited; there were accounts of new experiments and observations. But the moment this author found the most interesting was actually during one of the presentations in which no new research data was being cited. Speaking on how teachers' educational goals—what they want to achieve with their students in teaching them mathematics—informs everything they do in their classrooms, the speaker turned to address the audience:

"Tell me, what do *you* want to achieve?"

There was a moment's silence. Then there came a flurry of replies:

"To prepare students for future employment."

"To enable them to do well in tests."

"To make them mathematically literate."

"To motivate them to study mathematics."

"To show them how to apply mathematics."

"To help them get into the university they want."

"To get them to understand the significance of mathematics."

"To help them get skilled work."

Many other objectives were cited. The speaker concluded by making the point that all those who had spoken probably tried to incorporate these distinct goals into their teaching. The speaker continued with the presentation, but the audience kept thinking about what we had heard from the author. What really is most important to impart to our students?

Few would argue against mathematics being a necessary part of one's education. The leading organization of the profession, the National Council of Teachers of Mathematics (NCTM), lists the following areas where mathematics is of use:

- Mathematics for life
- Mathematics as a part of cultural heritage
- Mathematics for the workplace
- Mathematics for the scientific and technical community (NCTM, 2000, p.4)

In practice, however, ideas that people have of mathematics and of why it should be taught vary considerably, even among those who have taught it for many years (Bishop et al., 2003; Cooney & Viegel, 2003). This is hardly surprising. People are different—they embrace different perspectives and their views are based on different experiences. Objectives themselves can always be approached from different standpoints. What teachers want their students to be able to do in twenty years time is one thing; what they want them to achieve during a semester is quite another. Many different objectives for mathematics instruction that the teachers cite are obviously important.

Two particular responses mentioned at the conference however are most critical for us to consider:

Enabling students to realize their potential

Ensuring students become intelligent citizens.

Helping Students Realize Their Potential

The artist and the natural scientist, the mathematician and the historian, the businessman and the actor each think in a particular way. The style of historical research would not be considered appropriate in mathematics, and an accountant analyses a situation differently from an actor. Each discipline has its own principles for inquiry, for determining how to incorporate new ideas and drop deficient ones. The role of the school is to help students discover different, meaningful ways of perceiving the world. Some of these ways will prove more congenial to them in their future schooling and careers, but they will be able to determine this only after they have gotten to know each of them properly. If an education system deprives students of an acquaintance with authentic mathematics, it runs the risk of driving away or completely preempting latent mathematical talent. In Mark Twain's story (1992) "Extract from Captain Stormfield's Visit to Heaven," the most talented general turns out to be a bricklayer from Boston who has never been in battle. His talent was of the highest order, but he had never had the opportunity to display it. Something similar also happens frequently in mathematics—who can calculate the number of potentially gifted mathematicians who never happened to meet the right teacher to help their talent manifest itself?

Even those whose gifts and inclinations turn out to lie in other areas will miss out if they never get a chance to experience proper mathematical reasoning. If deprived of this experience, young people are denied the ability to see and analyze many important aspects of life around them.

Mathematics for All

For centuries underprivileged groups were denied proper mathematical education. Social and economic factors, along with racial inequity, made (and in some cases still make) mathematics inaccessible to many students. Large parts of the population are thus deprived of career opportunities and are prevented from a rich understanding of the world around them. This should not be tolerated in a modern society. It is for this reason that the NCTM calls its first principle—

The equity principle: high expectations and strong support for all students (NCTM, 2000).

Helping the Student Become an Intelligent Citizen

Mathematics teaches rational analysis and provides an approach to decision-making —precisely that which intelligent citizens need. One can cite numerous examples of situations where mathematics is vital (*For All Practical Purposes*, 2001), and where mathematical methods and procedures have been developed for specific purposes. It is neither possible nor necessary to teach every possible strategy at school. But it is desirable to inculcate in students a readiness to use such methods; to reason systematically in a balanced and considered fashion, rather than judge things by approximation only, or blindly, in the heat of passion.

Setting Serious Goals for Yourself and Your Students

How is a particular goal in teaching mathematics to be achieved? This is a rather complicated question, and in some measure, this whole book is an attempt to answer it. The teachers' tools are their interest in the subject, their energy, and their teaching skills; however, there is no foolproof system. Even the best teachers do not always emerge victorious. It is still useful, however, for you to consider what you want to achieve. And wanting to achieve something concrete with your instruction—that is, setting serious goals for oneself and one's students—is the most important consideration of all.

A teacher who goes from one lesson to the next without giving the teaching process any real thought ("Why complicate things? Let's just follow the textbook"), or who merely goes through the motions and does not believe in any real possibility of success in working with the students, will hardly achieve anything.

On the other hand, a sincere desire to teach does not go unnoticed by students. Here is what one pre-service student wrote about the teacher she liked the best, in contrast to most of her other teachers, whose teaching she described with some disappointment:

> Why was she so special? I think that the main reason why she stands out is that I could really feel that she *truly cared* for me and for the rest of my class. If we were having difficulties with our subject matter, most teachers just let things be and didn't really make any effort to help us out—if we didn't get it, we had to learn to swim on our own. That was not true of her. Many of my classmates had problems with Math. She tapped into this by creating a "buddy system" where those who were doing well in math were paired off with those who were not. This gave us many valuable opportunities to learn from each other and communicate in a simple language that we both understood.

While this situation only describes one instructor and one instance, it indicates a more general idea: a teacher with clear goals and a flexible plan to implement them in classroom instruction produces engaged students who will set meaningful goals for themselves.

Math Myth. Beliefs about Mathematics

"My class is not at all interested in mathematics," is a common lament among teachers. It is not that such statements are completely unfounded. Much has been written about false ideas that students form of mathematics—the so-called "math myth" (Kogelman & Warren, 1978). Many students sincerely believe that mathematics is either for "supergeniuses" or "supernerds" (De Bruxelles, 2001; Leder et al., 2002). They easily find excuses for their own lack of desire to study mathematics by describing this as something characteristic of a larger group ("girls don't understand math", "math is only for someone whose parents finished college", etc.).

In addition to other cultural factors and social norms (e.g., mass media depictions of mathematics and mathematicians), mathematics instruction at school often supports such judgments, creating the notion of mathematics as a difficult, boring, and, most of all, completely meaningless subject. Schoenfeld (1987) wrote:

> I argue that, largely as a result of their instruction, many students develop some beliefs about "what mathematics is all about" that are just plain wrong—and that those beliefs have a very strong negative effect on the students' mathematical behavior (p. 195).

This does not mean that teachers should resign themselves to the fact that their class will have little interest in mathematics. The overall goals teachers set for themselves, which include student interest, must be embodied in a series of smaller, specific goals: the goals of a course, a unit, or an individual lesson. Formulating these goals and accomplishing them demands careful thought.

Reflection

Assignments and Topics for Discussion

1. Study the introductory chapter of PSSM "A Vision for School Mathematics." Give examples that support the conclusion of the NCTM on the role of mathematics in four areas.
2. Consider what goals of teaching mathematics are especially important to you and what you would like to achieve. (Give your answer both for the short term—a semester or a year—and for the long term.)
3. Analyze the activity of your own mathematics teachers in school. What do you think they wanted to achieve?
4. Schoenfeld (1987) cites the following example in support of his statement about "wrong beliefs" current among students. In the course of the NAEP secondary mathematics exam, 45,000 students were given this problem: "An army bus holds 36 soldiers. If 1128 soldiers are being bused to their training site, how many buses are needed?" 30% of those who answered were not able to divide correctly, 29% answered that the number of buses needed is "31 remainder 12", 18% gave the answer "31 buses", and only 23% gave the correct answer, "32 buses." Analyze these results. What sort of assumptions about the students' perception of mathematics could you make? What do you think it was in the teaching of mathematics that led to such results? What changes would you recommend?

WHAT IS MATHEMATICS?

Strangely enough, the answer to this question is far from simple. The Merriam-Webster Dictionary (2006) defines mathematics as "the science of numbers and their operations, interrelations, combinations, generalizations, and abstractions, and of space configurations and their structure, measurement, transformations, and generalizations." There is a famous statement simplifying the definition to the effect that "mathematics is the class of all propositions of the form 'p implies q'" (Russell, 1903). It is clear that the author of this statement was deliberately exaggerating the role of logic and minimizing everything else. Another, probably also not quite serious statement, attributed to Felix Klein, states that "mathematics in general is fundamentally the science of self-evident things" (Moritz, 1942). Courant and Robbins (1996) might propose the best approach in their famous book, *What is Mathematics?* Throughout the book, the authors simply do mathematics. This is probably the best means of understanding what mathematics is.

For students, mathematics is not an abstraction. It is what they *do*, based upon the instruction they receive. But what mathematics should be taught, and how? Debates about what sort of mathematics instruction is needed in school are never-ending. They are so heated at times that they have occasionally been referred to as "math wars." (Reys, 2001; Schoen et al., 1999). These disputes concern all aspects of the reform that needs to be undertaken in mathematics instruction, starting with the role of training in basic skills, and ending with the issue of what form mathematical language ought to take (Becker & Jacob, 2000; Schmidt, 1999; Wu, 1997). One hotly debated question is what specific areas of mathematics need to be taught.

Examples of Changes in Mathematics Curricula

At times one has the impression that the content of the school course in mathematics is quite stable; indeed, that mathematics itself is a static discipline. Parents often expect to see virtually the same mathematics in their children's textbooks that they learned in their own studies. In fact, in recent decades, mathematics textbook content has not undergone any great changes (changes in language, approach and style are another matter.) The mathematics course taught today has not always been the norm, however. In the Middle Ages, knowing a selection of excerpts from the first four (out of thirteen) books of Euclid was considered a profound understanding of the essence of geometry. High school students in the late nineteenth and early twentieth century, on the other hand, were taught a far greater number of proofs of geometrical theorems than present-day students (Donoghue, 2003). It is important to keep in mind that what is taught today might very well not be taught tomorrow.

Until fairly recently, courses in mathematics devoted considerable time to teaching students how to use the slide rule—the computational aid of which present-day students have only a very dim idea. At that time, it was thought that this was something universally useful. Nowadays, there are different means of performing these calculations: calculators, computers, and tablets for example. It may be that in thirty years' time, the use of the graphing calculator in schools will seem no less antiquated than the slide rule does today.

Mathematics evolves, as do schools and society as a whole. Mathematics courses and content will inevitably change. Recently, when speaking of applications of mathematics, one had in mind primarily differential equations. Today the role of discrete mathematics is no less important (Report on Applied Mathematics in the Undergraduate Curriculum, 1972). These changes are reflected in the school curriculum.

Changes in our understanding of mathematics and of how it should be taught at school are reflected in the national standards. So what exactly do national standards tell us about the content of the mathematics course?

The Content Standards of NCTM

The current contents of school courses can be described fairly well by the content standards of the National Council of Teachers of Mathematics (NCTM, 2000), a summary of which is presented in Table 1.1.

Each of these standards requires a more precise description (these standards will also be discussed in greater detail later). As emphasized above, the content of these areas will inevitably change, but the same desire that motivated Archimedes, as well as contemporary mathematicians—to understand what is not understood, to discover new patterns and establish new laws—will surely drive the mathematicians of the future as well. Doing mathematics is a journey into the unknown, a process of discovery and reasoning for which one needs to be armed with a certain set of skills. But the process of mastering these skills is itself part of mathematics. It is to be accomplished not by cramming and meaningless drilling exercises, but by reflection and thoughtful work.

The Process Standards of NCTM

Process is just as important as product in mathematics instruction, a point easily lost on teachers and students alike. It is for this reason that The Process Standards suggested by the NCTM (2000) are so important:

- Problem solving
- Reasoning and Proof
- Communication
- Connections
- Representation.

Students should understand mathematics not as an established and finite body of knowledge that merely remains to be learned, but as a discipline open to creativity and problem solving. Students should see investigation of conjectures through reasoning and proving as the major tools of building

TABLE 1.1

Number and Operations	Instructional programs from pre-kindergarten through grade 12 should enable all students to: • Understand numbers, ways of representing numbers, relationships among numbers, and number systems; • Understand meanings of operations and how they relate to one another; • Compute fluently and make reasonable estimates.
Algebra	Instructional programs from pre-kindergarten through grade 12 should enable all students to: • Understand patterns, relationships, and functions; • Represent and analyze mathematical situations and structures using algebraic symbols; • Use mathematical models to represent and understand quantitative relationships; • Analyze change in various contexts.
Geometry	Instructional programs from pre-kindergarten through grade 12 should enable all students to: • Analyze characteristics and properties of two- and three-dimensional geometric shapes and develop mathematical arguments about geometric relationships; • Specify locations and describe spatial relationships using coordinate geometry and other representational systems; • Apply transformations and use symmetry to analyze mathematical situations; • Use visualization, spatial reasoning, and geometric modeling to solve problems
Measurement	Instructional programs from pre-kindergarten through grade 12 should enable all students to: • Understand measurable attributes of objects and the units, systems, and processes of measurement; • Apply appropriate techniques, tools, and formulas to describe measurements.
Data Analysis and Probability	Instructional programs from pre-kindergarten through grade 12 should enable all students to: • Formulate questions that can be addressed with data and collect, organize, and display relevant data to answer them; • Select and use appropriate statistical methods to analyze data; • Develop and evaluate inferences and predictions that are based on data; • Understand and apply basic concepts of probability.

mathematical knowledge. Students should see mathematics as useful to everyone, and its separate areas as not isolated from the rest, but as interconnected by hundreds of threads. Students should learn to formulate their thoughts using different mathematical representations (words, formulas, graphs, etc), to communicate their thoughts and knowledge with those around them and to understand in turn what others are saying.

Mathematics will hardly be understood any differently 100 years from now, and the above process standards will hardly become outmoded in 100 years, even if the content of classroom instruction changes. However, this should not be taken to mean that content is unimportant. To successfully instill the process standards there must be some content used to practice them. One does not solve problems in general—problems are always about something in particular. Teachers who do not see to it that their students master the relevant content in algebra, for example will not be able to teach them reasoning or communication in a general way either. Problem solving does not have to be organized solely around special problems devised for "problem solving" itself. It is the task of the teacher to know how to organize genuine mathematical activity around even the most ordinary school material.

| Examining |
| *an* Example |

Example of Classroom Practice

A student in Ms. Rodrigues' class added two fractions in the following way:

$$\frac{1}{2}+\frac{2}{3}=\frac{1+2}{2\cdot3}=\frac{3}{6}=\frac{1}{2}.$$

Instead of telling the student outright that the answer was wrong, Ms. Rodrigues gave him two further assignments. Firstly, she asked the student to check and see if his answer was plausible insofar as the first fraction did not appear to change by the addition of the second. She then gave him the sum

$$\frac{2}{4}+\frac{2}{3}$$

(in other words, the same sum as above only written down differently). By completing these two assignments the student was persuaded that he had added the fractions incorrectly. Ms. Rodrigues then proposed to the class to give a few more examples where such a "sum" of two fractions would be equal to one of them. By studying different examples the students did not only realize the erroneousness of the above algorithm and did not just practice working with numbers, but they were also taught a lesson in how to reason by checking their own work and results.

Common Core Standards for Mathematical Practice

Mathematics educators frequently have expressed concerns about the depth and quality of mathematics learning in the American educational system over the years. The National Council for Teachers of Mathematics, including the NCTM Process Standards and other documents, has greatly influenced the direction of mathematics education in response to these various concerns. Another recent, and important, step has been adoption of the Common Core State Standards in Mathematics (CCSS-M, 2010). Importantly, the standards include not only grade-level content standards, but also Standards for Mathematical Practice (SMPs). These eight practices, related to the NCTM Process Standards, were intended to help standardize and quantify some of the important desired processes and proficiencies in mathematics education:

- Make sense of problems and persevere in solving them
- Reason abstractly and quantitatively
- Construct viable arguments and critique the reasoning of others
- Model with mathematics
- Use appropriate tools strategically
- Attend to precision
- Look for and make use of structure
- Look for and express regularity in repeated reasoning

The primarily goal of both the Process Standards and the SMPs is to help specify some of the important ways and characteristics with which students should be engaging in mathematics—so that the *doing* of mathematics in education is aligned with what mathematics as a discipline is all about.

Reflection
Assignments and Topics for Discussion

1. Study Chapter 3 of the PSSM Standards for School Mathematics: Prekindergarten through Grade 12.
2. Read the descriptions and examples of NCTM's Process Standards and the Common Core SMPs. Compare and contrast the two.
3. Analyze an article on the reform of mathematical education from the website http://mathematicallysane.com. What is your position on the questions discussed here?
4. In old school textbooks when transforming trigonometric expressions one was usually required to give the answer in the form of a product (this was called reducing to a form convenient for taking the logarithm). Explain the reason for such a requirement, and why today it is outdated.
5. Imagine that a research mathematician were to criticize the formulation of the "Measurement" content standard, saying that mathematics is not concerned with measurement: the derivation of the formula for the volume of a sphere is not measurement. Would you agree with this criticism? Justify your position.

6. Analyze an old mathematics textbook (e.g., from the 1950s). Name some areas or problems that nowadays appear outdated.
7. Give examples showing that the topic of "quadratic equations" is related to geometry, physics, and problems of the real world. Choose any topic of a school mathematics course and show its connections with other areas of mathematics, or other fields of knowledge.
8. Give examples of various representations that can be used in the study of: a) multiplication of numbers, b) functions, and c) ratios between quantities.

THE NCTM PRINCIPLES

In addition to the Equity Principle the National Council of Teachers of Mathematics (2000) developed five other fundamental principles:

- The Curriculum Principle
- The Teaching Principle
- The Learning Principle
- The Assessment Principle
- The Technology Principle (pp. 14–27)

All of these principles are united by the effort to see mathematical education as a unified, coherent, and meaningful instructional process. A process based on general ideas whose development is aided by each lesson and in which students develop and enrich their understanding of mathematics. In order better to understand these principles it is important first to discuss existing concerns about American mathematics education.

Concerns about American Education

American education has long suffered the reproach of being "a mile wide and an inch deep." Although it is possible to name many teachers and courses that do not at all fit this description, there is clearly some basis for such a judgment. There are also grounds for concern about the coherence of the educational process.

The everyday incoherence of teaching became especially noticeable to many after the appearance of the videotape studies carried out during the Third International Mathematics and Science Study (TIMSS) (Clarke, 2003b). The main part of this study concerned the testing of students that was conducted in a number of countries (and subsequently repeated). As in a sports competition, a hierarchical list of participating countries was compiled based on student results in these tests, beginning with those countries whose students showed the best results and ending with those whose indicators came out lowest. The results for the United States were not comforting—eighth graders from the United States took 28th place in 1995 and 19th place in 1999. The TIMSS results naturally provoked concern among politicians and in society at large, as well as wide discussion (Baker, 1997; Gough, P. B, 1997; Keitel & Kilpatrick, 1999; Schmidt et al., 1997). However, no less important were studies that accompanied the testing itself. One of these studies involved the videotaping of lessons in different countries (Stiegler et al., 1999).

The researchers (Stigler & Hiebert, 1999), along with thousands of mathematics educators who watched the video recording of lessons in the eighth grade, as they were taught in several different countries, saw radically contrasting pictures in the US and Japan. The Japanese lessons focused around one single key idea, which was developed using different examples and a variety of methods. By contrast, the American teachers tried to develop several fairly unrelated ideas within a single lesson, and usually failed to do it properly as there was obviously insufficient time to cover all of them.

The Disconnectedness in Lessons

The unfortunate thing here is that it is not just a matter of disconnectedness within the lessons. Units contain lessons that clearly do not belong together, and the entire curriculum often reminds one of a song in which, after the first verse, the singers break off and begin to sing another song, then finish the last verse of the first song, then once more repeat what they have already sung, etc. Researchers (Yoshida et al., 1993) have shown that students understand and master the material better when it is presented to them in a coherent way. In such a presentation mathematical ideas become more visible, and the student's attention is not distracted by extraneous details. Sleep (2012), for example, characterizes this as "teaching to the mathematical point." Moreover, doing mathematics is a process of deep and focused investigation, and not a summary of one set of results followed by an immediate jump to some other, just as poorly substantiated set of results. The teacher who "skips" from one topic to the next cannot establish in any sensible way what students have really assimilated and cannot correctly plan what to do next.

A Call for Change

Finding support in numerous pieces of research, the NCTM announced the need for a change of approach to mathematics teaching in the United

States. The NCTM Principles are precisely a concentrated expression of the proposed new methods.

The Curriculum Principle

The Curriculum Principle says that "curriculum is more than a collection of activities: it must be coherent, focused on important mathematics, and well articulated across the grades. (NCTM, 2000, p. 14) This is a difficult task. It is not always easy to determine what "important mathematics" is—in other words, what parts of mathematics will be useful in the future and would therefore be relevant to the development of the schoolchild of today—and it is even harder to inculcate it in school practice. The task of combating the habitual incoherence of mathematics education referred to above is equally difficult, but essential if one wants to improve mathematics education.

The Teaching Principle

The Teaching Principle calls on teachers to understand what students already know and what they should know. In accordance with this principle, teachers should challenge and support students, determining precisely what each is capable of and what sort of tasks can be proposed to facilitate their further development. Clearly, in order to be able to do this, teachers must be armed with an understanding of the students' psychological peculiarities, with the mastery of a variety of educational strategies, and with deep knowledge of mathematics at a high level.

The Learning Principle

The Learning Principle requires that instruction be set up in such a way that students "learn mathematics with understanding, actively building new knowledge from experience and prior knowledge." (p. 20). This principle contrasts mathematical study with understanding to mathematical study given to rote learning and procedural automatism.

In other words, people are expected to produce what is truly human— thought and understanding, while computers are supposed to do what is automatic. This does not mean that people, and students in particular, should not possess procedural fluency; indeed, this is something often gained in the course of trying to understand the mathematical material studied. The NCTM also encourages the recognition of the fact that mathematics with understanding is accessible to everyone and not just a select few.

The Assessment Principle

The Assessment Principle advocates an understanding of assessment as a means of obtaining "useful information to both teachers and students" (p. 22). The above mentioned task of determining what the student knows is not possible without assessment. Just as students need to learn mathematics with understanding, as stipulated by the learning principle, they also need to be involved in self-evaluation, which assessment can provide. Assessment is thus understood primarily as a support for learning.

It should be further noted that assessment is ordinarily divided into *formative* assessment, carried out in the course of study, which helps both teacher and student to evaluate the progress of instruction and make various decisions with regard to perfecting it, and *summative* assessment, which comes at the end of instruction as a whole or at the end of one of its stages.

Nowadays, however, when the learning process is seen as practically lifelong, even summative assessment should probably be understood more flexibly than before, and should be carried out in a variety of authentic ways.

The Technology Principle

This Principle advocates an understanding of technology both as a support for learning and as a potential source of influence on mathematics itself, particularly as a source of change in what is considered significant and accessible for students of mathematics. (The investigation of the characteristics of complex shapes by using dynamic geometry software even in Middle grades provides just one example of what has become possible in school mathematics.) At the same time this principle warns that "technology should not be used as a replacement for basic understanding and intuitions" (NCTM, 2000, p. 25).

The Principles and Standards for School Mathematics, whose publication was based on the previous NCTM documents (*Curriculum and Evaluation Standards for School Mathematics* (1989), *Professional Standards for Teaching Mathematics* (1995), and *Assessment Standards for School Mathematics* (1995)) summed up a great deal of work already done by mathematics educators, but it also outlined new problems. The latter must be solved by the entire community of mathematics educators. They must be solved by every teacher and in every class. The planned reform is not straightforward and faces many difficulties (Price & Ball, 1997); you will be the ones fighting for its realization.

Reflection
Assignments and Topics for Discussion

1. Analyze the table of contents of any mathematics textbook. Does the presentation seem coherent? (If not, why not? How would you improve the presentation?) Why do you think this particular sequence was chosen?

2. Inspired by the call to challenge students, a teacher included in every homework assignment a problem from the American Mathematics Competitions (Schneider, 2000), offering extra credit to those who solved them. Since no one ever gave a correct solution the

teacher discontinued the practice. What do you think the teacher should have done instead?

3. How would you propose to judge whether the students have mastered some course unit with or without understanding? Consider, for example, the geometry unit devoted to the criteria for the congruence of triangles. Give several examples of possible situations in which it is clear that understanding has not been achieved. Give several examples of exercises that would make it possible to clarify whether or not the students understood the topic.

4. Name several forms and methods of evaluation with which you are familiar. Name some groups of students whose success would clearly be inaccurately judged, based on the results of written tests alone.

5. Give examples of some areas of mathematics whose study in school would become easier and more accessible through the use of graphing calculators or dynamic software.

ANALYZING LESSON CHARACTERISTICS: AN ATTEMPT AT LESSON STUDIES

The TIMMS videotape study, and the publications accompanying it (e.g., Stigler & Hiebert, 1999; Stigler & Stevenson, 1992; Fernandez et al., 1992) drew attention to the practice of detailed lessons studies that were current in Japan. Here groups of teachers worked together to prepare lessons. One member of the group would teach a prepared lesson in the presence of other members. During the subsequent discussion the weak and strong points of the lesson would be revealed, and recommendations for improving it would be worked out. Sometimes the same lesson was taught again to another class. The teacher would thus be involved in a system, quite uncommon in many countries that worked incrementally to increase professional mastery. Instead of lectures in which teachers are simply told "how it is done," they actually do it—not alone, but together with other interested professionals who are able to recognize both positive and negative aspects of a particular lesson.

Some (Stigler & Hiebert, 1999) are of the opinion that this method of teacher education is incomparably more effective than any other. Today there are many in the United States who are carrying out investigations along these lines, diligently observing the details of concrete lessons and analyzing the reactions of the students (Fernandez & Choksi, 2002; Kelly, 2002; Lewis, 2002).

In order to become an effective teacher you have to learn to analyze lessons—both those that you sit in on and observe, and your own. This is where lesson studies become useful. This section will examine some important characteristics of lessons, students and teachers, which you should consider and reflect upon.

Ability to See the Class

The first thing that lesson studies require is the teacher's ability to see the class. Novice teachers (and not only they) often conduct a lesson concentrating only on their own intentions: they remember what problems need to be set and what formula needs to be explained, but they do not observe how their students perceive this. Sometimes teachers do not even look at students, or if they do, they literally cannot see what goes on in front of them. They often do not realize that students are seldom occupied only with what the teacher has prepared for them.

Examining an Example

As an example let us cite the marvelous episode where Mark Twain's heroes spend the lesson trying to train a tick while appearing engrossed in their studies (Mark Twain, 1991).

So he [Tom] put Joe's slate on the desk and drew a line down the middle of it from top to bottom.

"Now," said he, "as long as he is on your side you can stir him up and I'll let him alone; but if you let him get away and get on my side, you're to leave him alone as long as I can keep him from crossing over."

"All right, go ahead; start him up."

The tick escaped from Tom, presently, and crossed the equator. Joe harassed him a while, and then he got away and crossed back again. This change of base occurred often. While one boy was worrying the tick with absorbing interest, the other would look on with interest as strong, the two heads bowed together over the slate, and the two souls dead to all things else.

Note that the children here created no special problem for the teacher—they simply ignored the lesson completely. They were not unhappy either—they just did not learn anything. Novice teachers are often bothered only by breaches of discipline that prevent them from carrying out their plan. It is important, however, to be able to see not only those who draw attention to themselves, but also those who are silently absent. It is the teacher's role to actively involve them too in class work.

Recognizing Student's Cognitive Development

The NCTM principles should be realized in actual lessons in the collaborative work of teachers and students. Indeed, the aims and objectives that you set out will never be realized unless you take into account the particularities and cognitive development of the students you are teaching.

Helping Students Construct Their Knowledge

Piaget (1952) has shown that cognitive development of students goes through several phases, from the sensorimotor stage, at which young children start to imitate and think, to the formal operational stage, where adolescents become able to solve abstract problems logically. It is not possible to leap through all these stages. If you demand of children something that they are cognitively unready to do you will simply drive them away from education. True knowledge cannot be crammed into someone by force. Children and adolescents should construct such knowledge for themselves. Thus, 'constructivism' is the term used to describe the kind(s) of teaching that aims to help students do precisely that.

In thinking about a lesson it is useful to consider how students acquire knowledge in it. You can guide students towards the realization of why proofs are necessary and develop their skill of proving, or you can simply present them with a proof and ask them to learn it by heart. You can give students the model of a solution and a couple of dozen identical assignments in order for them to practice solving similar cases, or you can present them with a situation where they would themselves have to look for different possible solutions and then select those that fit and reject those that do not. Which of these approaches seems preferable to you? The answer is hardly difficult. This way the understanding of the theory of human development is converted into more effective teaching practice.

Identifying Individual Learning Styles

Furthermore, students can have completely different learning styles. Kolb (1984) has noted that some children find active experimentation more comprehensible, while others learn better through reflective observation. While some tend to look for support primarily in concrete experience, others prefer abstract conceptualization. If you ignore these characteristics, you will prevent students from fully discovering their abilities.

Developing Students Through Collaboration

However, one should not think that a good teacher merely observes the students' process of development. Vygotsky (1982) spoke of the error of pedagogical theories that "relinquish the process of the development of concepts to its own intrinsic laws," thereby "condemning the teaching process to an utterly passive role in the development of concepts" (p. 190).

Children are often unable to perform this or that task all on their own. However, in collaboration with an adult they become perfectly capable of accomplishing it. The child's development takes place precisely in the process of this collaboration. Vygotsky (1982, 1986) used the term *zone of proximal development* to refer to those parts of a child's personality that are still underdeveloped but that can be developed in collaboration with an adult. "Instruction is adequate only if it comes ahead of development itself," wrote Vygotsky (1982, p. 252). "Only then is development awakened, only then is a whole range of functions, which are still only at a germinating stage and in the zone of proximal development, brought to life".

Teachers' skill lies in determining what sorts of tasks their students are ready for, yet would find new and challenging, and what, by contrast, is still not adequate for their stage of development. By working with students on such tasks the teacher ensures the students' proper development and assimilation of mathematics. It is important here for the teacher to analyze and carefully consider all the details of the lesson, including its structure, the choice of materials and the organization of activities.

Types of Activity in a Lesson

From the results of their investigations, Stigler and Hiebert (1999) distinguished the following most typical steps in a lesson in the United States (p. 80):

1. Reviewing previous material
2. Demonstrating how to solve problems for the day
3. Practicing
4. Correcting seatwork and assigning homework

Nobody takes this pattern to be law binding, but in the opinion of the researchers (Stigler & Hiebert, 1999), the pattern is deeply rooted in the culture of the American classroom. Of course, the above procedures can be carried out in various different ways. Take, for instance, the first of them— reviewing previous material. You can do this in any of the following ways:

- Briefly review the contents of previous lessons (*lectures*).
- Put several problems on the board and call on several students to solve them while the rest of the class would be solving them at their desks.
- Put several problems on the board and tell the class to solve them by themselves in their notebooks (sometimes with intent to collect the solutions later). This type of revision is employed at the beginning of a lesson in many schools, and is often called "*do now*";

- Choose several problems that can be discussed orally by the class as a whole (*class discussion*);
- Give some problems for *group work*.

This list could be added to further, of course. One could also investigate which of these ways are the most popular. The point is that the teacher always has a number of possibilities at each stage (even if the scheme provided is followed in its entirety).

Choosing the Appropriate Form of Class Work

One should not assume that some of the above types of activity are in and of themselves particularly good or bad. Formerly, the main type of class work used to be the lecture. The teacher described what needed to be done, the students wrote down what was said in their notebooks, learned it later, and, under the teacher's direct guidance, they were trained to complete assignments using the rules that they had learned. A poor listener, for example, could not meaningfully learn what was written down or cope with the assigned examples, and may then be considered lazy or incapable of learning.

Important discoveries in psychology and especially the emergence of new theories of learning and cognitive development (Bruner, 1966; Piaget, 1952; Vygotsky, 1986) have made it possible, among other things, to consider anew the types of class work used in lessons. In a constructivist classroom learners have come to be perceived not as passively acquiring (or not acquiring) the knowledge imparted to them, but as building their own conceptions of the material (Brooks & Brooks, 1993). Consequently, these days the lecture has become much less popular than it used to be. By contrast, today there is wide use of *teamwork*, which was practically never used in the past.

This does not mean, however, that teamwork is the only type of class work that should be employed. The process by which each individual learner constructs knowledge is complex and idiosyncratic. You can and should use all existing pedagogical forms in order to find a way to reach all of your students. However, the ability to explain mathematical ideas will never become unimportant for teachers. It is clear that a lecture, for instance, can prove to be an excellent pedagogical tool for summarizing a topic and for structuring what has already been discussed. A lecture is also useful when it is necessary to impart, in a condensed way, information that students cannot easily obtain on their own in class (for instance, historical information). There are other, similar, examples as well.

Teachers should have a sense of proportion, choosing the duration and place of each type of class work in harmony with their teaching goals and the peculiarities of the class. The teacher is not at all obliged, of course, to follow the scheme given above. In recent years a number of studies have appeared (Clarke, 2003a; Wilson et al., 2001) that analyze different patterns in the composition of lessons and the duration of different steps in different countries. Even in the United States, of course, teachers use a variety of schemes, and do not always follow the one outlined above.

Motivating Students

For instance, one important step in many lessons that has not yet been explicitly discussed here is the one that addresses the key question of student *motivation*. Clearly, a considerable role in motivating students is played by so-called *extrinsic motivators* (the fact that one needs education for a successful career, the praise that one gets from the teacher or the competition that one enters with one's classmates). But the *intrinsic motivators* that directly stimulate student interest in the subject play a role in involving students in active learning that is perhaps even more important (Malone & Lepper, 1987). Among these intrinsic motivators are:

- Being presented with an interesting and beautiful problem
- Finding out about an unexpected application of something studied earlier
- Being faced with a question that unexpectedly fails to yield an answer
- Learning about the history of this or that problem
- Being involved in an experiment that assumes the discovery of something new

All these are examples of activities that can awaken the interest of students and a place should certainly be found for them in the lesson.

The Lesson as a Complex Structure

Lesson studies also encourage the perception of a lesson (and of a series of lessons) as a complex structure where separate steps do not exist in isolation, but interact with one another, acquiring additional meaning from this interaction. Stigler and Hiebert (1999) compared well-formed lessons to well-formed stories. But while in literary studies there is a long tradition of analyzing how the content of a story is connected to its form, and how this connection and interaction is reflected in the reader's perception (Vygotsky, 1971), a similar analysis of how lessons work still remains inadequate. Very often researchers (and practicing teachers as well) concentrate either only on problems of content ("these are the problems I give", "this is the formula I show") or only on pedagogical procedures ("seatwork", "teamwork", "lecture"), but pay insufficient attention to their interaction. Meanwhile, it is obvious that not every problem is suitable for, say, teamwork. Similarly it is not enough just to note that the students were occupied with seatwork for 20 minutes. One must specify what material this was devoted to and how this work was structured. Such work can be set up in different ways depending on whether only one problem is given, or if twenty completely separate questions are posed, or if five interrelated assignments are given.

Maintaining Students' Interest

Like the author of a literary work, you as a teacher must strive to make your work (lesson) as relevant, attractive, and emotionally satisfying as possible. By switching from one type of class activity to another the teacher can regulate the level of tension the students need in order to stay involved in the lesson (for instance, replacing the lecture or group discussion with an individual activity in which students can work at their own pace). In the same way the teacher can vary the complexity of the material in order to avoid making the intervals where the material presented is too difficult (or too easy) excessively long. Through such "dramaturgical" devices the teacher can maintain the interest of students, and prevent the tired or over-active child from being excluded from the lesson.

When superimposed on a specific pedagogical procedure, particular mathematical content acquires additional aspects. When proposing to solve a problem in groups, the teacher increases the role of communication in the solution of the problem. Furthermore, a problem will be solved differently depending on whether it is presented as an exercise for written seatwork or as a problem for mental calculation (Sowder, 1990). For example, given as a written exercise, the task of finding the product of 35 and 4 will most likely involve multiplication in columns. By contrast, if the same problem were given as a mental exercise, the students are likely first to multiply 35 by 2, and then by 2 again.

The sequence of pedagogical procedures used and their correspondence to the material studied is determined by the goals of the lesson and the idiosyncrasies of the class. As a teacher be aware that there is a variety of possibilities open to you in the construction of a lesson and you should know when and how to make use of all of them. This is again something that lesson studies teach us.

Reflection
Assignments and Topics for Discussion

1. Give examples of situations in a lesson in which it would be useful to employ: (a) class discussion; (b) individual seatwork; and (c) teamwork.
2. Give an example of high school material that would be solved differently depending on whether it was given for mental or for written work.

3. Visit a mathematics classroom. Name the types of work used in the lesson. Did the lesson correspond to the pattern described by Stigler and Hiebert?
4. Visit a mathematics classroom and observe two students. Try to estimate the degree of their involvement in the lesson at each step. Try to imagine (write an essay) how this lesson looked from the standpoint of the students you have observed (for example, how they would describe it at home to their parents).

DEVELOPING THE ART OF TEACHING

Successful teaching finds support in insightful and multifaceted pedagogical research carried out over many decades, if not centuries. And still, far from everything in teaching practice can be derived from the findings of rigorous pedagogical science. Interpreted by two different teachers a text can be appreciated by one group of students and abhorred by another. A great deal in the teaching of even such an exact subject as mathematics depends on the elusive nuances of how a word is pronounced, on what sort of body language the teacher uses, on the teacher's posture and appearance, and on various other individual characteristics that are not easily expressed in precise terms. In educational literature it is generally acknowledged that teaching is not just a science, but also an art (Woods, 1996). Among the features of the artistic approach to teaching noted by researchers are multiple forms of understanding and representation (including situations in which, as the researchers put it, "we get to know through all our senses, not just the mind"), expression and emergence, emotion and creativity (Woods, 1996, pp. 21–26). It is not only in the planning of tasks and assignments, but also in their enactment, that teaching occurs.

The analysis of lessons and of assignments given by the teachers will be incomplete and imprecise if we lose sight of this individual component—the set of traits characterizing the behavior of the teacher in communication with students. You should think about the best way of preparing yourself in these terms as well.

Experience from Another Field

Long ago the famous Russian theatre director Konstantin Stanislavsky wrote a book on how to become a good actor. In English translation this work is known as *An Actor Prepares* (Stanislavsky, 1976), but the literal translation of the Russian title is "the actor's work on himself in the creative process of experiencing." It is written in belletristic form, as the story of a young actor studying with his peers under an old and experienced master. In the course of these studies, working on special exercises, they try to develop qualities essential to an actor. This is hardly just a matter of acquiring technical skills like how to speak in a loud voice or run quickly around the stage; it involves the ability to feel and to convey one's feelings. What sorts of characteristics Stanislavsky considers important is evident from his chapter titles: "Imagination," "Concentration of Attention," "Relaxation of Muscles," "Faith and a Sense of Truth," "Emotional Memory," etc.

Stanislavsky's belief that it was possible to teach someone how to be a good actor was occasionally ridiculed even during his lifetime (Bulgakov, 1968). Although it is true that this teaching how to be a good actor is by no means always possible, the book's influence was enormous. Unfortunately, we still do not have books on how to develop qualities necessary for a teacher, despite a great need for studies of this kind. Indeed, "Imagination", "Concentration of Attention", "Faith and a Sense of Truth", "Emotional Memory" would not be bad chapter titles for a book on teaching either. Even certain technical aspects, such as the question of how muscles should work in a lesson, ought to be considered by teachers. What a teacher should start with, however, would be an analysis of concrete teaching experience.

Qualities of an Effective Teacher

What sorts of characteristics are necessary for an effective middle school teacher? Having asked this question, Arnold & Clifford (1999) gave the following answer: "These teachers have the ability to be the Wild and Crazy Guy, but organized like Felix of the Odd Couple; caring like Mother Goose; flexible as Gymnasts; intellectually curious like Einstein, Edison, and Darwin; and team players like the Chicago Bulls and Boston Celtics."

Analyzing accounts by pre-service students of their best teachers, the authors distinguished the following qualities of effective teachers (the lists obtained are close to those proposed by other researchers, e.g., Young & Shaw, 1999).

- Truly cared for me and the rest of the class
- Loved his subject
- Enthusiastic
- Well organized
- Energetic
- Good sense of humour
- Intelligent and inspiring
- Fair and consistent, treated everyone equally
- Balanced between fun and discipline

- Encouraged student participation
- Expected a lot from students
- Interested in students' lives beyond the classroom
- Showed an interest when students were having troubles
- Gave each of the students individual attention
- Made it very easy to ask questions
- Very patient
- Never insulted your intelligence
- Offered help even during lunch
- Varied where he stood in the room
- Had animated voice and face

How does one cultivate such qualities in oneself? What sorts of exercises should a novice teacher perform to acquire them? There is hardly a simple answer to this. Experienced teachers are distinguished from beginners by the fact that they preserve in memory all their previous experiences of empathizing with students, and therefore understand better how to react in the next situation.

One teacher whose work one of the authors studied kept on his wall the following list of precepts that seem deserving of attention.

- Remember the importance of your actions—they can bring both joy and grief.
- Remember that you do not know everything and are not always right.
- Remember that it is your job to help overcome difficulties and not add to them.
- Remember that people are different, learn differently and behave differently.
- Remember that your student's view of what goes on in a lesson is different from your own.
- Remember that your student has a life outside the classroom.

It is always important to try to understand one's students better: the experiences they bring into class, what goes on in their daily lives, what motivates them, and what they like (one need not cater to it, but one should bear it in mind). It is also always important to try to understand yourself better: which of your qualities, knowledge and skills might be attractive to your students; what was it that interested you in mathematics—what did you think about then, what did you feel and how might you share this with your students.

This book deals mainly with the planning, organization, and carrying out of lessons, and with the selection, composition, and use of teaching materials. But neither lessons nor problems appear before the students by themselves.

It is the enactment of a lesson by and the personality of the teacher that plays the key role in successful teaching. By the same token, working on oneself is always important, and especially so for novice teachers.

Reflection

Assignments and Topics for Discussion

1. Talk with several students who have recently come to the United States. What was their previous experience of mathematics education? Try to draw a picture (based on their accounts) of how they see the study of mathematics in their new school: what they like about it, what causes them difficulties, what seems unfamiliar to them.

2. Talk with two or three students from one class. Find out what interests them, what books they like, what musical groups they listen to. Try to determine what subjects are interesting to them and why. Does this include mathematics? Try to devise an activity that could interest them in mathematics.

3. Arnold & Clifford (1999) say that effective middle school teachers "will dress up like historical characters, wear funny outfits, bounce off the walls, and are full of energy." Devise a dress-up game for middle school students. How do you think this could be of use in your own teaching? What role would you choose? Why?

4. Choose a topic and think about how you would talk about it to students. Record your talk on tape. Think about what you like and dislike about your mathematical explanation and the way the ideas come across.

CHAPTER 2

GETTING READY TO TEACH

The goal of this chapter is to discuss the planning of teaching and to recommend ways of organizing it.
This chapter discusses:

- How to begin work on a new curriculum or textbook.
- How to plan lessons and course units, including the basic stages and forms of class work.
- Examples of lessons, with a focus on difficulties experienced by the teacher, the causes of these difficulties and ways of eliminating them.

DEVELOPING A MATHEMATICS CURRICULUM

During their school years students ordinarily study at several educational establishments. We have already discussed how difficult it is to follow the curriculum principle of the NCTM, which calls for coherence. Each teacher is responsible for addressing this challenge, although a teacher is not ordinarily called upon to develop an entire curriculum.

The choice of curriculum and textbook is a difficult matter, since it is closely tied to the idiosyncrasies of the student body and the school's (or district's)

Mathematics in Middle and Secondary School, pages 29–55
Copyright © 2015 by Information Age Publishing
All rights of reproduction in any form reserved.

own ethos. A textbook that is excellent for one school might prove completely unsuitable for another. As always, the experience of others can be useful, and finding out what teachers working with one particular curriculum say is definitely useful. But the judgment of teachers who know the characteristics of the school in question ought to be decisive. Students can study in the same grade and take the same courses, yet at the same time have completely different educational experiences, be raised in completely different cultures, and be troubled by completely different educational problems. For this reason, it is desirable for the choice of both curriculum and textbook to be carried out only after a careful consideration of all the different options available.

At some point, however, the final choice will be made. The teacher will then face a semester's or a year's work with a class using one particular textbook. (The duration of the course taught by a single teacher can be entirely different in different schools.) Very often novice teachers, who have started a job at a new school, find themselves in this very situation. How are they to plan their work? Let us list five steps that might be useful. They are presented here in a particular order, although in real life, since the teacher must work simultaneously on several different fronts, they are naturally carried out in parallel.

Knowing the Curriculum, the Textbook and the Course Requirements

You need to thoroughly familiarize yourself with all the teaching materials. It is naïve to think that it is sufficient for the teacher to be only one step ahead of the student; that the teacher can prepare the topic just before it is scheduled to be studied and only vaguely guess what comes next in the textbook. One has to try to understand the overall scope and sequence of the material, as well as what is characteristic of the textbook's overall approach, what is good and bad about it, and what materials might be lacking. Ask yourself:

- How should you work with slow learners using this text?
- What could it offer to those with more ability and interest in mathematics?
- Are the assignments it gives varied enough and could they be used for students with different learning styles?
- Where could one find materials that would stimulate students' interest in the subject matter?
- What problems would help students practice using the concepts and methods introduced?
- What would help them understand the application of these methods in practical situations?

The teacher will have to find answers to these questions in the course of teaching. It is not possible or necessary to answer them all at once definitively in the overall planning of the course, but one must outline approximate answers, at least, and estimate the degree to which additional sources will have to be brought in.

Not Teaching To Tests yet Ensuring Good Results on Them

It is absolutely essential to become familiar with the state standards and exams, the requirements envisaged by the school and the most widely used departmental exams. Many have spoken of the harm caused by merely teaching to tests, where the whole sense and beauty of mathematics is replaced by one single sentence: "This will come up on the test." Moreover, such a narrow-minded approach usually has no pedagogical benefit whatsoever. That which is not interesting will simply not be learned. It is impossible to retain in one's memory recommendations and procedures if there is no understanding of what lies behind them. But to ignore established standards and requirements is equally naïve. Students, teachers, and school administrators are all very interested in having students pass tests successfully. Therefore, your challenge as a teacher is to think of how to include in your overall teaching plan exercises that would help your students acquire skills necessary to pass the test in such a way that these exercises still form part of the process of meaningful study rather than something special or additional.

Examining *an* Example

Many states tests include the problem of solving equations with an absolute value, such as $|x-1| = 3$. Some teachers draw the conclusion from this that they must first give students the rule for solving such equations and then set them as many exercises as possible to ensure that the rule is properly learnt. However, a creative teacher would instead draw the conclusion that this problem provides in fact another great opportunity to discuss different representations in mathematics and would plan the lesson so that students would have to examine the problem from different perspectives. They could be asked to discuss a verbal problem reducible to the equation $|x-1| = 3$ (for example, the question of finding points on the number line for which the distance to the point at 1 equals 3), to examine the intersection of the graph of the function $y = |x-1|$ and the straight line $y = 3$, and finally, to work with formulas. This would enable the teacher to connect different types of material and to obtain a better, more multifaceted understanding of the problem, something that would inevitably manifest itself in the exam as well.

Learning from the Experience of Others

No one can do your work for you—prepare your lessons or teach the course on your behalf. However, it is no doubt very useful, in preparation for teaching, to familiarize oneself with the teaching experience of others. Publishers commonly publish teachers' manuals that reflect current teaching experience based on corresponding textbooks. One can also often find useful advice and lesson plans on the internet. Finally, colleagues at school can also tell you a lot about what worked or did not work for them and in what way. Remember though that your class (like any other) is unique, and it would hardly be possible to find readymade the exact plans that you would need. At best you might be able to borrow one or two interesting ideas, problems or activities that you can then incorporate in your own lesson plan. It is possible that you will gain little from what you read and hear (at least at first glance), and some suggested lesson plans or pieces of advice might seem totally inappropriate. Nevertheless, they will make you think— they will draw your attention to this or that aspect of your material and they will help you develop your own point of view on the matter. In other words, they will still be useful to you in one way or another.

Knowing Alternative Materials

A different textbook and a different curriculum as a rule imply a completely different approach. This means that different materials cannot be combined at random—the logic and coherence of the course would thereby be lost. But familiarizing yourself with materials other than your own is no doubt worthwhile, because they still might be able to provide you with ideas that you can logically weave into your teaching. In particular, you might find in them problems or activities that you are lacking. It is also useful to read over the basic documents relating to the course you are teaching, such as the NCTM standards, the CCSS-M standards, or the standards of your state.

Knowing Your Class

Your class is unique, because all children are unique. The sooner you analyze their idiosyncrasies, the more precise your lesson planning and the more successful your teaching will be. Try to learn about your students even before the course begins. If you have the opportunity to observe how they work with another mathematics teacher, do not miss it. It is also useful to visit lessons in other subjects as well. The novice teacher is sometimes astonished to discover that a student that seems completely uninterested, in addition to being an inveterate troublemaker, works with enormous enthusiasm in lessons taught by a colleague. How can this be explained? In some cases this is due to the fact that the other subject is simply more interesting to the child. This information might still give you some indication of how to attempt to interest the child in mathematics as well. In other cases the child's interest can be explained by the strategy and behavior of this other teacher. In that case you must think of how to incorporate in your teaching some of the approaches used by your colleague. Sometimes, however, it is a matter of the student having, for one reason or another, adopted a particular pattern of behavior specifically for mathematics lessons. In that case it is important to figure out what the reasons for this are and to try to change the student's attitude. Advice and accounts from colleagues who have worked with the children in your class can also be useful.

Learning about Students from Themselves and Their Parents

In working with a class, it can also prove useful to ask students directly about their interests, expectations, and assumptions with respect to studying mathematics. Such questions help students understand their own views better and also help you prepare for further work with them.

It is important for the teacher to treat meetings with students' parents as one more opportunity to learn about the children they are going to teach and their living conditions, aiming to help them realize their potential. Parents can help attentive teachers see sides of their students that have for some reason remained unnoticed. Parents can bring to the teacher's attention feelings and impressions that children are sometimes not even fully aware of themselves.

The influence of parents is extremely important to children. Consequently, in planning the course you should also think about how to make your approach comprehensible to parents and how to win their support and understanding.

Pedagogical literature (Civil, 2000) provides accounts of work with parents as the means of involving them in the teaching of mathematics to their children. In this particular case, the mathematics educator worked directly with the parents, involving them in mathematical activities, and helping them discover the mathematical dimension of things that previously seemed far removed from mathematics. This work helped bring about a change in views about mathematics within the family and the community at large. The child consequently proved much more motivated to study it. Clearly, teachers are by no means always in a position to undertake such large-scale actions all by themselves, but thinking about possibly working with parents, as part of teaching their children, is important and meaningful.

Knowing the Classroom and Teaching Supplies

For a teacher just starting to work in a new school, it is important to consider carefully the environment where teaching is to take place. Sometimes the classroom itself will determine how class work will be organized; at other times, the organization of furniture within a classroom can be either prohibitive or supportive for specific activity or movement during lessons. For instance, in a small, crowded room, it will be difficult to conduct group work. Consequently, the teachers should ask themselves: What sorts of pedagogical strategies can be employed in this room? What audiovisual equipment and other technology can be used in it? What capabilities and resources does the school have available? You should try to obtain an answer to these questions well ahead of time. You must find out what supplies the school library and the mathematics department have to offer. Sometimes planning will include asking the administration to obtain additional materials, to make certain changes, or to re-arrange furniture to ensure a teacher's (and students') ease of movement around the room.

Having carefully considered all the available materials and supplies, and having accumulated as much information about the class as possible, the teacher draws up his plan for teaching the course. (This presupposes the formulation of serious, challenging, but at the same time realistic goals, as well as an approximate scheme of how to accomplish them and what specific methods of assessing progress to use.)

Establishing "Class Rules"

It is important also to think about laying down certain "rules of the class"—rules of daily classroom practice one plans to follow throughout the course. These include rules for both daily classroom procedures as well as norms for classroom activity and interactions. For example, it is useful for the teacher to think beforehand about the order of homework assignments, when and in what form homework will be given and checked, what requirements will be involved in specific assignments (for example, an answer with no work shown obtains only one-third credit), as well as other norms such as how students should engage in collaborative work, what students are expected to do as they enter the class (such as, get out homework, work on a "do now" problem, etc.). Such rules should be discussed in class and subsequently adhered to for the duration of the course—this helps students better to understand the requirements involved, to develop the habit of being organized, and it also makes the teacher's work easier. Of course, some subsequent changes are likely, but such amendments and additions should be reduced to a minimum since new rules, introduced at a later date, tend to be taken in less easily by the class than those established at the outset.

Reflection

Assignments and Topics for Discussion

1. Choose a textbook and analyze it, guided by the list of questions given on p. 30.
2. Compare how a certain topic is studied in two different textbooks. What differences are there in approaches and materials? Which approach do you find more congenial? Why?
3. Chose a topic and analyze the questions given on this topic in your state's exam.
4. Imagine that you are working in a school where in each lesson every student has a laptop computer. Specify in what way this would affect your lesson planning.
5. Make a draft of "rules of the class" that you would like to propose in middle school and in high school.

DEVELOPING A UNIT PLAN

What is Unit Planning and Why Is It Necessary?

A course can be divided into a number of units each of which is devoted to a separate topic. The study of each unit can take days and sometimes even weeks. To divide a course into units is no doubt quite conventional. One teacher can think of a course as consisting of a few large units, and another one may try to think in terms of a greater number of smaller units. In any case, the planning of a course and the specification of its general goals usually compel the teacher to look for some intermediate unit of discussion that would lie between the course as a whole and an individual lesson, such that the lessons that form such a unit are closely related to one another. When working from a textbook it is usually convenient to take one chapter as equivalent to a unit. A unit can also be devised as a set of interrelated activities.

For example, in the inductive approach to geometry, working with shadows could be taken as one unit. In the course of a particular series of interconnected lessons, students can be involved in a variety of different activities. By performing experiments, observations and measurements they can discover for themselves the various properties of projections. These lessons are all united by a single object that all the different observations have in common. This is why in planning these lessons it is natural to treat them as a whole and to think through the overall goals of study for the entire unit.

The overall goals of the course determine the specific requirements with respect to each unit. The textbook or other materials available to you in turn prompt you to follow one particular system. All this, however, does not substitute for detailed planning. In the course of such planning the teacher sets goals and objectives for the study of a unit and determines how they will be accomplished. In the process the teacher must answer the following questions:

- What are the basic concepts and ideas studied in this unit?
- What skills should the students acquire?
- What should the student performance outcomes be from studying the unit?
- How and when will assessment for the unit be carried out?
- How and when will the material studied in this unit be used in the course of further instruction?
- What knowledge and abilities are needed to successfully study the given topic?
- What advantageous moments and opportunities for getting students interested in mathematics and for showing them its true character does this topic include?
- What knowledge and abilities necessary for studying the given topic do the students of a particular class have at their disposal?
- Do they have any experience in working with the concepts and assignments that will be given them in the new unit, and if so, how can they use this as a guide?
- What are the fundamental difficulties that might be encountered in studying the given topic in this class?
- How many lessons are needed to study the material in this unit?
- In what order should the study of the unit be set out?
- What mathematical tools and manipulatives are needed to carry out the teaching of the topic?

Planning Helps to Be Flexible!

It is naïve to think that everything can be planned beforehand. What is more, it needs to be said straight out that very often when having to choose between following one's pre-prepared plan and reacting to what emerges during the lesson, the teacher ought to opt for a direct response to what actually occurs. The teacher's mastery consists to a great degree in listening to and understanding the student, and in capitalizing on those situations that, even if unplanned, emerge during the lesson. It is clearly wrong to prevent students from voicing their views or to ignore their remarks and questions simply in order to be able rigorously to follow one's own plan. A well thought out plan, however, usually enables one to anticipate certain questions, to remove likely difficulties, and also to allow room for further discussion.

Setting Performance Objectives in Planning

The order and style in which teachers set out the issues that their students will be expected to deal with is utterly individual. But it is desirable to imagine these issues not only in their general verbal form (e.g., "students will learn to perform arithmetical operations with negative integers"), but also in the form of specific problems that students can be asked to solve. There are students who will not necessarily see the problems "find the product $-2 \cdot (-3)$" and "find the product $-32 \cdot (-23)$" as essentially the same thing. The teacher needs to be specific; you must think in terms of concrete problems, so to speak, and not just in terms of descriptions of general requirements. In setting out one's teaching goals, it is desirable always to specify exactly what mathematical content stands behind the words and exactly how one can judge the attainment of these goals. The precise outline of what students will be able to do at the end of the course or one of its parts is what is meant by "performance objectives."

Unit Plan Examples

It is possible to work on one and the same unit from various different perspectives. Let us examine the work of three groups of pre-service and in-service teacher learners on one of the units in an Algebra course.

Preliminary Information

The teacher learners were asked to plan the study of the chapter on Systems of Linear Equations and Inequalities. In the textbook this chapter included the material in Table 2.1.

TABLE 2.1

Number	Content of section
1	Concept of a system of linear equations. Solution of a system of linear equations. Point of intersection of two lines as a graphic illustration of the solution of a system of linear equations. Solution of a system by graph and check method (only for systems having a unique solution)
2	Solving Linear Systems by Substitution (only for systems having a unique solution)
3	Solving Linear Systems by Linear Combinations (only for systems having a unique solution)
4	Applications of Linear Systems. Solution of word problems (some examples of which have been given in preceding sections as well). Solution of systems by all methods.
5	Special cases of Linear Systems (cases in which a system has infinitely many solutions or has no solution).
6	Solution of systems of linear inequalities (shadowing region, consisting of solutions on a graph)

The chapter is preceded by chapters devoted to graphing linear equations and inequalities, and is followed by chapters devoted to operations with powers.

After establishing all this, the teacher learners also analyzed the exam problems given in their state and noted that these generally included three types of problems:

1. The solution of the system of equations

$$\begin{cases} -x+8y=5 \\ 2x+3y=9 \end{cases}$$

   is which of the following:

   (A) $(1, 1)$ (B) $(-3, 1)$ (C) $(3, 1)$ (D) $(3, 3)$.

2. Solve the system of equations

$$\begin{cases} 2x+y=3 \\ 3x-y=2 \end{cases}.$$

3. Rodrigo collected stamps. He has 942 stamps in all, and twice as many American stamps as foreign ones. How many foreign and how many American stamps does he have?

Different Versions of Unit Planning

Each group of teacher learners then proposed their own version of sequencing lessons and gave their reasons for it.

GROUP I

The students already know that a linear function is an important means of modeling real processes. In this chapter they study systems. Systems are also a very important means of modeling. (One could say that a generalization of the material in this chapter forms the basis for linear programming, widely employed in economics.) From studying this chapter the students can also better understand that the same problem can be solved in different ways. Accordingly, these are the goals of study for this chapter: to familiarize students with systems of linear equations as the means of modeling and to demonstrate the variety of approaches to the solution of a problem. Students can be assigned activities using material from the textbook, though without following it literally, and they can be involved in these activities during solution of word problems. In the course of discussing this problem they will see how it can be reduced to a system of linear equations, and they will learn the appropriate terminology. They will then be guided to the solution of a system by all three methods. Subsequently they will be given several more word problems. The graphic method employed in this chapter enables one to make the material more visual. The last three lessons will be devoted to this. Student assessment will rely on the final project, in which students must complete several assignments in modeling real world problems by various methods, as well as on their journals, where they will write about the ideas they discovered in the process and that were new to them.

Accordingly, the lessons can be sequenced as follows:

- Posing the word problem from Section 4 (Applications of Linear Systems). Its discussion. The writing of a system of equations. Working out the concepts from Section 1 (Concept of Linear System) (1 day).
- Discussion of approaches to the solving of the equation obtained—Sections 1–3 (Solving Linear Systems) (1 day).
- Problem solving—Section 4 (Applications of Linear Systems) (5 days).
- Section 5 and Section 6 (Special Cases and Inequalities) (1 day).
- Discussion of projects (2 days)—10 days all in all.

GROUP II

The purpose of this unit is to learn how to solve systems of linear equations. The main difficulty encountered in this consists in the fact that students often do not have the necessary degree of algebraic and graphing skills. It can easily happen that in solving the system of equations

$$\begin{cases} 2x + y = 3 \\ 3x - y = 2 \end{cases}$$

they will grasp that it is appropriate to solve by linear combination, but they will make errors in performing the operations. Or else, in solving it by substitution, they will mistakenly express y in terms of x. In solving it graphically, they might make mistakes in graphing. In particular, students always experience difficulties in the solution of word problems. They may fail to solve them, not because they have not learned how to solve linear equations, but because they do not know how to set up these equations. It is therefore important, first of all, to give them more practice, and second, always to review at the beginning the algorithms that will be used in what follows.

It is important to show from the outset how the process of solving systems of linear equations is applied. The discussion of applications should therefore not be put off until later. One should use word problems in class from the very beginning.

At the end of study of the second, third, and fourth sections students need to be given 10–15 minute quizzes that will enable both them and the teacher to evaluate how well the basic concepts have been mastered. After studying the unit students will be able to solve problems of the type given in state exams.

The final test should include each of the following types of problem: using substitution, using linear combinations, etc. At the same time one should have a system of evaluation where students can get partial credit if they apply the algorithm in a basically correct manner, but have difficulties with technical details. Accordingly, the lessons can be sequenced as follows:

- Review: graphing of a linear equation, operations with variables that are part of a linear equation. (2 days)
- Section 1 (Concept of Linear System) and discussion of examples of word problems reducible to systems of linear equations (2 days)
- Section 2 (Solving Linear System) (2 days)
- Section 3 (Solving Linear System) (1 day)
- Word problem reducible to linear equations (1 day)
- Section 4 (Applications of Linear Systems) (3 days)
- Section 5 (Special Cases) (1 day)
- Section 6 (Inequalities) (1 day)
- Review (1 day)
- Test (1 day)—15 days all in all

GROUP III

The unit contains both purely technical aspects—methods for solving systems—and very important conceptual ones—the concept of a system of equations, its solution, and the number of solutions. These concepts are needed to be discussed: it is not at all obvious to students, for example, that a problem can have many solutions, and that in guessing an answer, they have by no means completed the solution. The study of conceptual questions should not concern difficulties related to students' insufficiently developed computational skills: the examples used can be computationally very simple.

This chapter is also important as a way of showing the interrelatedness of different parts of mathematics and especially how the same phenomenon may be described both algebraically and geometrically. It is natural to keep in close proximity the study of sections devoted to "qualitative" aspects.

Here it will be necessary to add appropriate exercises that are lacking in the textbook. In particular, it is useful to begin with the discussion of certain word problems that have already been solved earlier in class, in order to remind students how unknowns are introduced and how an equation is set up. Starting from real world problems (adding one more convention—the equation), one can move on to the discussion of new questions, having shown the importance of their solution in various applications.

On the other hand, students must have enough time to familiarize themselves with all the methods employed. It might be possible, therefore, to save time by devoting less attention to section 6, which stands somewhat apart. It will clearly be used far less in what follows. The teacher can, for example, show one example in a lesson devoted mainly to the solution of other problems, and ask students to acquaint themselves with the material in this section on their own.

Over the course of instruction micro-quizzes (3–5 minutes) can be given, as a form of formative assessment. These are especially important in the first qualitative part, when it is vital to monitor how well the basic concepts are being learned. For instance, questions like the following may be asked: "Think of a system of equations whose solution will be the pair (0, 0)", "Nick says that the pair (2, 3) works for a certain system of equations, and Kate says that the pair (–3, 4) works for her. Can they both be right?", "Can a system of two linear equations have exactly two solutions?" Summative assessment can include several brief quizzes (10 minutes), given after the study of different methods of solving systems, a final test, in which one should find space for qualitative questions, and a small project devoted to problem solving (word problems or guided solving of more complex systems, for example, of three equations).

Accordingly, the lessons can be sequenced as follows:

- Review: Analysis of a word problem that entail linear equations with two variables (1 day)
- Section 1 (Concept of Linear System) (2 days)
- Section 5 (Special Cases) (2 days)
- Section 2 (Solving Linear Systems) (2 days)
- Section 3 (Solving Linear Systems) (1 day)
- Section 4 (Applications of Linear Systems) (2 days)
- Review (1 day)
- Test (1 day)—12 days all in all

Discussion

The participants of these three groups had varied experience in teaching. Some of them were still pre-service students and had just begun to visit schools and observe lessons. Others were already thoroughly experienced teachers. Even more importantly, their experience, both as students in their time and as teachers, was very different depending on the schools in which they happened to study and teach. There are also great differences in the philosophies that lie behind each of the approaches described, and it would be naïve to seek a single correct one among them. Moreover, they are all hypothetical: they proceed from a number of speculative notions about the class. Teachers normally find themselves in a better position than these teacher-learners for they know their classes and can better imagine what the students need and are able to do. There is something of value in each of the approaches presented, and each of them could be used successfully under favorable conditions. But it is important to understand what sorts of demands are implicitly made on students and what the gains and losses might be with any given approach.

The First Group's Plan

It strikes one immediately that the first group, to a certain extent, went against the textbook. Even though the text offered various activities and exercises that could be incorporated in their plan, the overall study scheme implied in it was completely different. Accordingly, one can immediately question the sheer practical inconvenience of this plan. A lot of the required exercises need be formulated by the teacher herself, and she would need to be very accurate in the way she does this, making sure that the work she sets is both within the class's powers and beneficial to them. This plan is also inconvenient for students who wish to learn more about the material from the textbook. Probably a teacher whose approach and philosophy differ so strongly from those adopted in the textbook should simply choose a different text.

The lesson sequence of the first group could be seen as appropriate to the goals set. But the goals themselves do not include the students' confident mastery of the skills required for solving linear systems. It is no doubt very important to show the open character of these problems—the possibility of different solving strategies. At the same time it is clear that for some students it will not be easy to master the three different methods for solving systems when they are given to them all at once, with no time properly to assimilate and "get used" to each one. Not every student will be able, either, to evaluate the advantages of a given method in different situations. This approach will facilitate the development of skills for solving systems only if the students are sufficiently well prepared and interested (and get additional support in their studies). On the plus side, all the students would gain experience in the mathematization of specific real-world situations and have ample opportunity figuring out applications for the mathematics being taught. In addition, given the real-world approach, students may be more interested in the class.

The Second Group's Plan

The second group, in contrast, makes the question of developing skills paramount. For them, the solving of applied problems is also, in essence, a skill that must be consistently molded, reinforced and practiced. The group realistically approached the evaluation of students' knowledge, pointing to the need for reviewing material on which further exposition will be based. However, one might raise the question of the time needed to carry out this program. This group required more time than the other two and it is not at all clear if, even after this time, the desired effect would be achieved. Why, for instance, will two days of review at the beginning prove effective, when previous study has not helped much? Generally speaking one can expect that "practice makes perfect," but the reality of school life is such that the duration of such practice is invariably limited. In addition, students may, from the outset, get the idea that they already know the content of this unit, and therefore disengage from class.

This group did not set itself (at least not obviously) any goals other than developing skills. Even in the course of such work there can and should be room for demonstrating the conceptual nature of mathematics, and it would be wrong to make the presumption that the proposed plan does not allow for it. It is important, however, that no "indices" of understanding are provided—the object of assessment is solely the mastery of the algorithms studied.

The Third Group's Plan

The third group singles out this conceptual aspect. Having started with practical problems, the members of this group propose then to move to a deeper analysis of the mathematical side of the question, so that later, having developed among the schoolchildren the necessary understanding of mathematical ideas and the necessary skill in applying the algorithms, the teacher can return to real life problems. This approach involves a certain flexibility—the desire to show interesting mathematics even to those who experience difficulties in the face of its computational aspects, and accordingly to evaluate not just skills, but understanding as well.

At the same time it is clear that the success of such an approach will largely depend on how much the teacher is able to interest the class in the investigation of the conceptual aspects of mathematics. It is easy to imagine a negative attitude towards these on the students' part ("What do I care how many solutions a system can have?"). The teacher must be highly professional and inventive to alter such an attitude. On the other hand, the decision to actually eliminate the study of one of the sections of the unit cannot fail to raise questions. The effort to keep within the time frame and still find time for the main part of the chapter is understandable. Still, the omission of any section, and particularly such a conspicuous one as solving systems of inequalities, could be criticized.

Summary

To sum up, we repeat that it is hardly possible to find one ideal approach to unit planning. The approach must be judged from the standpoint of its conformity to a chosen philosophy (evaluating this philosophy, obviously, is in every case a separate, much more general and complex question)—in other words, by evaluating how well a particular plan helps achieve the general educational goals one has set oneself and one's students. Regardless of the approach, however, it would be useful for the teacher to give some thought to the issues mentioned above. More specific considerations would then be carried out in actual lesson planning.

Assignments and Topics for Discussion

1. In what order would you consider it appropriate to study the unit devoted to systems of linear equations? Explain your position.
2. Describe how you would plan to realize the connections and communication standards of NCTM in studying the unit devoted to systems of linear equations.
3. Describe at least one way you would incorporate each of the Common Core SMPs into study of the unit.
4. Imagine that you have in your class several mathematically gifted students. Construct a lesson plan for working with them on the unit devoted to systems of linear equations. Then think how you would work on this same unit with other learners.
5. Put together the final tests on systems of linear equations for a course of study that follows the plans of group II and group III above. Make up assignments for study projects according to the plan of group I above.
6. Choose a unit and describe the order in which you would teach it. Indicate the assumptions you are making about the class for which you are preparing the unit plan.

DEVELOPING LESSON PLANS

Lesson Planning

Lesson planning is a key moment in a teacher's preparation. At this stage, you carefully consider everything that will take place in class: both your own actions and those of the students. The overall goals of instruction, the goals of the course, and the goals of the unit are finally made concrete in the form of goals and objectives for each individual lesson. In a certain sense one could say that this entire book is devoted to the planning and carrying out of lessons, which means that in this section we will confine ourselves to a few general statements and examples.

All teachers work on their plans in their own way. Some write everything out in great detail, while others write down only key moments, keeping in mind what will really be taking place. In any case, it must be understood that every seemingly minor step entails an answer to a whole number of implicit questions.

| Examining _an_ Example | **Examples of Details that Require Careful Consideration** |

Let us imagine that a teacher plans during a lesson to acquaint students with a formula. Teachers (especially if they are experienced) can briefly write this down in their plans, but the note leaves a lot unsaid. Where will the formula be written? Will there be room for it on the board? Sometimes one might not wish to erase what one has done before. The teacher might want to refer to what is written there while showing students the formula. Should the students remember the formula? If so, will there be time for them to copy it down? (Students will hardly be listening to the teacher's explanations while copying the formula from the board.) Where will they write the formula down? The teacher might recommend that they keep a list of basic formulas in the back of their notebooks. Ideally students should be organized enough themselves to record everything where they need to; however, by helping them get into the habit of being organized, the teacher is also educating them, and therefore some reminders may be needed. How will the formula be read out? There may be some letters or terminology for which the pronunciation or meaning will cause students some difficulty. How exactly will it be written out? A bare formula without a verbal explanation of its contents invites errors on the part of students. (For example, the fact that students remember the formula $(a+b)^2 = a^2 + 2ab + b^2$ does not at all guarantee that they will be able to use it to expand the expression $(c+d)^2$, let alone $(2a+b)^2$.)

The list of questions can go on, and failing to provide answers to them creates many potential pitfalls in a lesson. The same applies to many aspects of every lesson. An experienced teacher almost automatically approaches a lesson in a way that takes into account potential problems, but a novice teacher must be prepared for the fact that lesson planning can be a long process. It begins, as always, with the setting out of the lesson's goals and objectives.

Setting Goals and Objectives

Carefully rereading the teaching materials and thinking about the place of the given lesson in the unit, you should determine what you would like to achieve as a result of this one lesson—the goals and objectives for the lesson. A very important step, as in unit planning, is determining performance objectives–what students will be able to do as a result of the lesson.

For instance, the performance objectives for a lesson devoted to solving systems of linear equations by substitution might be formulated as follows:

Students will be able to solve systems of the type

$$\begin{cases} 2x - 3y = 2 \\ y - x + 2 = 0 \end{cases}$$

by substitution, choosing which variable is most convenient to isolate.

Performance results can be measured relatively easily and fairly quickly—ideally during the lesson, and in the worst case over several lessons. However, in setting the goals of the lesson, you should not limit yourself to this.

Learning outcomes, as is well documented in pedagogical literature (Gagne & Briggs, 1979), can be very different. The goals and objectives of a lesson cannot be reduced to performance objectives. The goals you set yourself may include ones like awakening interest in the subject, showing the significance of mathematics, developing the intellectual skills of students, and many others. The achievement of such pedagogical results is sometimes difficult to measure instantly and in a strictly numerical way, but such results can nonetheless be significant.

Currently in many textbooks the authors directly indicate the goals of instruction for each section. It should be noted that even though your own goals for a lesson will usually include these, they should not be exhausted by them. You can be much more specific in relation to your own class, seeing, on the one hand, the textbook material that must be studied, and, on the other, your class and the problems that each of your students is experiencing in his or her development.

Useful Tip! **Discuss your goals with the class.**

It should be noted that teachers achieve their goals not in isolation from the class but in collaboration with students. Thus, it is natural to allow time in a lesson for a discussion of what will be done and what is the importance and necessity of doing it. This can be done either through direct discussion or by involving students in solving a problem that makes them aware of the need to study the new material. In any case students should understand what they are doing in a lesson and why.

Then, in accordance with their goals, the teachers choose suitable exercises and activities and types of work for their lessons. Let us repeat what was said earlier: the interaction of the mathematical content and the organizational and pedagogical procedures to be employed must be carefully thought out. The planning of assignments includes establishing what materials, manipulatives, and supplies will be needed. One has to order them (especially to make sure there is minimal interruption during class transitions), make sure they are in good condition, or sometimes make them oneself.

Reminder: Think through carefully how you would work with special needs students.

In planning a lesson, the teacher also has to think about how to work with children that have special needs. Will there be a special needs teacher in the lesson? In any case one must consider (together with the special needs teacher when there is one) how to work with these children in a way that will be fruitful, directed to the achievement of the basic goals of the lesson and in harmony with it.

Vary activities!

It is important to vary the types of activity during a lesson. This is crucial for maintaining the interest of the class. In addition, as noted before, it is useful to alternate steps that require students to work under pressure with those in which they can work at a more comfortable pace, and not allow them to become overtired. The teacher, too, needs some sort of break during a lesson—it is hard to stay attentive, artistic, and energetic for almost a whole hour. But it is important for all the steps and elements of the lesson to be interconnected—only a single lesson is being given, not five little ones. Accordingly, the transition from one step to the next during the lesson must be justified, motivated, and comprehensible to students.

Collect feedback

All possible feedback that the teacher can obtain during a lesson is important, including direct questions by students and the observation of how they work and answer questions. In planning a lesson, the teacher must consider ways of obtaining such information, including, for example, some sort of exercises for the formative assessment of students. Based on the feedback obtained, you should be ready to introduce changes into your plan during the lesson itself.

Don't forget about the reality of your school!

In your plan you must take into account the reality of the school in which you work. If from 1:00 p.m. to 1:05 announcements are made on the loudspeaker in your school, it would hardly be reasonable to set up a lesson in such a way that key aspects of an explanation would come at precisely this time. Here one needs activities where interruption would be reasonably painless. Clearly, if the interval before the lesson is only three minutes long, not all students will be able to get right to work on something that requires full concentration. The teachers themselves cannot always switch over that quickly. Some sort of activity that permits a gentle transition to more intense labor is appropriate here (this, of course, does not imply that these first few minutes should simply be wasted, as sometimes happens).

The Anatomy of a Lesson

Conventionally, a lesson can be divided into three parts:

Introduction. Here, for example, there can be a brief review and/or evaluation (of one type or another) based on what was studied previously, and a reminder of the information that will be needed in the lesson; a motivational activity or problem can be given; finally, the key question of the lesson can be posed and its basic structure outlined.

Main part. Here the class becomes acquainted in one form or another with the basic content of the new material. The basic facts, formulas, and assertions are introduced. The basic algorithms are developed. Students have a chance to work with the new material, to practice on it.

Conclusion. Here a summary is given. There is a statement of what has been achieved. Questions might be outlined that will be needed in further study. Homework assignments are given.

Not all lessons are set up according to this scheme; however, a great many lessons are set up in precisely this way. The main challenge for many teachers is to work out the time needed for each step. Sometimes it can happen that the introduction stretches into the whole lesson. Sometimes, on the contrary, everything planned is accomplished in half the time and the novice teacher then agonizes over what to do next. At the root of this are usually mistakes in evaluating the material to be studied and, most of all, the class itself.

Examining *an* **Example** **Learning from Mistakes**

Let us analyze the experience of one student teacher. She gave a lesson in middle school on the "area of a circle." This lesson was part of a unit devoted to area. Up to that point the school students had become familiar with how to find the area of a square, a rectangle, and a triangle. This was her lesson plan.

Topic: Area of a circle
  Goals:

• to develop the knowledge of how to find the area of a circle;

Objectives:

- students will know the formula for the area of a circle;
- students will become familiar with the number π;
- students will learn to carry out approximate calculations with π in determining the area of a circle;
- students will learn to solve problems with real world objects in which finding the area of a circle is required.

Performance Objectives:

- students will evaluate the area of a circle with a given radius (1, 2, 0.5) in terms of π and up to two decimal places.
- students will evaluate the area of a given model of a circle, using measurements.

Introduction

- The students will solve in their notebooks and later discuss in open class the solution of the following motivational problem. Find the pattern: 1, 8, 27, 64, 125,...
- The students will be told that the study of the area will be continued.
- The students will be divided into groups for further work.

Main part

- Squares will be passed out to students (Figure 2.1) and they will be asked to inscribe a circle, color it and cut it out.
- Rectangles will be passed out to students (Figure 2.2). They will be asked to cover as many as possible of the smaller squares making up the rectangle by cutting the cutout circles into pieces and placing these onto of the rectangle.

Figure 2.1

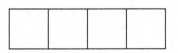

Figure 2.2

- Students will see that the area of a circle is greater than the area of rectangle consisting of three smaller squares.
- Students will notice that with the pieces of the circle it is possible to cover at least the rectangle of area $3r^2$ and will deduce that the area of the circle is greater than $3r^2$ and less than $4r^2$.
- The teacher will inform them that the area of a circle is equal to πr^2, and the students will see that π is greater than 3 but less than 4. In fact, $\pi = 3.14\ldots$
- Students will find in their notebooks the area of circles with the radius 1, 2, 0.5 in terms of π and up to two decimal places.
- Students will discuss these results on the board.
- Models of circles will be passed out to students and, again in groups, they will measure their radii and find their area. The results will be discussed within groups.

Conclusion

- The teacher will give the results of the lesson and assign homework.

(The homework consisted of exercises in finding the area of circles analogous to those analyzed. As models students were given cardboard cutouts of circles with marked centers.)

The lesson thus planned went as follows.

At the beginning nobody could solve the pattern problem. After prompting by the teacher one of the students correctly said that the numbers 1, 2, 3, etc. had been cubed. This was repeated by the teacher and written down by several students in their notebooks.

Afterwards students spent a very long time inscribing circles and, especially, coloring them diligently, discussing and commenting on how to color them. When the rectangles were passed out the students did not understand straightaway what was expected of them. The teacher had to explain and show them several times that the idea was for them first to cut up the circle, and afterwards cover the rectangle with the pieces. Finally the teacher started doing this herself, showing the class, and then the class too started to do something like it, which also took some time. After this the teacher asked what the area of each of the small squares making up the rectangle was equal to if the radius of the inscribed circle is r. No one could answer. The teacher showed that the side of the square was r, and reminded them that for any rectangle the area was found as the product of the sides. After this someone said that the area was $2r$. The teacher said that it was r^2, for example, if $r = 3$, the area was $3^2 = 9$. In discussing how great an area could be covered by the pieces of the circle, the students were supposed to say $r^2 + r^2 + r^2$, but again no one could find what this was. The teacher explained that it was equal to $3r^2$. During the last minutes of the lesson the teacher concluded that the area of the circle was by the same token less than $4r^2$, but greater than $3r^2$, and equal to πr^2, and π was a number whose first digits were 3.14. Homework was not assigned; instead the students were told it would be handed out at a later stage.

Why did the lesson turn out like this?   One of the reasons why the lesson was not a success was because there was simply not enough time. However, even if by some chance the teacher had another hour at her disposal and was able to carry out the whole plan to the end, the lesson could still not be considered successful. The work that students did with the materials the teacher gave them was not what led them to understand how to work out the area of circles. They simply took the formula for the area of the circle as something that had to be memorized.

What is the cause of failure here? Probably, if one were to look for the chief cause, it would be the fact that the teacher did not start either from the goal of the lesson, or from the peculiarities of the class, but from a desire to use certain activities and types of work. It is clear why these activities appealed to the student teacher: it is good for students to have the chance to do something, measure something, experiment with something themselves in order to be visually persuaded of the correctness of an assertion. Such activities can be useful for attaining pedagogical goals, but do not in themselves guarantee success. This reiterates the work of Stein, Smith, Henningsen & Silver (2009), who distinguish between the planning of good tasks and the enactment and maintenance of good tasks.

It is clear why the problem about the sequence 1, 8, 27,…appealed to the student teacher: she wanted to emphasize the role of patterns in mathematics. But such a problem would have been effective only as part of a unified strategy, not as a detached piece that bears no relation to other things discussed. Let us identify a number of errors of judgment committed by the student teacher.

- *The student teacher did not realistically assess the previous knowledge and skills of the students.* The elements of algebra, which seem completely natural to a person with a higher mathematical education, are not natural at all to a middle school student. Students usually experience difficulties in working with variables. Confusions and mistakes of the type $r \cdot r = 2r$ and even $r^2 + r^2 + r^2 = r^6$ are encountered quite often. Nothing was planned to anticipate possible errors. Accordingly, students had to be corrected on the fly, which is less effective and distracted their attention from the basic result of the lesson. The teacher also did not anticipate that inscribing a circle into a square would cause difficulties, bringing further loss of time.

- *The student teacher did not succeed in making the problems in the lesson comprehensible to the students, and did not succeed in making the lesson coherent or directed towards the solution of the goals she had set.* The "motivational" problem was in no way connected to the rest of the lesson. For most of the lesson students were engaged in an activity whose goal they did not understand. Why the study of the area required students to color and cut out a circle became understandable only at the end of the lesson, when it was explained that by doing this one could compare the area of a circle with the radius r with $3r^2$ and $4r^2$. But at the end of the lesson the children were no longer in a position to think about this—they were overwhelmed by other difficulties.

- *The student teacher did not succeed in organizing productive student work during the lesson.* The work in groups was only an imitation of group work. There was not, and indeed could not be, any division of labor in the group, any discussion or joint work. The set tasks—cutting out, coloring, etc.—were carried out by one person, whom the rest of the group could only hinder and distract. The tasks the students were given were not comprehensible enough to them. The work was not at all structured and no time frame was specified. This is why most of the time was spent on the fairly needless coloring.

Even though the lesson plan appeared to follow the standard format and contained all the usual headings, the plan was not sufficiently well thought out to accommodate for its implementation. Realistically, it is overly ambitious to try to teach in one lesson the elements of algebra, how to inscribe a circle, how to work with sequences, and how to find the area of a circle (a difficult topic in itself, which one can only begin to study in middle school). Having set herself the goal of developing the knowledge of how to find the area of a circle, the teacher should have tried to anticipate the possible difficulties and alleviate them beforehand.

A More Successful Lesson on the Same Topic

Let us describe a lesson that took place in another class and was taught by an experienced teacher using practically the same ideas and materials.

At the beginning of the lesson the students were given review problems: find the area of the figures given in the diagrams (Figure 2.3). The students completed them and their solutions were discussed. The error $r \cdot r = 2r$ cropped up here as well, but it was corrected by the students themselves, based on a previous exercise, where $r = 3$. The teacher briefly commented on their discussion, using a poster on which the definition of a^n was given.

The teacher formulated the lesson's objective as that of learning how to find the area of a circle. It was emphasized that a great many objects have

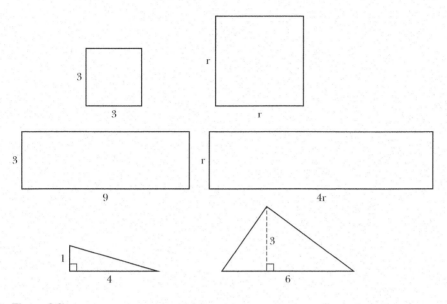

Figure 2.3

this shape (several such objects were shown), so it was important to know how to do this.

A square was displayed in which a circle with the radius r was inscribed (Figure 2.4). These questions were asked: Which is greater, the area of the circle or the area of this square? The area of the circle or the area of one of the small squares? The area of the circle or the area of the rectangle consisting of two small squares? The students were able to answer by looking at the picture. In the course of discussion it was noted that the area of the small square was r^2, and the area of the rectangle consisting of two small squares was $2r^2$.

The teacher proposed to students to compare the area of the circle with $3r^2$, i.e., the total area of the three small squares. For this the students were divided into pairs, and each pair was given several copies of Figure 2.4. They were asked to discuss how best to compare these areas,

Figure 2.4

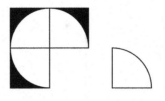

Figure 2.5

e.g., by cutting out the figures, and then to make necessary observations and discuss the results.

The students mostly cut up one quarter of the circle and tried to cover with the bits that they obtained the three "remainders" (shaded parts on Figure 2.5). A few pairs, on the contrary, cut up the squares and tried to fit the bits inside the circle.

The result was that the area of a circle is greater than $3r^2$, and they were told that to determine the approximate area of a circle one could multiply the area of the small square by 3.14. They were shown the formula πr^2 and were told that $\pi \approx 3.14$. It was emphasized that this is an important number, about which more would be said later.

Then problems that involved finding the area of circles with a given radius were solved. Students were then asked, working in pairs, to find the area of circles from models. The students had to take turns carrying out measurements and calculations, and fill in the table they were given.

At the end of the lesson the teacher summarized the results, noting that whereas all the figures studied previously had sides—line segments—this lesson had been devoted to a figure that had no sides, but was bounded by a curve. Yet for it as well a formula had been derived in mathematics. Homework was assigned.

Discussion

Let us reiterate that the topic considered here is undoubtedly a very difficult one. For instance, the comparison of the area of a circle with $3r^2$ is not easy, since the difference is small. There are many other activities that could have been used here. What is important, however, is that this lesson was free of the mistakes noted in connection with the first lesson. The role of the problems given at the beginning of the lesson should be emphasized, in particular the fact that they prepared the class for further work on the topic. The teacher here gave the class a series of problems that she could make use of later in tackling the main problem of the lesson. By working on a series of specially chosen interconnected problems, the children were able to cope even with the more difficult one much better than if these had appeared unexpectedly, without any preparation. When necessary, one could simply refer to what had just been done. In later chapters this method will be discussed further.

Assignments and Topics for Discussion

1. Think of a few more activities that one could use to establish the area of a circle. How would you use them in a lesson?
2. The lesson on the area of a circle analyzed in this section was given in a class that was not familiar with the formula for finding the length of a circumference. Prepare a lesson plan on the area of a circle for middle school, under the assumption that students are familiar with the formula $2\pi r$.
3. Discuss how your lesson plan for assignment #2 fulfills the Common Core State Standard CCSS.M.7.G.B.4, which includes that students should be able to "give an informal derivation of the relationship between the circumference and area of a circle." What SMPs are incorporated in your lesson plan?
4. How would you plan a lesson on the topic "area of a circle" for those familiar with Calculus? What would be different and what similar?
5. Prepare a plan for the concluding lesson on the topic "Area" in which you would sum up and revise everything that was studied previously.
6. Give an example of a lesson whose goals might include developing skills of mathematical communication. Draw up a plan for such a lesson.

PART II

This part introduces the reader to the theory of problem solving and problem posing and to its possible applications in class activities.

CHAPTER 3

WHAT IS PROBLEM SOLVING AND HOW IT IS CONCEPTUALIZED IN MATHEMATICS?

The purpose of this chapter is to acquaint the reader with the most important approaches and conclusions of classical works in the theory of problem solving. The chapter discusses:

- The concepts of "problem," "exercise" and "problem solving."
- Different approaches to describing the process of problem solving, especially the four-stage schema of George Polya.
- Examples of different heuristic strategies.

WHAT IS A PROBLEM?

The Meaning of the Word "Problem"

One comes across the word "problem" so often, in mathematics as well as everyday life, that this inevitably leads to misunderstandings. In ordinary

Mathematics in Middle and Secondary School, pages 59–89
Copyright © 2015 by Information Age Publishing

speech "problems" generally refer to obstacles that hinder the achievement of a particular pursuit. In the classroom "problems" sometimes refer to so-called "word problems"—tasks that appear as a verbal description of some situation, but which then needs to be translated into a mathematical language in order for the solution to be reached. "Problems" are sometimes, explicitly or implicitly, linked to the mathematical modeling of real life situations. Occasionally, by "problem solving" one means the solution of particularly difficult mathematical tasks, like those set in mathematical competitions, while tasks found in school textbooks are then called "exercises." In other cases, however, it is precisely the completion of these school tasks that is dubbed "problem solving."

Schoenfeld (1992) highlights this plurality of meanings, citing Webster's (1979) definitions for the term "problem":

> Definition 1: In mathematics, anything required to be done, or requiring the doing of something.

> Definition 2: A question . . . that is perplexing or difficult.

NCTM on Problem Solving

What is then being discussed in the "Problem Solving Standard" of NCTM (NCTM, 2000)? The latter states that "problem solving is not only a goal of learning mathematics but also a major means of doing so." What kinds of problems are being referred to here? NCTM explains that "problem solving means engaging in a task for which the solution method is not known in advance." This definition considers problem solving from a fundamentally different perspective—the issue is not just what a problem itself is, but also what sort of relation the problem solver forms with it.

The Psychological Definition of the Problem

This approach essentially defines mathematical problems in general psychological terms, insofar as "a problem is defined generally as a situation in which a goal is to be attained and a direct route to the goal is blocked" (Kilpatrick, 1985). It is precisely in this way that the concept of "problem" is considered by specialists in different fields (Newell & Simon, 1972; Resnick & Glaser, 1976), who analyze the actions of those engaged in solving not just mathematical, but also other kinds of problems. By contrast, tasks for the solution of which it is sufficient to apply an established method are then called "exercises" (Schoenfeld, 1992). In the latter case one could say that the path to the solution is known and direct.

It is clear that in this sense a "problem" can take a whole variety of forms. It can appear as a word problem, as an equation, as a calculation problem, or as any other type of problem from virtually any sphere of mathematics. At the same time, one can formulate exercises in every part of mathematics.

Furthermore, it is possible for the same task to appear as a problem in one particular set of circumstances, but not in another.

Examining *an* Example

Nineteenth-century village schoolchildren depicted in the picture (Figure 3.1) are clearly engaged in problem solving. If we take a closer look, we see that the problem they are trying to solve is the following: Calculate

$$\frac{10^2 + 11^2 + 12^2 + 13^2 + 14^2}{365}.$$

It appears that the students are asked to perform this calculation mentally. The trick on which the teacher has based the task lies in the fact that $10^2 + 11^2 + 12^2 = 13^2 + 14^2 = 365$. Once these equalities are established, it becomes easy to perform the division and obtain the result 2. But to come to this realization is not that straightforward, even for a student who has memorized the squares of all the numbers between ten and twenty. Even if one calculates that the sum of the first three items $10^2 + 11^2 + 12^2$ is 365, it is easy to miss that this coincides with the denominator. It is likely that students would then simply carry on adding to this $13^2 = 169$, and so on, which is rather difficult to do mentally.

Figure 3.1

Let us now assume that the students were allowed to do the task on paper, or that the task was set in a modern classroom where students were allowed to use calculators. It is clear that in these cases the task would cease to be a problem and would become more of a routine exercise. Moreover, let us imagine that a student from the class depicted in the picture finds himself a month later in a different class where the same task (or one sufficiently similar) is given, again to be performed without pen and paper. For this student the task would no longer be a problem because he would already be familiar with the method to be adopted.

Summarizing

Thus, in order to determine whether a task is a problem or not, one has to know both the conditions in which the task is performed and what those asked to perform the task have been taught beforehand. Kilpatrick (1978) distinguished three sets of independent variables that influence (or can influence) the way in which a task is interpreted and is being solved: subject variables, which comprise characteristics of the one performing the task; task variables, which comprise characteristics of the task and of the context in which it is set; and situation variables, which describe the conditions in which the task is completed. These variables influence the success in solving the task, but they also influence whether the task should be understood as a problem or not in a given case.

What Does "Problem Solving" Mean?

Naturally, the subtleties involved in defining a student task as a "problem" as opposed to an "exercise" are not important in and of themselves, but the overall issue is important. (Where the issue is unimportant, such as in everyday speech, the word "problem" is used as a synonym of the word "task.") The definition in question is simply a language that seems particularly convenient for describing the processes that take place in the classroom. Understanding these processes is crucial for ensuring success in mathematical education.

Examining *an* Example	**Examples of Different Approaches to the Same Problem**

Let us now describe how the same equation was solved by two different students. Both of them were given a fairly unusual-looking task: Establish how many numbers x there are if $3^x + 4^x = 7$, and find these numbers.

The first student saw straight away that $x = 1$ fits. As he was writing down the answer that there is only one x, he read the question again and asked himself why indeed there should be only one x. He then tried using loga-rithms and began writing "log..." but clearly could not establish which base to use and started looking for a different idea. He then tried out other num-bers for x and, realizing that $x = 2$ did not fit since one evidently got more than 7, he concluded that nothing higher than 2 would work either. He then tried out numbers between 1 and 2, taking 1.5 as a test case. Using a calculator he established that $3^{1.5} + 4^{1.5}$ was more than 7. Afterwards, he said that one could, in fact, manage without a calculator since it was obvious that $3^{1.5} > 3^1$ and $4^{1.5} > 4^1$, and that this was going to be the case with all numbers between 1 and 2. He then corrected himself and said that this would gener-ally be the case for all numbers higher than 1. After that he was able to write down quite quickly that for $x < 1$ it was true that $3^x < 3^1$ and $4^x < 4^1$, and that $3^x + 4^x < 3 + 4 = 7$ was therefore also true, which meant that x could not be lower than 1 either. After this he answered that there was only one solution and that this solution was $x = 1$.

The second student almost instantly made the following argument:

> This is a problem about the properties of a function. As the sum of two in-creasing functions, the function $y = 3^x + 4^x$ is itself an increasing one. Con-sequently, its graph crosses the horizontal line $y = 7$ only once. Where does it cross the line? Let us guess: $x = 1$. The solution is that x can only be one number and that this number is 1.

It is clear that both students were well prepared and fluent in using the appropriate mathematical apparatus: they were both members of their re-spective schools' competitive mathematics teams and took part in competi-tions. Both of them successfully arrived at the solution. The second one did so immediately, but even the first one got to it reasonably quickly. The second one's solution appears more mature and mathematically impecca-ble, and probably makes a better impression. However, the main difference between them does not lie in the form of their solutions.

The second student had been taught this method of solving problems—the analysis of corresponding functions. For him this was a routine pro-cedure for dealing with equations that are difficult to solve by standard means. Thus, he was able almost instantly to go through all the different approaches he knew and he quickly found the one that worked in this par-ticular case. He then completed the exercise by applying the method re-markably well.

The first student came across this kind of equation for the first time. He did not know in advance how to proceed and he tried out different ap-proaches, including those that led to an impasse. Eventually, he discovered the right path. To do this he had to perform quite subtle mental opera-tions all on his own, including establishing connections with other parts of mathematics (inequalities and function properties) and finding the appropriate form to write down the solution.

This was the fundamental difference between the two: the first student learned something new and did this all on his own, while the second merely applied prior knowledge. The first was active, while the second was essentially passive. The first built his own knowledge, while the second reproduced what he had learned earlier. The task was of significantly more value and importance to the mathematical development of the first than of the second student. A good teacher, knowing that the latter already knew how to perform such tasks, ought to have given him some other task—a genuine problem, in the above definition—so that the student would use the lesson in the most valuable way possible and truly progress in his mathematical development.

Giving Students a More Active Role

The call to recognize problem solving as a key activity in mathematical education, and the appeal for this education to be organized on the basis of problem solving, is effectively a call to give students a much more active role in the learning process, and to see them actually doing mathematics, rather than simply reproducing what they have learned. The fact that the student is completing certain tasks, even quite complex ones (in the sense, for example, that the completion involves a number of different steps), is no guarantee that the student is actively learning, as the above example clearly shows. Conversely, doing mathematics can be achieved in tasks that do not necessarily require great mathematical knowledge or virtuosity.

Problem Solving for Everyone and Not Just Mathematicians

Stanic and Kilpatrick (1989) rightly claim that: "Problems have occupied a central place in the school mathematics curriculum since antiquity, but problem solving has not." Humanity has accumulated an enormous store of problems that are able to challenge even the most mathematically gifted student. These are, however, usually left out of the standard curriculum, or else are used in classes or textbooks simply in the form of exercises based on a general, pre-learned rule. Only a few isolated individuals—essentially only creative mathematicians and, as a rule, outside the school environment—tend to do things the opposite way. By starting with the problems themselves, they create radically new methods in the process of trying to solve them. From medieval tournaments in problem solving (Eves, 1990) to our own times (as evident by the statement of the outstanding contemporary mathematician Israel Gel'fand that "theories come and go, but examples stay with us forever" [Arnol'd, 1998]), creative mathematics has continued to use problems as *the* source of the discipline's progress.

The community of mathematics educators is today challenged to try and introduce this approach into mass education. The NCTM (2000) calls for the creation of programs that should enable all students to:

- Build new mathematical knowledge through problem solving
- Solve problems that arise in mathematics and in other contexts
- Apply and adapt a variety of appropriate strategies to solve problems
- Monitor and reflect on the process of mathematical problem solving

What Does a Good Mathematical Problem Look Like?

The argument that one needs to engage students in an activity that has traditionally been considered accessible only to professional mathematicians does not mean that every student needs to be confronted straight away with the kinds of problems that professional mathematicians encounter. It is clear that such problems would not, in fact, be of any use to students because the path to the goal would be too hard, while the purpose of the problem would remain unclear. For the same reason it is difficult to expect, in ordinary conditions, the active participation of students if one tried to give too many of those otherwise truly remarkable problems, which have been used for decades in specially selected classes as the principal means of preparing future mathematicians. Such problems need to be arrived at only gradually. In an ordinary class the teacher needs to strike the right balance between, on the one hand, merely repeating what is already known and routinely following pre-learned methods, and on the other, immersing students into complete obscurity, from which they would be unable to emerge all on their own.

Additionally, the problem needs to be of a mathematical nature. In other words, one must assume that the solution to it would require the application of mathematical methods and the use of a mathematical language.

Examining *an* Example	**Recalling an Earlier Example**

The answer to the question above about the roots of the equation $3^x + 4^x = 7$ assumed the students' ability to reason and carry out proof in a mathematical way, to apply various specialized means of communicating and representing information (with the help of functions or inequalities, for example) and to discover connections between different parts of mathematics. In other words, the solution to this problem demanded that students apply all of NCTM's Process Standards. In terms of the Common Core SMPs, the task required students to engage in many different practices, such as making sense of and persevere in solving a problem, reasoning abstractly and quantitatively, constructing viable arguments, and using structure. This was therefore, undoubtedly, a good mathematical problem.

The mathematical value of the other problem discussed in this section—that of calculating

$$\frac{10^2 + 11^2 + 12^2 + 13^2 + 14^2}{365}$$

mentally—is rather more debatable. One is dealing here with a special trick that in itself seems to have a very narrow application. In order to use it, students still need to demonstrate that they have a certain number sense—the ability to group numbers in an appropriate way and to perform division term by term. But in the understanding of modern mathematicians, this could be understood as no more than a curiosity that has little to do with important mathematics. The village schoolchildren in the picture are undoubtedly engaged in problem solving, but hardly everyone would agree that the problem in question deals indeed with deep and interesting mathematics.

Developing a Problem

And yet, the task has potential for developing activities that have far more mathematical content. Problems can be given not in isolation but in a particular sequence. Thus, the teacher can perform a transition from a non-mathematical (or not entirely mathematical) problem to a properly mathematical one.

Let us take a closer look at the above task. What exactly strikes one about it above all else? The answer given above was that we are dealing with a mere trick—an unexpected device that one is unlikely to use in any other situation. But is this situation really as unusual as that? Before providing the answer, the question needs to be formulated more precisely and to be translated into a more rigorous mathematical language. Such activity could in itself have significant mathematical value. Let us describe the fragment of a lesson organized in just this way, on the basis of the above problem.

At the beginning of the lesson Ms. Pinkovsky showed the students the reproduction of the picture (Figure 3.1) and formulated the problem set there. She asked the students to solve it using a calculator and then think how it could be solved if they had to do it mentally (assuming that they already knew the squares of all the numbers between ten and twenty).

When the class provided the answers, the teacher remarked that the problem was based on an arithmetic trick, but then, feigning hesitation, asked if this really was a trick after all. Are there perhaps other, similar numbers? The next question was: Can one name any other sequence of five whole numbers, where the sum of the squares of the first three would be equal to the sum of the squares of the last two?

The students began working on this in pairs, mostly using their calculators. Soon someone came up with the sequence $-2, -1, 0, 1$ and 2, for which it was clearly true that $(-2)^2 + (-1)^2 + 0^2 = 1^2 + 2^2$. The next question was whether there were any other such sequences of five numbers. The students answered that probably not, because "when the numbers are greater, the squares of the last two numbers are only slightly higher than the squares of the first three, while there are three squares to the left and only two to the right."

Ms. Pinkovsky praised this argument, but said that it was not precise enough—what did "slightly" mean? The squares of 14 and 15 were enough to balance out the extra square on the left. Could this work for any other numbers too?

One pair of students came up with the equation $x^2 + (x + 1)^2 + (x + 2)^2 = (x + 3)^2 + (x + 4)^2$, where x was the first number in the sequence. The class then worked together on this equation and found that $x = 10$ or $x = -2$.

In conclusion it was argued that the effort to solve the equation was, in fact, unnecessary, because its two solutions had already been found by other means and because one could not have more than two solutions for a quadratic equation.

For homework the students were asked to think whether it was possible to name a sequence of six natural numbers so that the sums of squares of the first and the last three were equal. (The problem was solvable without algebra since the last three numbers in a sequence would always be higher than the first three and the sum of their squares would therefore also inevitably always be higher).

Thus, the original arithmetic problem was substantially developed and expanded. The students were drawn into analyzing the situation so that they could explore problems both in different directions and by different methods. The wealth of possibilities for discussing, generalizing and further developing a question is the principal quality of a good problem.

New Possibilities: The Role of Technology

Today you have far more means of posing good problems in class than before. Technology in particular comes to the teachers' aid here. Many situations that were previously inaccessible to students due to technical difficulties now become suitable for discussion even in middle school. NCTM (2000) notes that "technology can alleviate much of the drudgery that until recently often constrained middle-school mathematics to using only problems with 'nice numbers'." This limitation had made many problems artificial for students and prevented the discovery of connections within mathematics. Most importantly, it did not permit the development of problems and the investigation of what happened when variables or parameters change, thereby revealing mathematical patterns. In fact, one of the Common Core Standards for Mathematical Practice is using appropriate tools strategically, which includes this relatively modern day school phenomenon of utilizing various technologies to facilitate solving problems.

Easy-to-use computer software and graphing calculators allow us to process far more information than before; and not just for the purposes of mere algorithmic calculation, but precisely as a means of investigation. Dynamic software technologies (such as Geometers Sketchpad, GeoGebra, SketchUp, Fathom, TinkerPlots) in particular, have fostered student investigations across a variety of domains. Dynamic interaction produces real-time changes and modifications based on direct input, such as "dragging," from students; these interactions allow students to conjecture about what remains invariant across thousands of examples, or how certain changes impact other changes, etc. Such technologies allow exploration of connections across geometry and algebra, as well as intuitive ways to interact with statistical data. Indeed, such technologies can open up avenues for students to understand what was perhaps years of a historically significant mathematician's work; for example, Archimedes' methods for bounding π or determining the surface area and volume of a sphere can be quickly simulated and recreated using technology, allowing students to literally rediscover these concepts (e.g., Wasserman & Arkan, 2011). This in itself vastly expands the source-base of 'good problems'.

Learning How to Select Good Problems

In what follows, much will be said about how to select and construct problems. No ready-made collection of problems is likely to cater fully to all the teacher's needs. It is important that you have the ability to create problems independently. The work of teaching frequently involves creating problems (or sequences of problems) that develop particular mathematical content, but that are also crafted with particular pedagogical motivations in mind. The founder of the modern science of mathematical problem solving, Polya (1973, p. 4), has argued that "we acquire any practical skill by imitation and practice." This is how one learns how to solve problems, and this is also how one learns how to select and create them.

Polya himself co-authored a remarkable collection of problems (Polya & Szego, 1976) prior to writing his main methodological works (1973, 1954, 1981). As both scholar and educator, he was developed under the influence of the Hungarian tradition of intensive pedagogical work with students (Vogeli, 1997), which included the preparation of the most talented for mathematical competitions (Kurchak et al., 1963).

It is not at all necessary for teachers to reach perfection in solving extremely difficult problems, or to be ready to compete and win in international competitions. The work of the teacher lies elsewhere. However, familiarity with collections of "good problems" that contain true masterpieces of school mathematics, and an acquaintance with the culture of formulating fundamental mathematical questions, is likely to be beneficial to teachers even if they end up never using these problems in regular lessons. This book cannot provide even a remotely exhaustive list of such problems, though some remarkable examples will be cited in what follows.

Reflection

Assignments and Topics for Discussion

1. The Principles and Standards for School Mathematics analyze the following task: find out whether there are more boys than girls in the four second grade classrooms (in a given school). Can one consider this to be a problem for second grade students? Why? What about the tenth grade?
2. Think up a task that could be solved by using the same method as the one used for the equation $3^x + 4^x = 7$. Could one consider such a task a problem for the two students in the example above?
3. The arithmetic problem with squares could also be developed in other directions. For example, one could ask students whether 365 could be represented as a sum of squares of a different sequence of numbers. How should one go about solving such a problem? Where would one be able use this problem in teaching?
4. Look through the journal *Mathematics Teacher* and find one example of what you think is a 'good problem' that can be solved with the help of technology. Explain why you like this problem.

HOW TO SOLVE A PROBLEM

How Does a Problem Solver Think?

Polya (1981) argued that "the greater part of our conscious thinking is concerned with problems" (p. 117). It is therefore not surprising that the experience of successful problem solvers, from Plato onwards, has been the subject of thorough investigation. Problem solving has been studied by outstanding philosophers, psychologists and mathematicians.

Thorndike on Problem Solving

Debates and arguments about problem solving and human thought processes more generally have, inevitably, not been immune to ideological controversy. Thorndike (1921) claimed that "problems of a certain degree of complexity and abstractness they [certain students] simply cannot solve, just as they cannot jump over a fence five feet high or lift a weight of five hundred pounds." Such pessimism has prompted some notorious objections among other psychologists (Krutetskii, 1976).

Also with reference to Thorndike the German psychologist Max Wertheimer (1959) wrote: "Many psychologists would say: ability to think is the working of associative bonds; it can be measured by the number of associations a subject has acquired, by the ease and correctness with which he learns and recalls them" (p. 9).

Gestalt Psychologists on Human Thought

Wertheimer and other scholars of the same school who were opposed to this "mechanistic" view of thinking formed the so-called *Gestalt* (in German, meaning an image, structure) model of human thought. According to this model, the most important characteristic of thought is the realization of structural properties and necessities, while the most important stage in this realization is *insight*—a sudden leap in understanding. This theory is to some extent confirmed by the experience of a number of outstanding mathematicians (Hadamard, 1945), who observed in their practice particular moments of insight, which often took place in the middle of an activity that had nothing to do with the solution of the problem in question. (Such moments normally occurred, however, after prolonged conscious efforts at clarifying the problem, which inevitably resulted in, among other things, partial solutions to some of the less difficult parts of the problem.)

However, the Gestalt model in turn seems vulnerable, because it lacks a "plausible theory of mental mechanism" (Schoenfeld, 1992). It is also inadequate for the needs of practicing teachers, since it fails to provide any sort of intelligible advice on how to reach the moment of insight (in contrast to Thorndike's theory, from which it is easy to conclude that one simply must train harder).

Looking for a Way to Organize Problem Solving

Even centuries ago Descartes (1952) tried to devise a universal method of problem solving. In essence, he proposed to translate all problems into the language of equations, and then develop ways of solving these. While noting that "there are more obstacles and more intricate details than Descartes imagined in his first enthusiasm," Polya (1981, p. 22) insisted that Descartes' project was truly grand. This is indeed true, not simply because analytical geometry was born in the process, but also because subsequent attempts to formulate general methods of problem solving (usually far less ambitious than those of Descartes) took his ideas as a starting point.

Among philosophers who made a particular contribution to problem solving one must cite especially John Dewey. Using a terminology slightly different from the one currently in use—referring to "reflective thinking," rather than "problem solving"—Dewey distinguished "five phases, or aspects of reflective thought" (1933, pp. 107–114). According to Dewey, the problem solver makes the following five steps: (1) becomes aware of the existence of a problem and of the impossibility of solving it in a routine way; (2) conceptualizes and formulates the problem; (3) works out propositions and hypotheses; (4) realizes the plan; and (5) in conclusion, tests the solution.

According to Thorndike (1921), students in the fifth or sixth grade could be taught the following principles of problem solving (pp. 138–139).

1. If you know surely how to solve the problem, go ahead and solve it.
2. If you do not at once see how to solve the problem, consider the question, the facts, and their use, asking yourself: What question is asked? What am I to find out? What facts are given? From what am I to find it? How shall I use these facts? What shall I do with the numbers, and what I know about them?
3. Plan what you are going to do and why, and arrange your work so you will know what you have done.
4. Check the answer obtained, to see if it is true and reasonable according to what the problem says.

Polya's Scheme of Problem Solving

Polya's own scheme of problem solving (which became famous after the publication of his book *How to Solve It?*) appears very close to Dewey's and Thordike's schemas. Polya (1973) refers to four distinct stages in problem solving:

1. Understanding the problem
2. Devising a plan
3. Carrying out the plan
4. Looking back

What made this schema so well known and so frequently cited is probably the fact that Polya was able not only to provide the schema itself, but also to fill it with concrete mathematical content. Polya has formulated a series of questions that problem solvers—not just a major scholar, like Hadamard, but any schoolchild—can ask themselves at each of the four stages. He has also provided a series of suggestions and recommendations, together with examples of how to use them.

It would be naïve to expect any book or article, including Polya's work, to teach one how to solve every single problem, or, in the above terminology, how to transform every problem into a routine exercise. No theory—neither the old ones mentioned above, nor the more modern ones—can make such claims, even in cases where they offer many subtle and valid statements and observations about problem solving. Finding support in both his own experience as a mathematician and in studies of problem solving by other scholars (including those mentioned above), Polya has been able to show teachers how a mathematician thinks. It is now up to the teachers to find the appropriate forms and examples of such thinking that could be of particular use to their students.

EXAMPLE OF PROBLEM SOLVING

Let us analyze a problem in the spirit of Polya.

Problem

Various non-vertical straight lines are drawn through point A that lies on the ordinate (y) axis above the abscissa (x) axis. Each of these lines intersects the parabola $y = x^2$ in two points. Prove that the product of the abscissas of these two points of intersection is the same for all the straight lines.

Stage I

At this stage Polya asks the following questions and makes the following recommendations.

What is the unknown? What are the data? What is the condition? Is it possible to satisfy the condition? Is the condition sufficient to determine the unknown? Or is it insufficient? Or redundant? Or contradictory? Draw a figure. Introduce suitable notation. Separate the various parts of the condition. Can you write them down?

The obvious first step is to do a drawing. One can select an arbitrary point A and draw an arbitrary non-vertical straight line through it. It is now seen that the line genuinely crosses the parabola in two places. Let us note down their abscissas (Figure 3.2.a). The assertion (requiring proof) is that the product of the abscissas of the two points of intersection would be the same for any straight line that goes through point A. The problem solver can then, for example, draw another line (deliberately selecting a special case, such as a horizontal line), taking note of its points of intersection with the parabola (Figure 3.2.b). One could then say that the product of the abscissas of the points where an arbitrary line intersects the parabola ought to be the same as for the horizontal line.

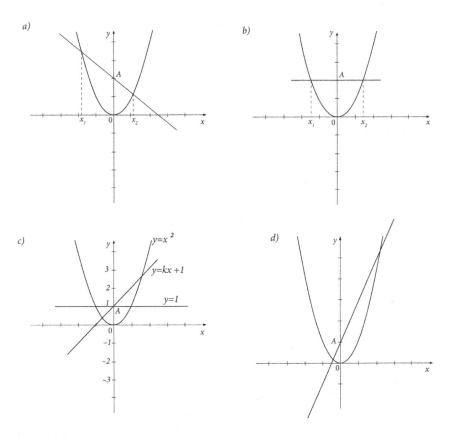

Figure 3.2

But what is this product in the case of a horizontal line? By asking this question we move on to the second stage (which is closely linked to the first one).

Stage II

At this stage Polya recommends the following:

> Find the connection between the data and the unknown. You may be obliged to consider auxiliary problems if an immediate connection cannot be found. You should obtain eventually a plan of the solution.

> Have you seen it before? Or have you seen the same problem in a slightly different form?

> Do you know a related problem? Do you know a theorem that could be useful?

Look at the unknown! And try to think of a familiar problem having the same or a similar unknown.

Here is a problem related to yours and solved before. Could you use it? Could you use its result? Could you use its method? Should you introduce some auxiliary element in order to make its use possible?

Could you restate the problem? Could you restate it still differently? Go back to definitions.

If you cannot solve the proposed problem try to solve first some related problem. Could you imagine a more accessible related problem? A more general problem? A more special problem? An analogous problem? Could you solve a part of the problem? Keep only a part of the condition, drop the other part; how far is the unknown then determined, how can it vary? Could you derive something useful from the data? Could you think of other data appropriate to determine the unknown? Could you change the unknown or the data, or both if necessary, so that the new unknown and the new data are nearer to each other?

Did you use all the data? Did you use the whole condition? Have you taken into account all essential notions involved in the problem?

Following this advice, let us try, for example, to understand what happens in a concrete case—for example, when point A has the ordinate 1 (Figure3.2.c). It is clear that in this case the horizontal line that goes through point A is the line $y = 1$, and that the abscissas of the points where it intersects the parabola $y = x^2$ are $x_1 = -1$ and $x_2 = 1$. Their product is -1. It transpires that one must prove that the product would also be -1 for all other lines that go through point A. But how does one find the abscissas of the points of intersection with the parabola for these other lines? The answer is -1 in the same way as for the horizontal line, though the matter becomes technically more complicated. Each straight line that goes through point A $(0, 1)$ can be given as the equation $y = kx + 1$ where k has an arbitrary value. The abscissas of the points of intersection with the parabola $y = x^2$ can be found from the equation $kx + 1 = x^2$. It turns out that there is no need to speak of abscissas of points of intersection but rather of roots of equations. These can be found through the coefficient k, and are generally easier to work with. The same can be done if point A is selected arbitrarily along the ordinate axis.

Stage III

At this stage one carries out the plan outlined above. Polya gives the following advice here:

Carrying out your plan of the solution, check each step. Can you see clearly that the step is correct? Can you prove that it is correct?

Let us say that the ordinate of point A is c ($c > 0$). In that case the arbitrary straight line that goes through point A can be given as the equation with the form $y = kx + c$ where k has an arbitrary value. The abscissas of the points of intersection of such a line with the parabola $y = x^2$ are the roots of the equation $kx + c = x^2$ and can be found by solving the equation $x^2 - kx - c = 0$.

One needs to prove that the product of these roots is constant for all k and the same as for $k = 0$ (the horizontal line). In the latter case the equation looks like this: $x^2 - c = 0$. Its roots are $-\sqrt{c}$ and $\sqrt{c}$, while their product is $-c$.

It is obvious that in the general case as well, where $k \neq 0$, the product would be the same. For, if x_1 and x_2 are the roots of the equation $x^2 - kx - c = 0$, then it is possible to write that $x^2 - kx - c = (x - x_1)(x - x_2)$. It follows that $x_1 \cdot x_2 = -c$.

Stage IV
At this stage Polya recommends:

> Examine the solution obtained. Can you check the result? Can you check the argument? Can you derive the result differently? Can you see it at a glance? Can you use the result, or the method, for some other problem?

The problem analyzed here is set in such a way that the solver is to some extent not required to check the validity of the result. However, it could still be useful to try out different straight lines. While doing so one would see, for example, that for all lines that go through point A $(0, 1)$, if the abscissa of one of its points of intersection with the parabola is very large than the other will be very small. It is therefore unsurprising that their product is only -1 (Figure 3.2.d).

In the solution above we did not use the formula for quadratic equations. Many solvers of this problem fail to notice that one does not need to use this formula and first write out the solutions of the equation as

$$x_1 = \frac{k - \sqrt{k^2 + 4c}}{2} \text{ and } x_2 = \frac{k + \sqrt{k^2 + 4c}}{2}.$$

Only after multiplying these do they realize that the result could have been obtained by other means.

In solving this problem the most important step was to shift from the language of geometry (straight lines, parabolas, points of intersection) to the language of algebra (roots of equations). To do so we made use of the fact that the product of the roots of a quadratic equation where the leading coefficient equals 1 is equal to the constant term. In fact, matching this assertion, and using the same logic, one must also assert that the sum of the roots of the quadratic equation $x^2 + px + q = 0$ equals $-p$. In order to devise a problem similar to the one discussed above, and make use of this assertion, one needs to note that parallel lines are the ones that have the same slopes. We therefore arrive at the following result.

> All possible parallel lines that traverse the parabola $y = x^2$ in two points are examined. The sum of the abscissas of these two points is the same for all such parallel lines.

We could continue analyzing and generalizing the problem further, but what has been said so far should suffice. Naturally, the above path of reasoning is not the only one possible. Experienced problem solvers shift to equations almost automatically and often cannot tell at what point exactly they went through the first or the third stage in the schema. Furthermore, Polya's recommendations do not in themselves guarantee the solution. For example, following Polya's advice to look for connections with already known problems, an inexperienced solver could end up wasting a lot of time trying to remember various assertions to do with parabolas in the hope of finding something of use. And yet Polya's schema is still of use to problem solvers, helping them organize their efforts.

Heuristic Problem-Solving Strategies

In dealing with the above problem a number of typical mental operations were used that helped us reach the solution. These operations are called heuristics.[1] Polya has provided a range of models of heuristic reasoning, the knowledge of which ought to help one reason. It would be fair to say that it was Polya who drew the contemporary public's attention to heuristics, of which he rightly said that it had been "as good as forgotten today" (Polya, 1973, p. 112).

As Schoenfeld (1985) writes, "Polya's success in reviving what he called 'modern heuristic' was anything but modest" (p. 69). Thanks to Polya's influence, heuristic strategies are now widely used in many classrooms, while entire books and courses are being specially devoted to them (Posamentier & Krulik, 1998; Wickelgren, 1974). A number of such strategies were used in the above example: the strategy of considering a special case (when the point on the ordinate axis had the ordinate 1, or a horizontal line as one of the non-vertical lines), or that of reformulating the problem, for example. We could name several other important ways of using heuristic strategies.

Drawing a Picture

The idea that underlies this heuristic device of drawing a picture could be expressed in a slightly more general way. It consists essentially in representing the given information in a different way, in "translating" it into a different mathematical language (this device has been used above). This heuristic involves the Common Core SMPs of modeling with mathematics and using appropriate tools (e.g., representations) strategically, which are related to NCTM's Representation and Connections standards. More specifically though, the device enables the solver to visualize what has been given as information.

Example: Find all numbers a, such that the equation $1-|x|=|x-a|$ would have exactly two solutions for x.

Discussion

The problem can undoubtedly be solved using standard algebraic methods by examining different cases (when the number x is not negative and larger than a, when it is negative and larger than a, etc.). But let us instead try and solve it by drawing a picture. We could graph the functions $y=1-|x|$ and $y=|x-a|$ for various a (Figure 3.3.). It now becomes apparent that these graphs have exactly two points of intersection when the point $(a,0)$ lies inside the right angle formed by the graph of the function $y=1-|x|$. This happens only when $-1<a<1$.

Solving an Analogous Simpler Problem

This device consists in analyzing a problem that is similar to the original one, only simpler. The solution obtained for the latter provides us with clues for solving the more complex problem. Let us first give a very simple example.

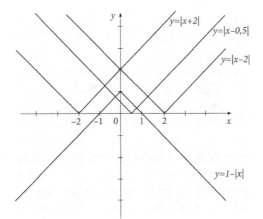

Figure 3.3

Example: How many ways are there of distributing 10 different pencils among 5 boys (so that each pencil can go to any of the boys)?

Discussion

Let us first solve an analogous simpler problem: How many ways are there of distributing only 1 pencil among the 5 boys? And what about 2 pencils?

For one pencil the solution is straightforward—there are 5 different ways since the pencil can be given to any one of the 5 boys. What if we then try to distribute the second pencil? It is clear that the second pencil can similarly be distributed in five different ways. This means that there are in total $5 \cdot 5 = 25$ ways of distributing 2 pencils. If we now return to the original problem, it is easy to conclude that the same will happen with each additional pencil. The answer for 10 pencils is therefore 5^{10}.

This device does not always work as straightforwardly. Let us give a rather more complicated example.

Example: Solve the equation $3^x + 4^x = 7^x$.

Discussion

A simpler analogous problem was examined earlier. We were able to solve the equation $3^x + 4^x = 7$ by guessing the answer ($x = 1$) and by showing that there were no other answers because the function $y = 3^x + 4^x$ was an increasing one and its graph could therefore not intersect the horizontal line $y = 7$ more than once. To guess the root of the more complex equation is also simple. The answer is again $x = 1$. However, the old method no longer works, because instead of the horizontal line we have the graph of the function $y = 7^x$. Generally speaking, two graphs of increasing functions can intersect each other twice, three or, in fact, any number of times (Figure 3.4). Of course, with the help of a graphic calculator it is easy to see that this is not the case with the above function (Figure 3.5). But how would one reach this solution without the use of an electronic device?

The question could be posed in the following manner: Would it be possible to reduce the problem to another, simpler one that has already been solved—to the situation where we would be dealing with a monotonous function and a horizontal line? The answer to this question (which Gestalt psychologists would say requires insight, though the latter undoubtedly needs to be prepared by prior reasoning) is as follows: If we divide the left- and right-hand side of the equation by 7^x we get

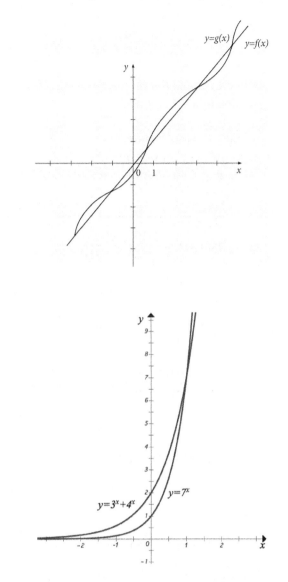

Figure 3.4

Figure 3.5

$$\left(\frac{3}{7}\right)^x + \left(\frac{4}{7}\right)^x = 1.$$

The problem now becomes absolutely identical to the one we solved above. The root of the equation is evidently $x = 1$. There are no others since the graph of the decreasing function

$$y = \left(\frac{3}{7}\right)^x + \left(\frac{4}{7}\right)^x$$

(and the function is decreasing as the sum of decreasing functions) cannot intersect a horizontal line more than once.

Considering a Special Case (finding a pattern)

This strategy is close to the previous one and consists in establishing a general pattern by analyzing a number of concrete cases. Let us look at an example.

Example: Simplify the expression $\dfrac{1 \cdot 1! + 2 \cdot 2! + ... + n \cdot n! + 1}{(n+1)!}$.

Discussion

Let us begin by considering the above expression if $n = 1$. In that case the expression has the form:

$$\frac{1 \cdot 1! + 1}{2!} = \frac{2}{2} = 1.$$

If $n = 2$ it has the form:

$$\frac{1 \cdot 1! + 2 \cdot 2! + 1}{(2+1)!} = \frac{1+4+1}{6} = 1.$$

If $n = 3$ it has the form:

$$\frac{1 \cdot 1! + 2 \cdot 2! + 3 \cdot 3! + 1}{(3+1)!} = \frac{1+4+18+1}{24} = \frac{24}{24} = 1.$$

The hypothesis emerges that the result is always 1, or rather, that $1 \cdot 1! + 2 \cdot 2! + ... + n \cdot n! + 1 = (n+1)!$. What remains to be done now is to prove this hypothesis, for example by means of mathematical induction. This is now a standard exercise. As usual, one has to assume that the assertion is true for n and then prove that the equality $1 \cdot 1! + 2 \cdot 2! + ... + n \cdot n! + (n+1) \cdot (n+1)! + 1 = (n+2)!$, obtained by the substitution of n with $n + 1$, is also true.

With this assumption we get the desired result:

$$1 \cdot 1! + 2 \cdot 2! + \ldots + n \cdot n! + (n+1) \cdot (n+1)! + 1$$

$$= (1 \cdot 1! + 2 \cdot 2! + \ldots + n \cdot n! + 1) + (n+1) \cdot (n+1)!$$

$$= (n+1)! + (n+1) \cdot (n+1)!$$

$$= (n+1)!(1 + n + 1)$$

$$= (n+1)!(n+2)$$

$$= (n+2)!$$

Working Backward

This strategy presumes a careful analysis of the outcome that needs to be reached (proven). The advice is to consider where exactly the assertion that one wants to reach could come from.

Example: Two boys are playing the following game: There are two piles of pebbles—one pile has 2014 pebbles, the other 2013. A move consists in a player getting rid of one of the two piles and splitting the remaining pile into two new, not necessarily equal, piles. Players take turns and the loser is the one who can no longer move. Who will win if both players play the game correctly—the one who goes first or the one who goes second?

Discussion

In which situation would a player not be able to move? It is clear that if at least one pile has at least two pebbles, a move is possible. The losing position is when each "pile" contains just one pebble. Correspondingly, the winning position is when one pile has two pebbles, while the other can have any random number of them. Who can create such a position? Or, put differently, who can prevent the opponent from creating this winning position?

The answer is—the player who goes first. The first player simply needs to play in such a way that the second player is always left with both piles containing an odd number of pebbles. This can be achieved in the following way: The player who goes first removes the pile with 2013 pebbles and splits the remaining one into two piles, each containing an odd number of pebbles. The second player will then be unable to avoid splitting whichever pile he chooses to keep into two, one of which would have to have an even number of pebbles. This would allow the first player again to split this pile into two with an odd number of pebbles each, and so forth. Since the number of pebbles is always decreasing, the winning position will emerge sooner or later, and never for the second player. It follows therefore that the winner is the first player.

Classical examples of working backward are construction problems.

Example: Construct the triangle ABC, knowing its perimeter *p*, and its angles ∠A and ∠B (Figure 3.6a).

Discussion

Let us begin from the end. Let us assume that the triangle is already constructed (Figure 3.6b). Let $m\angle A = \alpha$, $m\angle B = \beta$. Let us now try and visualize the given value *p*. Since we are given a segment, the length of which is equal to the perimeter, let us construct it on the drawing. To do so we construct the segments

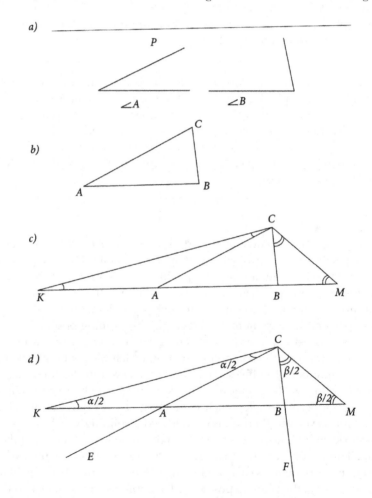

Figure 3.6

$\overline{\text{AK}}$ and $\overline{\text{BM}}$ so that AK = AC and BM = BC (Figure 3.6c). In that case KM = p. Let us look closer at the picture obtained in this way. The triangles AKC and BCM are isosceles. Consequently $\angle$AKC $\cong$ $\angle$ACK and $\angle$BMC $\cong$ $\angle$BCM. Moreover, $\angle$CAB is the external angle of the triangle AKC (and $\angle$CBA of the triangle BCM). As a result, since the size of the external angle of a triangle is equal to the sum of angles not adjacent to it, we get that $m\angle$AKC $+ m\angle$ACK $= 2m\angle$AKC $= \alpha$ and $m\angle$AKC $= \frac{\alpha}{2}$, $m\angle$BMC $+ m\angle$BCM $= 2m\angle$BMC $= \beta$ and $m\angle$BMC $= \frac{\beta}{2}$. Thus, we know two angles of the triangle KCM and we know the base $\overline{\text{KM}}$. Such a triangle can indeed be constructed!

The solution then consists first in constructing the triangle KCM with the base p and the angles CKM and CMK, the measures of which are equal to $\frac{\alpha}{2}$ and $\frac{\beta}{2}$ respectively. It then remains to draw rays $\overrightarrow{CE}$ and $\overrightarrow{CF}$ so that $m\angle$KCE $= \frac{\alpha}{2}$ and $m\angle$MCF $= \frac{\beta}{2}$, obtaining points A and B where $\overrightarrow{CE}$ and $\overrightarrow{CF}$ intersect the segment $\overline{\text{KM}}$ (Figure 3.6.d). (Other solutions are also possible.)

Accounting for All Possibilities

In some problems it is possible simply to go through all the different possibilities. Such a process does not appear particularly creative and seems more appropriate for a machine than a human being. It may not, however, be that easy to isolate these different possibilities or indeed analyze them.

Example: Prove the inequality $x^4 - x^3 + 1 > 0$.

Discussion

Term x^4 is certainly not negative while number 1 is positive. If the third term $-x^3$ is also not negative, and this would be if $x \leq 0$, then the sum is evidently positive. What remains to be done is to see what happens with all cases where x is positive. If $x \leq 1$, then $x^3 \leq 1$, which means that $-x^3 + 1 \geq 0$ and that the entire sum is positive as the sum of one non-negative and one positive value. If, on the other hand, $x > 1$, then $x^4 > x^3$, which means that $x^4 - x^3 > 0$, and therefore the entire sum is positive.

Adopting a Different Point of View

As already noted above, the headings used for particular heuristic strategies allow a fairly broad interpretation. The strategies of using a different mathematical language or of representing a problem in a different way, which were examined earlier, could also be dubbed "adopting a different point of view." Let us, however, give one more example of a problem that could be solved by such a strategy, though this time understanding it in a somewhat different sense.

Example: Written on the board are numbers 1, 2, 3,…2014, 2015. Students are asked to take turns in wiping out any three numbers (let us call them x, y and z) and writing down instead of them two new numbers:

$$\frac{2x+y-z}{3} \text{ and } \frac{x+2y+4z}{3}.$$

This is done until only two numbers remain on the board. Could it be that these last remaining numbers are 1,001,010 and 1,012,005?

Discussion

The conditions of the problem tell us about changes taking place in the process. We are told that some numbers are essentially replaced by others. Problem solvers are therefore tempted to pick out different combinations of three numbers and see what pairs of numbers they get instead. But one could also ask a diametrically opposite question: what is it that remains constant in the process? It is easy to note that

$$\frac{2x+y-z}{3}+\frac{x+2y+4z}{3}=\frac{3x+3y+3z}{3}=x+y+z.$$

This means that even though we are constantly replacing a trio of numbers, we do not, however, replace their sum. This means that the sum of all the numbers written on the board remains the same despite the changes. This sum can be calculated by using the formula for calculating the sum of the members of an arithmetical progression. The latter is equal to

$$\frac{2015\cdot(2015+1)}{2}=\frac{2015\cdot2016}{2}=2015\cdot1008=2,031,120.$$

This does not equal the sum of the numbers 1,001,010 and 1,012,005. It follows that these two numbers cannot be the last ones remaining on the board. (However, we note that if the remaining two numbers did equal the arithmetic sum that would not be sufficient to prove they could be the last numbers remaining on the board.)

Developing Recommendations for Teaching Heuristic Strategies

The point of heuristic strategies lies in the fact that they prompt steps that help problem solvers reach their goal. Polya and his followers were basically saying this: Do not just sit there and wait for insight to come (or not, as the case may be). It is better to examine some concrete case or some simpler but analogous problem. It is better to look ahead to the final, desired result and think of how one could get to it. It is better to try and reformulate the problem, and so forth. As we have seen in the examples above, such strategies can be deployed in practically all spheres of mathematics—geometry, algebra, analysis, and discrete mathematics. In this sense, they represent strategies, rather than algorithms or rules of thumb that apply only to a limited number of concrete objects. Such concrete rules of thumb can be used extremely effectively in accomplishing tasks typically set in school textbooks. (Hundreds if not thousands of teachers all over the world tell their students, for example, that when solving word problems, one can assume that x is what one is asked to find in the end. Students regularly follow this advice, happily avoiding the need to think through what the problem is actually about, and they in fact very often successfully arrive at the solution, since textbook problems where such rules of thumb do not apply are rare indeed.) Heuristic strategies are nothing like that. Their purpose is to help one think rather than to replace one's thinking or make thinking redundant.

Reflecting on Research: Is heuristic practice helpful or not?

Research (Schoenfeld, 1985) shows that explicit heuristic practice on the whole helps students become better problem solvers. In experiments conducted to test this, students whose attention was specially drawn to heuristic strategies of the kind described above showed better results in problem solving than students who were asked to solve the same problems without learning about these strategies. The habit of considering how a problem can be solved also seemed to be transferred to new problems. This indicates that it would be particularly useful to devote lessons not simply to solving problems, but also to discussing strategies for how they can be solved.

At the same time, familiarity with heuristic strategies does not in itself guarantee success (at least not as much as one might wish). Research (Smith, 1973) has also shown that the habit of applying heuristics is hardly ever transferred to different domains. Begle (1979) has even claimed that research into heuristics provides "no clear-cut directions for mathematics education," insofar as the application of particular strategies depends too much both on the problems themselves and on the students who are asked to solve them. It is clear from the above examples at least that heuristic strategies point one in the direction of the solution in only a very general way.

Specifying heuristic strategies. Schoenfeld (1985) has remarked that "carrying out a strategy such as 'exploiting an easier related problem,' for example, involves six or seven separate major phases, each of which is a potential cause of difficulty. Training in the use of the strategy must involve training in all of those phases" (p. 73).

Schoenfeld (1985, 1992) has consequently campaigned for more prescriptive variants of heuristics training. He has recommended that each strategy be articulated in a more concrete form, with much more specific recommendations regarding its application. The strategy of examining special cases could be rendered more concrete in the following variants:

Strategy 1. When dealing with problems in which an integer parameter n plays a prominent role, it may be of use to examine values of $n = 1, 2, 3 \ldots$ in sequence, in search of a pattern.

Strategy 2. When dealing with problems that concern the roots of polynomials, it may be of use to look at easily factorable polynomials.

Strategy 3. When dealing with problems that concern sequences or series that are constructed recursively, it may be of use to try initial values of 0 and 1—if such choices don't destroy the generality of the process under investigation." (Schoenfeld, 1992).

The recommendation of reformulating a problem is developed by Schoenfeld (1985) in the following manner:

1. Replace givens or goals with equivalent conditions (e.g., "closed" with "compliment of open" or "contains all its limit points", "parallelogram" with "opposite sides equal and parallel," etc.)
2. Try to reformulate the problem using
    a. a more convenient notation or a different perspective.
    b. a logically equivalent form (e.g., argument by contrapositive)
3. Reorganize the problem by
    a. arranging things in a different way (e.g., infinite series)
    b. introducing something new (lines in a diagram, for example) (p. 112)

In this way one gets something in-between rigid prescription of algorithms typical of routine problems and the vagueness of overly general recommendations. Heuristic strategies thus become more closely associated with particular subject domains. They appear as typical ideas of use in frequently encountered situations. (Note that isolating typical ideas and situations is useful in problem solving more generally and not just in mathematics. Such ideas play a particularly important part in chess training, for instance (Silman, 1997), where players plan how to counter particular opening moves.)

In preparing lessons, the practicing teacher should consider which typical strategies would be especially useful in studying a particular domain of mathematics, by what means students should be introduced to these strategies, and how one should teach their application.

Reflection

Assignments and Topics for Discussion

1. Analyze your own practice of problem solving. Can you recall a situation from your own problem solving experience that you would describe as insight?

2. K. Duncker (1945) conducted experiments with the following problem: Why are all six-digit numbers of the form 276,276; 591,591; and 112,112 divisible by 13? (The reason is that all such numbers are multiples of 1001). Duncker noticed that the problem is solved more easily if as examples one gives the numbers 276,276; 277,277; and 278,278. How would you explain this?

3a. The problem is set in the following way: "Prove that the point lying on the bisector of an angle is situated at an equal distance from its sides." Reformulate the problem to reveal the sense of concepts such as "bisector" and "distance between a point and a straight line."

b. Give other examples of reformulating problems that consist of exposing the content of the terms used in the original formulation.

4a. The condition of a problem specifies that the graph of a quadratic function intersects the abscissa axis in two points $x = 1$ and $x = 2$. Translate this condition into the language of algebra.

b. The condition of a problem contains the equation $|x-1| = 2$. Reformulate this condition using the term "distance."

c. Give other examples of reformulating problems that consist in establishing connections with other parts of mathematics.

5. Recommend how to use substitution in order to solve an equation below. Which auxiliary problem would one then need to solve?
(a) $2\sin^2 x - \sin x - 1 = 0$; (b) $4^x - 2^{x+2} = -3$.

6. The same equation is expressed in two different ways. Which of the two is easier to solve? Why?
(1)(a) $4x - x^2 - 3 = 0$, (b) $x^2 - 4x + 3 = 0$;

(2)(a) $\dfrac{(x+1)^4}{x^2} - 3x = 10 + \dfrac{3}{x}$, (b) $\left(x + \dfrac{1}{x} + 2\right)^2 - 3\left(x + \dfrac{1}{x}\right) - 10 = 0$.

7a. From the assertion that in every triangle the bisectors of its angles intersect in a single point, the student assumes, by analogy that the same would also apply to every quadrilateral. Is this assertion true? How would you advise the student to go about testing this assumption?

b. Give examples of other assertions that are arrived at by analogy that are themselves (1) true; (2) untrue.

8a. A student is asked to determine the area of a figure, for which it is known that the distances between several of its points equal a, b and c. The student arrives at a formula for the area:

$$\frac{ab\sqrt{a^4+b^4+c^4}}{c}.$$

Immediately you recognize the formula cannot be valid. How would you advise the student to check this formula?

b. Solving the system of equations

$$\begin{cases} x^5+y^5=1 \\ x^2+y^2=1 \end{cases},$$

the student answers that the solution is the pair $(0, 1)$. How would you advise the student to check this solution?

c. The student has come up with the following formula for the area of an arbitrary triangle ABC:

$$AB \cdot BC \cos\frac{m\angle A + m\angle C}{2}.$$

How would you advise the student to check it?

9. Give an example of a problem that you know has several solutions. Which solution do you like best and why?

10. Cite or invent a problem that can be solved in the same way as the two examples above: a) the one about proving the inequality $x^4 - x^3 + 1 > 0$; and b) the one about replacing three numbers with two new ones derived from the three that are being substituted.

11. Take any problem and analyze how its solution could be realized according to Polya's four-stage schema. (Suggest how solvers should reason at each stage and what questions they should answer.)

12. Study the book Posementier & Krulik, 1998, and select examples of problems that would particularly benefit from using some of the heuristic strategies examined in this section (give one example per strategy).

13. The following problem is being examined: Prove that for all points that lie on the base $\overline{AC}$ of the isosceles triangle ABC, the sum of the distances between such a point and the other sides of the triangle would be the same. (a) Use the strategy of considering special cases in order to reformulate the problem and thereby clarify what this sum is supposed to be; (b) Examine the specific case of the right isosceles triangle. Do a precise drawing and formulate assertions, the proof of which would enable you to obtain what is required. Carry out the full proof; (c) Solve the problem (ideally in two different

ways); (d) Prove that for all points that lie inside an equilateral triangle, the sum of the distances between such a point and the sides of the triangle is one and the same; and (e) Think of another such generalization and elaboration of the problem.

NOTE

1. "Heuristic reasoning is reasoning not regarded as final and strict but as provisional and plausible only, whose purpose is to discover the solution of the present problem" (Polya, 1973, p. 113).

CHAPTER 4

INTEGRATING PROBLEM SOLVING INTO THE CURRICULUM

The purpose of this chapter is to acquaint the reader with the way in which problem solving is being used in school practice and to show how this can be developed further.

The chapter discusses:

- Examples of difficulties experienced by students in the process of problem solving.
- The role of the resources and beliefs of problem solvers, as well as the latter's capacity to control and monitor their activity.
- Ways of organizing problem solving in the classroom and the role of the teacher in such activities.
- Various purposes that problem solving can serve in class work, and in the learning process in general, with illustrative examples.

Mathematics in Middle and Secondary School, pages 91–128
Copyright © 2015 by Information Age Publishing
All rights of reproduction in any form reserved.

EXAMINING SCHOOL REALITY

Solving an Unfamiliar Problem

The Case of the Area of a Parallelogram

The procedure of working with problems in the classroom is often very remote from that dreamed of by Polya and his followers. The psychologist Max Wertheimer (1959) gave a classical description of a lesson devoted to parallelograms (pp. 13–16). What follows is a summary of this description with some abbreviations.

At the beginning of the lesson the teacher reminds the class that in the previous lesson they have learned how to determine the area of a rectangle and checks that the students remember the appropriate formula. He then "gives a number of problems with rectangles of varying sizes, which all solve readily."

The teacher then moves on to the new topic. He draws a parallelogram (Figure 4.1a) and reminds the class of its definition. At this point a student asks what lengths the sides of the parallelogram would be and the teacher replies that "the sides may be of very different lengths." He continues by saying that "In our case [on the drawing], one side measures 11 inches, the other 5 inches." The student then guesses that the area of the parallelogram is 5 · 11 square inches. "No" answers the teacher. "That's wrong; you will now learn how to find the area of parallelogram."

The teacher then completes the drawing (Figure 4.1b), marking it with letters and accompanying each step with appropriate explanations. He conducts a thorough proof that the triangles ade and bcf are congruent, from which he reaches the conclusion that the areas of the parallelogram abcd and of the rectangle edcf are equal, since they both consist of the same figure edcb plus the congruent triangles. "In each case he [the teacher] states the previously learned theorem, postulate, or axiom upon which the equality or congruence is based." The teacher concludes that it has been proven that the area of the parallelogram is equal to the base times the altitude.

After that the class is asked to find the area of different parallelograms and the class accomplishes these assignments without any problems. Similar problems are given for homework, along with reading the section of the textbook that contains the proof of the theorem.

In the next lesson Wertheimer asks permission from the teacher to set the class the problem of determining the area of the parallelogram depicted in Figure 4.1c and observes the reaction of the class.

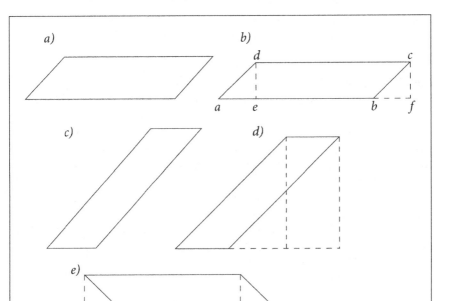

Figure 4.1

Some are obviously taken aback.

One student raises his hand: "Teacher, we haven't had that yet."

Others are busy. They have copied the figure on paper, they draw the auxiliary lines as they were taught, dropping perpendiculars from the two upper corners and extending the base line. Then they look bewildered, perplexed (Figure 4.1.d).

Some do not look at all unhappy; they write firmly below their drawing: "The area is equal to the base times altitude"—a correct assumption, but perhaps an entirely blind one. When asked whether they can show it to be true in this case they too become perplexed."

Only very few students do what Wertheimer is looking for—having rotated the drawing, they drop the perpendiculars onto the other side (Figure 4.1. e), after which they are able to apply the kind of reasoning previously demonstrated by the teacher.

Wertheimer wrote that during the first lesson he had asked himself the following questions about the children: "What have they learned? Have they done any thinking at all? Maybe all that they have done is little more than blind repetition?" Their reaction to the picture he gave them hardly dispels such concerns. When faced with a suddenly changed situation, the vast majority of students either did not know what to do or simply tried to ignore the obvious differences. The kind of reasoning that worked in situations already encountered by students clearly failed to provide a solution in the new case; it was not possible in the new drawing to construct the rectangle in the way used previously. But the students simply did not grasp this because for them the proof was clearly just a formality that bore no relation to reality.

Is the teacher to blame for what happened? This is what one of the students thought. The student had attended the same lesson in a different class and whispered to Wertheimer that his class had, in fact, discussed the above drawing. Indeed, there is no doubt that if the teacher had shown the students how to reason in this somewhat different case, the class would have had no difficulties in reproducing the solution and the researcher would have been obliged to think of another example. However, it is impossible to show students the solution to every single type of problem, and doing so in one additional case would hardly have changed the way students thought.

The Teacher Misses an Opportunity

Wertheimer was interested in studying patterns of thinking far more than methods of teaching. For this reason his book provides no commentary on how the teaching was actually conducted (in fact, he invariably emphasizes how conscientious and thorough the teacher was). Let us, however, look more closely at the moment where the student formulated the hypothesis that the area of the parallelogram with the sides of 5 and 11 inches equals 55 square inches. This is, of course, incorrect. However, this is the only moment in the lesson where a student exhibited any sort of active thought and desire to engage with the problem. A new situation had arisen (the case of the parallelogram). The student formulated a hypothesis (incidentally, the student, in Polya's terms, sought the solution through analogy), and engaged the class and the teacher in considering this problem. This student, as well as the class as a whole, would probably have been able to draw various parallelograms with 5- and 11-inch sides (Figure 4.2a), had the teacher decided to entertain the student's thought. If they then compared them, they would have been able to conclude that the areas were different and that the hypothesis was therefore untrue, which would have been a clear attempt at solving the problem. Alternately, the teacher could have explored what there were 55 of in the parallelogram—namely rhombi not squares (Figure 4.2b). But the teacher was not interested in solving problems. He simply stated that the student's approach was wrong and demonstrated to the class how to proceed correctly.

It would be wrong to say that if the teacher had reacted differently to the student's remark (in this and even all other similar cases) all students would necessarily start acting like true problem solvers whenever they encountered a new problem. The case discussed by Wertheimer confirms, however, that if teachers do not work on developing the habit of problem solving,

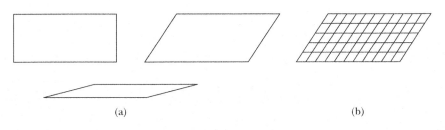

(a)   (b)

Figure 4.2

and limit their teaching to a conscientious reproduction of the textbook, then students will not acquire such habits and will abandon any attempt at genuine thinking.

Studying the Practice of Problem Solving

Researchers have recorded many situations of problem solving in the classroom. This allows one to study in some detail what causes students the greatest difficulties. Basing his study on such protocols, Schoenfeld (1985, p. 15) has distinguished the following four categories of "knowledge and behavior necessary for an adequate characterization of mathematical problem solving performance": Resources, Heuristics, Control, and Beliefs. Their content is elaborated in the Table 4.1.

Examining *an* **Example**   **Example of a Problem**

Let us, for example, analyze the problem that Schoenfeld has used in his research.

> You are given two intersecting straight lines and a point P marked on one of them. Show how to construct, using straightedge and compass, a circle that is tangent to both lines and that has the point P as one of its points of tangency (Figure 4.3a).

The solution consists in constructing the bisector of the given angle and then constructing the perpendicular to the given straight line at point P, taking point O where the two intersect as the center of the circle. Its radius would be OP (Figure 4.3b).

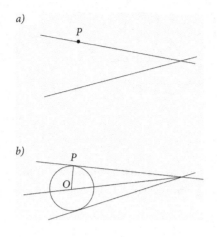

Figure 4.3

TABLE 4.1

Resources: Mathematical knowledge possessed by the individual that can be brought to bear on the problem hand.
- Intuitions and informal knowledge regarding the domain
- Facts
- Algorithmic procedures
- "Routine" non-algorithmic procedures
- Understanding (propositional knowledge) about the agreed-upon rules for working in the domain

Heuristics: Strategies and techniques for making progress on unfamiliar or nonstandard problems, rules of thumb for effective problem solving, including
- Drawing figures; introducing suitable notation
- Exploiting related problems
- Reforming problems: working backwards
- Testing and verification procedures

Control: Global decisions regarding the selection and implementation of resources and strategies
- Planning
- Monitoring and assessment
- Decision-making
- Conscious metacognitive acts

Belief systems: One's "mathematical world view," the set of (not necessarily conscious) determinants of an individual behavior
- About self
- About the environment
- About the topic
- About mathematics.

Which Resources are Required Here?

It is obvious that in order to solve the problem one needs to understand what it means to make a construction using compass and straightedge. It is also necessary to know the algorithms for constructing the bisector of an angle and the perpendicular to a straight line. The following facts were also used:

- The tangent of a circle is perpendicular to the radius at the point of tangency.
- The center of the circle inscribed in an angle lies on the angle's bisector.

All these are the resources that one needs in order to solve the problem. Some of these can be obtained in the process of solving the problem, which suggests that an accurate and exhaustive description of necessary resources is hardly possible. It is clear, however, that without the support of existing knowledge the problem cannot be solved.

Reflecting on Research: Having the resources is not enough!

As demonstrated by experiments conducted by Schoenfeld, the presence of resources does not guarantee the solution of the problem (this is also confirmed in other research (i.e., Garofalo & Lester, 1985), which shows that students are sometimes unable to solve problems even when they have all the knowledge required). Research protocols have recorded a fairly wide-range of disordered activity that problem solvers undertook in the above case. Some performed a number of different operations, while others drew different straight lines and expressed a whole variety of suppositions, usually without pursuing any of them to the end and without evaluating whether it was worth going down a particular path or not. The steps that these solvers took were very remote from the heuristics strategies examined above. What is most important, however, is that they did not know how to establish control over what they were doing. They acted as if they were hoping that the solution would just suddenly turn up all on its own. They had no plan or system for organizing what was being done, which is precisely what led to failure.

Furthermore, the students often did not perceive any connection between the problem and what they already knew. In their minds, mathematical theorems were one thing, while problems were something completely different. Schoenfeld concluded that at the root of this lay a particular system of beliefs. He has described this system, articulating in a somewhat exaggerated form the beliefs of a typical student (p. 43):

Belief 1. Formal mathematics has little or nothing to do with real thinking or problem solving.

Consequence. In a problem that calls for discovery, formal mathematics will not be invoked.

Belief 2. Mathematics problems are always solved in less than 10 minutes, if they are solved at all.

Consequence. If students cannot solve a problem in 10 minutes, they give up.

Belief 3. Only geniuses are capable of discovering or creating mathematics.

First consequence. If you (a typical student) forget something, too bad. After all, you are not a genius and you will not be able to derive it on your own.

Second consequence. Students accept procedures at face value, and do not try to understand why they work. After all, such procedures are derived knowledge passed on "from above."

Hardly anyone would ever seriously express his/her views about mathematics in this way. However, even if we concede that many students unconsciously conceive of mathematics in this way, then no heuristics or planning or observation of results would be possible, or even necessary, while problem solving in general would become futile.

Conclusions for Teachers

The above analysis points to the fact that the teacher's task is not simply to enrich the students' resources (which is considered to be the traditional role of teaching) or teach them how to apply the various heuristic strategies we examined above. The teacher's task is also to develop the habit of controlling the activity of problem solving, while also forging in students' minds a system of beliefs that would allow them to see themselves as active and creative participants in school mathematics.

The Principles and Standards for School Mathematics specify that "effective problem solvers constantly monitor and adjust what they are doing"—in other words, that they are constantly in control of what they are doing. The teacher needs to know how to develop this habit in students. Fostering and forming students' beliefs is even more complicated since its success depends on a radical transformation of the usual school routine.

The Roots of Students' Beliefs about Problem Solving

It is perfectly clear that students derive their beliefs from everyday school practice. Schoenfeld (1985) has studied this practice, including how problems are solved in class, what sorts of commentaries are made by teachers, what sort of advice is given to students, and so forth. He has isolated the following dichotomies that the teacher is confronted with:

- Empiricism versus deduction
- Meaning versus form
- Problems versus exercises
- Passive versus active mathematics

Schoenfeld's conclusions were quite depressing. What seemed to be constantly emphasized in one form or another was the role of practice, memorization and accuracy. This was done in such a way that the rational and properly mathematical basis of what was being studied became completely obscured. What teachers were essentially telling their students was the following: "This is how this or that is done; and this how you too should do it; just make sure you do it properly." Why something was done in a particular way and what lay at the basis of a particular approach, became utterly inconsequential.

Most tasks set in class took little more than 2 minutes to solve. Schoenfeld rightly concluded that students were thereby denied the opportunity to engage with problems of any sort of substance and that this was precisely where they acquired the belief that if the solution did not come quickly there was no point in even considering it further.

Finally, Schoenfeld noted that instruction usually boiled down to the teacher simply communicating the results and then justifying their correctness. Solving problems amounted to step-by-step procedures that students were meant to memorize. Consequently, the teacher's efforts in helping students solve problems practically always only consisted of asking questions such as "what should the first step in solving such a problem be?" or "what should the next step be?" Students were condemned to the role of passive recipients of knowledge.

Changing Students' Beliefs: You Can Make a Difference!

As noted above, students' beliefs can have a negative influence on school practice, while these beliefs in turn emerge precisely from school practice itself. When referring to school practice, what is important is not the rhetoric—what one *claims* should happen in class, but what *actually happens* there—the daily routine of the classroom. Teachers need to recognize how important organizing the class actually is, and, especially, to be aware of the manner in which the four dichotomies mentioned by Schoenfeld are being negotiated. This is important not just in dealing with this or that particular topic, but in the way the teacher develops the students' general attitude towards the study of mathematics (this may be particularly significant for teachers of the middle school, which is the stage at which such attitudes frequently are formed).

How to Teach Problem Solving?

Some Practical Recommendations

Teachers tend to work in conditions of fixed external requirements. It is hardly possible, for example, to propose to the teacher not to spend too much time on two-minute exercises, if it is precisely that sort of exercise that is on the tests by which the work of both the children and the teacher is judged. There are, however, other reasons for why it is difficult to organize problem solving properly in regular lessons.

Let us take as an example the exclusion of "long" problems—problems for which the solution presents certain difficulties and may therefore require more time. Teachers are often worried that they will be unable to control the class in such circumstances and that the class will lose interest in the problem if it is not being solved immediately. To be fair, such concerns are often justified, because schoolchildren very often do not know how to work with complex problems. The teacher who simply throws a difficult problem at the class will indeed not only fail in furthering the students' habits of problem solving, but will actually scare schoolchildren away from mathematics for good.

Reflecting on Research: The case study of a novice teacher.

The lack of a proper theoretical understanding of what problems and problem solving actually are, which was discussed above, can have a direct impact on teaching practices. Cooney (1985) cites the case of a novice teacher, Fred, who started his first job with the conviction that problem solving was important in the classroom, but who, after only three months of teaching, renounced his views and became a firm believer that a teacher should, in the good-old-fashioned way, simply spell out the rules and drill students in their application.

In Fred's mind, problem solving referred merely to the solution of special problems devoted to recreational mathematics and he opposed this to the study of mathematics content. Cooney writes that Fred "appeared to view problem solving as a layer of a cake. It may be a thick layer, but nevertheless it is a layer and not an ingredient like sugar that might be mixed homogeneously in the cake." Fred believed that by giving students a few recreational mathematics problems, which had little connection with what was being studied in regular classes, he was initiating his students into real mathematics and opening up to them this allegedly remote world. In practice, students did not take these problems particularly seriously and saw their teacher as someone who only wanted to play games. This is how, faced with a wall of incomprehension, Fred decided to radically change his approach. Beginning teachers not infrequently encounter difficulties when attempting to arrange genuine problem solving instruction (Karp, 2010).

On Teaching Problem Solving to Different Audiences

Kantowski (1980) has written about the need for teachers to work differently with various audiences, depending on the students' previous experiences with problem solving. She has distinguished four levels of development in problem solving skills.

First level—

Students have little or no understanding of what problem solving is, of the meaning of strategy, or of mathematical structure in the problem. Most students at this level do not know where to begin to solve a non-routine problem.

Teacher assumes the role of *model*.

Second level—

Students understand the meaning of problem solving, of strategy, and the mathematical structure of a problem. They are able to follow someone else's solution and can often suggest strategies to be tried for problems similar to those they have seen before. Although they will participate actively in group problem solving activities or instructional episodes, many feel insecure about independent problem solving.

Teacher acts as *prosthesis*, or *crutch*.

Third level—

Students begin to feel comfortable with problems. They suggest strategies different from those they have seen used. They understand and appreciate that problems may have multiple solutions and that "no solution" may be a perfectly good solution.

Teacher becomes problem *provider*.

Fourth level—

Students are able to select appropriate strategies for most problems encountered and are successful in finding solutions much of the time... They suggest variations of old problems and are constantly searching for novel problems to challenge themselves and others.

Teacher serves at *facilitator*.

(Kantowski, 1980, pp. 198–199)

Most frequently the teacher assumes the first two roles—that of a model and that of a prosthesis, or a crutch. These two roles require teachers to pay special attention to their actions while solving problems and to have the skill to demonstrate in class how one reasons in mathematics. The teacher here does not simply communicate the result, but demonstrates how one can arrive at it, and frequently re-enacts or imitates the process of discovery (even in cases where the teacher acquired this knowledge passively).

Examining an Example   **Recalling an Earlier Example**

Let us return to the class studied by Wertheimer and to the question of how the teacher, who decided to state immediately the formula for the area of the parallelogram, could have acted instead. He could have

- Highlighted the difference between the new situation and the one already learned
- Formulated a new problem
- Discussed resources (knowledge and formulas), that could be of use
- Dwelt on various possible ideas for the solution, showed how they were used in other, related problems, and then imitated the thought process of trying to apply them to the new situation (e.g., "Shouldn't we perhaps try to cut up a rectangle and make a parallelogram out of its pieces? Didn't we do something similar with a triangle (Figure 4.4.) when we constructed it out of the pieces of a square?").

Getting Students to Reach the Final Result Themselves

It is obvious that the teacher telling the students the result was not (and is not) the only, nor probably the best, pedagogical solution. Teachers can organize a lesson in such a way that the students themselves actually perform

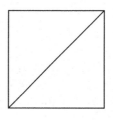

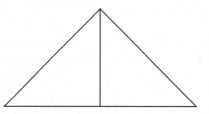

Figure 4.4

actions that would be part of genuine problem solving. While serving as a *crutch*, the teacher *structures the lesson*, and includes in it a sequence of interconnected activities, each of which could be quite brief. These could be both individual and group activities, and they could also include the teacher's explanations. It is in fact crucial that the sequence is accompanied by the teacher's questions or explanations, as this would enable the students to grasp what has actually been achieved and how their various actions were mutually connected. Care, however, needs to be taken to make sure that the teacher breaking down a problem into smaller concrete steps is only the beginning of developing problem solving rather than its final result; indeed, always specifying smaller tasks and sub-steps toward solving a problem does not necessarily instill problem solving, but can hinder it, creating a dependence for the student on someone else providing an outline of concrete steps to complete.

Students would therefore not remain one-on-one with a problem that, to begin with, may have appeared to be beyond their capabilities. Instead, they would gradually learn what sort of questions to ask and what sort of action to take. One could say that this way their system of beliefs would be gradually transformed.

Examining *an* Example	**Returning Once Again to the Lesson on the Area of the Parallelogram**

Let us again return to the area of the parallelogram. Students will almost certainly be unable to derive the formula for it independently. Recall what has been said above about students not being accustomed to dealing with problems that require more than two minutes to solve. Yet what the teacher can do is give students several such 'two-minute problems' in a series, which would together lead to the desired conclusion. In order to achieve this one needs to think about how to *split one large problem into parts, isolating intermediary results.*

What exactly does one need in order to realize that the area of a parallelogram is equal to the product of its base and its altitude? The reasoning conducted by the teacher included an additional construction (that of the parallelogram's altitudes), the proof of the congruence of the triangles, the realization of the equality of the areas of the parallelogram and the rectangle, and the conclusion about the formula (Figure 4.5a).

What intermediary problems could the teacher have given? There are various ways of going about this. One possibility would be to give students, as an initial assignment, models of a triangle and a trapezoid and ask them to construct both a parallelogram and a rectangle using the two shapes (Figure4.5b). The following assignment would then be to compare the areas of the parallelogram and the rectangle. Next, students could be asked

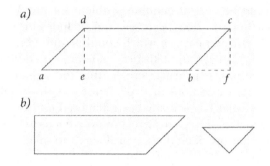

Figure 4.5

to examine a random parallelogram, to draw its altitudes and to prove the congruence of the triangles obtained in this way. And finally, in conclusion, students could be asked to explain how to find the area of a parallelogram, knowing its altitude and base. (Note that in giving such activities and questions you should not always demand a formal proof that uses impeccable notation. This, in fact, should be required relatively infrequently.)

Using Structured Problem Solving

The sorts of questions that can be asked depend considerably on what the class is like. Classroom organization and management in this type of teaching (which Stiegler and Hiebert (1999) have aptly called "structured problem solving") is actually easier than if students were asked to work individually on a problem that could take a relatively long period of time to solve. Even more important, though, is that by splitting the problem into parts, by suggesting a plan for its solution or discussing the results obtained in the process, and by summarizing the outcome of a series of activities, the teacher shows and models for students how to control the process of problem solving. Students receive models of questions that they can then ask themselves and they become accustomed to the process of reflecting on what has been accomplished.

Teaching an Entire Course Through Problem Solving

In what follows, considerable attention will be devoted to general questions of problem posing and to concrete examples of splitting a complex problem into a number of simpler ones and then formulating questions on a variety of topics. Let us again stress that instruction in problem solving needs to be introduced gradually and in stages, but in a systematic way and throughout the course as a whole, and not just in exceptional cases and with the use of special material.

In particular, the teacher needs to be able to take any situation as open to further exploration. In the above description, Kantowski (1980) rightly observes the importance of students being aware that different solutions to the same problem can exist. We believe that even the most inexperienced students (those situated on Kantowski's level one) should be made aware of this.

Teachers who aim to help students develop the habit of problem solving need to transform the routine of merely learning an algorithm into a useful problem solving activity. They should not only show examples of how to apply a rule but also discuss different possible algorithms, comparing their respective strengths and weaknesses, and then rejecting those that did not work.

At the same time, even those parts of mathematics that offer the greatest scope for mathematical creativity (such as, for example, the creation of formulas for areas of polygons) can, in practice, be turned into thoughtless subjects, learned by rote. Indeed, the beliefs and attitudes of students towards mathematics are to an inordinate extent determined by the beliefs and attitudes of their teachers.

Reflection

Assignments and Topics for Discussion

1. How would you organize a lesson devoted to the area of parallelograms and how would you engage students in productive thinking? Prepare a plan for such a lesson.
2. Wertheimer (1959) states that he finds it surprising that some textbooks provide a detailed explanation of how one should reason in the case of a drawing like the one seen in Figure 4.6, by producing multiple cuts and translations of the parallelogram to fit into a rectangle with dimensions equal to the parallelogram's base and altitude. In his view, this is not necessary because the solution could also be found by dropping the altitude onto the other side. Do you agree with this argument? Explain your position on the matter.
3. What resources are required for the solution of the problem about the abscissas of the points of intersection of the parabola and the straight line (pp. 56–57)? Analyze the resources necessary for solving the problems discussed in Chapter 3 (pp. 59–65).

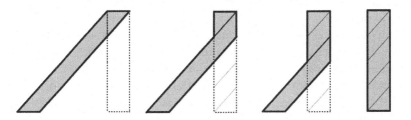

Figure 4.6

4. How do you think the belief is formed that only geniuses are capable of discovering or creating mathematics? How could one amend his/her teaching practice in order to change this belief?

5. The following problem is examined: work out the last digit of the number 7^{2014}. Solve the problem. How would you retell its solution to students who are not very experienced in problem solving? Compile a series of problems that would help students solve this problem independently.

6. Suggest several ways of multiplying the numbers 125 and 32. Give another example of a situation where, in addition to the most widespread algorithm, one could also propose another.

WHAT ROLES CAN PROBLEM SOLVING PLAY IN TEACHING MATHEMATICS?

Problem solving can be woven into the texture of the education process in a number of different ways; it can perform a variety of roles and produce a variety of results. Stanic and Kilpatrick (1989) distinguish three general themes that characterize the role of problem solving in the school mathematics curriculum:

- Problem solving as Context
- Problem solving as Skill
- Problem solving as Art.

They relate the first theme to situations where the solution to the problem plays a somewhat auxiliary role and where problems are used as the means of achieving this or that concrete educational aim in the context of mathematics. The second and third types refer to situations where problem solving is, to some extent, understood as an aim in and of itself or as the means of achieving certain general aspects of human development (such as the development of thought or of aesthetic feeling or of the ability to orientate oneself to and function in the real world). In this context, those who understand problem solving primarily as a skill usually concentrate on routine problems (which really ought to be called exercises), while the view of problem solving as Art, which comes especially from Polya, is usually associated with work on non-routine problems.

Let us examine some examples of different ways in which problems can be used, dividing these into situations where the problems serve as means for achieving other goals, and where the problems serve as aims in and of themselves.

Problems as Means

Following Stanic and Kilpatrick (1989), let us distinguish several main possible ways of using problem solving (these are closely interconnected and to some extent mutually overlapping).

Problem Solving as Justification

Problems can be introduced into the lesson in order to show the value of studying mathematics in general or to demonstrate the importance of a particular part of mathematics. For example, in preparation for the study of areas of polygons, the teacher can give students a problem of comparing two pieces of land (Figure 4.7a), asking which of the two would be better to own? In some cases the answer is fairly obvious, since one of the pieces of land is visibly smaller than the other (Figure 4.7b), or the two are obviously of the same size even though they have different shapes (Figure 4.7c). In other cases the answer is not as straightforward. One can discuss in class the fact that even when all the sides of a polygon are measurable, establishing the area is not necessarily straightforward. One could mention, for example, that in Ancient

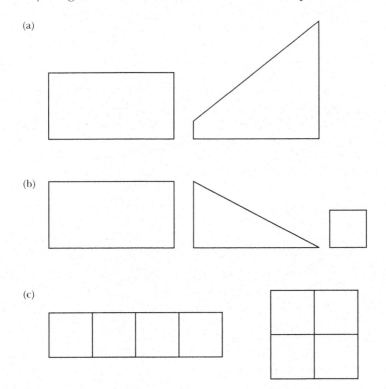

Figure 4.7

Egypt it was sometimes believed that polygons with equal sides also had equal areas (Eves, 1990). One could ask the class to consider whether this is plausible. (The parallelograms in Figure 4.2., already discussed, have equal sides but visibly unequal areas.) Conversing with students about such problems demonstrates the importance of deducing formulas (rules) for finding the areas of polygons and serves as a justification for studying the topic.

In particular, the history of mathematics provides plenty of examples of problems whose solution has become of great importance to humanity. As a source of problems that can be used to justify the study of this or that topic, one could also use specific case studies, where a protagonist is prompted to seek a mathematical solution to some problem. In this regard, situations taken from famous novels or movies may be particularly effective.

Examining *an* **Example**   **Using Literature as a Source of Problems**

Arthur Conan Doyle's, *"The Adventure of the Musgrave Ritual,"* in which Sherlock Holmes needs to find the hidden crown of the British kings, offers some potentially useful problems. In this story, an ancient ritual provides instructions about the exact spot where the crown is buried. It gives the direction and the distance needed to walk from a particular point—the far end of the shadow cast by an elm tree, at the time when the sun was clear of the oak. However, the elm is no longer there. The owner of the land, Musgrave, recalls from childhood that it was 64 feet tall. This information alone allows Holmes to solve the problem. (When he later told Watson about it, the latter could not refrain from the comment: "That must have been difficult, Holmes, if the elm was no longer there.") So how did Holmes solve the problem? He placed a pole where the elm used to stand, measured its shadow when the sun was clear of the oak, and multiplied this length with the ratio of 64 feet and the length of the pole. He essentially used triangle similarity.

The teacher could suggest to the students to read the story at home and then discuss in class how mathematics was used in that particular case, and why the method proposed by Holmes was correct. The discussion of the solution to this problem could serve as a justification for the study of similar figures.

Issues to consider: Some recommendations.   In thinking about the way to teach a particular topic, the teacher should consider what students would benefit from the most in studying it. What substantially new problems would they be able to solve afterwards? Why is that important? The most significant and illustrative problems could then be given at the beginning of studying the topic. In doing so, it is also useful to draw students' attention to these problems later on, both during the study of the topic, and at the end, at the point where one discusses what exactly has been achieved and why it is important. Ideally, students should be able to see the relevance of what has been learned quickly. Telling them that they need to do something for the sake of exams or because it will be of use to them in two-three years time, when they are in a higher grade, usually fails to convince.

At the same time, however, while realizing the significance of using problem solving as justification, the teacher should avoid abusing it. School mathematics has its own logic of development. One should not avoid parts of school mathematics with the excuse that this or that small section of the textbook does not in itself have any practical use. (Nor should one try to think up artificial uses for such sections.) Students are perfectly capable of accepting that particular parts of mathematics are of an auxiliary nature. What is really important is for problems that serve as a justification of a particular topic not to be postponed for too long.

Problem Solving as Motivation

Using problems solving as motivations could also incorporate problems similar to those discussed above; indeed, by demonstrating the various uses of mathematics, the teacher inevitably works on strengthening students' motivation. However, the problems that we actually include here are those specifically intended to arouse the students' interest and curiosity towards a particular topic (whether one immediately perceives their practical usefulness or not).

Examining *an* Example   A Mathematical Trick

The example of such a problem is the following simple mathematical trick that could be shown in a pre-algebra class. You could ask the class to think of a number, without revealing it, and then conduct the following operations on it: (1) add 3; (2) multiply the result by 4;(3) take away 9; (4) take away the student's own original number; (5) divide this by 3; and (6) again, take away the original number. At this point, to the great surprise of your perplexed class, you could pensively announce that everyone's final result must be 1.

The trick's mechanism is simple: let us write down what takes place after each instruction, taking x as the number that a particular student in the class has chosen.

Instruction	Result
Add 3	$x + 3$
Multiply by 4	$4(x + 3) = 4x + 12$
Subtract 9	$4x + 3$
Take away the original number	$3x + 3$
Divide by 3	$x + 1$
Take away the original number	1

The trick would be a good way to open a lesson dedicated to the use of variables and (or) the distributive property. Depending on whether the lesson is situated at the beginning or the end of a unit, the teacher could either immediately ask the students to find an explanation for why the trick has worked, or else postpone such discussion by informing the class that the topic to be discussed in the lesson is precisely what will help them understand the trick.

A variant of the same trick can also be given later on when discussing how to solve equations. In this case, instead of asking students in the end to subtract the number they have thought of, you can lead them to the result of, say, $5x$. After students share their particular result, you can then tell them immediately what their original number was (having divided the result by 5 in your head). This kind of introduction could be used as a way of getting students interested in solving linear equations.

Generally speaking, students' attention is especially drawn to what is surprising, unexpected and counterintuitive. Cognitive conflict produced in this way inevitably prompts students to think about the problem. A similar effect is achieved by problems where students are asked to locate the error on a particular path of reasoning that ultimately leads to an unmistakably wrong result (such as 1 being equal to 2).

| Examining |
| *an* Example | **A More Advanced Example**

In considering how to motivate students to determine the exact limit of an expression, the teacher can look for examples where carelessness in reasoning, or an over-reliance on the obvious, leads one to make evident mistakes.

Let us give an example of such reasoning (Bradis, et al., 1999).

> Let us divide the hypotenuse of a right triangle into n equal parts and draw through each of the dividing points two segments—one parallel to one leg of the triangle and the other to the other, up to their point of their intersection. One thereby gets a graduated broken line (Figure 4.8a). It is easy to see that the sum of the lengths of all the links parallel to the side $\overline{AC}$ equals AC, while the sum of the lengths of its links parallel to the side $\overline{BC}$ equals BC. The sum S_n of the lengths of all the links of the broken line equals AC + BC. We will now gradually increase the number n. By examining the drawing (Figure 4.8b) it is easy to see that the broken line is closer and closer to the hypotenuse when n is increasing and that when n is approaching infinity it coincides with it. We therefore get $\lim_{n \to \infty} S_n = AB$, while, at the same time, $\lim_{n \to \infty} S_n = \lim_{n \to \infty}(AC + BC) = AC + BC$. Consequently we seem to get that AC + BC = AB, or, in other words, that the sum of the lengths of the legs is equal to the length of the hypotenuse.

Clearly, the "visibly obvious" assertion that $\lim_{n \to \infty} S_n = AB$ is simply not true. The value S_n is constant. The eye genuinely does not distinguish the

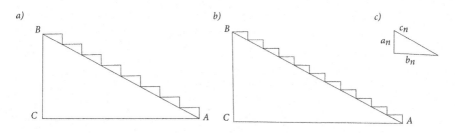

Figure 4.8

broken line from the hypotenuse when n is particularly high. Furthermore, if one denotes the lengths of the sides of the small triangles when dividing the hypotenuse into n equal parts as a_n and b_n, and the length of the hypotenuse c_n (Figure 4.8c), then it is possible to write this down as

$\lim_{n\to\infty}(a_n+b_n-c_n)=0$. But the difference S_n-AB does not change at all with the increase in n.

Examining an Example — Using an Interesting Story

A problem can also be successfully used for the purposes of student motivation in situations where the story of how the problem first emerged and was eventually solved, and the people who were involved in solving it, happen to be familiar and of interest to students. For example, in trying to interest students in logarithms the teacher could tell them the story of Benjamin Franklin's will (Van Doren, 1965).

> Franklin left a thousand pounds each to Boston and Philadelphia. This money was to be used for loans administered to "young married artificers [or craftsmen] under the age of twenty five years," to be repaid with an annual interest of 5%. "If this plan is executed, and succeeds as projected without interruption for one hundred years, the sum will then be one hundred and thirty-one thousand pounds"—wrote Franklin. Franklin stipulated that 100,000 pounds of this money should then be spent on social needs, while the rest would be invested in the same way as before for another one hundred years. Franklin further concluded that: "At the end of this second term, if no unfortunate accident has prevented the operation, the sum will be four million and sixty one thousand pounds sterling, of which I leave one million sixty one thousand pounds to the disposition of the inhabitants of the town... and three million to the disposition of the government of the state, not presuming to carry my views further.

The class can then be asked to consider how exactly Franklin got these figures. If the sum that accumulates in 100 years is x, then one can formulate the equation $x=1000\cdot1.05^{100}$, because each year 5% is added to the sum, or, in other words, the sum is multiplied by 1.05. Nowadays, the student could use a calculator to raise 1.05 to the power of 100; however, this brings up the question as to how Franklin may have calculated this result. Franklin had to rely on logarithms and logarithmic tables. By using, for example, decimal logarithms and corresponding logarithm tables, one can write

$$\log_{10} x = \log_{10} 1000 + \log_{10} 1.05^{100}$$
$$= \log_{10} 1000 + 100 \log_{10} 1.05$$
$$= 3 + 100 \cdot 0.021189$$
$$= 5.1189$$

By again using the same tables and by rounding the figure, one gets that *x* equals 131,000. Calculations for a further 100 years are done in the same way (Franklin performed them with only a minor error).

In general, teachers should seek out and collect problems with interesting, vivid formulations, capable of engaging students either by their unusual outcome or by their history.

Problem Solving as Recreation

One could say that using problem solving as recreation also involves motivating schoolchildren, since we are again dealing with a means of arousing interest. However, while in the previous group problem solving was used to stimulate interest in a particular domain of mathematics, what we are dealing with here is the use of problem solving as a source of fun. Such problems are particularly useful if only to show the "human face" of mathematics and thereby encourage a more positive attitude towards it among schoolchildren. Entertaining problems have been used in teaching and learning from time immemorial. Examples can be found in Ancient Egyptian papyruses and medieval manuscripts. It is important, however, to think through the methodological underpinnings of using such recreational problems. We mentioned above the work of Cooney (1985), who discussed the unsuccessful experiment of a young teacher who used recreational problems regularly, but without any connection to his regular teaching. This did nothing to improve the students' attitude towards mathematics, but only caused bewilderment.

Using recreational problems: Some recommendations.   Teachers should always have in reserve a few interesting recreational problems that they could give (in basically any class, though especially in middle school) as a kind of prize, particularly in situations where regular work has been completed sooner than planned or to dispel a negative atmosphere in the classroom, which could have formed for whatever reason. Recreational mathematics can also have great uses in extracurricular work. A good way of doing this is to use poster problems (Karp & Vogeli, 2002).

Posters with a variety of recreational problems should be provided on a regular basis (once a week, for example). Students could be encouraged to submit their solutions, with the best solutions posted for everyone to see. The teacher could reward active participants in various ways, including giving extra points in class, though such problems should generally be solved outside normal school hours.

It is obvious that problems selected for this kind of work need to stand out and be attractive in the way they are presented. The level of difficulty of the problem needs to be estimated with great care in order not to frighten students off by offering problems that may appear to be beyond their capabilities.

Examining an Example

Let us take a look at two examples of poster problems with different levels of complexity (Figure 4.9).

The first of these works is something of a joke (Figure 4.9a). The door of the bus is not visible—it is on the other side. Consequently, the bus is traveling to New York.

Students from a school in New York took a trip to Washington, D.C. When they returned, one of them drew a picture. Is the bus in this picture going to New York or to Washington?

A certain street gang member loved to tear up newspapers to threat a newsstand owner. Once he grabbed a newspaper and tore it up into 4 parts. Then he grabbed one of the pieces and tore it up into 4 parts. And then he continued grabbing pieces and tearing them up into 4 parts until the police came and stopped him. Could he have ended up with 2015 pieces?

(a)   (b)

Figure 4.9

The other assumes the use of more serious mathematics (Figure 4.9b). The gangster adds three pieces each time, starting with 1. Consequently, the difference between the number of pieces and 1 must be divisible by 3. But 2015 − 1 = 2014 is not divisible by 3. So, he could not have ended with 2015 pieces.

Problem Solving as Vehicle

In the words of Stanic and Kilpatrick (1989): "Problems are often provided not simply to motivate students to be interested in direct instruction on a topic but as a vehicle through which a new concept or skill might be learned." This use of problem solving is the most important one in teaching. The study of mathematics through problems, or rather, through the process of seeking answers to questions set either by the teacher or by the students themselves, involves students in active mathematical labor. Problem solving is here not opposed to the study of content, but, on the contrary, becomes the means of its study. Practically every aspect of studying new material can take the form of problem solving (Karp, 2007). Let us look at a few examples.

Examining *an* Example	**Preparing the Study of a New Phenomenon (the discovery of a new phenomenon)**

Mr. Paolucci plans to devote a particular lesson to studying the law of cosines. He believes it is important to ensure that students do not merely get acquainted with yet another formula but that they recognize that such a result is genuinely sensible, even expected. The congruence axiom guarantees that all the angles and sides of a triangle can always be determined from two sides and the angle between (i.e., its side-angle-side). In other words, from two sides of a triangle and the angle between them, one can always find the third side. How can one demonstrate this to students? The teacher has decided to engage students in an activity that requires them to find the third side of a triangle by using the two sides and the angle between them, and to tell them in advance that this can be done in all the cases.

At the beginning of the lesson the students were given the following problems:

For the triangle ABC, $m\angle ACB = 90°$, AC = 5, BC = 3, find AB (Figure 4.10a)

For the triangle ABC, $m\angle ACB = 60°$, AC = 5, BC = 5, find AB (Figure 4. 10b)

For the triangle ABC, $m\angle ACB = 120°$, AC = 2, BC = 2, draw its bisector of $\angle ACB$ and, by using this additional construction, find AB (Figure 4.10c)

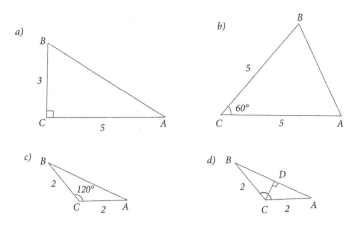

Figure 4.10

The first of these problems can be solved using the Pythagorean theorem ($AB = \sqrt{34}$). For the second, it is sufficient to notice that the sides $\overline{AC}$ and $\overline{BC}$ are equal, while the angle

$$m\angle ABC = m\angle BAC = \frac{180° - 60°}{2} = 60°,$$

which means triangle ABC is equilateral and that AB = 5. Finally, in the third problem one can use the fact that the bisector $\overline{CD}$ is both the altitude and the median (the triangle is isosceles), and that, consequently,

$$AB = 2AD = 2 \cdot AC \sin 60° = 2 \cdot 2 \cdot \frac{\sqrt{3}}{2} = 2\sqrt{3}$$

(Figure 4.10d).

While discussing these problems, the students were asked to consider whether it is always possible to find the length of the third side, knowing the other two and the angle that they form. Mr. Paolucci then asked them another question, which they were supposed to work out mentally without writing anything down.

For the triangles ABC and $A_1B_1C_1$ it is known that $m\angle ACB = m\angle A_1C_1B_1 = \alpha$, $AC = A_1C_1 = b$, $BC = B_1C_1 = a$. Is it possible that $AB \neq A_1B_1$? (Figure 4.11) The answer, no, follows directly from the congruence axiom.

The teacher then went on to reason that since the third side is determined on the basis of the data provided, one needs to find a way of expressing the length of the third side in terms of this data. He then formulated the law of cosines.

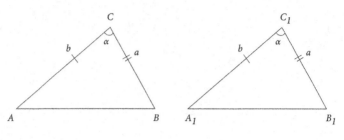

Figure 4.11

In this particular case, the teacher, along the lines of the heuristic strategies discussed above, approached the problem by first providing concrete examples of the general rule he wanted to demonstrate. The students were able to formulate the necessary hypothesis by basing their thinking on these concrete cases. Only after finding answers to these problems were the students ready to assimilate the main theorem.

Understanding Definitions

Communication in mathematics includes the use of specialized terminology, which is introduced through definitions. Working with definitions incorporates a series of elements and stages during the process. Students usually need to:

- Understand the need for the new term, or, in other words, the existence of particular situations and objects which require description (e.g., to realize that there are quadrilaterals with a pair of parallel sides—trapezoids; that there are numbers that cannot be expressed as a ratio of whole numbers—irrational numbers; that there are numbers for which a function has the value zero—zeros of a function, etc.)
- Understand the meaning of all the words and expressions used in the definitions and the way they are mutually related (for example, the definition of a trapezoid assumes an understanding of the words "quadrilateral," "side," "parallel," "pair," etc.)
- Know how to determine whether a particular object fulfills the definition; or, similarly, come up with objects that would not fulfill the definition for one reason or another
- Know how to "read" a given text that includes the new term and be able to "translate" it into another mathematical language by utilizing another means of representation (for example, to be able to sketch a drawing that would help solve problems involving trapezoids)
- To be able to construct mathematical propositions using the new term.

All these skills can be both fashioned and tested through problem solving. Problems can actively engage students in working with such specialized terms, which allow concrete difficulties to manifest themselves and prompt students to look for ways to overcome them. In this context, problems can be structured in such a way that students do not confront all of the difficulties at once, but gradually, and in parts. Let us examine the definition of the median value for a collection of numbers.

> *Definition:* For an odd number of data points the median is the middle number in a set of data when the numbers are arranged in order. For an even number of data points the median is the average of the two middle numbers when the numbers are arranged in order.

The need for considering the concept of the median could be demonstrated by discussing problems where one is asked to describe a "typical" value in some data set (skewed data sets, such as income, for example, make the median particularly relevant as a "typical" value). For instance, the class can be given a table of income values from some town and asked to identify the typical income of a person who lived there. From there, the "middle" number can be discussed as an important indicator of typical.

By focusing on the text of the definition above, one can note that it is comparatively difficult insofar as it contains two distinct cases and assumes an additional operation on the data—namely, placing the values in order. If you want to help students overcome potential difficulties, you can propose a set of questions of the following type:

- The following data set is given: 2, 4, 6, 7, 9, 13, 15. Is it arranged in order? Which number is the middle one? How many middle numbers are there? What number is the median?
- The following data set is given: 1, 5, 7, 11, 15, 19, 21, 53. Is it arranged in order? Which number is the middle one? How many middle numbers are there? What number is the median?
- Could the average of two whole numbers be fractional? Replace any number in the previous data set so that the median would become a fraction.
- The following data set is given: 2, 7, 4, 5, 6, 3, 1. Is it arranged in order? Is it true that the number 5 is its median?
- The following data set is given: 1, 5, 4, 2, 2, 1, 3. The assertion is made that its median is number 3 because it is precisely in the middle between the highest (5) and the lowest number (1) in the set. Do you agree with this assertion?

You can then also pose other problems. For example, students could be given several bar graphs and then asked, knowing the median of a data set, to determine the bar graph on which this set was represented. You can later give problems that require more complex operations with the new term.

Substantiating Assertions

Even a comparatively difficult proof can be carried out as a sequence of problem solutions. Let us examine a classical proof of the Pythagorean theorem, based on operations with the areas of figures that form a square with the sides a + b. The following tasks can be given:

Figure 4.12 depicts a square with the sides a + b, divided into four triangles and a quadrilateral.

1. Prove that all four triangles are congruent to the given right triangle, with sides a and b, and hypotenuse c.
2. Prove that $m\angle AMN + m\angle QMD = 90°$.
3. Prove that the quadrilateral MNPQ is a square.
4. Express, only in terms of a and b, the areas of the square ABCD, the triangle AMN, and the square MNPQ.
5. Prove the Pythagorean theorem: $c^2 = a^2 + b^2$.

Alternately, the proof can be divided into stages in other ways as well. Each of the above problems can be split into smaller problems and be followed up by various additional instructions, or else they can be grouped into fewer more complex problems. For example, the proof that the quadrilateral MNPQ is a square presumes, first of all, proof that it is a parallelogram, something that can be formulated as a separate problem. On the other hand, in some classes students could do without task 2, because they may be able to realize for themselves that this needs to be established before they can accomplish task 3. The teacher's skill and knowledge of the class consist precisely in the ability to determine the students' levels of knowledge so

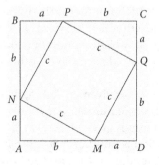

Figure 4.12

that the task is both within their capabilities and yet present a problem for them in the truest sense of the word.

In most cases it is impossible to conduct a rigorous proof of any assertion in class due to lack of time. However, this does not mean that teachers should limit their teaching merely to formulating general rules. For example, before telling students the rule for multiplying negative integers, you could ask them to try and guess for themselves what the product of the numbers –3 and 2 would be. You could model the values of integers using some context, such as someone having to pay a fine of 3 dollars twice, or instead make the connection between multiplication and repeated addition.

Generally speaking, when giving problems where concrete cases of some general rule are examined, or where the question is being modeled in some way or another, the teacher can engage students in what Polya called *plausible reasoning*. Here an assertion is affirmed by articulating strong arguments in its favor, even if the assertion is never rigorously substantiated.

Anticipating Errors

Among errors committed by schoolchildren, teachers need to distinguish those that are systematic in nature, not explained by some isolated inaccuracy but rather by the fact that students are following some erroneous strategy. The teacher can intentionally select problems that allow such strategies to manifest themselves early, in order to—at least to some degree—forestall future potential mistakes.

While studying the transformation of expressions, for example, one could provide the following task: "Test the conclusion of the following transformation of expressions

$$\frac{3x}{x-3} - \frac{x-6}{x-3} = \frac{3x-x-6}{x-3} = \frac{2x-6}{x-3} = \frac{2(x-3)}{x-3} = 2."$$

This task provides an opportunity to discuss the typical mistake that emerges in the course of this transformation, since $-(x-6) = -x+6$ and

$$\frac{3x}{x-3} - \frac{x-6}{x-3} = \frac{3x-x+6}{x-3}.$$

The teacher can draw the students' attention to this false reasoning, describing typical situations in which it may occur. In general, tasks that ask to analyze a particular mathematical text and correct it often become a useful instrument, not only of fostering a particular habit, but, more broadly, of instilling the habit of verifying one's own results.

Diagnosing Student Difficulties

The following is a fairly standard problem: "A translation moves P (1, 7) to P_1 (3, 5). What are the coordinates of the image of point Q (2, 3) under the same translation?" A student's inability to solve it may occur for a variety of reasons. The student could:

- Not understand what a "translation" or "the image under a translation" is
- Not know how to communicate the coordinates of a translation
- Find it difficult to perform the necessary arithmetic operations
- Isolate the change in only one direction
- Not understand the structure of the problem.

These difficulties can be encountered in different variants and combinations. Sometimes the student can experience them all at once; at other times, they may arise separately. Often, discussing the entire solution from the beginning is counterproductive because the students rarely encounter all the difficulties in the same place, and the superfluous information only detracts from the real issues. Students are certainly not always capable of formulating independently what they find difficult, nor are the difficulties always visible from what they write down.

Teachers often need to give separate tasks in such a way that specific difficulties would then manifest themselves. Ideally, such problems should be constructed to isolate (i.e., diagnose) one specific difficulty, while removing or substantially reducing the others (it might be impossible to do away completely with calculations, for example, but one could always formulate them in such a way that they are extremely easy.)

In the case of the difficulties encountered in the translation problem, the following questions could be used:

A translation moves point $(0,0)$ to $(0,1)$.

- Which of the following assertions is true: a) point $(0,0)$ is the image of $(0,1)$ under this translation; or b) point $(0,1)$ is the image of $(0,0)$ under this translation.
- Mark points $(0,0)$ and $(0,1)$ on the coordinate plane. Indicate the image of $(0,1)$ under the same translation.
- Represent the above translation in terms of its coordinates.
- A translation is defined by the vector <2,3>. Show the point to which it would translate the point $(1,1)$.

Diagnostic problems, in addition to helping isolate specific difficulties, can also have an instructive role. It is obvious, for example, that a student who has solved all the above problems will find it easier to tackle the original problem. Generally speaking, the ways of using problems as a vehicle in class are closely interrelated.

Problem Solving as Practice

Drill and practice are probably the two principal uses for which problem solving has been exercised, not only in contemporary education, but for decades, if not centuries of schooling. One could hardly cite a more typical school situation than the scenario where students are given a worksheet that has a long set of repetitive, nearly identical, problems. Using the terminology elaborated above, it would be more appropriate to describe this as an exercise than a problem solving activity, since children are not presented with anything unfamiliar but are merely asked to regurgitate and repeat what they have already learned.

Emphasizing the role of problem solving should not be understood as a rejection of exercises—they too are necessary to a certain degree. But to limit practice to exercises only is pointless. Dewey argued that: "In reference to material already learned, questions should require the student to use it in dealing with a new problem rather than to reproduce it literally and directly" (1933, p. 266). Mere training in applying a pre-learned algorithm does not in itself guarantee that the student will correctly use it in solving a problem where the application of the algorithm is not the intended goal but only a path to something else; furthermore, learning an algorithm in one context does not guarantee success on problems where the task is formulated in a way sufficiently different from the one used in training. The teacher should therefore find it useful to set genuine problems that would differ one from the other, both in the way that they are formulated and in terms of information given or of any other detail relevant to the solution.

Practice is important, however, not simply because it helps develop particular technical or calculation skills: the development of any intellectual habit assumes the practice (or experience) of applying it. We discuss a rather subtle example, using the research of Wertheimer (1959).

Practice applying the same strategy. Wertheimer asked participants in his experiment to determine the area of the golden frame of an alter window (Figure 4.13a). Interestingly, the solution does not actually require any

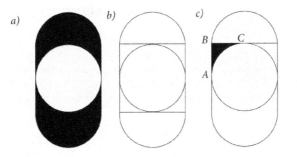

Figure 4.13

calculation, since the area of the circular glass window equals the area of the two semicircles that form the upper and lower part of the frame (Figure 4.13b). All one needs to do is determine the area of the square. However, this kind of reasoning seemed to be beyond a large number of Wertheimer's subjects. Most segmented the figure into parts and then tried to work out how to determine the area of the curvilinear triangle ABC (Figure 4.13c).

The difficulty here lay in Wertheimer's subjects not knowing how to restructure the data. The question being asked is to determine the whole *without* determining its parts, which to a certain extent contradicts the experience of most solvers, who normally proceed in stages—first one calculates this, then that, and so forth. In order to develop the flexibility of thought among students, the teacher can give similar sorts of problems as practice. We provide some examples of problems with a similar underlying idea.

EXAMPLE 1

A circle is inscribed in a triangle with sides of length 10, 13 and 13. Another circle is inscribed in the upper portion of the figure thus obtained, and then another in the remaining space, and so forth (Figure 4.14). The horizontal diameter is drawn in each of the circles. Determine the limit of the sum of their lengths.

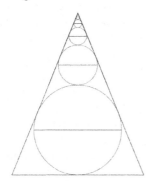

Figure 4.14   **Figure 4.15**

EXAMPLE 2

A donut is depicted in Figure 4.15 The radius of the larger circle equals 10. Two tangential circles are inscribed inside the ring. Determine the perimeter of the triangle, the vertices of which lie in the centers of the circles.

EXAMPLE 3

A circle is inscribed in a triangle with base BC = 8. The sum of the distances from vertex A to the points of tangency on the two sides (i.e., AM + AN) equals 6. Determine the perimeter of the triangle (Figure 4.16).

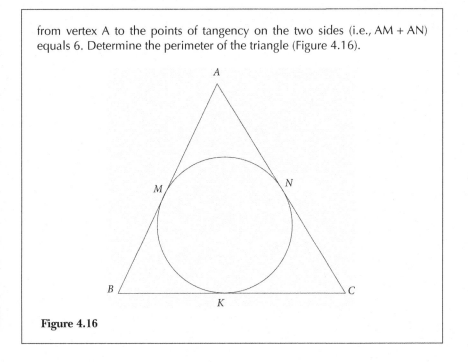

Figure 4.16

In all these and similar problems one is asked to determine the sums, whereas determining its parts is either impossible or difficult. Students need to realize this and find a way of transforming the information provided. In the first example it is sufficient to imagine other diameters (Figure 4.17). The sum of the diameters evidently approaches the length of the altitude, which is 12. In the second problem one can see that parts of one side of the triangle complement those of the other up to the radius of the

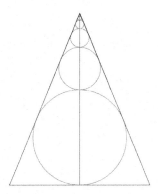

Figure 4.17

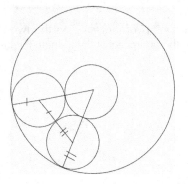

Figure 4.18

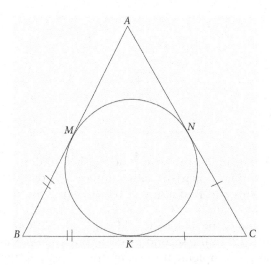

Figure 4.19

larger circle, twice (Figure 4.18). The answer is 20. The same idea (though expressed differently) works in the third problem (Figure 4.19), giving a perimeter of 22.

Solving this kind of problem and, in general, problems where one has to apply the same strategy, is itself an example of practice. One can practice thinking and not just the routine application of rules.

Problems as Aims

Historically, the aim of mathematical training has been first and fore-most to enable people to solve certain practical problems, such as how to calculate the sum of money owed by a debtor, or how to perform navigational calculations. At the dawn of capitalism, volumes of so-called "commercial arithmetic" started to be published on a massive scale, by the standards of the times. Published charts and tables (such as tables of logarithms or sine values) helped people cope with specific mathematical problems that they faced in their everyday life. Even today, one of the aims of mathematics education is to prepare students to deal with practical problems that arise in the real world. It is important to realize, however, that the nature of such problems is changing before our eyes.

Changes in the Everyday Life Use of Mathematics

There are far more people today than in the sixteenth century—at the dawn of capitalism—who need to perform calculations. These calculations also tend to be more complicated than they used to be then. However, the number of people who need to perform something like long division has hardly increased (if at all). Even people who fill out their own tax forms rarely do this without the help of a special computer program, while those who do any sort of calculation without a calculator today are hard to come by.

What is required from a problem solver today is very different from what used to be the case centuries or even decades ago. Today it is more often necessary to:

- Understand that a particular problem can, in principle, be solved by mathematical means (which often implies that the solver then simply needs to find the appropriate mathematical instrument, without wasting time on any further considerations)
- Understand the language of mathematics—its various means of communication and representation
- Be able critically to evaluate the final outcome, rejecting clearly erroneous results produced by technology.

Consequently, skills in which a schoolchild needs to be trained in order to solve practical problems successfully are also changing. Today these skills do not just involve familiarity with a particular algorithm; in fact, they are something radically different from algorithmic activity (which, however, does not imply that schoolchildren should not be trained in something like long division).

Furthermore, contrary to the past, when a person who learned how to solve a particular set of practical problems was then able to use this knowledge throughout his/her life, today, the "necessary problems"—the problems that ought to be the purpose of mathematics education—are, in fact, changing all the time. This again does not mean that in vocational schools students should not examine concrete practical problems and contemporary ways of solving them; indeed, the general cannot be learned without the concrete. However, the teacher's attention, even when explaining problems that are significant in practical life, should not concentrate on merely imparting particular rules.

The ability to evaluate a result critically or to analyze a text, which was previously considered to be of use only to a few specialists, has become an essential part of the everyday practice of most people today. Problems that form and develop such skills therefore become valuable.

Problem Solving as an Art

Similar changes are also taking place in people's ability to appreciate the beauty of a problem and its solution. Delight in the beauty of a particular mathematical solution used to be accessible only to the elite (as was the case with paintings and sculptures). Today, the teacher's task is to acquaint all schoolchildren with this sentiment.[1]

Stanic and Kilpatrick believe that an understanding of problem solving as Art first emerged within the work of Polya. They also recognize the significance of Dewey's work, who, contrary to erroneous and conflicting interpretations, wrote substantially about the value and importance of abstract thinking.

In his book, *How We Think*, is a section entitled precisely "Developing Delight in Thinking." Dewey wrote:

> Children engage, unconstrainedly and continually, in reflective inspection and testing for the sake of what they are interested in doing. Habits of thinking thus generated may increase in amount till they become of importance on their own account. It is part of the business of a teacher to lead students to extricate and dwell upon the distinctively intellectual side of what they do until there develops a spontaneous interest in ideas and their relations with one another—that is, a genuine power of abstraction, of rising from engrossment in the present to the plane of ideas. (1933, p. 226)

What we have here is essentially a concise outline of an agenda that a teacher should follow in order to involve students in problem solving as a form of art. The first stage of such work is to address the intellectual and even artistic side of what takes place in problem solving. Teachers cannot and should not confine themselves to solving particular problems simply because it is useful for some practical purpose, even if this purpose is indeed the principal motive for assigning the problem in the first place. Teachers must also, without fail, make precisely the way in which a problem has been solved comprehensible and interesting to students. They need to show why a particular solution is efficient, elegant and beautiful, and why it may be better than another.

According to Dewey, such activity can and should prepare students for appreciating problem solving (and more generally, thinking) for its own sake. At this stage the teacher ought to provide examples of problems that are truly worthy of detailed study and could be seen as works of art in their own right. The teacher could also discuss with the students the importance and beauty of a mathematical result or method that was developed specifically for the solution of such a problem. In order to stimulate the development of mathematical curiosity and creativity, as well as understanding the evolution of mathematics as a discipline, the teacher can discuss the history of some famous problems, including those that have never been solved.

It is easy to note the similarity of such work with the above cited schema of teaching roles (Kantowski, 1980), according to which the teacher at the lower levels serves as a model, while at the higher ones, becomes a problem provider and facilitator. Of course, the transition from one to the other is neither quick nor simple. Let us reiterate, however, that active problem solving and the understanding of problem solving as Art, or more precisely as a creative activity, are certainly not accessible only to the elite—a place for it should be found in every classroom.

Reflection

Assignments and Topics for Discussion

1. During a lesson a student asks: Why should I learn about linear functions? Give examples of problems that one could present to the class in order to prevent such questions.
2. A lesson is to be devoted to uses of proportions. Select problems that could be assigned to motivate the class.
3. Find examples of mathematical problems from books and movies. In which situations could you foresee them being used in a classroom setting?
4. Find some recreational problems that, in your opinion, are good. Why do you like them?
5. Create a set of problems that could be used for work conceptualizing and defining the limit of a sequence.
6. Choose a theorem. Create a few problems that you could give to students as a way of preparing them to carry out the proof of the theorem independently.
7. A student is unable to complete the following task: Determine the domain of the function

$$f(x) = \frac{x}{x^2 - 6x + 5} + 1.$$

Create a set of problems that would help you establish which stage of the solution is the one that causes the greatest difficulty for the student.

8. Propose a set of problems (on the topic of your choice) that would help students practice the use of different forms of mathematical representation.
9. Cite some mathematical problems for which the solution is important in everyday life. Does school teach students how to solve them? If so, in which course?
10. Give examples of problems, the beauty of which has left an impression on you. What is it that makes them beautiful?

NOTE

1. It is interesting to mention that different systems of mathematics teaching can develop different understandings of what is beautiful in mathematics and what is not (Karp, 2008).

CHAPTER 5

MATHEMATICAL INVESTIGATION AND HOW TO ENGAGE STUDENTS IN IT

This chapter is devoted to the role played by problem posing in the teaching of mathematics.
The chapter discusses:

- Why the skill of posing problems is useful to both teachers and students.
- What role problem posing plays or could play in different lessons.
- Organizing class work in a way that helps students learn to pose problems.

WHY POSE PROBLEMS?

The Art of Problem Posing

The study of mathematics is inseparable from solving problems. The previous chapter has shown that practically every stage of working on

Mathematics in Middle and Secondary School, pages 129–145
Copyright © 2015 by Information Age Publishing

mathematical material in class can be realized by means of problem solving. It would not be an exaggeration to say that teachers spend practically every lesson in mathematics either trying to explain to students how to solve particular problems, or getting them to look for solutions to problems themselves. But where do these problems come from?

Why it is Important for the Teacher to Know How to Pose Problems

Problems for lessons are primarily culled from textbooks (or some other type of auxiliary teaching materials). However, teachers often find themselves in situations where there are simply not enough ready-made problems and questions at hand. They then need to construct new problems themselves. Depending on what the class is like and what actually happens in a lesson, a good teacher looks for new approaches and new types of problems accordingly—even if these remain within the confines of established patterns and ideas. If you limit yourself entirely to a published collection of problems, and forfeit your right to construct problems yourself, your teaching will likely become rigid, missing opportunities to capitalize on crucial teachable moments that arise during a lesson. Silver, et al. (1996) rightly observed that: "Problem Posing is of central importance in the discipline of mathematics and in the nature of mathematical thinking." The art of problem posing is of equally central importance in the teaching of mathematics. This does not mean that problems posed by teachers need to be original, in the sense that they have never been posed before or that they are particularly unusual and difficult. Such problems could be something quite familiar, or equivalent to what one can find in most textbooks. What is more, a teacher does not necessarily need to invent a problem from scratch—the problem can simply be recalled from memory. And yet, even here teachers exercise a considerable amount of creativity. Particular problems (whether they are created independently, taken from a textbook, or recalled from memory) are especially useful at specific moments in the process of instruction, and a teacher needs to recognize this utility. An assignment that may be considered just a standard exercise can suddenly, in certain situations, become a genuine problem, capable of meaningfully developing the mathematical thinking of students, despite its technical simplicity. Every teacher needs the skill to formulate assignments in such a way and at such a time for this to be achieved.

Why it is Important for the Student to Pose Problems

It is just as important for students themselves to be introduced to the art of problem posing. English, et al. (1998) argue that problem posing activities can:

- Improve students' understanding and awareness of problem structures and enable them to distinguish good problems from poor ones
- Improve students' problem-solving abilities, as well as reinforce and enrich basic concepts
- Foster more diverse and flexible thinking
- Improve students' attitudes toward, and confidence in, mathematics and mathematical problem solving

It is clear, however, just as with any other creative activity, that it is not easy to master this art of problem posing or, indeed, the art of inspiring students to pose problems. Polya (1981) compared a teacher's skill in choosing the right question to the skill of choosing the right tool from a toolbox. It is impossible to describe in advance all possible uses for a tool, in all conceivable situations. An artisan acquires the speed and the skill in making the right choice of a tool primarily through experience and by observing peers at work. Similarly, a good teacher gradually accumulates experience and skill in constructing problems.

Different Aspects of Problem Posing: The Compound Inequalities Lesson

This and the following sections will analyze specific situations that arose in actual lessons. The analysis of these lessons will enable us to see what role problem posing can play in teaching. When analyzing lessons it is always useful to think about what kinds of problems were missing and what other student tasks might have been assigned.

The teacher first devoted a series of lessons to multi-step (linear) inequalities. In these lessons the teacher explained to students that with inequalities one must proceed as with equations, but that there are two important distinctions. Firstly, inequalities have not one but many solutions; and secondly, one needs to be especially careful when dividing both parts of the inequality by a negative number, because in that case, one needs to remember to change the inequality sign, writing "<" instead of ">" and ">" instead of "<". Students then practiced solving inequalities, and did so on the whole quite successfully.

The next lesson was then devoted to compound inequalities. The teacher explained that two inequalities can be joined by the word "and" or by the word "or". The teacher then demonstrated (solved) several examples. Students were then given worksheets with similar tasks and were asked to work on them in groups.

At this point, however, students started experiencing serious difficulties. For example, in trying to solve the compound inequality $2x + 4 < 6$ and $3x - 2 > -5$ one group did the following: Proceeding according to the pattern previously outlined by the teacher, the students began by solving the first inequality and obtained the result $x < 1$. They then solved the second inequality and got the result $x > -1$. They then wrote down the answer in the following form: $x < 1$; $x > -1$. Seeing this, the teacher told the class that this was wrong, and explained that one could not have this result. The compound inequality said "and," which meant that one must express x in such a way that both inequalities would apply, and not only one or the other. This meant that the solution should be $-1 < x < 1$.

Alas, when it turned out that the results of the next compound inequality were $x < 3$ and $x < 5$, the students in some groups, trying to adhere to the teacher's explanation, wrote down the solution as $3 < x < 5$, while others wrote $3 > x < 5$. Moreover, several groups actually made mistakes in solving individual inequalities because they had totally forgotten the rule about changing the sign of the inequality, even though they had previously assimilated this rule quite well. By the end of the lesson, most of the tasks on the worksheet remained unsolved, and the teacher had to postpone solving them until the next session.

Discussion of the Lesson

Two interrelated questions can be asked here: (1) Why did the lesson turn out to be such a failure?; and (2) What is the teacher supposed to do in the next lesson?

Laying aside comparatively minor details, one could say that the fundamental reason for the failure of the lesson (and what is more, of the entire series of lessons) is linked to the fact that the teacher had limited his/her instruction to giving out recipes on how to go about solving compound inequalities, without discussing why one must proceed in a particular way. In the short term, such an approach seems effective—without wasting time on elaborate discussion, the students simply memorize the rule and apply it. But when the situation becomes more complicated—when new problems and new rules come up—it is no longer possible to apply the rules without understanding their underlying premises. Confronted with new difficulties, students are distracted and even begin to forget the rules that they have already learned. Worst of all, since they are conditioned to follow rules blindly, they identify the teacher's demonstration of a solution to a single problem with a universal rule, an assumption that inevitably leads to very crude mistakes. In the above case students had worked out the "rule" that the presence of the word "and" means that the answer must entail a dual inequality. The teacher could have explained the solution to specific problems perfectly correctly, but this had not prompted students to think.

(It is also worth noting that the assertion made by the teacher above, that an equation has a single solution while an inequality has many, is simply untrue and only disorients students.)

On the one hand, students clearly found it difficult to understand what the solution of an inequality actually is, and how it is to be represented symbolically. On the other, the formality of their learning led to not understanding how the words "and" and "or" provide some meaning and logic to compound inequalities. Giving problems devoted to these specific aspects of compound inequalities could have prompted students to think actively about them. What was needed was not another round of routine exercises but rather genuine problems that would have stimulated thought and understanding. It is clear, however, that one cannot make such problems overly complicated because students have neither the necessary prior knowledge nor sufficient time to engage with them. So what sorts of problems could be posed here?

Problems That Can be Posed When Discussing Inequalities

Students could start off by working with the concept "the solution of inequalities." A comparatively simple, but vital question, which could nudge students in this direction, could be: "Give some numbers that could be the solution for the given inequality." Another related question would be: "Is it true that such and such a number is the solution of the given inequality." In both cases the student is invited to analyze the relation between concrete numbers and what is meant by the solution of an inequality.

A concept is always understood better if it is expressed through different means of representation. Sometimes teachers leave the application of mathematical principles to the surrounding world for much later, believing that one first needs to deal with the mathematics itself and only then tackle the more complex task of its application. However, for many students a concept remains incomprehensible if it is not related to the real world and applied to actual objects. This is why teachers should try to use problems that actively engage students in real scenarios, with concrete objects. For example: "Four identical sticks are laid out in a sequence so that the bottom of one is touching the top of the other, and the bottom of that one is the top of the next, and so forth. One knows that the length of the sequence as a whole is less than 12 inches. What could be the length of a single stick?" In this scenario, students can literally measure the possible answers with their hands, and they can also experiment with different lengths.

It is also important for students to be able to represent the concept they are studying graphically. One can ask questions of the following type: "Show all the solutions of the given inequality on a number line."

Students can also be given assignments where they are asked to move from one form of representation to several others, and not just in the conventional order, but also in reverse. For example, ask students not only to represent the solution to a given inequality graphically, but also to write down an inequality for which the totality of solutions is represented by a particular interval on the number line. Students can be asked not just to solve an inequality derived from a word problem, but also to formulate their own word problem on the basis of an inequality. Such problems are far more open-ended than the usual "straightforward" problems; they allow for multiple solutions, and require a more fluent mastery of the concept studied, for both the student and the teacher.

Problems That Can be Posed When Discussing Compound Inequalities

Such problems are also useful in solving compound inequalities. One can, for example, ask the following questions:

- Give some numbers that satisfy both the inequalities $x < 1$ and $-2 < x$.
- Represent on the number line all the numbers that satisfy both the inequalities $x < 1$ and $-2 < x$.
- It is known that six identical books weigh less than 3lbs and that 4 such books weigh more than 1lb. What does one book weigh?
- Construct a word problem based on a given compound inequality.
- Write down the compound inequality that would have the interval $x < 2$ as the solution (or, say, the interval $3 \leq x \leq 5$).

Useful Tip! It is important to anticipate the mistakes students are likely to make. For example, teachers must take care to avoid the creation of false associations (such as the above conviction that the word "and" in a compound inequality always means that the answer has the form (a, b) for some numbers a and b). To prevent this, one can give students a set of compound inequalities that contain a diverse range of results. Or one can simply ask the following question directly: "Is it true in solving compound inequalities containing the word "and" that one always gets an answer of the form (a, b) for some numbers a and b?"

Anticipating and correcting errors related to the use of symbols is also important for teachers. For example, one can ask the question: "Which of the following notations, representing the solution to a compound inequality, is definitely incorrect: (a) $x < 2$ or $x < 3$; (b) $-3 < x < -5$; (c) $x > 5$; d) $1 \leq x > 2$; e) all numbers."

What Sort of Problems Need to be Posed?

In the process of determining what sorts of problems need to be posed, we have essentially analyzed the steps that students need to take in solving these problems and what sorts of basic difficulties they are likely to encounter in the process. As discussed in the previous chapter, problems (understood as a fundamentally active form of study) can be used to achieve practically any methodological aim. Teachers should aim to present students with certain rules—such as the one mentioned above about changing the sign of the inequality when dividing both sides by a negative number—as they arise in the process of problem solving, rather than to offer the rule in advance as a given.

It is far better to ask this type of question from the very beginning, rather than wait for the lesson to fail before presenting it. However, it is impossible to predict all the difficulties that can arise. As such, teachers often need to formulate problems ad hoc, as a reaction to what happens in class. Both the proactive aspect of planning to orient lessons around solving certain problems, and the reactive aspect of altering lessons around those problems actually posed, form an important tension that the teacher must learn to navigate.

From the above questions, the students were prompted to work in the following domains:

- *Concretizing* assertions (either those given to them in advance or those obtained in the course of solving the problem)
- *Translating* one form of representation into another
- *Checking* said assertions
- Theoretically *exploring* a variety of possible situations.

Also, these are at least some of the strategies that could be used to construct new problems. How exactly can they be used in this context? What other strategies for constructing problems can be recommended? What sorts of questions does one need to ask oneself when posing problems? We find some answers to these and other matters through extant research; we discuss these ideas in what follows.

Lesson on Tangent Lines to the Graph of a Function

This lesson was used to open the study of differential calculus. Having dealt with organizational matters, the teacher marked on the graph of the function f two points with the coordinates $A(x_0, f(x_0))$ and $B(t, f(t))$. Students were divided into groups and were asked to solve the following problems in sequence:

- Write down the equation of the straight line $\overrightarrow{AB}$ (in a general form);

- Do the same for the specific function $f(x) = x^2$;
- Do the same for the specific function $f(x) = x^3$;
- For the function $f(x) = x^2$ and for $x_0 = 1$, find the limit of the slopes of the straight lines $\overleftrightarrow{AB}$ as t approaches x_0;
- For the function $f(x) = x^3$ and for $x_0 = 1$, find the limit of the slopes of the straight lines $\overleftrightarrow{AB}$ as t approaches x_0.
- For the functions $f(x) = x^2$ and $f(x) = x^3$, write down the equations of the straight line which occupies a limiting position in relation to the straight lines $\overleftrightarrow{AB}$ as t approaches $x_0 = 1$.

The teacher then told the class that such a straight line is called the tangent to the graph of the function f at the point with the abscissa $x_0 = 1$. The teacher gave the definition of the derivative and wrote down the equation of the tangent line in its general form. In the end, students were asked to write down the equations of the tangent lines of the functions $f(x) = x^2$ and $f(x) = x^3$, but for other points x_0.

Discussion of the Lesson

This lesson went well. The teacher was pleased with the results. Indeed, students obtained important results entirely on their own. The teacher was able to determine precisely what sort of problems were within the students' grasp. The teacher successfully used concrete examples of functions (for which students could easily find corresponding limits), and then guided the students toward the desired generalization. The lesson was built on problems and students were actively and independently acquiring new knowledge.

However, if we look at the lesson from the perspective of a person who is unfamiliar with Calculus (and this is precisely the students' point of view), one cannot avoid asking: "But why are we doing all this?" A few lessons later, students will see for themselves how useful the derivative is, and they will realize the need to understand its geometrical sense. But this happens only later; in the meantime, students are merely drawn into some incomprehensible procedure. Because this is so common in teaching mathematics, this fact did not, unfortunately, seem to baffle them at all.

Brown (2001) speaks of the need to find a balance between problem solving *in the small* and problem solving *in the large*. One could say from the point of view of problem solving in the small (and thus, problem posing in the small) that there was nothing wrong with the above lesson—the concrete problems given to students were selected well. What was lacking, however, was problem posing in the large, or, in other words, an understanding of the particular part of mathematics as a whole, or some greater mathematical problem, that provides the context for a specific problem.

Posing problems that require weeks to solve will be different from posing problems that can be solved straight away. Generally speaking, the ideal of problem posing in the classroom does not necessarily entail that problems be solved immediately (or even that they need to be solved in class).

The teacher of the above lesson could have used certain preparatory problems, such as the problem of replacing the segment of a curve with the segment of a straight line that comes close to it (which is essentially one of the fundamental ideas of Calculus). The teacher could then have said that the next part of the course would be devoted to the solution of that and related problems. This would have shown students what they would be working on in the lessons to come and what purpose or end these problems served collectively. It is important for teachers to understand the material studied as directed towards some larger goal, and to be able to convey this understanding to students through appropriate problems.

Examining a Lesson in Which the Students Are the Ones Posing Problems

Reducing Word Problems to Inequalities

After solving several problems mentally, Ms.Thompson gave the class the following problem: "Two cars travel from one city to another on the same road. The first car drives at a speed of 40 mph, while the second car drives at a speed of 20 mph the first half of the way, and at a speed of 80 mph the second half of the way. Which car will be the first to reach the destination?"

The problem was solved and then discussed. The teacher then asked the students to try out the same problem using different numbers. Ms. Thompson suggested the speeds of 60, 30, and 120 mph, respectively, and asked the students to explain why she had chosen these numbers. The students solved the problem and explained that, as in the previous example, the second number was two times lower than the first and the third was two times higher.

The teacher then asked the students to think up some other "similar or more difficult" problems. The discussion (conducted largely in groups and partly by the class as a whole) resulted in the following questions:

Solve the above problem as before when:

- The first number is 30, the second 15, and the third 60
- The first number is two times higher than the second and two times lower than the third (in a general form)

- The first number is twenty times higher than the second and twenty times lower than the third
- The first number is higher than the second by as many times as it is lower than the third

The following problems were also proposed:

Two cars traveled the same length of time. The first traveled at a constant speed for the entire journey. The second traveled the first half of the journey twice as slowly as the first car and the second half of the journey twice as fast as the first car. Which of the two cars went further?

Two cars traveled from one town to another along the same road. The first traveled all the way at the same speed. The second car spent the first half of the allocated time at twice the speed of the first car and the second half at half the speed of the first car. Which of the two cars reached the destination first?

In constructing these problems it was noticed that some of them could not be solved as easily as the original one and that one needed to introduce variables and use algebra. Having formulated the above problems, the class went on to solve them, introducing variables and noting the given conditions in algebraic form. Some of the problems were given for homework, while others were left for the next lesson.

Discussion of the Lesson

This lesson was radically different from those discussed earlier. Here it was not the teacher but the students who were posing problems. Their active participation in the lesson thereby necessarily increased. Their level of interest in solving the problems also became far higher than if the problems had been posed by the teacher. Even more importantly, in the process students were acquiring the ideal attitude towards problems: they were acting as mathematicians studying a mathematical situation and developing further what had already been established.

Some of the problems that they posed were simply a repetition of what had been discussed earlier. However, even in this case, the actual posing of problems by the students indicates greater engagement with the subject matter. Some of the problems that they had constructed were, in fact, quite hard (and the last of the problems actually turned out to be too hard for some of the members of the group that had posed it).

How problem posing by the students was organized. The teacher was able to organize the lesson in such a way as to actively engage students in the construction of problems. The first stage in this process involved solving a problem. The second stage involved posing a new problem and analyzing how it was constructed. The students first formulated questions by analogy (this is yet another established strategy of problem posing), but then gradually generalized the problem. It was crucial that students were able to realize in the course of the discussion that the solution to the problems they were posing required broadening their mathematical tools, so to speak. In other words, problem posing helped students see the need for further developing their mathematical skills and techniques.

Engaging students in problem posing and developing their investigative tendencies is an important task for teachers. This does not happen on its own accord but needs to be worked out systematically. Various strategies for organizing such work will be discussed in what follows.

Reflection

Assignments and Topics for Discussion

1. Give solutions to all the above problems devoted to compound inequalities and to secant and tangent lines.
2. Create a set of assignments intended to show students that the assertion, equations have a single solution while inequalities have many, is untrue. Is this assertion true for equations and inequalities of the first degree?
3. Give examples of problems that the teacher could give to students who are starting to learn about integral calculus, in order to provide students with a sense of the kinds of general questions that this part of mathematics tries to answer (i.e., problem posing *in the large*).
4. Solve all the problems posed in the last of the lessons discussed above. Think up some more problems that would further develop and generalize the situation.

ENCOURAGING STUDENTS TO POSE PROBLEMS

It is hardly possible to indicate a general strategy for encouraging students to pose problems, one that would bear fruit in every situation. It is possible, however, to outline a number of methods, alongside those already discussed, that could be of use in stimulating students' desire to ask questions.

Acting as a "Model" and as a "Crutch"

As in the case of problem solving, with problem posing the teacher's first role is that of a model. The teacher analyzes a particular situation and explains, through a series of questions, what governs his/her thinking: "See, we again got a whole number. It would be interesting to see if this is always the case." or "This is how we have solved the problem for a triangle. It would be interesting to see if this would also work for a quadrilateral."

As in the case of problem solving, the teacher also acts as a "crutch." On the one hand, teachers provide students with examples of possible questions and answers; on the other, they specifically provoke questioning by setting up a situation that prompts further investigation. Let us look at an example: the teacher can first give students a table of whole numbers from 1 to 100 and ask them to pick out numbers that are perfect squares or perfect cubes. The teacher can then ask whether there are numbers that are simultaneously both perfect squares and perfect cubes. It is extremely likely that the affirmative answer, which one can give quite easily (numbers 1 and 64), would prompt a further question from students: "But are there any more such numbers?"

Using Open-Ended Problems

There has recently been more and more research devoted to so-called "open-ended" problems (Becker & Shimada, 1997). What is usually understood by an "open-ended" problem, in contrast to a "closed" one, is that the problem has a number of correct solutions. Sometimes, however, the term is understood more broadly to refer to problems that have several fundamentally distinct ways of being solved correctly. For example, the problem of classifying a group of graphs is, generally speaking, open-ended insofar as the task can be completed in different ways, depending on the properties of graphs one takes into account and on the specific perspectives from which one examines them. By contrast, the problem that consists in calculating the value of the derivative of a given function at a given point with the help of the chain rule is a closed problem insofar as it has only one, unequivocal solution.

Experience in solving open-ended problems helps students develop the habit of problem posing. Silver et al. (1995) spoke about possible uses for such non-goal-specific, "open-ended" problems and of turning ordinary problems into them.

Examining an Example

A textbook gives the following problem:

The radius of a circle inscribed in a square is 6 inches, as shown in the figure below (Figure 5.1). Find the area of the square.

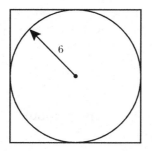

Figure 5.1

Instead of this problem the teacher gives students the following one:

> The radius of a circle inscribed in a square is 6 inches, as shown in the figure below (Figure 5.1). Find out all you can about the circle and the square.

In trying to solve such a problem the students themselves have to ask a series of questions and then look for answers to them.

It is very important to recognize explicitly the value of problem posing in student work. Extra credit is commonly given to students for solving especially hard problems; good problem posing by students deserves just as much extra credit and attention. Of even greater value, however, is the teacher's praise of a student's question and an explanation to the rest of the class about why the student's problem is so interesting and what is particularly good about the way it has been formulated. This may inspire other students to pose problems of their own. Finally, it is vital to treat problem posing as a regular form of class work.

Raising the Level of Student Activity: Examples from the Classroom

Concerns about the Low Activity of Students

Cangelosi (1984) has written about how, in ordinary problem solving lessons, only a small subset of the class actually responds to the teacher's questions. For this reason, despite the apparently high activity of student participation in a lesson, it is often the case that the majority of the class is, in effect, inactive and excluded from the process of solving and discussing problems. An analogous issue emerges in sessions devoted to problem posing: It is true that the teacher is not the only one asking questions here, but it is up to the teacher to always check whether it is all students or only a few students who are taking an active part in the exercise.

Cangelosi (1984) proposes several strategies for involving as many students as possible in discussing and solving a problem. One suggestion consists of asking the same question to all students, one by one, so that the discussion would not be limited to just one person but would involve everyone. In applying this strategy to problem posing, the teacher needs to hear problems posed by a number of students and not just one or two.

Examining
an **Example**   **A Lesson in Middle School**

The following describes a fragment of a lesson devoted to problem posing in middle school (Manouchehri, 2001).

Ms. S: OK, class, my comment for the day is "Even numbers!" What are some good questions to ask about them? You have ten minutes to write as many questions as you can in your notebooks. Remember, you need to be ready to share them with the rest of us.

[Students begin writing in their notebooks. Following a ten-minute individual work session, Ms. S. asks Jennifer to state the first question. Ms. S. records every question posed by the students on the board.]

Jennifer: What is the sum of two even numbers?
Ms. S: Good. What is the next question?
Nadine: What are four even numbers between 10 and 50?
Amy: I guess we could say, What is the product of two even numbers?
Ms. S: Good question. Next one?
Anne: I was going to say, Which even numbers are prime numbers, but I'd like to change that and say, What even [pause] . . . I mean, which even numbers are perfect squares?
Ms. S: I like both your questions. What is next? . . .

(This is how every student gets to ask his/her own question.)

Other Strategies for Increasing Student Involvement
Other ways of increasing the number of students engaged in answering questions include asking students to submit their answers in writing, and also group work. Both of these strategies can work well for problem posing.

During a lesson the teacher wanted to show the class how a situation can be studied from a variety of perspectives. The teacher presented the class with the following situation: a box contains 10 red, 8 white and 7 black marbles. Students were then asked to write down questions about this situation. The entire class analyzed the questions. Among them were arithmetical questions such as: "How many marbles are there in the box in total?" or "How many more red marbles than white marbles are there in the box?" or "How many fewer red marbles than marbles of other colors are there in the box?" Then there were questions devoted to constructing diagrams, such as: "Construct a pie chart that would represent the different shares of marbles of all three colors." There were also algebraic problems, such as: "The same number of white and black marbles is taken out of the box so that there are twice as many white ones as there are black ones remaining. How many white marbles have been taken out?" Finally, there were questions in discrete mathematics, such as: "One marble is taken out at random. What is the probability that this would be a black one?" or "Three marbles are taken out. How many different color combinations can one get?"

The fact that students were asked to formulate their questions in writing, and in advance, enabled everyone to become involved in the activity. It also allowed the teacher to examine the questions and answers beforehand and to plan the lesson accordingly.

This is how English, et al. (1998) describe the different stages of their work with students in sessions devoted to problem posing.

1. Students complete their problem creations, either individually or as a small group.
2. They then write a solution of their problem and hand the problem and its solution to the teacher. This step may be done as a homework assignment, if necessary.
3. In the next lesson, the teacher takes all the student-generated problems, but not their solutions, and distributes them to pairs of students. Along with the problems, the teacher gives students a critique sheet.
4. The students attempt the problem that they receive, showing all their work on the back of the critique sheet. After they have solved the problem, they fill out the critique sheet, which is then viewed by the teacher and returned to the author of the problem.

In such a sequence of steps the written form of the task allows the teacher to have different pairs doing different work. When a pair has finished with one particular task, it can be given to another pair. This means that all the students are working simultaneously on a large number of different tasks, which can then be discussed by the class as a whole.

It is also useful to develop the practice of problem posing in small groups. Small groups allow students to discuss the virtues and drawbacks of particular questions straight away, to make necessary corrections and to introduce essential clarifications. Small groups also give individual students a greater opportunity to express their own judgment and formulate their own questions. (The teacher needs to be careful when organizing groups, though, to avoid the domination of a group by a single student.)

Different groups of students can be given the same problem situation, which can subsequently be discussed by the whole class. In this case, members of different groups can make criticisms or request clarifications for particular problems. Another way of organizing group work would be to have different groups examine different situations. For instance, three groups could be given one situation, another three groups could be given a different situation, and yet another three groups could be asked to work on a third situation. Groups working on the same situation could then exchange each other's problems and try to solve them. There are, of course, numerous other ways of organizing group work of this sort.

Transforming the Class into a Site of Independent Research

It is very important to think through all the details of a lesson devoted to problem posing carefully. This should not be limited to technical details, such as the sequence in which problems ought to be posed and solved, or what sort of tasks one should do with the class as a whole and what sort of tasks on should give to small groups. What is far more important to consider is the general atmosphere generated in lessons involving problem posing. Brown and Walter (1990) write:

> There is a myth that it is the role of the expert or authority (textbook, teacher, research mathematician) to ask the questions and for the student merely to answer them. Of course, it is considered good pedagogy to encourage students to ask questions, but they are usually questions of an instrumental nature—questions that enable teachers to pursue their pre-conceived agendas. (p. 10)

Frequently, asking question is even highly welcomed, but usually only in order to assess whether the students have understood exactly what is required of them. Brown and Walter (1990) continue:

> Such an atmosphere neither leads to understanding the significance of an activity or a procedure, nor does it contribute to the development of a sense of autonomy and independence. (p. 11)

In order for problem posing truly to become the means of expressing (and forming) independent thought, the teacher must understand the classroom as a place of investigation rather than simply realizing one's own pre-prepared agenda (which itself commonly follows the dictate of some higher authority). What is more, the teacher needs to see the student as an active participant in this investigation and to respect the student's ability to ask unanticipated questions. A sincere attempt by the teacher to create such an atmosphere in the classroom, along with a genuine interest in the questions that students come up with, is usually noticed by students and may become a key factor in teaching them the art of problem posing and thinking like mathematicians.

Reflection
Assignments and Topics for Discussion

1. Prepare a series of assignments that would "provoke" students to ask further questions.
2. Take any textbook, select from it some goal-specific problems and then transform them into non-goal-specific problems (i.e., open-ended problems).
3. Give examples of situations in which the work of the whole class (middle or high school) could be based on students posing problems.
4. Give examples of situations in which students could pose problems when working in small groups.

CHAPTER 6

POSING PROBLEMS AND GROUPS OF PROBLEMS

This chapter is devoted to different ways a teacher can pose problems, as well as help students learn how to pose problems themselves.
The chapter discusses:

- Various methods for posing problems.
- The use of problems with unusual, "non-algorithmic" formulations.
- The construction and use of mental mathematics problems in both middle and high school.
- The construction and use of blocks of interconnected problems.

HOW TO POSE PROBLEMS

Problem Posing and Problem Solving

For students themselves, posing problems has its own value because it demonstrates student involvement in mathematical activity. For a teacher, however, posing problems is never an aim in itself, but a pedagogical

Mathematics in Middle and Secondary School, pages 147–172
Copyright © 2015 by Information Age Publishing

instrument. We talked above about the role that problem solving plays in the pedagogical process. The teacher poses problems in order to address certain concrete pedagogical aims. It might seem somewhat paradoxical that one of these aims would actually be to teach students themselves to pose problems. Recalling Polya's four-stage schema of problem solving, one could say that the ideal solver inevitably engages in forms of problem posing at two of Polya's stages—that of "devising a plan" and that of "looking back." In trying to find a solution to a problem it is often necessary to refer to problems that are similar to the one that is being solved. For example, one might need to reformulate the problem so that it fits some specific case. Also, once the solution has been reached it is worth considering what else can be achieved by using the problem's solution. In other words, what else can be said about the situation examined in the process of solving the problem? All of this effectively involves posing new problems.

Problem solving and problem posing invariably flow into and mutually stimulate one another. New problems are posed in order to solve existing ones, while solving existing problems prompts the posing of new ones. The teacher, playing the role of the ideal solver, needs to be able to demonstrate this interaction to students, thereby engaging them in the process of mathematical creation. Thus, both the teacher and the students need to be made aware of particular strategies of problem posing. Some of these will be discussed in what follows.

The "What-If-Not" Strategy

Everyone knows the formula for quadratic equations. But what about cubic equations? Or quadratic inequalities? Do formulas for such problems exist too?

What happens to the assertion: "Two triangles are congruent if two sides and the angle between them in one triangle are congruent to two sides and the angle between them in another triangle," when we take out the words "between them"?

Or what happens if we leave these words in, but instead of the word "triangle" we insert the word "parallelogram"? Is it true that when two sides and the angle between them in one parallelogram are congruent to the correspondent sides and angle of another parallelogram, that these parallelograms are congruent? And what if we take out all reference to "the angle"—in other words, if we simply say that two triangles are congruent if two of their sides are congruent?

It is known that $\sin 2x = 2\sin x \cos x$. But what about $\sin 3x$? Or $\cos 2x$? Or $\cos 3x$?

The Unified Strategy in Posing All of These Questions

One could carry on listing such questions indefinitely. Some of them are quite simple, but others are clearly much harder. It is even possible to come up with a problem for which the solution is unknown. All the above problems were obtained by a single method—starting off with some concrete situation, the question is then changed in some way by completely eliminating one of the conditions. Brown and Walter (1990) call this the "what-if-not" strategy. This is how they describe the different stages in constructing problems on the basis of this strategy:

- Choosing a Starting Point
- Listing Attributes
- What-if-Not-ing
- Question asking or Problem Posing
- Analyzing the Problem

Examining *an* Example	**Example of Constructing Problems with the Help of the Above Strategy**

Brown and Walter (1990) examine the following, deliberately routine, example (pp. 69—72):

> Calculate the area of a rectangle given that its width is 2 meters and its length is 3 meters.

Taking this as their starting point, the authors list the attributes, among which are the following (the list could, of course, have been compiled in a variety of ways):

1. The exercise is a request to calculate.
2. The exercise deals with a rectangle.
3. One is asked to calculate an area.
4. The width and length are specified.
5. One is given two numbers.

Next, start changing the attributes, one at a time only. Here are some examples of how the fourth attribute can be changed, for instance.

1. Only the width is specified.
2. The sum of the width and the length is specified.
3. The length and the width can be chosen from two given numbers.
4. The length of the diagonal is given, etc.

Next, concrete questions can be posed (third stage). Asking a question about calculating the area is an option, but in the specific instances listed (1–4), no definite numeric answer can be obtained. Alternately, the question itself could be modified. For example, in the second and fourth case it would be pertinent (if not entirely original) to ask about the largest possible area of the rectangle, while in the third case one could ask how many different solutions could be obtained for the area of the rectangle. New problems obtained using this "what-if-not" strategy can be solved and then analyzed further in order to pose yet more new problems.

Why This Strategy is Useful from a Pedagogical Point of View

Strategies for posing problems can also be analyzed from a pedagogical point of view. It is clear that "what-if-not" problems are useful at least for revealing to students the value and role that all the data in the formulation of a problem provide. Among the questions that can be asked at the first stage of problem solving, Polya proposed a question about whether the condition of the problem specifies the unknown. Playing with the question does the same thing—it helps to better understand the original conditions. In a somewhat broader context, this strategy (as well as most other problem-posing strategies that will be discussed) is valuable because it especially allows students to perceive mathematics not as a hermetic world with predetermined rules but as an aggregate of discovered situations that can be modified and explored.

Some Other Problem-Posing Strategies

While some may argue that other problem-posing strategies are, to a certain degree, all subspecies of the "what-if-not" strategy, it is worth distinguishing and discussing several more concrete methods of problem posing.

Dismantling a Problem into Parts

It would be fair to say that this is the most basic method used by teachers. In order to enable students to solve a more complex problem, the teacher often represents it as a chain of simpler problems. Chapter 4 discussed one example of such a chain of problems, which intended to enable students to prove the Pythagorean theorem independently. Similar work can be carried out on practically any problem (or theorem).

Here is an example.

Wanting to help students solve a word problem, the teacher first gave them several equations to solve (in the "do now" form) at the beginning of the lesson. Students were then assigned several word problems and asked to form the appropriate equations by expressing some of the values with a variable (introduced by the teacher). The equations they obtained were the same as

Concretization and generalization as methods of problem posing. The above method of problem posing could be seen as linked to the methods of concretization (mentioned briefly earlier) and generalization. By asking about the existence of something we are effectively asking the student to give examples (i.e., to find a concrete object to which a general assertion would apply [Watson & Mason, 2005]). Butt (1980) argues that problems that require the solver to give examples have certain pedagogical advantages over more traditional forms of recognition exercises. He argues that this stems from the fact that such problems prevent students from learning by rote without genuinely understanding the situation—with concrete examples. This also applies to certain unconventional formulations devised to enliven algorithmic exercises, such as the following: "Give an example of a number that satisfies the equation $2x^2 - x - 1 = 0$" (instead of the standard formulation: "find the solution").

Involving students in theoretically exploring the situation. Cases where it is difficult (or impossible) to give an example are equally useful. Here students engage in the theoretical exploration of a situation. For example:

- Can one construct a triangle for which two sides are shorter than 3 and the third is longer than 6?
- Can one formulate a quadratic equation so that it has three solutions?
- Can the logarithm of the sum of two numbers be equal to the sum of the logarithms of these numbers?

In situations where the answer is affirmative (as in the last question, where one can cite the example of the pair 2 and 2), it is easy to extend the problem further by asking whether the relation or assertion always applies. Questions with words such as "all" and "always" essentially assume (true or false) generalizations. Here are some examples:

- Having examined the right triangle with the sides 3, 4 and 5, the teacher can ask: "Is every triangle whose sides have the value of successive numbers right?"
- When studying numerical operations, one can ask: "If the sum of two numbers is positive, is it always the case that their product is also positive?"
- When studying properties of functions, one can ask: "If a function is increasing on a particular segment of the domain, is its highest value always situated at the far right of the segment?"

Using unexpected objects. Another method for transforming routine questions into non-routine ones is to use unexpected and unconventional

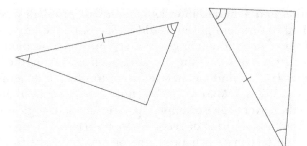

Figure 6.2

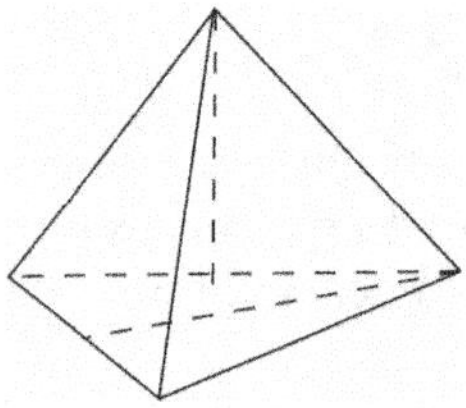

Figure 6.3

objects. The simplest example of this would be to formulate routine assertions about triangles, but place these triangles on the plane in an unconventional manner (Figure 6.2). Many students would find the equation $\lambda^2 - 5\lambda + 6 = 0$ different from $x^2 - 5x + 6 = 0$, and the problem of finding the area of one face of a regular tetrahedron (Figure 6.3) different from the problem of finding the area of a regular triangle. The teacher can and should use this method to get students to apply the algorithms that they have learned with greater understanding

Making Use of Mathematical Errors

Mistakes made by students also can become a brilliant source of new problems. These can be used to prevent mistakes from being made in the future, but they can also, just as importantly, be used as a way of turning errors into a positive experience—namely into the means of creating an unusual perspective for observing the given situation. An erroneous step generates a multitude of questions. Among them is, of course, the question of why the step happens to be a mistake. But this is certainly not all.

One can ask the question why the mistake was made in the first place— where it originated. Meyerson (1992) gives a series of "justifications" for the assertion that $(a+b)^2 = a^2 + b^2$. Among them is the application of the distributive property to the operation of squaring and a reference to the fact that $(a-b)(a+b) = a^2 - b^2$, which could suggest that by replacing the minus with a plus on the left, we ought to do the same on the right, and so forth. The very idea of trying to explain why a particular step was made, i.e., the request to make explicit the assumptions that were used in the process of solving a problem (such as those above, for example), is a mathematical task in the most profound sense.

One can also ask whether the step that caused the error is a mistake in every situation. For example, although

$$\frac{16}{64} = \frac{1}{4}$$

is correct, it is, generally speaking, untrue that

$$\frac{\overline{ab}}{\overline{bc}} = \frac{a}{c},$$

where a, b, and c represent digits, not variables (Borasi, 1992; Carman, 1971). Asking how often, and in what situations, can an error lead to a correct result is another way to use errors productively. For example, for which numbers a, b and c will

$$\frac{\overline{ab}}{\overline{bc}} = \frac{a}{c}$$

be true.

Examining *an* Example | Using the Error of a Movie Character

Below is another example of a whole series of pertinent problems that arise from a mathematical error.

> In the movie *The Wizard of Oz*, the Scarecrow, having been given a brain, asserts: "The sum of the square roots of any two sides of an isosceles triangle is equal to the square root of the remaining side." In other words the Scarecrow claims that if the two sides of an isosceles triangle are a and b and the third side is c that the following relation applies $\sqrt{a} + \sqrt{b} = \sqrt{c}$

It is obvious that poor old Scarecrow has got it all mixed up. Instead of "isosceles triangle" he meant "right triangle"; instead of any two sides of the triangle he meant the two legs; and instead of $\sqrt{a} + \sqrt{b} = \sqrt{c}$ he meant $a^2 + b^2 = c^2$. Let us now develop his errors and ask the following questions:

- Are there such numbers a, b and c for which $\sqrt{a} + \sqrt{b} = \sqrt{c}$ would actually apply?

- Does the Scarecrow's assertion apply to an equilateral triangle? And what about the isosceles right triangle with legs that equal 1?
- Is it possible to give an example of a triangle where it would be true to say that the sum of the square roots of two of its sides is equal to the square root of the remaining side?
- Is it true that in the case of a right triangle the sum of the squares of any two sides is equal to the square of the remaining side?

Why these problems are useful? These problems allow you to engage students in the kind of mathematical activity that is both highly varied and at the same time goes deep into the matter discussed. When solving these problems the students will need to:

- Give examples and check whether the assertions are correct by trying out concrete numbers;
- Transform algebraic equalities;
- Use the inequality of a triangle in an unexpected situation (if for some sides of a triangle it is true that $\sqrt{a}+\sqrt{b}=\sqrt{c}$ it would then follow that $a+b+2\sqrt{ab}=c$, which is impossible, because this would contradict the inequality $c < a+b$ which must be also true);
- Analyze the subtleties of the language and of the logical structure of the problem.

As already mentioned, the large variety of mathematical activities in which a solver is asked to engage is typical of a good problem situation.

"Translation"

Three of NCTM's process standards are in one way or another concerned with "translation" from one mathematical or ordinary language into another: communications, connections and representation. A form of "translation" is required when establishing connections between different types of knowledge, when looking for an appropriate way to express mathematical thoughts, and, more generally, when trying to find the means for representing specific information.

Students "translate" the conditions of a word problem into the language of equations. They "translate" their individual ideas, images and manner of reasoning into the conventional language of mathematics in order to explain their solution and "speak to others" (Pimm, 1987). Students "translate" when they move from one representation to another.

Students learn how to perform such "translations" mainly through solving problems. However, performing such "translations" can also serve as a valuable source of new problems.

Examples of assignments. You can ask students to engage in forms of "translation" when studying all sorts of mathematical concepts and results. Students can be asked to look for different ways of representing these concepts and results or they can be asked to clarify their meaning in the context of other areas of mathematics. When discussing some numerical relation, it is possible to ask what sort of geometry lies behind it, and vice versa. When some assertion is written down as a formula, it is natural to ask how such data would be represented as a graph or a table, and so forth.

Students can be asked to solve such problems if they are assigned by the teacher, or they can be asked to formulate similar problems on their own. For example, after examining the problem: "For which values of a does the equation $x^2 + 4x - a = 0$ have exactly one solution?" the teacher can also pose two further questions:

- For which values of a does the graph of the function $y = x^2 + 4x - a$ touch the x-axis?
- For which values of a is the polynomial $x^2 + 4x - a$ the square of a binomial?

The answers to the latter two questions evidently match the answer to the original question. In fact, they are all one and the same question only "translated" into other areas of mathematics.

You can also do something different. Instead of asking these questions yourself, as explained above, you can ask students to consider what problem about the graph they have solved while answering the first question. The activity thereby becomes one of problem posing.

On mathematical modeling. One could say that "translation" is the most important part of mathematical modeling. In modeling students are not given a finished problem but rather a situation that requires them to formulate the problem on their own (Pollak, 2003). This is how Pollak (2003) describes one of the stages in the construction of a mathematical model:

> We idealize the situation by deciding what is most important about the objects and their interrelations, and we translate this idealized version into mathematical terms to obtain a mathematical formulation of the idealized situation. This is called a *mathematical model.* (p. 58)

Mathematical modeling also includes other stages, among which is the solving of the mathematical problem obtained through modeling and exploring the plausibility of this solution: "We translate back to the real world and do a reality check" (Pollak, 2003). This means that situations from real life, in all their complexity, and each stage in constructing a mathematical model for them can serve as a source of new problems. A number of books have recently been published that help teachers construct an entire course in mathematics on the basis of mathematical modeling (Dossey et al., 2002). Modeling also remains extremely useful in courses organized around more standard bases as well. Indeed, within CCSS-M (2010) modeling is listed both as one of the SMPs as well as a conceptual category in high school, which has to some degree revitalized interest in mathematical modeling in the United States. COMAP, for example, has recently published a series of resources about incorporating mathematical modeling into classroom teaching (CITE).

Carrying out the "reality check." A great number of traditional word problems tend to fail the "reality check." Carrying out a "reality check" is often much easier than solving the problem itself, but it is nonetheless extremely beneficial to the students' development. In addition to questions that are usually given to students, one could also ask whether a particular solution is plausible or not in a given situation and whether a particular real-life word problem is a good one and why.

Pollak (1970) analyzed the following problem:

> An electric fan is advertised as moving 3375 ft³ of air per minute. How long will it take the fan to change the air in a kitchen 27 ft by 25 ft by 10 ft?

As the authors of the problem have conceived it, the solution simply consists in finding the volume of the kitchen and then dividing it by 3375. But this solution is evidently based on the assumption that one first sucks out all the old air and then pumps in new air, something that clearly bears no relation to what happens in real life. A proper solution to the problem can be obtained only with the help of Calculus methods. However, the very discussion of the inadequacy of the problem is useful in itself.

Developing and enriching problems. Starting from comparatively routine problems, it is possible to enrich them by taking into account certain aspects of the real life situations that the authors have sacrificed for the sake of simplicity. Let us look at an example of such a standard problem.

> You have $100. Let us assume that you want to spend the entire sum on paperbacks and/or CDs. The paperbacks cost $5 each, while the CDs cost $10 each. Write down a linear equation that describes the situation. Graph this equation. Give some of the possible solutions for how you spend your money.

In real life the situation described above tends to be rather more complicated. Few people would make it their specific aim to spend all the money to the last cent. It is another matter to assume that one cannot spend anything over the sum available—even by, say, a dollar. Paperbacks rarely cost exactly $5 but are usually $4.99 and this also applies to CDs. In addition, the final price for these items is usually taxed. When buying several books or CDs one can often get some sort of discount (buy four CDs get the fifth free, for example). It ought to be beneficial to students to construct further equations (or inequalities) to include these new, more complicated, aspects of the situation.

Summing Up: A Problem Is Not an Isolated Phenomenon

The above list of problem posing strategies does not pretend to be exhaustive. One could, for instance, say something more about constructing problems *by analogy*, a strategy that has only been mentioned in passing. The strategy involves examining a situation that is analogous to another familiar one. Or else, the new situation merely has certain specific aspects that are analogous to those encountered before. Or else, one examines problems that might have analogous solutions, and so forth.

There are other methods that could be used in constructing problems, but the most important factor in mastering the art of problem posing is not the knowledge of particular methods, but the attitude that one takes towards problem situations. What is important is that a problem is not viewed as an isolated phenomenon, but as a situation that belongs to a whole series of related problems; a series that can, moreover, always be extended further. Finally, nothing can replace the actual experience of constructing problems.

Formulating Questions

One way of looking at a mathematical problem is to see it as a particular type of question that is asked in class. Solving a problem involves asking a number of comparatively minor questions and looking for an answer to them. The practice of asking questions in class has been studied from a variety of perspectives (Wilien, 1986; Posamentier, Smith, & Stepelman, 2006) and many of the observations and recommendations that have been made about this practice are of great use in posing problems. Here are some of these remarks.

- Plan key questions. One cannot, of course, anticipate all that will happen in a lesson and the teacher always needs to remain as flexible as possible, following carefully how the lesson develops. However, precisely in order to be able to focus on what happens during the lesson, the teacher needs to prepare all the key questions in advance.
- Ask questions in a way that is accessible to students. The teacher of mathematics differs from a mathematician. The latter can explore all questions that are of possible interest. The former, however, can address only those problems that are of specific use to students. The teacher must be both an imaginative author who creates new problems and a ruthless censor who rejects anything that is too hard or in any other way inappropriate for students.
- Use clear and simple language. Do not ask your students, say, to provide a thorough classification of all the possible cases that apply to

a given situation. It is better to ask simply which specific cases apply. In general avoid the kind of complex mathematical phrasing that you have learned at university. What you need are not words but ideas that lie behind them and the experience of working with these ideas. Avoid complex verbal constructions. Where possible, accompany your questions with a drawing or a table, designing them to avoid confusion.

- Ask questions with precision and clarity. You are putting these questions not to yourself but to students who have little idea of what goes on in your mind. You must therefore formulate explicitly all of the details and conditions.

- Ask questions not in isolation but as part of a logical chain of questions. Students must have a clear picture of how your questions are emerging and how they relate to one another. By placing the questions in a sequence the teacher makes it easier for students to find the answer and it also teaches them how to ask questions themselves.

- Pay attention to student responses. You have your own list of key questions, but you must not simply adhere to your pre-prepared plan without taking into account what actually takes place in the course of the lesson. It is possible that the response of a student requires some further clarification. Perhaps this response also gives you an opportunity to ask a new and important question. Listen carefully to what students are saying.

- Ask questions in such a way that students have enough time to think about them. Even when it appears to you that what is required is quite obvious, do not rush the student with the answer. Students might not find it as simple as you do. Trying to hurry them up ("What's taking you so long! It's easy!") usually only disrupts their thought process. Also, do not rush to call on the first student who comes up with an answer (especially if it is always the same student). Most importantly, do not rush to provide the answer yourself.

- Ask questions in such a way that they contribute to the students' development. Polya (1973) highlighted the difference between a question such as: "Do you know a related problem?" and a question such as: "Could you apply the theorem of Pythagoras?" The latter does not teach students anything new and reveals the key to the solution straight away (provided, of course, that the students understand the tip—and if they do not, the question becomes useless anyways). Black et al. (2004) basically assert that the only point for teachers to ask questions should be to accomplish one of two things: to push student thinking or to probe student understanding. The teacher's aim is not to create the impression that everyone is and needs to be quick in responding to questions, but rather to help students learn how to think mathematically.

Assignments and Topics for Discussion

1. Solve the problems cited in the text above.
2. Analyze the assertion that the diagonals of a parallelogram bisect each other. Compose some problems on this topic using the "what-if-not" strategy.
3. Construct a few problems that would lead to the proof of the law of cosines.
4. Construct a few problems that would lead to the proof that the area of any triangle ABC (with sides a,b,c, across from their respective angle A,B,C) is: A = ½ absin C.
5. The assertion that "one can inscribe a circle in every triangle" is true. Using this as a starting point, pose a few problems using what has been described above as "logical games."
6. Students are familiar with the algorithm for solving linear equations. Think up some non-routine questions on this topic.
7. The following inequality is examined:

$$\sqrt{a^2+(a-1)^2} \le 1.$$

   Construct some problems that one can reduce to this inequality, so that they refer to: a) distances; b) complex numbers; and c) circles.
8. Analyze a selection of word problems from any chapter of a school textbook of your choice. Are these problems realistic? How are they solved in real life? Does this match the solution recommended in the textbook?
9. Choose a problem from a textbook and, using it as your starting point, construct new problems by making the situation more realistic.
10. Create some problems that would be based on the following error: $\sqrt{a+b} = \sqrt{a}+\sqrt{b}$.
11. Pose some problems that involve operations on matrices by analogy with problems that you already know and that deal with operations on numbers.

CREATING SETS OF PROBLEMS

It has already been argued that questions in class need to be asked not in isolation but as part of an interconnected sequence. Teachers often plan groups of interrelated problems for a particular lesson or for one of its parts. Such problems can be grouped on the grounds that they all focus on developing a single idea or that they all discuss a single object. They can also be grouped on the grounds that they assume the same type of activity on the part of students engaged in solving them. Here are some examples.

Problems for Various Types of Work

Traditionally, formulations of mathematical problems contain words like "find," "calculate," "simplify" or "prove." It is far more difficult to find problems that require the student to discuss and provide arguments in favor of this or that point of view, or to carry out an experiment, for example.

The absence (or very small number) of such assignments reflects the widespread view of mathematics as a subject where everything is predetermined and where there is nothing debatable that requires validation through experiments. It is true that in the final stage of their creative work mathematicians are asked to present the finished product in a logically immaculate form. But in the process of seeking the truth mathematicians do not refrain from plausible reasoning or from trying to come up with the correct solution through guesswork. This is why Polya (1954) purposefully called for the greater use of plausible reasoning in school mathematics.

Assignment That Requires Plausible Reasoning

Assertions commonly found in school mathematics provide ample material for work of this sort. For example, students can be asked whether they find plausible the assertion that the altitudes of *every* triangle intersect in a common point. In response to this question students can perform experiments by constructing different triangles and checking where their altitudes intersect. Or else they can look at certain special cases where the assertion is easy to prove (e.g., the case of a right or regular triangle). Other students might use analogy—if the bisectors of every triangle intersect in a single point, it is natural to assume that this also applies to altitudes. This type of discussion of the above assertion would be no less (and often more) useful than conducting its proof in a logically rigorous fashion.

Indeed, constructing and critiquing mathematical arguments is one of the Common Core SMPs—a way in which students should be practicing mathematics frequently. Such assignments need to be given to students regularly in order to get them used to this type of work. They do not need to be explicitly interlinked, neither by the conditions that they presuppose nor by the methods required for their solution. They can be spread over a relatively lengthy period of time. However, the teacher should still treat such assignments as a particular set in its own right and, where possible, remind students of their previous experience with this type of work.

Problems That Require the Solver to Imagine Something

There are also very few assignments in textbooks that ask students to draw or imagine something. Such tasks are clearly more difficult to check and their discussion is also more complicated than that of more straightforward or "closed" problems.

For instance, the problem: "Draw the graph of a function that goes through points $(0, 0)$ and $(1, 1)$" can have a large number of different solutions (although many students are happy simply to draw a straight line through the two points). It is precisely the conjunction of their open-endedness, on the one hand, and their visual nature, on the other, that makes such problems so valuable. They are particularly useful in developing mathematical imagination.

The teacher can pose problems in which students are required to imagine an object first and then perform operations on it mentally, or alternatively, they can be asked to shift from a mental representation to a drawing. Here are some examples of such problems.

- Imagine a polyhedron with 6 edges. Draw it.
- Imagine a cube. Do the diagonals of its neighboring faces intersect?
- Imagine the graph of a function that decreases over the entire set R and has only positive values. Draw a graph of such a function.

Ideally, such problems should appear regularly, although there is no need for lots of them in a single lesson—one or two is enough. Gradually this type of question will become habitual.

Problems in Mental Mathematics

Problems in mental mathematics, or mathematical tasks to be completed without the aid of a calculating or recording device, are becoming increasingly popular, in explicit contrast to problems that assume the use of a pen-and-paper algorithm or a calculator. Indeed, they seem to play an important role in the teaching process. Creating sets of mental problems can be of great help in constructing lessons and they will therefore be discussed in more detail in what follows.

Reflecting on Research

According to research (Sowder, 1990; Carroll, 1996; Reys et al., 1993), problems in mental mathematics are especially useful because they direct the focus of the lesson on genuinely understanding the subject rather than assimilating purely technical aspects of the solution. Other advantages of such problems are that they allow for greater flexibility in discussing a mathematical situation and that solution methods are also generally shaped by the individual—typically, in solving these problems, students are looking for their own approach rather than recalling some memorized algorithm (not to mention the fact that mental mathematics is especially useful in real life situations outside the classroom). Panasuk et al. (2002) consider mental mathematics as essential in middle school, emphasizing that children at this age construct their own world of mental representations and that the better teachers understand and use these representations the more successful their teaching will become. It is also important to note that the indication that a problem must be solved in one's head carries a certain metacognitive message: it hints at the fact that there must be a strategy to reach the solution in this way.

| Examining |
| *an* Example | **Problems that Help Develop Number Sense**

You can regularly devote particular parts of a lesson to problems in mental mathematics in order to develop students' number sense. Such problems can be quite diverse, despite having to be solved mentally. For example, you can assign certain tasks where it is convenient to use the commutative property of multiplication or the distributive property.

Calculate mentally:

1. $25 \cdot 1322 \cdot 4$
2. $1217 \cdot 13 + 783 \cdot 13$.

Faced with such an assignment, students will not perform calculations in an automatic way, without giving it any thought at all, but will instead start looking for those distinctive properties of the given example that allow them to perform the calculation mentally. This would enable them to practice using the laws of mathematical operations in a meaningful way. Indeed, Carpenter, Franke and Levi (2003) argued that explicit and implicit use of such arithmetic properties can help students develop numerical fluency.

In order to construct such tasks, the teacher can effectively proceed from the end result. The previous case, for example, was achieved by starting off with a pair of numbers that are easy to multiply mentally, such as, for example 2000 and 13. All that remained to be done now is to break 2000 into two items so that their mental multiplication by 13 appeared difficult.

One can also imagine some more interesting tasks where there are several possible paths to the solution and where the student has to choose how to proceed. For example, the mental multiplication $96 \cdot 25$ can be performed in the following ways:

$$96 \cdot 25 = (100 - 4) \cdot 25 = 2500 - 100 = 2400$$

$$96 \cdot 25 = 96 \cdot 5 \cdot 5 = 480 \cdot 5 = 2400$$

$$96 \cdot 25 = 24 \cdot 4 \cdot 25 = 24 \cdot 100 = 2400$$

It is clear that work on such assignments and their consequent discussion develops the students' number sense. These tasks are also useful because they allow the teacher, as well as other students, to observe the manner in which some students think. Additionally, in posing such problems the teacher should choose numbers that allow a variety of paths to the solution (this does not necessarily mean that the teacher should be able to anticipate all the paths that might emerge in the lesson).

Mental Mathematics in High School

In high school, mental mathematics is unfortunately much less popular (Karp, 2006; Rubinstein, 2001). But even in this context the teacher can pose problems that need to be solved without pen and paper, or without a calculator. Here, too, such mental assignments hint at and help students focus on finding the optimal strategy rather than get distracted with technical details.

For example, in order to highlight the geometrical aspect of integration, teachers can ask students to calculate the integral,

$$\int_{-1}^{1} \sqrt{1 - x^2} \, dx,$$

mentally. Such a problem is far too hard for high school students if they try to solve it by applying standard "written" methods. The problem is, however, reducible to finding the area of the semicircle with the radius 1. In order to realize this, the student needs to know that the graph of the function $y = \sqrt{1 - x^2}$ is a semicircle (Figure 6.4) and, most importantly, to link

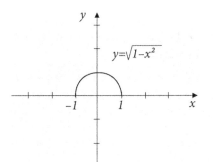

Figure 6.4

the question about calculating the integral to obtaining area (which can be repeated in one form or another during the lesson). By setting the task as a mental one, the teacher directs the student's thought process in the necessary "non-calculating" direction.

In solving mental mathematics problems, at both the high school and middle school levels, students usually feel less constrained by pre-learned algorithms: they are generally much bolder in proposing geometrical and other unconventional solutions compared to when they are asked to solve common "written" problems.

Using Mental Problems as a Tool in Lesson Construction

Mental problems can serve a few special purposes. They are particularly valuable as a means for training students to think without writing and drawing (as in the above examples that stimulated mathematical imagination). However, mental problems can also be used in teaching the most common parts of the course content and as a tool in constructing practically any lesson.

The teacher might, for instance, need to spend a particular part of the lesson reviewing key ideas from the previously studied material. In such cases, it is usually necessary to save time and not waste any of it on dealing with technical difficulties. These situations lend themselves particularly well to using a series of mental problems that deal precisely with the key ideas needing to be reviewed. The sequence of mental problems could then lead onto more demanding and labor-consuming problems that require a written solution.

On some occasions the teacher might want to use mental problems as the means for introducing certain key ideas relevant to the material studied. The lesson would in this case consist of two parts: first, one would examine the material quickly through a sequence of mental problems; and after that, one would move onto something weightier and technically more difficult. Here mental problems essentially model the content of the entire lesson on technically simpler material.

Examining *an* **Example** | **Lesson Devoted to Finding the Domain of a Function**

Let us look at one particular variant of a lesson devoted to finding the domain of a function that contains radicals. Students can experience difficulties in solving such problems for a variety of reasons: perhaps, because they might not understand the concept "domain of a function," or because they do not know how to solve the inequality that emerges in the process, or because they are unable to shift from the general concept of "domain" to concrete cases and inequalities. In devising the lesson, the teacher decided to deal with each of the above potential difficulties individually.

At the beginning of the class Mr. Jones gave students an inequality to solve. This was essentially a review assignment in the "do now" form. Students were asked to complete the assignment in writing and the inequality was then discussed on the board.

Mr. Jones then gave students the following series of mental questions.

1. Determine any number x for which the following operations would apply and another number x on which these same operations cannot be performed:

   a) $\dfrac{1}{x}$; b) $\sqrt{x}$; c) $\dfrac{1}{\sqrt{x}}$

2. Determine the domain of the following functions:

   a) $y = \dfrac{1}{x}$; b) $y = \sqrt{x}$; c) $y = \dfrac{1}{\sqrt{x}}$

3. Explain why the following graphs (Figure 6.5) cannot correspond to the above functions a)–c).

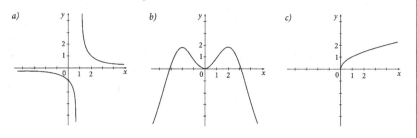

Figure 6.5

4. Choose the best answer out of the four possible solutions offered below and explain your choice. In order to determine the domain of the function $y = \sqrt{3x-5}$ one must: a) take only all non-negative numbers x; b) notice that there is a minus sign in the square root and therefore take all numbers from 5 upwards; c) solve the inequality $3x-5 \geq 0$; d) do something else that has not been proposed.

Students were then given written assignments analogous to these mental ones but technically more complex.

The above mental tasks were aimed at discussing the basic ideas, and they were devised in such a way that they could genuinely be solved mentally. Their discussion pinpointed a number of engrained misconceptions. To question 1b a student gave the answer $x = 3$, because one could not (allegedly) "extract a root from 3." The questions also involved a gradual shift to inequalities. This enabled students to be actively involved in apprehending inequalities and was helpful for solving further problems.

Mental problems can, of course, serve very different purposes in a lesson. It would be wrong to assume that it is the only useful pedagogical device for working on these ideas; however, the interaction of the mental and the written seems to help make mathematical ideas much clearer to students.

Determining if a Problem Can be Solved Mentally or Not

The series of mental questions in the example above was designed in response to an analysis of possible difficulties that students might encounter. This determined what aspects of the subject matter with which the specific questions should be concerned. The issue of whether these questions were actually suitable as mental problems was entirely dependent on the level of the class. In principle, a mental problem ought to be solvable in a reasonable number of steps, and that each assumes a reasonable number of calculating operations or (imagined) visualizations. What "reasonable" means, depends largely on the class itself. Psychologists (Krutetskii, 1976) have observed that talented students on average have a better mathematical memory and find it easier to establish connections between different parts of what they have learned than ordinary students. Consequently, in classes for talented students mental work can be done on problems that would be unsuitable in ordinary classes. At the same time, one can devise problems that would suit the above-described work in practically any type of class.

Blocks of Problems

In discussing problem posing, we have, in fact, invariably talked about problems as parts of particular blocks—aggregates of questions that refer to a single object (or a set of mutually related objects) where new questions are always based on old ones. It is particularly important, however, to grasp the importance not just of how to formulate individual questions within a block (however interesting these might be), but also of how to work with the block as a whole.

Even comparatively routine problems are often better organized not as distinct assignments (e.g., first solve ten equations, then construct ten graphs) but as blocks of interrelated problems. It is, in fact, much easier and quicker to ask students to determine the zeros of the function $f(x) = x^2 - 4x + 3$, then go on to graph the function, determine its range, and so forth, rather than

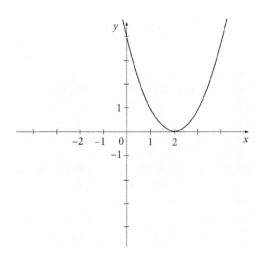

Figure 6.6

first give them one set of assignments to determine zeros of various functions, and then, separately, another set of assignments to graph these functions. This would merely make students repeat the same operations over and over again. By linking the different tasks together in a block, you can observe whether the students are able to relate one set of results with another, as obtained in different tasks.

Many students find this difficult in fact. For example, a student can wrongly graph the function $f(x) = x^2 - 4x + 3$ (Figure 6.6), but then correctly solve the equation $x^2 - 4x + 3 = 0$, using the formula for roots of quadratic equations. What is more, in this particular instance, the contradiction of the two results remained unnoticed by the student, something that is even more deplorable than the error committed in graphing the function transformation.

Some Recommendations

Blocks of problems are especially useful in developing the skill of establishing connections. This, however, is something that does not take place all on its own but requires systematic work. Here are some recommendations to teachers who want to compile blocks of assignments for work in class.

- One must choose objects that have a fairly rich structure. Since one will need to ask a whole series of questions, it is good to choose an object for which it is natural to ask so many questions. If one is studying a set, it must be an interesting one; if one is discussing a function, it needs to have a variety of properties; if one is describing a geometrical figure, it must involve reasoning and calculations.

- The teacher compiling a block of problems should think of the way to create connections between different points. This involves either a "translation" from one mathematical language to another, or checking what has already been done, or providing a concrete example of a general assertion. Whether to include a new problem to the existing block may be considered on the basis that it establishes some new connection. For example: "Is it possible to ask a question that would prompt students to check what they have already done?" This is just as important as thinking about how to include a problem that would deal with a particular property or theorem.
- In trying to create a rich network of connections within the block, one must not forget, however, about how accessible it is to students. Any complex points need to be carefully prepared, which means that the first steps need to be comparatively easy, designed primarily to clarify the subject matter.
- In solving problems in class it is important to highlight and discuss not just their purely mathematical dimension, but also the connections that one discovers between problems. This teaches students to seek such connections independently in the future.
- The block needs to be conceived of as open-ended, in the sense that student questions should be welcomed and encouraged. It is useful to ask students questions like: "Think of another question about this function." or "What more could you ask about this polygon?"

| Examining
 an Example | Set of Questions Intended for a
 Review Class |

Let us analyze the construction of a set of questions intended for a review class. The lesson was devoted to going over the material that was to come up on the exam. The teacher selected as the object of analysis a geometrical figure—a rectangle, both sides of which could be expressed through a single variable. This opened up the possibility of geometrical tasks, tasks involving the introduction of a variable, and also algebraic tasks. The teacher asked the following questions.

Let us examine the rectangle ABCD, where side $\overline{AB}$ is two inches shorter than side $\overline{AD}$.

1. Let us say that AB = 3. Determine all the sides and area of the rectangle.

---

2. Let us say that AB = x. Express the area of the rectangle in terms of x.
3. Find all values x, for which the area of the rectangle equals 35.
4. Construct a graph for the area of the rectangle based on the length of the side AB (x)
5. Let us say that AB = x. Express the diagonal of the rectangle, $\overline{BD}$, in terms of x.
6. Is it true that if AB = 6, the length of the diagonal of the rectangle, $\overline{BD}$, is an irrational number?
7. Is it possible to give a length for the side $\overline{AB}$ so that the length of the diagonal $\overline{BD}$ would be an irrational number?
8. Let us say that AB = x. Express the sides of any rectangle, in terms of x, for which the area would be the same as that of the rectangle ABCD.

As we can see, the level of difficulty of the first questions is fairly low—these are merely routine exercises. However, they too include an important shift (in the first two questions) from a concrete example to a general situation. The block of questions also includes "chaining" (where the result of one task is used for the solution of another, as in questions 2, 3 and 4, for example), "translation" into another language (in questions 4 and 8, for example; in the last one the solver is essentially asked to represent the expression $x^2 + 2x$ as the product of two factors different from x and $x + 2$) and finally, the "checking" of the obtained formula, coupled with its concretization (for example, in solving task 6, students either inserted number 6 into the formula or worked out the diagonal directly, thereby testing the formula).

Further Development: Questions Asked by Students

The above questions were asked in such a way that they provoked further inquiries by the students themselves. For example, during the lesson the students asked the following questions:

- Are there any other possible lengths for the side $\overline{AB}$, apart from 6, for which the length of the diagonal $\overline{BD}$ would be a rational number?
- Are any of the solutions [to the previous question] whole numbers?
- Is it true that if the width of a rectangle is 2 units shorter than its length and its area is the same as that of the above rectangle ABCD, then the rectangle is congruent to ABCD?

Some of the questions asked by students were, in fact, much more complicated than the ones asked by the teacher and they were therefore not discussed in class. Nevertheless, the very fact that the students were asking these questions is important. This is precisely why work with blocks of problems is so useful.

Assignments and Topics for Discussion

1. Create some tasks that have the following formulations: "conduct an experiment," "provide arguments in favor of a specific assertion."
2. Compile a set of assignments that would be used for practice in mental calculation.
3. Think up some mental problems for developing spatial imagination.
4. The teacher plans to spend a lesson on operations with radicals. Compile a set of mental mathematics problems that could be used at the beginning and end of such a lesson.
5. A lesson is going to be devoted to reviewing the properties of quadratic trinomials. Compile a block of problems for such a lesson.

PART III

This part discusses the teaching of algebra and some elements of precalculus. Its aim is to introduce the reader to the theoretical and practical aspects of teaching the basic topics of these courses.

PART III

CHAPTER 7

"THE SCIENCE OF TRANSPOSITION AND CANCELLATION"

This is the first of the chapters devoted to the study of algebra. Its general aim is to describe the content of a course in school algebra and particularly to shed light on the use of variables and algebraic transformations.
   The chapter discusses:

- The aims and objectives of teaching school algebra
- The principal difficulties and errors of students in the study of algebra
- What research has to say about the causes of these difficulties and about ways of overcoming them
- The process of studying algebra over the entire period of school education (K–12), including corresponding expectations and results (with reference to NCTM Principles and Standards)
- Some typical yet especially challenging problems based on algebraic transformations
- Planning lessons devoted to algebraic transformations as an example of working with such material.

Mathematics in Middle and Secondary School, pages 175–208
Copyright © 2015 by Information Age Publishing
All rights of reproduction in any form reserved.

ALGEBRA: WHY IS IT SO HARD TO TEACH?

What Does Algebra Teach Us?

The word "algebra" comes from the title of the work by the Arab mathematician al-Khowârizmî "Hisâb al-jabr w'al-mugâ-balah" that could be translated as "the science of transposition and cancellation" (Eves, 1990). Indeed, for decades, if not centuries, students associated school algebra with lengthy expressions where they had to cancel and transform everything correctly in order to get a 0 or 1 or some other simple expression. Today, however, the algebra course is understood far more broadly than before and the aim of teaching it now involves much more than just showing students how to manipulate symbols.

On the Content of the Current Algebra Course

Kieran (1992, p. 391) cites the following topics as typical for school textbooks in algebra:

---

a. The properties of real and complex numbers
b. The forming and solving of first- and second-degree equations in one unknown
c. The simplification of polynomial and rational expressions
d. The symbolic representation of linear, quadratic, exponential, logarithmic, and trigonometric functions, along with their graphs
e. Sequences and series

Kieran notes, however, that not all students study all of these topics.

Usiskin (1988) cites four different conceptions of school algebra: algebra as generalized arithmetic; algebra as a study of procedures for solving certain kinds of problems; algebra as the study of relationships among quantities; and algebra as the study of structures. The current course in algebra contains elements that reflect each of these conceptions.

This is how NCTM (2000) elaborates the core of the algebra standard:

Instructional programs from prekindergarten through grade 12 should enable all students to—

• Understand patterns, relations, and functions
• Represent and analyze mathematical situations and structures using algebraic symbols
• Use mathematical models to represent and understand quantitative relationships
• Analyze change in various contexts.

CCSS-M (2010) delineates various aspects of algebra throughout the standards, distinguishing between expressions and equations and functions in the middle grades, and building on each of those ideas in the high school standards.

- Algebra
  - Seeing structure in expressions
  - Arithmetic with polynomials and rational expressions
  - Creating equations
  - Reasoning with equations and inequalities
- Functions
  - Interpreting functions
  - Building functions
  - Linear, quadratic, and exponential models
  - Trigonometric functions

All these objectives are interrelated. One cannot, for example, speak of representing mathematical situations or of using symbols to this effect, without taking into account patterns and without mentioning relations and functions. Learning how to use symbols happens throughout the process of constructing mathematical models and clearly cannot be reduced only to practicing algebraic transformations, as was commonplace before. And yet, as was the case decades ago, algebra remains the gatekeeper to further mathematical study, mainly due to the fact that it is in algebra that students learn the particular language of mathematics—the construction and understanding of formulas.

The first, and in certain cases insurmountable, difficulty that students face in studying mathematics is with the use of symbols and variables, the need to be able to perform operations with them and to transform algebraic expressions. It is impossible to acquire such algebraic techniques without practice, but it is also not possible to achieve it through practice alone or through automatic memorization of rules. Here too, it is mathematical reasoning, specifically the understanding and solving of problems, that is the key to success.

Changes in the Understanding of Algebra as a Science and as a School Subject

Over the centuries, algebra changed not only as a school subject but also as a science. If at first the primary domain of algebra was the solution of equations, and its most important results were, for example, the proof that every polynomial equation has at least one complex solution, or (earlier still) the derivation of formulas for solving cubic equations and equations of the fourth degree, then later algebra became a science that studied the properties of operations in general and of systems where these operations are applied.

It is telling that the seminal work of van der Waerden (1950)—a watershed in the broad usage of such concepts as "group," "ring" and "field"—was called *Modern Algebra* in its first editions, but was later renamed simply *Algebra*, because the meaning of this word had itself become different, and not without the influence of Van der Waerden's book.

This transformation of algebra as a science does not mean that the schoolteacher can forget classical school algebra and start the course by immediately explaining "groups" to schoolchildren. Nevertheless, even when examining the same old problems that were part of algebra centuries ago, it is important for the teacher to remember the new essence of algebra, to understand that algebra is not simply a generalization of arithmetic, but also the means of describing and understanding many other processes and phenomena, from the transformation of geometrical figures to problems of economic development. This means that the old work on simply manipulating symbols now acquires a new sense and resonance.

Some Cases from School Practice: Discussion

Examining *an* **Example**

Katherine Merseth (2003) cites the following case.

A teacher, Mrs. Harper, gave her Intermediate algebra class the following problem from the textbook: Translate into an algebraic expression or sentence: "5 less than 2 times a number is 12 more than the number." Quite unexpectedly for the teacher, this, in her view, perfectly routine problem turned out to be beyond her students' abilities. During the lesson they gave a number of different answers, but none of them was the correct one.

The first variant of the solution involved the replacement of the ordinary words in the text with signs. Thus, instead of "less than" one of the students put "<", instead of "is"—"=", and instead of "more than"—">". The solution thus looked like this: $5 < 2n = 12 > n$.

The second student remembered that "less" means that one should subtract something and he therefore put a "minus" sign between 5 and the expression $2n$. The result became: $5 - 2n = 12 + n$.

The third student applied the same principle but interpreted the sentence differently. He decided that one must subtract five from two and then multiply this by the number. In other words, he wanted to write $(2 - 5)n$. However, since he forgot about opening parentheses (something he had learned the previous year) he wrote the following solution on the board: $2 - 5n = 12 + n$. Part of the class did not react to this at all, while others nodded approvingly. To Mrs. Harper's utter frustration the lesson ended with a debate about how the students could have come up with these formulas.

Examining *an* Example   The Case of Barry and Merry

Saul (2001) gives a different example of possible difficulties that students can experience, this time when working with ready-made algebraic expressions where no translation from ordinary to algebraic language is required.

Student Barry was able to solve linear equations only by trial and error. He knew how to insert concrete numbers into expressions and he could see perfectly well that $x = 2$ was not the solution of the equation $2x + 1 = 7$, but that $x = 3$ was. However, the teacher could not get him to subtract 1 from 7 and divide this by 2. Student Merry was able to factor $3x + 3y$, but the factorization of $3x + 7x$ was already causing her difficulties, while the expression $3x + 7x^2$ became much too hard. She knew the formula $x^2 - y^2 = (x - y)(x + y)$, but to make use of it in order to factor $(x + y)^2 - (x + 3)^2$ was simply beyond her.

Examples of Other Difficulties Experienced by Students
   One could go on citing many similar or more striking stories from school practice. Not all students are, in fact, able to insert numerical values into a given expression, as Barry did above. We have also already noted that many students confuse multiplication and addition, and that they write x^2 as the result of adding $x + x$; students also write $a + b = ab$, assuming that adding two letters means to write them next to each other (Booth, 1988). Teachers diligently, but often unsuccessfully, explain, for example, that $(-x)^2$ and $-x^2$ are not the same thing. Researchers (Boulton-Lewis et al., 1997) have recorded that in solving equations students often do not know how to shift from the expression $3x$ to x only, seeing $3x$ as a variable in its own right. There is a great deal of things that cause students' difficulties in algebra and it is not easy for teachers to keep their spirits up.

Manifestations of a Purely Formal Approach to Problem Solving
   After the lesson described above, Mrs. Harper felt genuinely upset. It has to be said, though, that she did achieve one pedagogical victory: at the end of the lesson students were able to explain how they reasoned while trying to solve the problem. This shows that students did in fact apply reason in order to reach their solutions, however absurd these solutions may seem to

us. This hardly happens all the time. As has already been observed, students often perceive what they are learning as simply a collection of established rules and they remain blissfully unconcerned about what sort of reasoning lies behind them. When faced with an assignment, they simply utter words that resemble those that the teacher has approved of in situations similar to the one they are presented with. In such cases, the teacher often has to deliberately provoke the students to think, by asking them to explain whether a solution is indeed correct and whether one can genuinely perform an operation in that particular way. In the case of Mrs. Harper's class, however, the students gave such explanations of their own accord.

And yet the manner in which they formulated the expressions shows that they were acting in a purely formal way. They understood the algebraic expression simply as an aggregate of stenographic signs that abbreviated ordinary language. They did not see any particular sense in the original verbal formulation or in the resulting algebraic expressions, let alone in their relation, and they did not seem to try to establish any such purpose themselves.

This happens all too often. Research shows that a large number of students respond to the question "write down in algebraic form that there is one professor per six students," by writing $p = 6s$, where p is the number of professors and s the number of students (Clement et al., 1981). They follow the same logic as the students in the example above: "to one professor"—we write $1p$, there are "six students"—we write $6s$.

Additionally, examples given by Saul (2001) show how difficult it can be for students to understand algebra as a science of operations that one can perform on a whole variety of objects and not just on numbers. The common idea that x (or any other letter) stands for an arbitrary number seems to baffle some students, let alone if they have to use a variable to designate an entire expression (as in the case of factoring the expression $(x + y)^2 - (x + 3)^2$ by applying the formula $a^2 - b^2$, assuming that $a = x + y$ and $b = x + 3$). What Merry failed to see is that she was performing an operation of finding the difference between squares of expressions. Barry failed to see that the expression $2x + 1$ is the sum of $2x$ and 1, and he did not understand that by adding -1 (i.e., by performing an inverse operation, he would find $2x$).

Dealing with Students' Difficulties

In trying to deal with the difficulties students experience when studying algebra, giving sets of specially selected problems could be of some help. It is worth noting that Mrs. Harper's students were able to overcome something that for many can be particularly difficult—they had no problem introducing the variable n and they all wrote down $2n$ for the expression that was twice the value of n. However, one could say that Mrs. Harper's question was probably too hard for the first question of the lesson. It is likely that if she had asked them first to write the expression for "the number five less than twice the given number," and then separately the expression for "the number twelve more than the given number," she would have given them some initial experience in translating verbal phrases into algebraic expressions and she would have made it easier for them to then move on to more complex problems.

Saul (2001) spoke of using "number stories" in teaching algebra to students: "There was the number x, and it got multiplied by 2. Then 1 got added, and the result was 7. What was the original number?" (p. 41). In other words, Saul presented problems verbally rather than by means of formulas. He also recommended problems that helped students understand expressions as units that one could add, for example. He gave the following problem as an example: "If $2x + 3y = 3$ and if $6x + 3y = 5$, how much do $8x + 6y$ equal?"

A selection of such problems would help structure the lesson. It would help students focus on questions that they are able to solve rather than force them immediately to tackle problems that are far too complex and general for them. Such a set of problems would also help the teacher pinpoint exactly what causes students most difficulties. It would help soften what is particularly hard for students. At the same time, one must be aware of the fact that the causes of student difficulties in algebra are most often deep-seated and that it would be vain to hope that they can be overcome in just a couple of lessons. What is needed is a systematic and carefully thought out teaching strategy that would be developed for all the different stages of an algebra course.

Diversity vs. Routine: Some Conclusions and Recommendations

Reflecting on Research: On the role of teaching arithmetic

It has been observed in pedagogical literature that many of the difficulties students experience in studying algebra could be explained by gaps in their previous study of arithmetic (Peck & Jencks, 1988). The experience of understanding the mathematical content of word problems ideally should be acquired through arithmetic problems, where concrete numbers are given.

Unfortunately, despite the apparent abundance of word problems for arithmetic, their uniformity makes students understand them simply as signals that prompt them to perform the particular action being studied. Students hardly ever go into the detail about the story contained in a word problem, instead performing actions on numbers in purely automatic fashion. Research (Bell, et al., 1981) also shows that a student's choice of operation required for solving a particular problem is governed less by the meaning of the problem itself and more by the student's own idea of what usually happens in similar circumstances. For example, if a problem requires the students to divide two numbers, they, as a rule, will prefer to divide the higher number by the lower one. Schools often use tables of key words that effectively tell students to memorize that if a problem says "more than," for example, one needs to perform addition, and if it says "times as many as," one needs to perform multiplication. On the part of teachers, the desire to make it easier for students to understand the structure of a problem and their attempt to create a kind of ready-made support for this is understandable. However, this produces results only in the short term; in the long run (as in the example above), it causes students to perform entirely formal and rote mathematical translations. It is essential to think through and discuss with the class what a word actually means, and in doing so to use different means of explanation including models and manipulatives. By setting a variety of arithmetic assignments and by stimulating a reflective attitude towards their content, the teacher facilitates the future study of algebraic word problems.

In effect, teachers inevitably work on algebra well before the name is ever mentioned to students. In elementary, and even more so in middle and high school, one needs to achieve the understanding of "meanings of operations and how they relate to one another" (NCTM, 2000). Without in any way underestimating the importance of achieving fluency in the performance of calculations, it must be said that performance on operations should not completely replace the explanation of their meaning.

In support of this let us look at an episode from a lesson taught by the student teacher, Anne.

| Examining |
| *an* **Example** |

Episode from a Lesson

The aim of the lesson was to teach students to divide fractions. After discussing the homework from the previous lesson and after working on some examples of multiplying fractions, Anne moved on to division and showed the class how this should be done. Students then successfully completed a few assignments on their own. As a conclusion, Anne was about to give them a word problem, when one of the students suddenly asked why division of fractions is carried out in that particular way. Anne was not prepared for this question. She first said that this was simply the established way of doing the division of fractions in mathematics and then she added that the most important thing was to learn to do it quickly and accurately, and that this would be of use to them both on tests and in life.

Discussion of the Episode
The student actually asked an excellent question, the kind that the teacher herself should have asked. Why do we do things the way we do them? And what for? These two questions all too often remain both unasked and unanswered.

The word problem appeared at the end of the class, as an appendix almost, and it was easy to recognize in advance that the solution to the problem would incorporate division since the whole lesson was devoted to this topic. It would have been more natural to give the word problem at the beginning of the lesson in order to demonstrate to students the need for division. Let us take the following problem:

A bucket is $\frac{3}{4}$ full of water. It is emptied into glasses the size of which are $\frac{1}{16}$ of the bucket. How many glasses will be filled using the water from the entire bucket?

One can say straight away that there will be more than 4 glasses because 4 times $\frac{1}{16}$ makes $\frac{1}{4}$, which is clearly less water than what we have. This way it is easy to show the link with multiplication: we are looking for a number that when multiplied by $\frac{1}{16}$ gives $\frac{3}{4}$. One can then mention that the operation of finding such a number is called division. The understanding of division as the inverse of multiplication allows the teacher immediately to justify the rule for carrying out division. Indeed, even without performing the multiplication $\frac{16}{1} \cdot \frac{3}{4}$, the teacher can ask students to perform the multiplication $\frac{1}{16} \cdot \left(\frac{16}{1} \cdot \frac{3}{4} \right)$. The result (clearing up any confusion between the associative and distributive properties) is obviously $\frac{3}{4}$, which means that the product $\frac{16}{1} \cdot \frac{3}{4}$ is indeed the result of dividing $\frac{3}{4}$ by $\frac{1}{16}$. After such a demonstration, along with a few more similar examples, the students would find the general rule well justified and fully substantiated.

Reflecting on Research: On student difficulties with more deep-seated causes
Such discussion in teaching arithmetic considerably facilitates the students' transition to the study of algebra. On the contrary, lack of facility with structures in numerical context is mirrored by issues in algebraic contexts (e.g., Linchevski & Livneh, 1999). Indeed, it is collections of arithmetic properties, such as the closure, associative, identity, and inverse properties that work collectively to form the foundations for algebra. Wasserman (2014a) describes the interaction and necessity of such assumptions for productive algebraic reasoning in even the most basic of algebra contexts.

There are, however, a number of difficulties that are specific to algebra. Indeed, even the simplest algebraic expressions can appear incomprehensible to students because they are new to them. For example, children sometimes see $x + 5$ as a process rather than a mental object, causing difficulties because they do not know how to carry on this process given that x is unknown. One could say that in order to work successfully with such expressions students must be able to perform a transition from procedural methods that are applied in arithmetic to structural methods as they are used in algebra (Kieran, 1992). Kieran notes the following distinctive characteristics of algebra: "the objects that are operated on are algebraic expressions, not some numerical instantiation. The operations that are carried out are not computational. Furthermore, the results are yet algebraic expressions" (p. 392).

The difficulties experienced by the student Merry, discussed previously, are linked precisely to her failure to understand algebraic structure. Pedagogical literature has registered difficulties that students experience, for example, when two variables are being introduced or when they need to grasp the meaning of the "=" sign, as well as in various other situations that require a deeper understanding of the structure of algebraic expressions (Byers & Herscovics, 1977; Nickson, 2000).

Nickson (2000) emphasizes the need to address structural aspects of algebra from the very beginning of getting students acquainted with its concepts. In particular, she says that "children need to recognize that the equals sign does not necessarily indicate that a numerical answer is required. They also need to be reminded of the requirement of balance on either side of the equals sign in any expression containing one" (p. 144). She also speaks of the need to pay more attention to the use of symbols in representing the unknowns at the earliest stages of learning. She especially argues that one needs to get students to understand that a symbol "can have a fixed value as in $2 + \nabla = 5$ or it can be a variable (as in $2l + 2b$ when describing how to find the perimeter of a quadrilateral)" (p. 145).

In a similar vein Schoenfeld and Arcavi (1988) speak of the "variable meaning of variable," seeing in it the cause of many difficulties students have in understanding algebra. Consequently, students must gain experience in using such variable meanings.

To sum up, from the very beginning students need to be confronted with a variety of situations and work on a variety of problems. Algebra is a language in its own right. Just as in learning a foreign language students need to be given as many different exercises in applying a particular expression (or symbol) as possible. The remainder of this section will discuss examples of using the following relevant methods:

- Translation from algebraic to ordinary language
- Use of the same symbols in different situations
- Use of different algebraic symbols in the same situations
- Use of different forms of representation in describing the same situation

Translation from Algebraic to Ordinary Language

In most problems students need to translate from "ordinary" language to algebraic language. However, in order to acquire fluency in using algebraic symbols, it is also useful to do *exercises in "reverse translation,"* in other words, to describe a situation represented by a particular algebraic expression or equation.

For example, in examining the expression $a + b$, one could say that it describes the number of fruits in a basket containing a apples and b bananas. Students here have to explain for themselves the meaning of the concrete symbols. This helps them better understand the expression and (or) exposes any problems that they might have in understanding it. For example, in answering the above question, students sometimes say that a are apples and b bananas, while $a + b$ signifies simply that there are apples and bananas in the basket. The teachers can then ask them what the expression $a + 2b$ means, or they can immediately discuss the meaning of the sign "+" or the frequent necessity for variables to represent numerical quantities. Either way, the exercise exposes the problem that the students appear to have had in grasping the variable expression and the problem can now be dealt with.

Use of the Same Symbols in Different Situations

Just as in the study of a foreign language, teachers of algebra need to present students with *a whole variety of situations* in which one can use the same expression (symbol), and they also need to discuss some of the different possible meanings that a single expression can have. This has to a certain extent already been discussed above: students can, for instance, be given the equation $4x = 16$, where x is the unknown. There can therefore be only one number that can replace x for the equation to be true. Students can then be given the expression $4x$ as expressing, for example, the perimeter of a square, the side of which has the length x. Here x can be any positive number.

Similarly, students can be presented with a situation that asks for the value or meaning of the expression $2x^2 + 2y^2$, where one first needs to find the values of x and y. For example, the problem could be formulated in the following way: if we know that $x = y$, and that $x + y = 4$, find $2x^2 + 2y^2$. Alternatively, students could be asked to try to find the value of the expression in a situation where one does not need to know either x or y but where the expression $x^2 + y^2$ must be comprehended as an object in its own right. For example, if x and y express the lengths of the two legs of a right triangle, the hypotenuse of which is 3, find $2x^2 + 2y^2$.

Use of Different Algebraic Symbols in the Same Situations

Students also need to be given assignments where *a variety of different symbols* are used. It has been noted (Wong, 1997) that students often experience problems linked to the stereotypical use of letters in algebra (say, the fact that the unknown is always *x*). It is therefore desirable to encourage the use of different symbols and to give examples of problems with such variable formulations.

Use of Different Forms of Representation in Describing the Same Situation

It is also desirable to give students assignments where the same concept would have *a variety of different* (synonymous) *representations*. This teaches students both to use these representations and to perceive their meaning in different parts of mathematics.

Swan (2002) cites assignments where students are given sets of algebraic expressions, explanations in words, tables and areas of shapes, and are then asked to determine their mutual relation. For instance, the expression $\frac{n+6}{2}$ corresponds to the explanation in words "Add six to *n* then divide by two," to the area of the shape in Figure 7.1 and to Table 7.1 (in which students must fill the empty cells themselves).

There are many other possible ways of formulating assignments that would be of use in the study of algebra. It is important to stress, however, that students must be presented with genuine problems and not just routine tasks. Practice required for the study of any language, including the language of algebra, should not be limited to uniform and repetitive

Figure 7.1

TABLE 7.1

Given	Result
2	4
3	4.5
4	5
6	
	7

exercises. Routine and repetition only breed boredom and generate fallacies, such as those discussed above, even if at first students appear to be successful in completing tasks that are analogous to dozens of others they have already done. One cannot promise swift and easy results in the study of algebra. The path is long and arduous, but what is clear is that in order to reach true success one needs to move in the right direction—that of diversity and problem solving.

Algebra: Step by Step

It is hardly possible to give a clear and precise description of exactly what sort of algebraic knowledge and skills students need to acquire in a given year: this is to be covered in middle school, that in high school, and so forth. Children differ greatly and each child has his or her own style and tempo of learning.

Karp and Vogeli (2002) reported on a six-year-old girl who discovered entirely on her own that in order to get the square of a whole number it is sufficient to take the square of the previous number, add to it twice the number and subtract 1. Using conventional signs the formula that she discovered can be represented as $n^2 = (n-1)^2 + 2n - 1$. The girl could not use letters and was unable to write down the formula, but she still noticed the pattern and was able to express it in words. Her mathematical development seems remarkable and is certainly considerably higher than average. Nevertheless, even such highly talented students need help and support from teachers, and it is essential for the teachers to be prepared to offer this help, by selecting different problems for them, ones that would be challenging enough yet still within their powers.

On the other hand, it is frequently the case that students are slower in learning algebra than teachers and authors of textbooks would expect them to be. This does not, however, mean that they are incapable of learning it or, worse still, that they should not be taught it at all. It simply means that you need to spend more time devising the right strategy for teaching such children and selecting additional assignments that would help them grasp the mathematics.

Despite all these provisions, some general goals and expectations for students to achieve at particular stages in the process of instruction can still be outlined. NCTM (2000) describes such expectations for one specific aspect of algebra; namely, the representation and analysis of mathematical structures by using algebraic symbols.

From the NCTM Principles and Standards:

- For Pre-K–2:
  - Illustrate general principles and properties of operations, such as commutativity, using specific numbers
  - Use concrete, pictorial, and verbal representations to develop an understanding of invented and conventional symbolic notations
- For Grades 3–5:
  - Identify such properties as commutativity, associativity, and distributivity and use them to compute with whole numbers
  - Represent the idea of a variable as an unknown quantity using a letter or a symbol
  - Express mathematical relationships using equations
- For Grades 6–8:
  - Develop an initial conceptual understanding of different uses of variables
  - Explore relationships between symbolic expressions and graphs of lines, paying particular attention to the meaning of intercepts and slopes
  - Use symbolic algebra to represent situations and to solve problems, especially those that involve linear relationships
  - Recognize and generate equivalent forms for simple algebraic expressions and solve linear equations
- For Grades 9–12:
  - Understand the meaning of equivalent forms of expressions, equations, inequalities, and relations
  - Write equivalent forms of equations, inequalities and systems of equations and solve them with fluency—mentally or with paper and pencil in simple cases and using technology in all cases
  - Use symbolic algebra to represent and explain mathematical relationships
  - Use a variety of symbolic representations, including recursive and parametric equations, for functions and relations
  - Judge the meaning, utility, and reasonableness of the results of symbol manipulations, including those carried out by technology

The CCSS-M (2010) outline similar progressions, beginning with operations and algebraic thinking in the elementary grades, moving on to ratios, and expressions and equations in the middle and high school grades.

Discussion

If we analyze the above expectations, we notice two interconnected directions of development: first, the shift from the concrete to the general and the abstract; and second, the increase in the diversity of situations where particular symbols are used and in the way they are applied.

- At first children can simply see that $2 + 3 = 3 + 2$, realizing that one gets the same result whichever way the numbers are placed. Later they learn that this represents a special property of addition; they become able to distinguish it, name it, and what is more, to notice that the same property applies to multiplication. Later still they can find different symbolic means of expressing this property.
- At first children learn about specific cases where letters or symbols are used. Later they not only begin to manipulate symbols but also become able to judge whether the symbols have been used adequately or not. In other words, they start thinking about the use of symbols in a general way.
- At first children examine individual examples of equations used in specific situations. Later they discuss general properties of equations, their equivalence and their different types.
- At first children learn only about linear equations, but gradually the range of equations they are asked to deal with becomes broader and broader. Algebraic symbols, which are initially used only to represent unknowns, become essential in explaining a whole variety of mathematical relations. The symbols themselves become more diverse and the symbolic language of mathematics becomes richer and more complex.

These developments do not happen all on their own, but rather in the process of working with new problems. It would be naïve to think that one can simply leap from one stage of development to another and instantly start working on more complex assignments. Even a highly talented child, such as the girl mentioned at the beginning of this section, would find it difficult to start manipulating algebraic symbols straightaway (e.g., if asked to expand the square of the expression $(n-1)$). This is why you would do such a child a disservice if you simply ran her through some particular section of the standard algebra course. At the same time, it would be equally a mistake to be constantly wary of telling students about something that they might not be familiar with at all. By assigning students a variety of different problems, the practicing teacher can diagnose what students are ready for and then give them precisely those new problems that would be beneficial to their development and their acquisition of new knowledge.

One could say that in order for the above expectations to be realized, much depends on teachers of middle school. It is precisely here that students make the most important step in assimilating the symbolic language of algebra. The teachers of middle school must be particularly careful to avoid boredom, uniformity and monotony. They must always take into account the youth of their students, while at the same time striving to communicate the richness and significance of algebra, revealing the depth and substance of the problems studied, and genuinely involving students in solving them. This is a difficult but vital task.

Reflection

Assignments and Topics for Discussion

1. Read the NCTM Algebra standard for all school years. Inspect some examples of assignments in algebra. What sorts of difficulties could students have in solving them?

2. In the attempt to simplify the expression $5x + 4y + x$, your student, John, came up with $10xy$. How would you explain his mistake to him?

3. How would you explain the algorithm for the multiplication of fractions? And what about the algorithm for the multiplication of negative numbers? What model(s) are consistently useful for understanding multiplication across different number sets?

4. Give examples of situations which can be described with the help of the following equations:

   a) $5x - 1 = 2x$; b) $x^3 = 4x$; c) $\dfrac{5}{x-2} + \dfrac{5}{x+2} = 6$

5. Give examples of situations where it is common to represent unknowns by letters other than x and y.

6. Using the model discussed above, provide a table, an explanation in words, and the area of a shape that all correspond to the expression $(n + 1)(n - 3)$. Find another, different, shape.

7. One of the greatest mathematicians of the twentieth century, Andrei Kolmogorov, spoke about how he experienced the joy of mathematical discovery for the first time. When he was 5–6 years old, he noticed that: $1 + 3 = 2^2$, $1 + 3 + 5 = 3^2$, etc. Formulate this pattern in a general way and prove it. Imagine that the parents of such a child have asked you for advice. What would you recommend they do with the child to develop his talent?

8. How would you tell students about the distributive property in middle school and how would you do the same thing in high school?
9. Discuss some possible confusions that students may have in distinguishing between the distributive, associative, and commutative properties of addition and multiplication, and when they apply.

HOW TO SOLVE IT? A SELECTION OF PROBLEMS

This section analyzes a number of relatively difficult algebra problems. Most of them are undoubtedly harder than what is usually given in class, but it seems particularly useful to look more closely at the type of reasoning they entail and to see the depths of mathematical study that standard school material can potentially reach.

Example 1

Let us look at an arbitrary two-digit number, which is a number whose ones digit is not zero (35, for example). If we transpose the digits of this number we get another two-digit number (53). Let us now subtract the lower of the two numbers from the higher one. In our example this would be $53 - 35 = 18$. We note that $(5 - 3) \cdot 9 = 18$. In other words, the difference between the two numbers is equal to the difference between the tens digits of the two numbers, multiplied by 9. One has to prove that this is the case for all such numbers.

Discussion and Solution
Start by trying out a few more examples (e.g., $61 - 16 = (6 - 1) \cdot 9 = 45$ or $84 - 48 = (8 - 4) \cdot 9 = 36$). However, in order not to have to go through all possible cases, the proof requires the use of algebraic notation and manipulation. What this means is using a different form of representing the information, one that entails a more general standpoint.

Let us say that the first digit of the number is a, and the second is b. The number then equals $a \cdot 10 + b$. The number that one gets after transposing the digits equals $b \cdot 10 + a$. Let us say that $a > b$ (the same argument can be applied in the other cases). In that case the difference examined is as follows: $a \cdot 10 + b - b \cdot 10 - a = 9a - 9b = 9(a - b)$. The difference $9(a - b)$ is precisely the difference of the tens digits of the two numbers, multiplied by 9.

Example 2

Nick and John love juice. On Sunday they drank a total of 28 glasses of three different juices: orange, cranberry and apple juice. The number of glasses of orange juice which Nick consumed is equal to the number of glasses of cranberry juice which John consumed. The number of glasses of cranberry juice which Nick consumed is equal to the number of glasses of apple juice which John consumed. The number of glasses of apple juice which Nick consumed is equal to the number of glasses of orange juice which John consumed. It is known that Nick and John consumed 10 glasses of orange juice altogether. How many glasses of apple juice has John consumed?

Discussion and Solution

In this humorous problem, it is important not to get muddled up in the data and to introduce the unknowns properly. One could, of course, introduce six unknowns that would correspond to the number of glasses for each juice drunk by each of the two boys, and then write equations that express the fact that some of these numbers are the same. However, one could also straightaway introduce three unknowns. Let us represent this in form of a table, where each cell contains the number of glasses drunk by each child for each juice.

	Orange	Cranberry	Apple
Nick	x	y	z
John	z	x	y

Now one can write down the equations. First of all, the total number of glasses drunk (which can be expressed through the above variables as $2(x + y + z)$) is 28. In other words $2(x + y + z) = 28$. Secondly, the total number of glasses of orange juice (which can be written down as $x + z$) is 10. Thus, we get the equation $x + z = 10$.

We have obtained the system of equations

$$\begin{cases} 2(x+y+z) = 28 \\ x+z = 10 \end{cases}$$

that cannot be solved in such a way that there is a single solution for all three numbers x, y and z. However, we are not asked to find x, y and z, but only the value of y.

By dividing the left and the right side of the first equation by two we get the system

$$\begin{cases} x+y+z = 14 \\ x+z = 10 \end{cases}.$$

What remains to be done is simply to subtract one equation from the other: $(x + y + z) - (x + z) = 14 - 10$. We get that $y = 4$.

The answer is therefore: John drank 4 glasses of apple juice.

Example 3

Simplify the expression:

$$\frac{1}{1-x}+\frac{1}{1+x}+\frac{2}{1+x^2}+\frac{4}{1+x^4}+\frac{8}{1+x^8}+\frac{16}{1+x^{16}}.$$

Discussion and Solution

The standard algorithm for adding fractions recommends that all the fractions should be rewritten with a common denominator. In the above case, however, this algorithm does not bode well: the common denominator is the product of the denominators of all the given fractions, and it is clear that this would make the expression in the numerator very difficult to work with. An alternative strategy that would be of use here is first to try and tackle an easier problem and then look for a more general pattern. Let us begin by adding the first two fractions.

$$\frac{1}{1-x}+\frac{1}{1+x}=\frac{1+x+1-x}{(1-x)(1+x)}=\frac{2}{1-x^2}.$$

We see that the resulting fraction is "almost" like the third. Let us add to this the third fraction:

$$\frac{2}{1-x^2}+\frac{2}{1+x^2}=\frac{2+2x^2+2-2x^2}{(1-x^2)(1+x^2)}=\frac{4}{1-x^4}.$$

By then adding the fourth fraction we get

$$\frac{4}{1-x^4}+\frac{4}{1+x^4}=\frac{4+4x^4+4-4x^4}{(1-x^4)(1+x^4)}=\frac{8}{1-x^8}.$$

Similarly, by adding the next one we get

$$\frac{8}{1-x^8}+\frac{8}{1+x^8}=\frac{8+8x^8+8-8x^8}{(1-x^8)(1+x^8)}=\frac{16}{1-x^{16}}.$$

Finally, if we add the last one, we get

$$\frac{16}{1-x^{16}}+\frac{16}{1+x^{16}}=\frac{16+16x^{16}+16-16x^{16}}{(1-x^{16})(1+x^{16})}=\frac{32}{1-x^{32}}.$$

Example 4

Factor $x^2y + xy^2 + x^2z + xz^2 + yz^2 + y^2z + 2xyz$.

Discussion and Solution

The common factor is not immediately obvious. One needs to be particularly observant to notice the equalities and interrelations that are relevant for factoring. One of the possible approaches to this problem would be to break down the expression into groups and then examine each group more closely. Let us, for example, separate all the terms containing *x*. One could then write:

$$x^2y + xy^2 + x^2z + xz^2 + yz^2 + y^2z + 2xyz = x(xy + y^2 + xz + z^2 + 2yz) + yz^2 + y^2z$$

We now have an easier problem to deal with, namely the expression in the brackets: $xy + y^2 + xz + z^2 + 2yz$. The sum $y^2 + z^2 + 2yz$ stands out immediately. It can be expressed as the square of the sum $y + z$. By grouping the remaining terms we get $xy + xz = x(y+z)$. Consequently, we can write:

$$xy + y^2 + xz + z^2 + 2yz = x(y+z) + (y+z)^2 = (y+z)(x+y+z).$$

We therefore get:

$$x^2y + xy^2 + x^2z + xz^2 + yz^2 + y^2z + 2xyz = x(y+z)(x+y+z) + yz^2 + y^2z.$$

Now we need to transform the sum of the last two terms: $yz^2 + y^2z = yz(y+z)$. The common factor of the entire expression becomes visible at last:

$$x^2y + xy^2 + x^2z + xz^2 + yz^2 + y^2z + 2xyz = x(y+z)(x+y+z) + yz(y+z)$$

$$= (y+z)\big(x(x+y+z) + yz\big)$$

What remains to be done is to factor the expression $x(x+y+z) + yz = x^2 + xy + xz + yz$. However,

$$x^2 + xy + xz + yz = (x^2 + xy) + (xz + yz)$$

$$= x(x+y) + z(x+y)$$

$$= (x+y)(x+z)$$

In the end we get

$$x^2y + xy^2 + x^2z + xz^2 + yz^2 + y^2z + 2xyz = (x+y)(x+z)(y+z).$$

This is not the only way of solving this problem, of course. It is possible to group the expressions differently, though the outcome will be the same. It is also possible to approach the problem from a completely different perspective.

In order to factor the expression $x^2+xy+xz+yz$ it is not necessary to group and extract common factors. One could start off by working backwards, by asking oneself what would the final result of the factored expression for $x^2y+xy^2+x^2z+xz^2+yz^2+y^2z+2xyz$ look like. The expression is symmetrical in relation to the variables x, y and z in the sense that if one replaced x with y, y with z, and z with x throughout, the expression would remain the same. This means that the expression obtained through factoring is also going to be symmetrical. As has already been shown, the expression contains the factor $(y+z)$. This points to the fact that it also ought to contain as factors $(x+y)$ and $(x+z)$. Finally, we see that it cannot contain other polynomial factors apart from these, because otherwise the expression would not be of the third degree.

Example 5

Factor $x^4 + 4$.

Discussion and Solution
Methods commonly used to perform factoring are clearly of no help in this case. The formula for the difference of squares cannot be applied, there is nothing to group and nothing to "guess." As possible solutions students sometimes propose variants like $x^3 \cdot x+4$ or

$$x \cdot \left(x^3 + \frac{4}{x} \right).$$

This only shows that the very concept of factoring is not entirely clear to them. One could, of course, take this as a positive pedagogical result, because it gives the teacher the opportunity to explain to students that one must represent the given polynomial as a product of two polynomials of degree not less than 1.

The idea that leads one to the solution of the above problem consists in making use of the fact that there are two squares in the expression: $x^4 = (x^2)^2$ and $4 = 2^2$. Consequently, we can complete the square by adding the doubled product of 2 and x^2, and, of course, by subtracting the added expression. $x^4+4=x^4+4x^2+4-4x^2=(x^2+2)^2-4x^2$. It is now easy to see that $4x^2 = (2x)^2$. We have therefore been able to represent the given expression as a difference of squares. Let us continue:

$$(x^2+2)^2 - 4x^2 = (x^2+2)^2 - (2x)^2$$
$$= (x^2+2-2x)(x^2+2+2x)$$
$$= (x^2-2x+2)(x^2+2x+2)$$

The fact that we were able to factor the above expression is not that surprising since the fundamental theorem of algebra implies that any polynomial of the third degree or higher, with real coefficients, can be represented as a product of some polynomials of the first or second degree. It is true, however, that although one can prove the existence of such polynomials it is often impossible to determine what they are. This was not the case with the above expression, however.

Example 6

Prove that for any numbers a, b and c if $a + b + c = 0$, then $a^3 + b^3 + c^3 = 3abc$.

Discussion and Solution

This and similar problems that involve the manipulation of variables also include a logical dimension. Historically, in school algebra proofs are examined very rarely, although they are just as important here as in geometry. In the above problem one is dealing precisely with proof—moreover, the proof is one that requires an argument rather than pure computations. Let us carry out the necessary argument.

Since $a + b + c = 0$, then $c = -(a + b)$. Consequently, $a^3 + b^3 + c^3 = a^3 + b^3 + (-(a + b))^3$. By performing the necessary steps we can write:

$$a^3 + b^3 + (-(a+b))^3 = a^3 + b^3 - a^3 - b^3 - 3a^2b - 3ab^2$$
$$= -3a^2b - 3ab^2$$
$$= 3ab(-(a+b))$$

By replacing $-(a + b)$ with c, we continue to write: $3ab(-(a+b)) = 3abc$, which completes the proof.

This problem is a good exercise in logic as well as algebraic manipulation. It can, in fact, be developed further. The proved assertion leads one to see that the expression $a^3 + b^3 + c^3 - 3abc$ can be represented as a product, with one of the factors being $a + b + c$. By using, say, the algorithm for dividing one polynomial by another (Usiskin et al, 2003), the following can be shown:

$$a^3 + b^3 + c^3 - 3abc = (a+b+c)(a^2 + b^2 + c^2 - ab - ac - bc).$$

Using this expansion one can prove the famous inequality between the arithmetical and the geometrical mean of three positive numbers

$$\frac{x+y+z}{3} \geq \sqrt[3]{xyz}.$$

This will be discussed later.

Example 7

Operation * is performed on a set of positive numbers. It is known that for any positive numbers x, a, b and c, two equalities hold:

$$x * (2x) = \frac{1}{2},$$

$$a * (bc) = (a * b) \cdot \frac{1}{c}$$

Find $12 * 15$.

Discussion and Solution

Solution of this problem assumes a very high level of algebraic development. The solver must understand operations in an abstract sense, not limited to only addition, multiplication, subtraction and division. One could say that an operation is defined on a set if, being given any two elements of this set, a third is then defined (where not all the elements are necessarily different). In the above case the link between operation * and multiplication allows one to describe this operation in an alternative form. By taking a closer look at the above equations, solvers can remark that they are familiar with an operation that has such properties—this operation is division. Indeed,

$$x \div (2x) = \frac{1}{2},$$

$$a \div (bc) = (a \div b) \cdot \frac{1}{c},$$

which means that division has this property. However, this is not a proper answer, because it still remains possible that there are other ways of defining operation * for the above conditions to remain fulfilled. This would indicate that there might be other variants of the answer apart from $12 * 15 = 12 \div 15 = 0.8$.

To reach a solution let us show that for any positive numbers x and y it is true that $x * y = x \div y$. To do this we can use the fact that any positive number y can be written down as the following product

$$(2x) \cdot \frac{y}{2x}.$$

Now, by using first the second and then the first property, let us write down

$$x * y = x * \left((2x) \cdot \frac{y}{2x} \right) = (x * (2x)) \cdot \frac{2x}{y} = \frac{1}{2} \cdot \frac{2x}{y} = \frac{x}{y}.$$

The proof was carried out in a general way, although to reach the solution of the problem it was enough to do it on the concrete numbers given. This might actually be simpler. Indeed:

$$12 * 15 = 12 * \left(24 \cdot \frac{15}{24} \right) = (12 * 24) \cdot \frac{24}{15} = \frac{1}{2} \cdot \frac{24}{15} = \frac{12}{15} = \frac{4}{5}.$$

The key difficulty of this problem lies in the fact that one must be able to manipulate algebraic objects freely—for instance, to represent y in the necessary form or to take the expression $2x$ as a component of the operation.

Reflection

Assignments and Topics for Discussion

1. Analogous to the assignment in Example 1, formulate and prove the assertion about the difference between an arbitrary three-digit number and a number obtained by transposing the first and last of its digits.

2. An arbitrary two-digit number is given. The same two digits in reverse order are appended to the end to form a four-digit number. Prove that the number thus obtained is divisible by 11.

3. From Example 4 above, group the terms of the expression in a way different to the one shown and generate another path to the solution.

4. Explain how one can know, purely by mental reasoning and without performing any computations, that the factored expression of $x^4 + 4$ cannot have a linear factor (with real coefficients).

5. Factor the following expressions: a) $x^4 + x^2 + 1$, b) $x^4 + 1$, c) $x^2y + xy^2 + x^2z + xz^2 + yz^2 + y^2z + 3xyz$

6. Prove that if $a + b = 1$, then $a^2b^2 + 3 = (a^2 + a + 1)(b^2 + b + 1)$.

7. If we know that $x + y + z = 5$, and $xy + xz + yz = 3$, find $x^2 + y^2 + z^2$.

8. Operation * is performed on a set of positive numbers so that the equation $(m*(4n)) \div n = m$ applies to any numbers m and n. Calculate: a) 3 * 8; b) 5 * 7.

PLANNING AN ALGEBRA LESSON

This section analyzes the plan of a lesson taught by a student teacher, Elizabeth, and it discusses how she prepared for the lesson. Elizabeth discussed her plan at the student teachers' seminar. She incorporated in her plan some of the observations and ideas expressed by her fellow student teachers.

Preliminary Information

For her student teaching, Elizabeth was assigned to an algebra course. Her specific task was to teach the part devoted to operations with polynomials, specifically factoring polynomials and solving equations with polynomials. The cooperating teacher described the class Elizabeth was supposed to teach as fairly interested in mathematics, but she warned Elizabeth that many students were experiencing problems in performing operations on variables and that some even had difficulties in performing operations on numbers. Elizabeth herself noticed, for instance, that many students made crude mistakes when they were asked to subtract the polynomial $3x^2 - 2x$ from the polynomial $5x^2 + 4$: some students got $5x^2 + 4 - 3x^2 - 2x = 2x^2 - 2x + 4$, and another got $2x^2 + 2x$, evidently subtracting 2 from 4. Elizabeth was asked to teach lessons devoted to the multiplication of polynomials.

The Textbook
The section in the textbook devoted to the multiplication of polynomials contained an analysis of several examples with explanations and references to the distributive property. The textbook then provided the algorithm for multiplying binomials and showed some forms of writing down polynomial products.
Under the heading "The Application of Polynomials in Real Life," there was an example of finding the area of a rectangular figure. For this purpose the variable x was introduced, with the length and width of the figure expressed as $3x + 8$ and $2x + 4$. These expressions were then multiplied (although the advantages of the answer $6x^2 + 28x + 32$ over the answer $(3x + 8)(2x + 4)$ were not elaborated on). The section "Practice and Application" contained around 40 assignments in the multiplication of polynomials (mostly binomials) as well as a few assignments devoted to finding the areas of various figures.

The Goal of the Lesson

The first question that Elizabeth asked herself in preparing the lesson was the following: What is the purpose of learning how to multiply polynomials? What sorts of problems can one solve with the help of multiplying polynomials? Her answers to these questions, which were later discussed and clarified at the student teachers' seminar, amounted to the following:

- Knowing how to multiply polynomials is essential in deriving formulas that are of use in mathematics, science, economics and sometimes even everyday life.
- Knowing how to multiply polynomials is necessary for the future study of the factorization of polynomials, which is itself necessary for solving many types of problems, including equations.
- The multiplication of polynomials teaches students that multiplication need not be performed on numbers only. This develops the students' algebraic thinking.

The goal *to develop the students' mastery of multiplying polynomials* thus emerged as significant and valuable. However, this immediately prompted the question of how exactly one ought to demonstrate to students the significance of this part of mathematics. In discussions that Elizabeth had with the cooperating teacher while preparing for the lesson, the fact that students' ability to multiply polynomials would be checked in state exams was stressed by cooperating teacher. Indeed, students clearly wanted to pass the tests, which meant that there would be no harm in telling them that such questions were going to be part of the exam. However, what was desirable for Elizabeth was to show them that the multiplication of polynomials was also important in mathematics itself.

What also concerned Elizabeth was that students not forget or confuse what they had learned previously, namely the addition and subtraction of polynomials.

There is no doubt that the multiplication of polynomials is very much a question of developing certain technical skills. However, Elizabeth believed that lessons devoted to developing such skills should also simultaneously develop students' mathematical thinking. She remembered that when she was in school herself, her teacher would simply demonstrate an example on the board and then distribute worksheets with nearly identical versions, asking the class to answer these during class. She remembered how excruciatingly dull this was. Although Elizabeth was aware that many other topics, such as linear equations or even factoring, would provide more opportunities for developing her students' mathematical thinking, she was keen to find space for reasoning and proving, as well as problem solving, even when teaching a predominantly technical part of mathematics, such as the multiplication of polynomials.

Lesson Objectives

Consequently, she came up with the following lesson objectives:

- Students will be able to review the material already studied
- Students will be able to see the importance of performing the multiplication of polynomials correctly
- Students will be able to engage in problem solving activities that will help them acquire the habit of applying learned algorithms with thought and understanding

Formulating Key Assignments for Students

Elizabeth observed that in order to fulfill these objectives she must modify the assignments provided in the textbook, either by adding something new to them or by borrowing something from other parts of the book. The textbook contained many good example problems to consider, but it was impossible to do all of them in the time available. Also, Elizabeth wanted to do some things different from the textbook's presentation. It was therefore impossible to follow the textbook completely. Elizabeth isolated the following key assignments that she wanted the students to be able to solve by the end of the lesson:

- Multiplying expressions of the following type: $(2x + 1)(x - 2)$, $(x + 1)(x^2 + 3x + 1)$, $(a + 2b)(a - b)$
- Explaining how to apply the distributive property when multiplying polynomials
- Applying the multiplication of polynomials for the purpose of deriving formulas

The Lesson Plan

Elizabeth had two days to spend on the multiplication of polynomials. She decided that the second day would be devoted largely to practicing and problem solving, while the first day would be spent mainly on learning the appropriate algorithm and on demonstrating its significance.

On the *first day* Elizabeth decided to start off with an assignment that the students would work on while she took attendance that dealt primarily with organizational matters.

The "Do Now" Assignment

The assignment was supposed to be devoted to what was done in the previous lesson, although it was natural to do something that would enable the class to move on to the new topic. Elizabeth thus planned to start the lesson with the following assignment (for which she allocated 5 minutes):

Calculate the values of the following expressions:
a) $x(x-1)-x^2+x$, b) $x^2+3x-(x+1)(x+2)$, if $x = 0, 1, 2$.

Elizabeth assumed that most of the students would simply insert the values provided and that they would eventually come to the conclusion that in the first expression one always gets 0 and in the second −2. She hoped, however, that some students might remember the rule for multiplying a polynomial by a monomial, which they had learned at some point in the past, and that this would help them reach more quickly the common value of 0 for the first expression. Either way, as part of the discussion of this assignment she planned:

- To show how important it is to multiply polynomials, since it was easier to work with specific numbers rather than bulky expressions
- To remind students about the distributive property and show them how to use it in order to see that $x(x-1) = x^2 - x$

She allocated 5 minutes to the discussion of this assignment.

Working in Pairs

Elizabeth wanted students to realize for themselves how the distributive property is used to prove that $(x+1)(x+2) = x^2+3x+2$, and also to grasp independently the geometrical meaning of this formula. To achieve this she planned to give the class the following two assignments for work in pairs, spending approximately 10 minutes on them:

- Find and express in terms of x the areas of all the rectangles into which the rectangle ABCD is divided (Figure 7.2). Write down the expression for the area of the rectangle ABCD in two different ways.
- Show how one can get that $(x+1)(x+2) = x^2+3x+2$ by using the distributive property.

Elizabeth planned to discuss these assignments and to formulate the FOIL pattern for multiplication (5–7 minutes).

Concluding the First Day

To end the first day she thought of giving the following assignments (around 15 minutes):

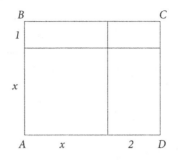

Figure 7.2

1. Find the following products:
   a) $(x+2)(x-3)$;
   b) $(a-4)(a-1)$;
   c) $(2y+1)(y-5)$;
   d) $(3t+1)(2t-4)$;
   e) $(a+b)(2a-b)$;
   f) $(x^2+2x-1)(x-3)$.
2. Simplify $(x+1)(x-4)-x^2+4$

She planned to have students do these simultaneously both in their exercise books and on the board. While working on these assignments she would discuss and comment on anything new (e.g., the appearance of coefficients together with the unknowns in assignments 1c and 1d, or the expression with two variables in assignment 1e). The solution of assignment 1f, which entails the multiplication of a trinomial by a binomial, was to be conducted thoroughly, with full commentary and notation.

For her closing remarks Elizabeth planned to highlight what had been learned in the lesson and to reiterate that this could be used to derive formulas in various parts of mathematics as well as its applications.

Homework Assignments
Homework included assignments from the textbook. Students were to use the problems to practice multiplying binomials and trinomials, and to explain how the distributive property is used in multiplication. One of the assignments was geometrical and involved finding the area of a given figure.

For the *second day* Elizabeth planned to select a variety of assignments in which students would be required to multiply polynomials. At the student teachers' seminar, during the discussion about what sorts of assignments a teacher could give here, it was argued that one ought to choose assignments that would enable students to establish connections between different areas of mathematics, including geometry and graphs. Assignments that enabled students to prove the presence of some pattern were also recommended. As the means of improving the students' technique in multiplying polynomials it was also considered beneficial to use assignments that would require an analysis of possible errors.

The following lesson plan was formulated as a result.

Warm-Up (approximately 5–7 minutes)

Working in pairs, students would be asked to analyze how multiplication was performed in the following four cases, to detect errors (if there were any) and to correct them.

a) $(2x+3)(x+2) = 2x \cdot x + 3 \cdot 2 = 2x^2 + 6$

b) $(t+4)(t+2) = t^2 + t \cdot 2 + 4t + 4 \cdot 2 = t^2 + 6t + 6$

c) $(3x+1)(x-2) = 3x \cdot x + 3x \cdot (-2) + 1 \cdot x + 1 \cdot (-2)$

$$= 4x^2 - 6x + x - 2$$

$$= 4x^2 - 5x - 2$$

d) $(a-1)(a^2 + 3a - 2) = a \cdot a^2 + a \cdot (3a) - 1 \cdot a^2 - 1 \cdot (-2)$

$$= a^3 + 3a^2 - a^2 + 2$$

$$= a^3 + 2a^2 + 2$$

The next 4–5 minutes would then be spent, as a whole class analyzing each of the problems and repeating what had been learned in the previous lesson.

Trick-Question (about 15 minutes)

The main part of the lesson would then open with the following trick-question that each student would solve individually.

- Write down any four successive numbers of your choice (for example, 1, 2, 3, 4 or 15, 16, 17, 18)
- Multiply the first and the last of the four numbers (you can use a calculator)
- Multiply the second and the third (you can use a calculator)
- By how much is the second product greater than the first?

When the students realize that they all got the same answer (by 2) they would be asked to introduce a variable and prove that the fact that their answers were identical was not a coincidence (the activity together with the discussion was supposed to take 15 minutes).

Two More Assignments (about 15 minutes)
Two further assignments were planned (another 15 minutes approximately):

- What is the graph of the function $f(x) = (2x-1)(x+1) - 2x^2 - x$? Provide the solution without a graphing calculator, but then use it to check your answer.
- Which of the two rectangles has a greater area (Figure 7.3)? Give the value of the difference of their areas if $x = 1, 2, 5$.

Conclusion
The conclusion would consist of bringing to the students' attention that the solution to all of these problems involved multiplying polynomials and then discussing homework. Apart from assignments involving straightforward multiplication, the homework was to include the following problem:

Prove that if n is a whole number then the number $(n-3)(n+4) - (n-6)(n+2)$ is divisible by 5.

Assessment
Elizabeth did not plan to do any tests or quizzes in these two days (she planned a quiz for the third day). However, she noticed plenty of opportunities to assess students' progress. While in pairs, she was ready to observe how they worked, what methods and approaches they used and what sorts

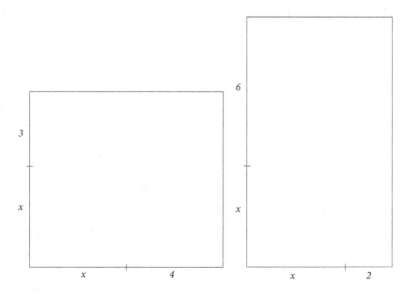

Figure 7.3

of mistakes they made. The discussion of problems by the class as a whole then gave her the opportunity to remark and spur on the most active students, as well as to take note of those who experienced the most difficulties, providing encouragement for them too. Following the example of her cooperating teacher, Elizabeth planned to award extra points for active participation in class discussion.

Discussion

Contemporary scholarship reiterates that, regrettably, the question "Why?" is asked all too rarely in classrooms, while giving students ready-made recipes seems to be the method of preference (Howson, 2005). Elizabeth confronted this issue from the very beginning, discussing and demonstrating why it was so important to learn how to multiply polynomials and why they are multiplied precisely as they are. This is the only way to give proper meaning to this part of mathematics—to make students understand why they need to study it and what sorts of problems it helps them solve.

The evident merit of this lesson plan is the fact that the multiplication of polynomials is not examined in isolation from the rest of mathematics but in close interaction with it. Elizabeth strove to establish connections, in accordance with the recommendations of the NCTM (2000), including connections with the concept of functions, which in many ways unites the whole of algebra and even the whole of mathematics itself (Chazan & Yerushalmy, 2003). The plan also allowed for a pertinent revision of old material during the study of new topics. The subtraction of polynomials, for example, was not just forgotten about. It was not just left for lessons devoted specifically to this topic, but was incorporated in subsequent lessons. In the same way, the multiplication of polynomials will continue to be used and will be revised in lessons to come.

Again in accordance with the recommendations of the NCTM (2000), Elizabeth used different means of representing the material, including geometric ones. The lesson also incorporated a variety of different kinds of problems. By assigning the class such a variety of questions, the teacher engages students in proper mathematical activity. In the above case, students were able to reflect independently about the grounds on which the rule for multiplying polynomials was based. Furthermore, insofar as they were given assignments that helped them along the path of reasoning, these assignments were also within their current capabilities. What also contributed to the success of the lesson were the shifts in forms of class work—work in pairs was followed by discussion with the class as a whole, accompanied by the teacher's brief commentaries. Another of the virtues of the above lesson plan was that it permitted some flexibility in the organization of the lesson—if one stage happened to take longer than expected, it would be relatively easy to do away with one of the assignments from the following section without jeopardizing the main aim and without failing to prepare students for their homework. Finally, informal assessment—the observation and collection of information about students' progress, as well as verbal praise and encouragement, which are no less important than established forms of formal assessment—was given due attention in the lesson.

Debatable Aspects of the Lessons

The above plan, however, contains certain debatable aspects. Elizabeth devoted a lot of attention to problems that can be solved by means of multiplying polynomials, but she devoted considerably less time to the technique of multiplication itself. In the first lesson, the series of assignments that gradually increased in difficulty certainly gave students the opportunity to acquaint themselves with the basic types of questions that tend to be asked in connection with the topic, but most of the actual practice was left for homework.

At the student teachers' seminar, someone proposed to give the class only one of the three assignments that followed the warm up session on the second day, and instead give a collection of assignments that would specifically ask students to multiply polynomials, including those with complex coefficients, such as

$$\left(\frac{2}{3}n+\frac{1}{7}\right)\left(\frac{3}{5}n-\frac{2}{7}\right).$$

In order to make this more interesting, it was suggested to divide the class into teams and organize a competition where the team that solves the most problems correctly by the end of the lesson is the winner.

It is fine to want students to acquire the technical skill of multiplying comparatively complex expressions, such as the one above, but one must be aware that such problems are likely to shift the focus of the lesson to something totally different—most of the time would then be spent on performing operations on fractions rather than on polynomials as such. This could, of course, be taken as a useful way of reviewing fractions, but it is hardly appropriate to have this review obscure the principal goal of the lesson. Besides, the algorithm for the multiplication of polynomials was used sufficiently frequently in the lesson as it stands.

The teacher must always be aware that there is never enough teaching time. It is essential to strike an appropriate balance between the different types of class work. The study of algebra assumes the mastery of many different technical skills and habits. It is important, however, not to limit one's teaching only to developing these skills. Skills should be acquired in the course of authentic mathematical activity, which is precisely what the student teacher, Elizabeth, was hoping to achieve in her lesson plan.

Reflection

Assignments and Topics for Discussion

1. Write down your impressions of Elizabeth's lesson. What did you like about it, and what do you think should have been done differently?
2. Construct a few more problems similar to the ones examined above, for which polynomials would need to be multiplied.
3. The following expression is examined: $vt - (v+2)(t-1)$. Simplify it. Think up a problem from physics whose solution would require an analysis of this expression.
4. Create a lesson plan that would follow the two described above and that would be devoted to the special products of polynomials: formulas of squares of sums and differences, and the difference of squares. Use Elizabeth's lesson plan as a starting point (in particular, try to answer the kinds of questions she asked herself when planning her lesson).
5. A student asks you: "Why does the textbook speak only of the multiplication, addition and subtraction of polynomials? Why are we not studying the division of polynomials?" How would you answer?

CHAPTER 8

PATTERNS, FUNCTIONS AND GRAPHS IN MATHEMATICS AND IN SCHOOL

This chapter starts off the discussion of the study of functions and graphs (to be continued in the next chapter). Its aim is to acquaint the reader with the principal difficulties encountered in studying this topic and with ways of dealing with them.

The chapter discusses:

- The mathematical essence of the concept of "function," different ways of defining it and the history of the concept.
- How patterns, functions and graphs are studied at school, the content of this topic and its role in secondary education.
- What research has to say about the causes of difficulties experienced by students in studying this topic.
- Possible ways of introducing the concept of "function" to schoolchildren and the subsequent study of related topics.
- Ways of establishing connections with this topic when studying other topics, especially equations and inequalities.

Mathematics in Middle and Secondary School, pages 209–241
Copyright © 2015 by Information Age Publishing

WORK ON THE CONCEPT OF "FUNCTION"

What Are Functions and Why Are They Important?

In contemporary school mathematics the words "pattern" and "function" have become especially popular. NCTM (2000) stresses that "Instructional programs from prekindergarten through grade 12 should enable all students to understand patterns, relations, and functions." This recommendation is not arbitrary. There are all kinds of regularities in nature, society, and mathematics itself. The best tool for expressing and describing these regularities are functions and graphs, which is why it is so important to study them at school.

We do not always recognize the extent to which functional language and its applications are part of our daily lives today. We use it practically every time we try to understand some process that is being described on the internet or in newspapers and we commonly use functional graphs and diagrams in other circumstances as well (Figure 8.1). However, people have been establishing patterns and regularities for a long time now.

Examples of Famous Regularities

Teachers who want to show their students how mathematics developed historically could make use of the fact that various numerical regularities had already been discovered in Ancient Egypt and Babylonia. Many assignments on the topic of patterns that are found in contemporary school textbooks were, in fact, discovered centuries ago. Among these are problems dealing with so-called figurate numbers, which show how many points are required in order to construct triangles (triangular numbers), squares (square numbers) and other polygons (Figure 8.2).

Lessons become more interesting if you allow schoolchildren to explore the patterns for these numbers or to derive formulas for obtaining such numbers. Pythagoreans also knew how to work with figurate numbers (Eves, 1990). They can even be used to reveal and prove other interesting

1 US Dollar equals

0.78 Euro

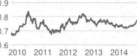

Figure 8.1 *Source:* Google.

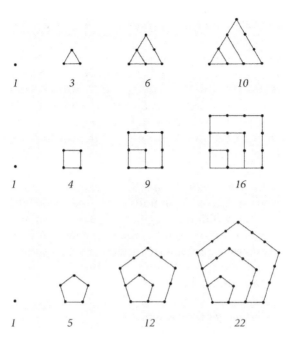

Figure 8.2

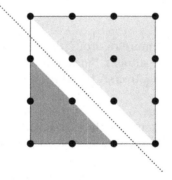

Figure 8.3

patterns, such as the fact that every square number is the sum of two consecutive triangular numbers (Figure 8.3).

How to Describe Regularities?

Students encounter these and other patterns all the time. Intuitively, most children understand that if they buy a can of soda for themselves as well as for a friend, they will need to pay twice the amount. This sort of pattern is universally familiar. However, any deeper investigation of patterns is far from simple.

Some years ago, Hamley (1934) observed that in the course of experimental tests many children correctly continued the series 2, 4, 6, ... with the numbers 8 and 10, and the series 2, 4, 8, ... with the numbers 16 and 32, but when the students were asked why they did this, they initially said that they did not know. As a teacher, you need to be prepared to teach students how to explain and express (by different means) the patterns that they establish.

Functions: The Mathematician's Perspective

A contemporary mathematician finds it easy to use the language of functions to describe many different regularities. For example, in the case of the arithmetic progression 2, 4, 6..., the sequence can be described by a function that matches the number of a term n with a value a_n, defined by the formula $a_n = 2n$. Thus, $a_4 = 8$ and $a_5 = 10$. But how is the actual concept of "function" defined in mathematics?

Set-Theoretic Definition of the Function

This is how one college textbooks explain what a function is:

> Let A and B be sets and let A × B denote the Cartesian product of A and B. A subset f of A × B is a function if, whenever (x_1, y_1) and (x_2, y_2) are elements of f, and $x_1 = x_2$, then $y_1 = y_2$.

If the explanation is yet more rigorous, then textbooks usually specify that a function is not just the subset f, but that it is made up of three entities: f, the set X made up of all x from A for which one can find the pair (x, y) in f, and the set B.

Using simpler language, one can say that a function is the totality of pairs where one element is taken from the first set and the other from the second set, so that for each element from the first set there is only one pair. Simpler still, one can say that each element from one set is matched by exactly one element from the other set and that when this relation is established, we have a function.

What are the pros and cons of such a set-theoretic definition? The value of such a definition lies in its generality (i.e., sets need not be only numerical but can contain elements of any kind). By placing in pairs the names of countries and their respective populations, one can define a function from the set of countries to the set of positive whole numbers. Or, say, a function from a set of triangles to a set of circles can be established, where each triangle corresponds to a circle with a center in a given point O, which has the same area as the triangle (its radius being $\sqrt{\frac{A}{\pi}}$, where A is the area of a given triangle). According to the above definition, the totality of all pairs where one first specifies a triangle and then its corresponding circle is a function.

However, as Tall (1992) rightly observes, a set-theoretic definition can hardly be considered a good cognitive root. Even a student who has mastered all the finer points of such a definition will not find it easy to see why such a complex and abstract concept happens to be so important. And yet, functions are the best means for expressing and studying changes and dynamics, crucial to everyone who inhabits a modern world that is anything but static (Lennes, 1932). Freudenthal wrote (1982, p. 12):

> Our world is not a calcified relational system but a realm of change, a realm of variable objects depending on each other; functions are special kinds of dependencies, that is, between variables which are distinguished as dependent and independent.

Instead of giving a pure set-theoretic definition, the Common Core Mathematics Standards describe the concept of function as follows: "Understand that a function from one set (called the domain) to another set (called the range) assigns to each element of the domain exactly one element of the range" (CCSS.M.HSF-IF.A.1).

The Emergence and Development of the Concept of "Function"

The concept of "function" emerged in the seventeenth century within the context of studying the mechanics of motion. Until then the concept had not been dealt with properly, even if some examples of correspondences and dependencies were already familiar in Classical Antiquity. The first explicit definition of the function was articulated at the beginning of the eighteenth century by Johann Bernoulli, a student of one of the creators of the Calculus—Leibniz. Bernoulli and others that followed treated functions as exclusively numerical in the sense that all the variables were numbers, while it was assumed, explicitly or implicitly, that a function was invariably expressed by a formula. Mechanics provided classical examples of functions. One variable (e.g., distance traveled) was expressed by means of another (e.g., time) through a formula, and what was studied was how one variable changed depending on the changes in the other.

Gradually, the concept of a function started to be defined in a more and more general way. When defining a function in 1837, Dirichlet pointed out that it was not important exactly how the relation was established—by a formula or by other means. Non-numerical functions also started to be examined. The language of functions became widely used in mathematics in general. The creation of set theory and the increase in rigor in mathematical reasoning eventually led to the modern, set-theoretic definition of function mentioned earlier. First appearing to describe mainly processes of movement, functions later became a useful tool for describing all sorts of different processes, such as changes of economic indicators, for example, and many others as well.

A different view of functions. And yet, gradually, a different interpretation of functions appeared. Functions emerged as useful and interesting *objects* with which one can perform operations. One can add functions; one can examine whole aggregates of functions and study the properties of such aggregates. One can even work out distances between functions. For example, even without referring to any rigorous definition, by simply looking at a drawing with the graphs of the functions f, g and h (Figure 8.4) one can say that function g is closer to function f than function h.

Today we know about functions far more than what is included in school programs. However, what is studied at school should not stand completely isolated from scholarly mathematics—that which emerges in mathematical research invariably (if only gradually and indirectly) influences school mathematics.

Functions and Patterns at School: Past and Present

Functions started to be introduced into school mathematics from the end of the nineteenth century. A decisive role in their inclusion was played by Felix Klein, who considered the function to be the soul of mathematics and the unifying principle of school mathematics (Hamley, 1934). Indeed, it was Klein who had the idea to approach the study and classification of geometry on the basis of the concept of "transformation" (and therefore, in a way, on the basis of functions). The key concept in modern

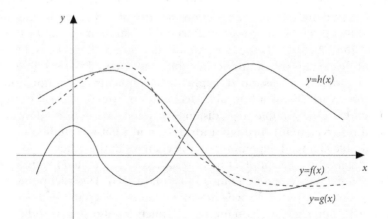

Figure 8.4

algebra—"operation"—is also described by means of functions. Graphs (yet again functions) are essential to the description and understanding of problems about probability, not to mention numerous real-world problems.

As a result of the abundance of applications of functions, mathematics educators have gradually afforded them more and more attention in the classroom. In school mathematics, functions are, on the one hand, used as the means of modeling and describing patterns (the NCTM and CCSS-M both state that students should generalize patterns using explicitly defined and recursively defined functions), and on the other hand, studied as objects in their own right.

What is Studied in School? The content of contemporary school mathematics relating to functions can therefore be divided provisionally into two parts. First, one studies the concept of "function" itself together with the graphs and the various properties of functions, such as domain and range, whether (or where) the function is increasing or decreasing, and its periodicity. Second, one studies concrete functions.

A special place in the school curriculum is occupied by linear functions. This is not accidental. Proportional growth (that is growth which can be described by the linear formula $y = kx$) can be observed in biology, economics, physics and everyday life. Moreover, linear functions are also an important means of modeling in cases where a process is, in principle, not exactly linear (i.e., where it is not described exactly by an equation of the first degree), but where the deviation from a linear function is negligible. The convenience of working with linear functions is so great that they are commonly used as the easiest way to describe what is happening, at least in approximate terms (e.g., how sports announcers sometimes describe the progress of a game in terms of, for example, points per quarter, effectively linearizing the progress of the game).

An important place in the curriculum is also given to quadratic functions. They too are very useful in describing many different processes in the real world. In the language of Calculus, quadratic functions are the anti-derivative of linear functions. In other words, if the speed at which a certain process is changing is described by a linear function (and there is a fair amount of such processes), then the process itself is described by a quadratic function. The value of quadratic functions is not exhausted by the fact that one can use them to model other processes; graphs of quadratic functions provide one of the simplest examples of curves on a plane.

Many other functions are also studied in school, including, for example, functions of the type $y = \frac{k}{x}$, polynomials of higher degrees, power, exponential, logarithmic and trigonometric functions.

The subdivision of school study of functions into the study of general properties of functions and the study of concrete functions is provisional insofar as both usually take place at the same time and in connection with one another. General properties are studied based on concrete examples. In addition, one can also distinguish another aspect of the study of functions at school, namely when functions and graphs are examined as objects of certain operations, such as transformations.

The study of functions takes place in stages. Your task as a teacher is to establish exactly the level of generality and abstraction accessible to students at each stage so that new concepts will expand and enrich their experience and will not seem artificial and unconnected to their practice.

Forming the Concept of the Function

Historically, the set-theoretic definition of function was developed much later than when functions were used. Such a definition is comprehensible and convenient only for those who have first done work on a large number of concrete examples of dependencies between different sets of values.

Kieran (1992) observes that the definition of function in many contemporary school textbooks makes no mention of the notion of dependency. This means that teachers themselves must be responsible for preparing students to understand the definition through examples that would make its essence clear to them.

Elementary School: Introducing Patterns

In order to do meaningful work with patterns in later grades, it is desirable to introduce students to patterns in elementary school. Ferrini-Mundy et al. (1997) observe that "teacher's questions can foster the habit of looking for patterns and relationships." Appropriate questions can encourage students to perceive dependencies between magnitudes. To give the simplest of examples—

the number of sticks used to form a particular quantity of triangles is always three times greater than the number of triangles (Figure 8.5).

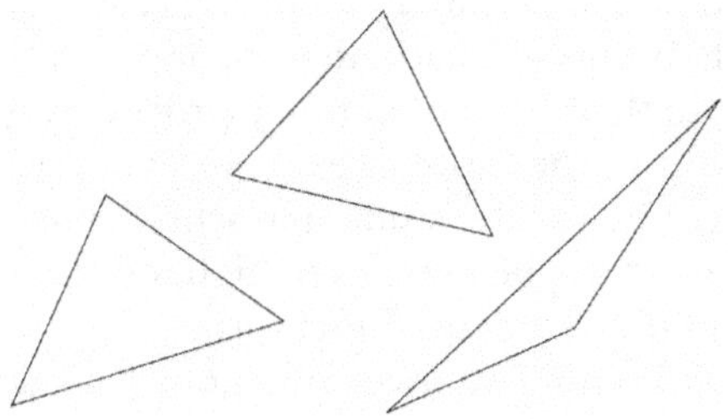

Figure 8.5

Andy is ten years old, and his sister is now eight. When he reaches the age of 15, she will be 13, and, more generally, her age will always be two years less than his.

In using any formula it is natural to emphasize the dependence of one quantity upon another. When examining the formula $P = 4a$, where a is the length of the side of a square and P its perimeter, you can suggest that your students fill out a table with the values of P for different values a, or to write down the pairs (a, P) for different values of a. You can then ask what happens to the perimeter if the length of a increases, say by one unit. You can also discuss the fact that the perimeter P will be shorter by 12 if the side becomes shorter by 3, and so forth. Students would therefore effectively be working with functions well before being introduced to their formal definition.

A widespread means of introducing students to functions is the so-called "function machine" analogy, which is a kind of box such that each time an object is inserted into it, another object comes out. Willoughby (1997) discusses active participation as a possibility, literally placing a student inside the box and asking her to throw out certain objects in response to those thrown into the box (Willoughby, 1997). For example, inserting a card with the number 3 written on it, the student may throw out a card with the number 9 on it; then, when the card with the number 5 on it is thrown in, you would expect the student to throw out the number 15, etc. The dependence between the input and the output is obvious. Indeed, such activities can be used as early as elementary school.

Middle School: Working with Dependencies

Literature (McCoy, 1997) describes the use of laboratory work in middle school as a way of demonstrating to students some of the dependencies that exist in the world around them. Usually such work consists of performing certain measurements (e.g., measuring the weight of pencils depending on their number x, or, as a more complex example, the weight of grain in cylindrical silos with a fixed base, depending on the height x of the silo), followed by drawing tables of values and discussing the dependency between the magnitudes examined.

The act of measuring allows students to "feel" the dependency. Subsequent work is then devoted to its expression by different means—tables, graphs and possibly symbols. In such lab-work, examining dependencies that are non-linear can also be assigned (e.g., investigating the weight of grain in silos with a fixed height depending on the size (radius) of their base). At this stage students usually cannot understand non-linear functions in detail, or indeed write them down symbolically, but they can see on a graph that the relationship is not linear. This is useful if only to prevent them from forming the false impression, so often found among students, that dependencies are invariably linear (this will be discussed in further detail later on).

Useful Tip! It is worth noting that even in cases when the dependency is linear (as in the two examples above) students can, due to measurement errors, still obtain points that do not lie exactly on the straight line of the graph of the linear function. You should be prepared for this. It is hardly worth choosing activities where a large number of errors are expected—which necessarily departs into asking questions of a more statistical nature—if the intent is to continue working with the exact function. (This type of activity is fine, however, if it is used simply as a way of demonstrating the presence of a dependency.) Let us examine and learn from a lesson taught by a student teacher.

Episode from a Lesson

> Wanting to introduce certain linear functions and then study their slopes, the student teacher gave students some bouncy balls and asked them to study the dependency of the height of the bounce y from the height of the drop x. After spending a long time performing measurements, students obtained points on a graph that, in the majority of cases, did not lie along a single straight line. The student teacher then explained that the inaccurate drawings were obtained due to measurement errors and that the drawings should have looked more like the graph that the teacher had done himself. He then continued with his lesson plan using his own drawing.

Discussion

It is clear that by pronouncing the measurements made by students inadequate, the teacher undermines the whole purpose of the activity (not to mention sets himself up for unproductive, tangential arguments with students). Instead of supporting what the teacher is seeking to demonstrate, the activity as completed is actually contradicting it. (It is worth noting that the above function should not in fact be seen as linear in the proper sense since the dependency would be different if the drop x were much greater. What one is dealing with here is the use of the linear function as an approximation, something not easy to explain to students who are encountering linear functions for the first time.)

Reflecting on Research: What research says about the use of symbols

When moving from general observations to the use of symbols, being very thorough and precise is important. Willoughby (1997) writes that, "the purpose of new symbolism should be to reduce necessary work—not add mysticism." Research has noted that functional symbolism, created in principle to facilitate work with functions, often becomes a source of great difficulties. For example, students find it far easier to complete the assignment: evaluate $a + 7$ when $a = 5$, than the assignment: determine $f(5)$ if $f(a) = a + 7$ (Kieran, 1992; Carpenter et al., 1981). Difficulties are also caused especially by abstract expressions such as $f(2x)$, etc.

One can say that the introduction of symbols takes place according to the following scheme: study of examples—verbal description—use of symbolism—study of examples. For instance, one first uses the "function machine" that turns 2 into 4, 3 into 6, and 5 into 10. This is followed by a discussion of the fact that the output is always twice the input. Only then will students understand that the function can be expressed by the formula $y = 2x$. After that, students can examine what the result would be if the function were applied to the number $x = 4$. In other words, the verbal and the symbolic generalize a large quantity of examples, while the sense of the symbols is then clarified by investigating their meaning when applied to concrete examples.

Graphs without symbols.   Literature (Nemirovsky, 1993) has also explored the way in which functional dependencies are studied at school with the help of graphs but without the use of symbols (at least at first). Students were given computer-based motion detectors attached to plotters (similar to calculator-based rangers [i.e., CBRs]) set up so that certain movements made by students translated into graphs. Students could then see clearly how the specific curve appeared depending on what actions were performed.

The role of graphs during the formation of the concept of function needs to be increased. Today, students come to school already familiar with all sorts of graphs, and while their knowledge is largely informal, these graphs can still be used to demonstrate the notion of dependency.

| Useful
Tip! |

High School: Moving to a Formal Definition

Moving to a more and more formal definition of function requires additional work. For example, if the definition given to students is based on the concept of "relation" (as is often the case in modern textbooks) students should first be acquainted with that concept (i.e., they should see different examples of relations, both those that represent functions and those that do not). It is also useful to give assignments that show the connection between the way the concept of relation is used in mathematics and the way in which this word is used in everyday life. Here is an example of such an assignment:

> Examine the relation of being brothers. Write down several pairs of people who are in this relation. Is this relation a function? Is it true that if certain "elements" a and b are in this relation then the elements b and a will also be in the same relation. Answer the same question for the father–son relation.

It is also important for students to see the transition from dependencies to pairs and relations. For example, students can examine several dependencies from the same set and to discuss sets of pairs of independent and dependent magnitudes that arise in the process. One can then move on to the discussion of what sets of pairs can be obtained in this way and an examination of the concept of "relation" in general. As a rule, new terms should be explained based on examples and should be justified by the fact that they facilitate subsequent comprehension.

Students must continually be given examples of different forms of representation when working with functions—graphic, verbal, formulaic and "arithmetic" (such as tables, ordered pairs etc.—Verstappen, 1982). This will help students notice the different aspects of the concept they are studying, and it will help them apply it to different situations. It will also enrich and develop their use of mathematical language.

Examining _an_ Example **How to Use Different Representations**

In order to emphasize the key idea in the definition of a function—that each input object is matched by exactly one output object—the teacher can give students assignments where this idea has to be analyzed in situations expressed through different means:

1. Show which of the graphs below are graphs of functions (Figure 8.6).
2. Show which of the following sets of pairs represents a function from the set $\{1,2,3\}$ to itself
   a. $(1,1)$, $(1, 2)$, $(2, 2)$, $(3, 3)$;
   b. $(1,1)$, $(2, 2)$, $(3, 3)$;
   c. $(1,1)$, $(2, 2)$, $(2, 2)$, $(3, 3)$;
   d. $(1, 1)$, $(2,1)$, $(3,1)$.
3. Show which of the following formulas defines the function y in terms of x:
   a. $y = x^2 + 3x - 11$;
   b. $y^2 = x - 1$;
   c. $y + x = 1$.
4. Let us examine all the first names of students in a certain class. Can we say that by mapping each first name to a student bearing this name we are defining a function?

The work on introducing the concept of "function" is not accomplished in one or two lessons. The concept of "function" pervades the whole of mathematics and the teacher must return to it time and again in different

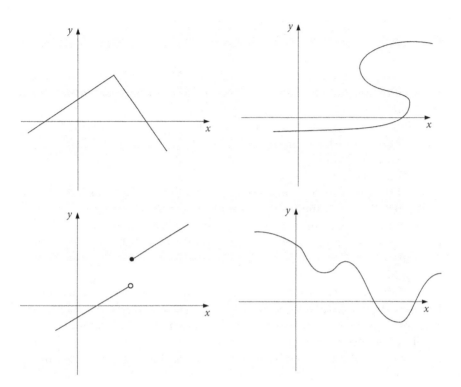

Figure 8.6

lessons, clarifying its essence and adding new aspects to its meaning. As a teacher, you should prepare problems for students that would help diagnose their level of comprehension of the concept and those that would further develop their understanding.

Analyzing Patterns: An Example from Practice

A description of a lesson taught in a Precalculus course is discussed. The lesson was devoted to patterns familiar to students from before, but that were now going to be studied on a deeper level.

At the beginning of the lesson the teacher, Ms. Cabral, gave the students two sequences:

1, 3, 5,.. and
1, 4, 9,..

The students were asked to provide the next term of each sequence and to try and explain their answer.

Students were ready to answer very quickly. Several hands went up instantly. Ms. Cabral asked one student, Nick, for his answers and the results he gave were 7 and 16, respectively.

"OK...,—said Ms. Cabral,—and what do you think, Loretta?

"7 and 16,"—Loretta replied.

"And you, Julie?"

"7 and 16"...

At this point bewilderment started to build up in the class. Why had the teacher given them such a simple assignment? And why did she continue to question them as if expecting a different answer?

The students were even more surprised when Ms.Cabral, feigning doubtfulness, said that for the second sequence she got 22 as the next number.

"But how?" cried the students. Instead of answering the teacher asked them to explain how they reached their own answers. The students explained that the first sequence was made up of odd numbers, while the second sequence was the sequence of squares starting with 1. Ms. Cabral then asked them to write down the formulas that would express this. The students gave the formula $a_n = 2n-1$ for the first sequence and $b_n = n^2$ for the second.

"Oh, I see...,—said Ms. Cabral, again feigning some confusion, but I chose for the second sequence this formula: $b_n = n^2+(n-1)(n-2)(n-3)$. When $n = 4$, you get 22. Is this formula wrong then?"—asked the teacher.

The students spent a few minutes checking the formula proposed by the teacher and thinking about it. They then discussed the situation, making brief comments, which mostly amounted to: "One can write dozens of formulas that would fit!" and "Our formula is better!"

Summing up the discussion, Ms. Cabral first asked the students to consider the first of these statements and to write a few other formulas that would fit the first sequence. Students worked on this in pairs. They came up with the following possible formulas for the first sequence: $a_n = 2n-1+(n-1)(n-2)(n-3)$, $a_n = 2n-1-(n-1)(n-2)(n-3)$ and $a_n = 2n-1+2(n-1)(n-2)(n-3)$.

Ms. Cabral then asked the students to represent these answers in graphic form by using a graphing calculator. She asked them to mark the points $(1,1)$, $(2,3)$, $(3,5)$ and to construct the graphs of the functions $y = 2x-1+(x-1)(x-2)(x-3)$, $y = 2x-1-(x-1)(x-2)(x-3)$ and $y = 2x-1+2(x-1)(x-2)(x-3)$ (Figure 8.7).

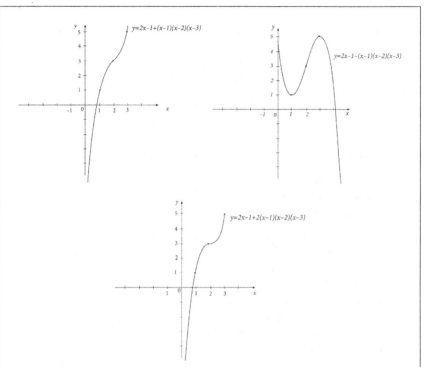

Figure 8.7

Students could then see clearly that the graphs of these different functions all went through the marked points, i.e., that $y(1) = 1$, $y(2) = 3$, $y(3) = 5$. This meant that all the formulas fit the first sequence 1, 3, 5.

In the course of the discussion, students observed that one could draw an infinite number of graphs through these three points and that these could be expressed by a whole multitude of different formulas. The teacher drew the attention of the class to this statement and said that other formulas could also be obtained by introducing, for example, roots or exponents into them and not just polynomials.

With the conclusion that an infinite number of formulas could be written to satisfy the first sequence, the teacher proposed to move onto the second statement.

"Why do you think that the two functions which you came up with initially were the best ones?"—she asked.

Students first argued that their formulas were the best because they were the shortest. But the question then emerged about whether it was always possible to write down a short formula. For example, the formula $x_n = n^2 - 5n + 6$ expresses the sequence 2, 0, 0, ... and there is no shorter formula that would do this.

One student remarked that the expressions of the first two formulas were of the first and second degree, while the other formulas were of higher degrees. The teacher agreed with this and pointed out that one could prove, in fact, that it would be impossible to write another formula of the first or second degree in the above case. She then gave students as homework the following problem for extra credit:

> The first three terms of a sequence are given. Prove that it is impossible to come up with two different formulas of the first or second degree, which would fit these terms.

Finally, Ms. Cabral pointed out that nothing in the assignment specified that one should choose the formula of the lowest degree, which meant that the problem, though simple and familiar in appearance, was probably not formulated accurately enough since it allowed for a multitude of different solutions. Finally, the teacher concluded that even seemingly simple problems of this sort can provide material for study and that even here providing thorough answers is needed to avoid inaccuracies.

Discussion

This lesson was taught in a fairly advanced class. Apart from dealing with the purely mathematical issue of demonstrating the role of functions in describing patterns, Ms. Cabral also had the psychological task of showing students the importance of accurately describing the situation that was being studied.

Useful Tip! You should realize that widely-used problems of this sort, where one is given only the first few terms of a sequence and then asked to continue it, are, generally speaking, misleading. As a rule, the first few terms of a series do not determine subsequent ones. (It is another matter that in elementary and even in secondary school one does not necessarily need to get bogged down in all the subtleties of this issue.)

Making use of the fact that such problems, otherwise familiar to students, had never been studied in full, the teacher constructed the lesson as a kind of puzzle (this of course presumed a certain artistic touch on the part of the teacher as well as the readiness (the habit) on the part of the class to accept the lesson as a form of exploration). The exploratory activity of the students need not be reduced to their performing empirical lab-work; in the above case the students were engaged in a form of *theoretical* exploration.

More on the given problem. Addressing the more general problem, if the first n terms $(a_1, a_2, \ldots a_n)$ of a finite sequence are given then it is always possible to find a polynomial P of the degree no higher than $n - 1$, so that $a_k = P(k)$ for all $k = 1, 2, 3, \ldots n$. At the same time, there will be no other polynomials of the degree less than or equal to $n - 1$ that have this property, but there will be an infinite number of polynomials of a higher degree than $n - 1$ that do have this property.

In class, while the discussion was based on concrete examples, the attention, however, was primarily focused on the existence of various polynomials that could fulfill the three terms of the sequence provided (which precisely demonstrates the fact that problems devoted to continuing sequences normally have many solutions). Only in the problem set for homework was the question raised about there being only one polynomial of the degree no higher than two, which applies to the first three terms of the sequence. In fact, this problem demonstrates two generally important mathematical queries: existence and uniqueness. While the class discussion focused on the existence and, particularly, the non-uniqueness of functions that generate the sequence, the homework narrows in on the uniqueness of the polynomial with degree less than $n - 1$. Here is the solution to this problem.

Let us say that three terms of a sequence are given as a_1, a_2, a_3. We can assume that we have found two different polynomials P and Q of the first or second degree so that $P(1) = Q(1) = a_1$, $P(2) = Q(2) = a_2$, $P(3) = Q(3) = a_3$. We then examine the difference of these polynomials P – Q. This should be a polynomial of the degree no higher than the second and also different from zero, but acquiring the value zero when 1, 2 and 3 are substituted. This, however, is impossible since equations of the first and second degree (with nonzero leading coefficients) cannot have three solutions.

On teaching methods used in the lesson. The lesson was devised in such a way that it prompted students to ask questions. What sorts of methods did the teacher use for this purpose?

From the very beginning Ms. Cabral sought to grab the attention of pupils, to pique their curiosity and even surprise them. She chose a problem that, to a certain extent, provoked incomplete answers and cognitive conflict for students. The teacher's acting abilities had an important role to play in this—Ms. Cabral was able to draw students into this game by showing interest, bewilderment and doubt herself.

What did the teacher do in order to stimulate the students' exploratory activity in the course of the lesson? Ms. Cabral encouraged her students to use different methods of representing information—verbally, formulaically and graphically. In this way, students were prompted to work with and relate different representational forms, thereby independently revealing facts that were new to them. The discussion of the fact that one could draw an infinite number of graphs through the three points made students see clearly that the problem of continuing a sequence had many solutions. Moreover, it stimulated students to realize that the terms of a sequence did not have to be expressed just with polynomials but also by means of completely different types of functions. This was useful as a way of broadening the students' understanding of the use of different functions in describing patterns and modeling processes.

What was the teacher's role in this lesson? Ms. Cabral gave very few explanations herself. Instead she created situations that allowed students to ask questions and seek answers for themselves. The teacher also played the role of editor and evaluator, highlighting the most significant assertions and helping students bring their thoughts into a more finalized form.

Reflection
Assignments and Topics for Discussion

1. Derive formulas for the triangular, square and pentagonal numbers.
2. Give examples of some functions that map: (a) from the set of polynomials to the set of numbers; (b) from the set of people to the set of countries; and (c) from the set of books to the set of libraries.
3. Analyze (write an essay on) the historical development of the concept of function using the books by Eves (1990) and Boyer (1989).
4. Define the concept of "operation" with the help of the concept of "function."
5. Let us define for a set of students the relation μ in the following way: we say that students a and b are in this relation if they sit at the same desk in their mathematics class. Is this relation a function? Is it true that if the two elements a and b are in this relation then the elements b and a will also be in this relation? Is it true that if the elements a and b are in this relation and the elements b and c are in this relation then the elements a and c will also be in this same relation? What properties are being discussed in the last two questions?
6. Give examples of patterns that middle school students would be familiar with from their daily lives.
7. The first three terms of the sequence (a_n) are given: 3, 8, 15. a) Find a polynomial P, of the degree no higher than two, so that $P(\kappa) = a_\kappa$ for $\kappa = 1, 2, 3$. b) Find another two polynomials Q so that $Q(\kappa) = a_\kappa$

for $\kappa = 1, 2, 3$. c) Find an expression of the type $T_n = a \cdot 2^n + b \cdot 3^n + c$ so that $T_k = a_k$ for $k = 1, 2, 3$.
8. Let us say that the first n terms of a sequence are given $(a_1, a_2, \ldots, a_n)$. Prove that there cannot exist two polynomials P and Q of degree no higher than $n - 1$, so that $a_k = P(k) = Q(k)$ for all $k = 1, 2, 3, \ldots n$. (Use the consequences of the fundamental theorem of algebra.)
9. A single journey on the subway in one city costs \$2.50, but if you buy four tickets, the fifth ticket is free. Devise a lesson plan for middle school devoted to the study of the corresponding pattern (possibly including other analogous assignments).

OVERCOMING DIFFICULTIES IN STUDYING FUNCTIONS

While teaching your students about functions, you may find that they experience difficulties in the process of studying specific functions. Zaslavsky (1997) described various obstacles that students may encounter when learning about quadratic functions:

- The interpretation of graphical information (e.g., when students take in only the visible part of the graph, ignoring the fact that the function is defined for the entire numerical axis);
- The relation between a quadratic function and a quadratic function (e.g., when students think that the zeros fully define a quadratic equation);
- The analogy between a quadratic function and a linear function (e.g., when students assume that the assertions they learned for linear functions apply to quadratic functions as well);
- The seeming change in form of a quadratic function when one parameter is zero (e.g., when students think that the graph of the function $y = ax^2 + bx$ does not have a y-intercept, since the parameter c is absent);
- The over-emphasis on only one coordinate of special points (e.g., when students think that the vertex of the parabola is defined by a single coordinate).

Researchers (Kieran, 1992; Tall, 1992) have examined the way that students study other functions as well, including some more general difficulties, such as neglecting the domain and the range of the function (Markovits et al., 1986). We have already discussed above some of the key difficulties that students experience when studying functions, and we have also looked at ways of overcoming them. Some other difficulties, which teachers encounter regularly in their practice, will be examined in greater detail in what follows and some recommendations for dealing with them will be provided.

Broadening the Range of Functions Studied

When studying functions, students often have a tendency to overemphasize their prior experience obtained in the study of arithmetic and linear functions. Students often believe that the equality $f(a+b) = f(a) + f(b)$ applies not just to linear functions, but to all functions f, something akin to a universal distributive property (something that causes many mistakes in the study of trigonometric functions, for example). This is not all. In answering the question of what a function can be and what sorts of properties it can have, students often unwittingly imagine only linear functions.

In answering the question: "Graph a function that passes through two marked points (Figure 8.8). How many such functions are there?" many students simply draw a straight line and assert that there is only one such function (Even, 1993). When faced with the situation where one has to imagine a function that increases along the entire number line, but all the values of which are, say, less than three, many students assume that this is impossible. There are also other questions that cause problems: for example, at how many points can the graph of a function cross the abscissa axis (students assume that there can only be one such point, as is the case in linear functions, or two, as is the case in quadratic functions); or the question about what the domain and range of a function can be, etc.

Useful Tip! It is useful to acquaint students with different functions and show them that their properties can be quite different from those of linear functions. We have mentioned above that it is important to give significant attention to

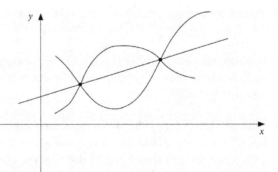

Figure 8.8

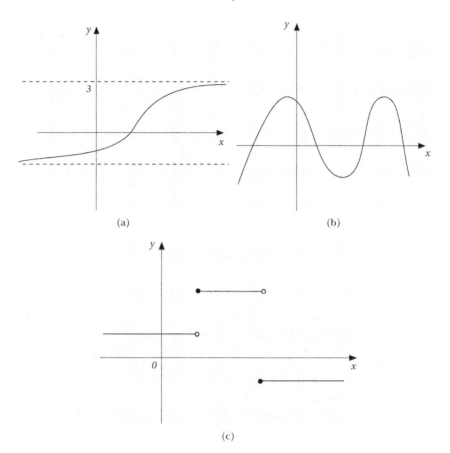

(a)

(b)

(c)

Figure 8.9

the graphic representation of functions. It is much easier to draw a bounded but increasing function (Figure 8.9a) or a function that has four points of intersection with the abscissa axis (Figure 8.9b), or a function that has a range that consists of three number (Figure 8.9c), than to provide a formula for such functions.

Use Examples From The Real World

Examples that would be interesting to study from this perspective can be obtained by constructing graphs of changes that take place in the real world. For instance, Figure 8.10 represents a graph showing the distance between the classroom wall and the student moving along the wall perpendicular to it during some time interval. Have one group of students observe

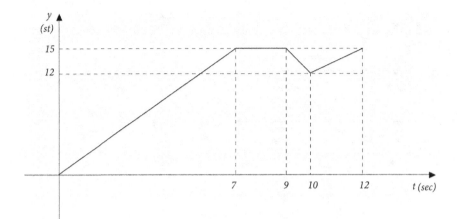

Figure 8.10

the student, and then construct such a graph, and have another group (not observing the student) give directions for how the student moved. Have both groups answer questions about the zeros of the corresponding function, about its range or about the intervals of monotony, etc.

Sometimes Use "Atypical" Functions

In order to broaden the students' understanding of what functions can be, it is useful to examine a few "atypical" functions expressed by "unusual" formulas, such as piece-wise functions (one should not, of course, overuse them or waste too much time on them, however). For instance, one could examine the functions:

$$y = \begin{cases} -2, & \text{if } x \le 0 \\ 0, & \text{if } x > 0 \end{cases} \quad \text{or } y = \begin{cases} 1, & \text{if } x \le 0 \\ x, & \text{if } x > 0 \end{cases}$$

(Figure 8.11). Work with this type of function is useful as an exercise in functional symbolism and also, to a certain degree, in logic, while at the same time showing how unusual (from the students' point of view) functions can be.

Generally speaking, questions of the type "is it possible that..." or "give examples of...," which have already been mentioned earlier, are particularly useful in the study of functions and graphs. Thinking up examples makes students use different forms of mathematical exploration and representation, and enables a deeper understanding of the concept studied.

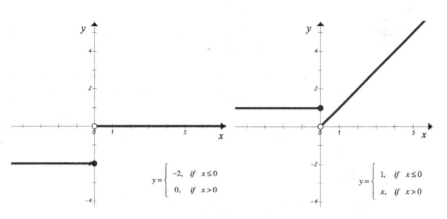

$$y = \begin{cases} -2, & \text{if } x \le 0 \\ 0, & \text{if } x > 0 \end{cases}$$

$$y = \begin{cases} 1, & \text{if } x \le 0 \\ x, & \text{if } x > 0 \end{cases}$$

Figure 8.11

Studying the Connection Between Equations and Functions

NCTM (2000) says: "Mathematics is not a collection of separate strands or standards, even though it is often partitioned and presented in this manner. Rather, mathematics is an integrated field of study." Unfortunately, at school different mathematical topics are often studied in isolation. This makes it much more likely that students will forget what they have learned previously, and also—no less importantly—it gives them a false impression of mathematics as a discipline and how it work. A direct consequence of this isolated study of different topics is the seemingly absurd errors that students tend to commit when they are asked to solve essentially the same problem by different means (for example, by using graphs and by manipulating symbols). They obtain different solutions and remain completely oblivious to the contradiction.

Establishing Connections

The study of functions and graphs allows one to discover connections between the different parts of the school mathematics course. In particular, functions and graphs are an efficient tool for the study of equations and inequalities. Here we shall dwell on some details of this teaching method. Other examples of such assignments will be given in the following chapters.

Graphs provide a far clearer visual representation of the solutions to equations. They also make the study of equations more productive and accessible. The natural first step here is to give assignments where students would be asked to solve and study equations on the basis of a given graph.

Examining an Example | Assignment Example

For instance, give your students the graph of a function *f* for the interval [–2, 4] (Figure 8.12). You can then ask your students the following questions:

- Solve the equation $f(x) = 1$.
- Solve the inequality $f(x) > 1$.
- Determine the values a, for which the equation $f(x) = a$ has solutions.
- Determine the values a, for which the equation $f(x) = a$ has exactly two different solutions.

The answer to the first question amounts to finding the abscissas of the points of intersection of the graph of the function *f* and the straight line $y = 1$ ($x = 1$, $x = 3$, $-2 \leq x \leq -1$). To answer the second question it is sufficient to indicate the abscissas of the graph lying above the straight line $y = 1$ ($1 < x < 3$, $3 < x < 4$). The third question is essentially about establishing the values a, for which the straight line $y = a$ intersects the given graph ($0.5 \leq a \leq 4$). Finally, in order to answer the last question it is sufficient to indicate the values a, for which the straight lines $y = a$ have exactly two points of intersection with the given graph ($0.5 < a < 1$, $a = 3$).

Such exercises help students acquire the skill of reading graphs and teach them to translate from the language of graphs to the language of equations, and vice versa.

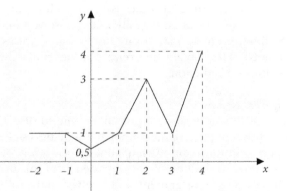

Figure 8.12

Using the same method with other assignments.

In the future you can use this skill, proposing to your students exploratory questions about how many solutions a particular equation has, as well as questions about certain properties of equations. Such assignments are especially useful when students are using a graphing calculator. What one has to do is simply to see how many points of intersection the constructed curves have with one another or with the abscissa axis. For instance, in order to answer the question about how many solutions the equation $x^4 = 4x - 2$ has, it is enough to graph the functions $y = x^4$ and $y = 4x - 2$ (Figure 8.13a) and see that these graphs have only two points of intersection. It is also possible to graph only one function: $y = x^4 - 4x + 2$ (Figure 8.13b), and get the same answer—two solutions, since the graph has two points of intersection with the *x*-axis.

In the next section we examine some other problems that can be solved by using the link between equations, functions and graphs. Let us reiterate that teachers should strive to demonstrate to students the connection between different parts of mathematics and the usefulness of deploying a variety of mathematical resources and methods. To do this, the teacher should get students to work on and discuss a large number of different kinds of problems.

Function as Object vs. Function as Process

We have discussed above the dual role of functions in mathematics—functions can be used to model processes and they can also be examined as objects of operations. This distinction is also present in the study of functions at school.

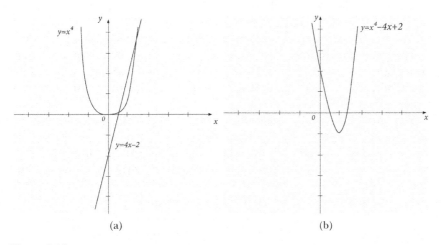

(a)   (b)

Figure 8.13

Reflecting on Research

Researchers (Kieran, 1992) observe that students understand functions primarily as descriptions of processes. For this reason, when students are asked to think of functions as entities with which one can perform operations, they usually start to experience difficulties. Work with this aspect of the concept of "function" is useful not only as a way of developing students' abstract thoughts or as the means of preparing them for college courses in mathematics; it also serves as an aid in solving many typical "school" problems. Research (Sfard, 1991) shows that the work on functions "as objects" is successful when it is not opposed to the study of functions "as processes" but instead develops out of it. The transition to functions "as objects" should be based on a large number of examples examined beforehand. This would allow students to focus not on the algorithm for obtaining a particular value of a function but on the result as a whole. It is also important to present everything as clearly as possible by using graphs, diagrams and, if possible, technology.

Examining *an* Example | Constructing Graphs by Means of Transformations

Let us examine the construction of graphs by means of transformations. As we know, in order to, say, graph the function of the type $y = f(x) + b$ it is enough to apply a vertical translation of the graph of the function $y = f(x)$. Graphing the function of the type $y = f(x + h)$ amounts to a horizontal translation of the graph of the function $y = f(x)$. Other less frequent assertions about the construction of graphs include, for example, the assertion that graphing the function of the type $y = -f(x)$ amounts to a reflection about the x-axis, while graphing the function of the type $y = f(-x)$ amounts to a reflection about the y-axis.

The use of these and other similar assertions allows students not only to construct certain graphs more easily, but it also helps them reach important conclusions about the material studied. (For example, with the help of such assertions, it is easy to see that the graphs of all quadratic functions are curves of a single type.)

You should gradually gear students towards making independent discoveries of such assertions. To do so, you can ask students to graph several functions (say, $y = x^2$, $y = x^2 + 2$ and $y = x^2 - 1$) on a single drawing, filling out tables of values beforehand and articulating hypotheses about how one such graphs can be obtained. Graphing calculators and dynamic technologies are also useful here since they allow one to quickly examine a large number of different graphs. You can also ask students to construct graphs with the help of a pre-prepared model, such as the parabola $y = x^2$, which then can be bent in different directions; for example, the use of dynamic software such as Geometers Sketchpad can allow students to drag the parameter b in the function $y = f(x) + b$ and immediately see the resulting transformation on the function's graph. Eventually, reverse problems can be given, where, for example, two curves would be given and the student is asked to identify which transformation could be used to obtain one curve from the other and how to write down one of these functions symbolically if the other is expressed by the equation $y = f(x)$. In this way, students can move from understanding a graph as something obtained in the process of placing points onto a coordinate plane to its conception as an entity in its own right.

Studying Properties of Operations with Functions

The same scheme can be used to study properties of operations with functions (which in itself develops students' understanding of operations, since students thereby learn that addition can be performed not only with numbers but also with functions, and also that this addition possesses properties such as the commutative and associative laws). Initially, different examples can be used to show how to define the sum (or difference) of two functions, after which the discussion can gradually move to the properties of the operation in question, as well as the properties of the function composed of the sum of the two other functions (for instance, the fact that the sum of two increasing functions is also an increasing function). Here again graphing calculators or dynamic technologies can be of use since it allows students to observe a large number of examples without creating any technical problems.

Don't Forget to Study Functions as "Processes"

There are other examples of the study of functions as "objects" (probably the most important of these are found in the geometry course where transformations are studied). In all these cases the conception of the function as "object" should not replace its understanding as "process." Researchers (Dubinsky, 1993) have noted cases where students, on the contrary, perceive the graph as something static and find it difficult to derive from it the values that a function has at one point. Indeed, one must also give students exercises that proceed from the "object" to the "process."

It is important to keep a constant balance between the abstract and the concrete, and to avoid overloading the students with too many symbols and general assertions. At the same time, you must try to go beyond what has already been studied and work towards a more general understanding of function, without forgetting to demonstrate how this general conception is embodied in concrete examples.

How a Graphing Calculator Helps in the Study of Functions

Graphing calculators were one of the first modern technologies used widely in mathematics education (not without considerable debate, however). And while many other technologies exist today, which undoubtedly can also foster learning mathematics, we discuss in more detail some of the specific features of and literature on the use of calculators (or other technologies that can mimic their capabilities) in mathematics education. We discuss some additional technologies, such as dynamic geometry software, in other sections of the textbook.

A number of situations where the use of graphing calculators is particularly helpful have already been mentioned. There now also exists a vast body of literature on the use of graphing calculators in school mathematics in general, and in the study of functions and graphs in particular (a survey of this literature can be found in Romberg et al., 1993, Lagrange et al., 2003). Teachers can find a large number of recommendations and activities in articles that describe the use of graphing calculators in teaching practice (e.g., cf. Hansen, 1994, Holmes, 2000; Lovinelli, 2000; Lum, 1995; Van Dyke, 2003; etc.). Of course, in addition to graphing calculators, dynamic software technologies such as Geometer's Sketchpad or GeoGebra can be used similarly to explore and interact with functions in real time.

Reflecting on Research

The use of calculators radically reduces computational issues and quickly makes available the necessary objects and evidence. Gage (2002) rightly observes that, "the immediate feedback provided enables students to challenge misconceptions as they form, so making their acceptance less likely. The calculator also forms a learning environment by providing a model for a variable that is concrete and easily understood by even quite young children."

The calculator substantially expands the limits of what is traditionally studied and allows students to become familiar with concepts and methods that would otherwise be inaccessible to them within the traditional framework. For example, students can be acquainted immediately with graphs of non-linear functions and thereby broaden their understanding of functions from the start, considerably increasing the possibilities of the global visualization of the overall behavior of functions (Tall, 1992). With the help of a calculator one can perform experiments by quickly constructing a large number of graphs that the class can then analyze. The calculator permits different methods of representing functions and thereby helps students form a clearer picture of what they are studying (Piez & Voxman, 1997).

Maximizing Positive Use of Calculators and Avoiding Pitfalls

At the same time, the appearance of the calculator (and technology in general) in school practice creates new challenges for the teacher. In particular, calculators open new possibilities for student error linked to incorrectly inputting data. Also, the window of the calculator is inevitably restrictive because it cannot display the entirety of the graph, or all its necessary elements, leading students to form incorrect ideas about the properties of particular functions.

Perhaps even more important than all of this is the fact that the calculator forces one to take a radically new look at many traditional school assignments. Literature (Greenes & Rigol, 1992; Harvey, 1992) distinguishes three types of assignments from the point of view of using calculators:

- calculator-inactive problems, for which there is no advantage (or disadvantage) to using a calculator;
- calculator-neutral problems, which can be solved without a calculator, although a calculator might be useful;
- calculator-active problems, which require the use of calculators for their solution.

The availability of calculators allows teachers to give students calculator-active problems, thereby expanding teaching options. However, it also turns many traditional problems into routine and pointless exercises. Certain exercises that involve calculations or even the construction of graphs, which without the use of calculators could be seen as expanding the students' understanding, have now become little more than a mechanical completion of operations. (To give the simplest of examples, a function is graphed not by studying its properties but simply by typing in a given formula). The same problem arises in the evaluation of the students' understanding of the material (Beckman et al., 1999).

Of course, the teacher always reserves the right to require students to complete certain assignments without a calculator. However, it is hardly natural or effective to do so too often. There is no doubt that the appearance of calculators has radically shifted the focus of teaching and of assignments given to students. What has now become far more important is the skill of evaluating the plausibility of one's results and the habit of critical thinking.

Examining an Example **Assignment Examples**

You must be prepared to make use of mistakes made by students in order further to develop their critical thinking. In a situation where a student is graphing the function $y = (x+1)^2 - 4$, and gets Figure 8.14, it is possible

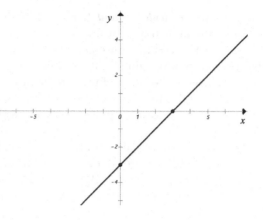

Figure 8.14

simply to observe that the student has incorrectly entered the expression $(x + 1)^2$, and then to demonstrate how it should be done. However, it would be much better to ask a series of questions that would compel the student to realize independently that the graph is incorrect. You can ask this student in which points the graph intersects with the abscissa axis, which are the zeros of the function, and then to check if, according to the formula, these numbers are the zeros of this function, etc.

Equally useful are assignments where the student is asked to "guess" what the graph of a particular function is supposed to look like and then to test this hypothesis by using a calculator. Such problems often work as games, but they undoubtedly play an important role in developing the students' understanding of the properties of functions.

For example, it is easy to determine that the graph of the function $y = (x - 1)(x - 2)(x - 3)$ ought to intersect the abscissa axis in three points with the abscissas $x = 1$, $x = 2$, $x = 3$, and that it is supposed to lie above the abscissa axis in the intervals $1 < x < 2$ and $x > 3$. It ought to disappear "into infinity" when x itself is approaching infinity, since it is clear that the expression $(x - 1)(x - 2)(x - 3)$ becomes greater when x becomes greater, etc. Having realized all this, it is not difficult to assume that the graph ought to look something like the one in Figure 8.15. This hypothesis, then, can be tested by using a calculator.

Problems based on having to translate from one representation to another and, in particular, on the modeling of real-world processes, are particularly useful in this new calculator environment. Calculators open up new possibilities by substantially reducing technical difficulties, yet they do not in any way reduce the need for understanding the material studied (without which the proper solution of problems based on real-life situations would be impossible). Let us imagine, for instance, that a certain process is modeled by the

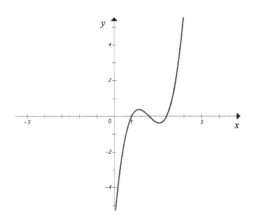

Figure 8.15

function $y = f(x)$. Students can then be asked questions about whether the value y increases or decreases on a specific interval, something they can answer with the help of a calculator well before learning Calculus. By formulating the answer in the terminology of a real-life situation, students can show that they are using the calculator with understanding and that they are aware of the properties of the function they are studying.

New Challenges and New Possibilities

As we can see, the use of graphing calculators in class demands additional work on the part of the teacher. The teacher needs to look for and construct new types of assignments and analyze a considerable amount of pedagogical literature. Such work is justified, however, by the new possibilities that the use of calculators can provide for teaching and learning.

Assignments and Topics for Discussion

1. Students often experience difficulties when they try to imagine functions that do not have the same properties as linear or quadratic functions. For example, the question: "Can there be a function such that its graph crosses the *x*-axis in three different points?", might seem complicated to them. Think up some questions of the type "can there be a function such that…." and provide answers to them.

2. The most frequently used piece-wise function is

$$y = \begin{cases} x, & \text{if } x \geq 0 \\ -x, & \text{if } x < 0 \end{cases},$$

i.e., $y = |x|$. The study of this function and the solution of the equations associated with it usually cause students difficulties. Why do you think this is the case?

3. Give examples of questions about inequalities that can be successfully solved with the help of graphs. Say how you would solve them and how you would use such questions in class.

4. Show that the graph of any function of the type $y = x^2 + px + q$ is the same kind of curve as the graph of the function $y = x^2$.

5. How would you show students that the composition of two reflections is a translation or a rotation. Formulate a set of assignments to illustrate this.

6. Analyze the articles on the use of graphing calculators that have been mentioned in this section. Which assignments and activities did you find the most interesting?

7. Figure 8.16 represents a graph constructed by a student based on the formula

$$y = \frac{3}{x+2}.$$

What do you think has happened? Which assignments would you propose to help the student realize and correct his mistake?

8. Think up some problems that require a graphing calculator for their solution, but where the size of the viewing window can lead to erro-

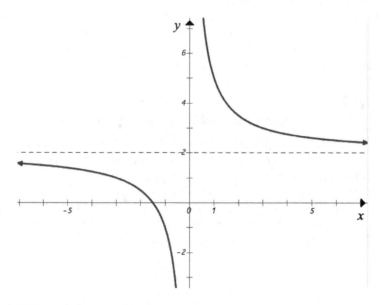

Figure 8.16

neous answers. Using such situations, formulate a set of assignments that would help evaluate the students' understanding of the topic "Functions and Graphs" in a calculator environment.

CHAPTER 9

PATTERNS, FUNCTIONS, AND GRAPHS

Problem Solving and Lesson Planning

This chapter continues the discussion of the study of functions and graphs (started in the previous chapter). Its aim is to help the reader make the most of practical work with students on this topic.
This chapter discusses:

- Some particularly challenging assignments on functions, graphs and patterns.
- How to conduct assessments while teaching the unit devoted to linear functions and graphs.

HOW TO SOLVE IT? A SELECTION OF PROBLEMS

This section will examine some interesting problems devoted to patterns, functions and graphs. These problems aim to indicate some particularly interesting directions for exploration that are available to students while studying this topic.

Mathematics in Middle and Secondary School, pages 243–268
Copyright © 2015 by Information Age Publishing
243

Example 1

Give examples of functions for which the domain is the interval $[0, 1]$, while its range consists of: a) the intervals $[-1, 1]$ and $(2, 3]$; b) just the interval $(-1, 1)$; c) the intervals $[-1, 1]$ and $[2, 3]$.

Discussion and Solution

a) It is easiest to represent the given function graphically. Figure 9.1a provides one possible answer. Let us note that it is also not difficult to represent this function algebraically (though this is not required in the conditions of the problem). To do so it is enough to derive the equations of the straight lines going through, respectively, points $(0, -1)$ and $\left(\frac{1}{2}, 1\right)$, and points $\left(\frac{1}{2}, 2\right)$ and $(1, 3)$, while taking into account the domains of each of their corresponding linear functions. The answer is:

$$y = \begin{cases} 4x - 1, & \text{if} \quad 0 \le x \le \dfrac{1}{2} \\[2mm] 2x + 1, & \text{if} \quad \dfrac{1}{2} < x \le 1 \end{cases}.$$

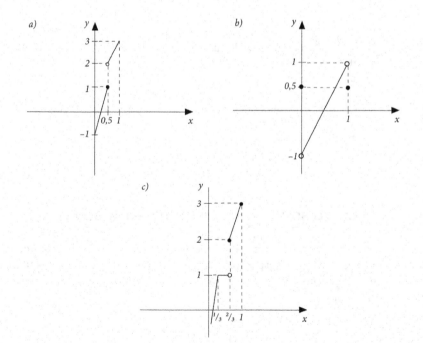

Figure 9.1

b) The difficulty in this assignment lies in the fact that the domain consists of a closed interval while the range is an open interval. Students usually unconsciously look for a continuous function that conforms to the given conditions, which is, however, impossible (the range of a continuous function, the domain of which is a closed segment, can either be a closed segment or a single number). After abandoning the idea of a continuous function, it becomes quite easy to construct the necessary graph. Figure 9.1b. provides one possible answer.

c) Here too it is impossible to find a continuous function that has the required properties. But even if one gives up on continuity it is not so easy to see how and where to make a "break." The solution to part A cannot be replicated, because for a function, the value at $x = 0.5$ must be unique. Figure 9.1c. provides one possible answer. (Let us note that both in this and the previous assignment it is equally easy to formulate the respective functions symbolically.)

These and similar assignments are useful as a way of expanding the students' understanding of what functions can be and also as a way of acquainting them informally with discontinuous functions.

Example 2

Determine the range of the function $y = x^2 - 2x$.

Discussion and Solution

This type of problem is usually solved in a Calculus course in the following manner: with the help of the derivative one first establishes that the given function has the minimum value -1; one then notes that $\lim_{x \to \infty}(x^2 - 2x) = +\infty$; finally, by referring to the continuity of the given function one concludes that its range is the interval $[-1, +\infty)$.

For the above function it is, of course, not difficult to reach an answer even without the use of Calculus. One can construct the graph of the function (Figure 9.2) and by simply looking at it give the same answer: $[-1, +\infty)$. Such a solution could, however, be considered not entirely rigorous. For example, it is not "visible" on the graph that the function takes all the values in the interval $[-1, +\infty)$. It is possible, however, to suggest one other solution that makes use of the strategy of adopting a different point of view and that connects the above topic with equations.

The definition of the concept of "range" states that a value for y is contained in the range of a given function if and only if there is a number x such that $x^2 - 2x = y$. In other words, a value for y is contained in the range of the given function if and only if the equation $x^2 - 2x = y$ has a solution. Now, this

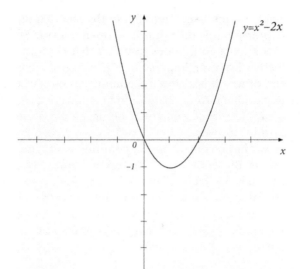

Figure 9.2

equation (or, rather, the equation $x^2 - 2x - y = 0$) has solutions if an only if its discriminant $2^2 - 4 \cdot (-y)$ is not negative. By solving the inequality $4 + 4y \geq 0$, we get $y \geq -1$, which are precisely all the values for y that are contained in the range of the given function. The answer is therefore: $[-1, +\infty)$.

Example 3

a) Prove that the function $f(x) = x^2 - 2x$ increases on the interval $[1, +\infty)$ and decreases on the interval $(-\infty, 1]$.
b) Determine the intervals of monotony of $g(x) = \dfrac{1}{x^2 - 2x}$.

Discussion and Solution

a) A rigorous solution of this type of problem is usually given in a Calculus course as well. However, in order to understand the essence of where a function is monotonous, it is useful to try and solve such problems with more basic methods. In order to prove that the given function f increases on the interval indicated, it is sufficient to prove that for any x_1 and x_2, such that $1 \leq x_1 < x_2$ the inequality $f(x_1) < f(x_2)$ is satisfied, or, stated in another way, that $f(x_2) - f(x_1) > 0$ applies. Let us prove this:

$$f(x_2) - f(x_1) = x_2^2 - 2x_2 - x_1^2 + 2x_1$$
$$= (x_2^2 - x_1^2) - (2x_2 - 2x_1)$$
$$= (x_2 - x_1)(x_2 + x_1) - 2(x_2 - x_1)$$
$$= (x_2 - x_1)(x_2 + x_1 - 2)$$

We can now note that insofar as $x_1 \geq 1$ and $x_2 > 1$, then $x_2 + x_1 - 2 > 0$. On the other hand, according to the condition of the problem: $x_2 - x_1 > 0$. It is clear from the two factors both being positive that the product $(x_2 - x_1)(x_2 + x_1 - 2)$ is also positive. This proves that $f(x_2) - f(x_1) > 0$. In an analogous fashion one can prove that $f(x_2) - f(x_1) < 0$ for $x_1 < x_2 \leq 1$, which proves that the function f decreases on the interval $(-\infty, 1]$.

b) The given function in part B, g, is undefined for $x = 0$ and $x = 2$. These points and the point $x = 1$ (where the function $f(x) = x^2 - 2x$ changes from increasing to decreasing or vice versa, which corresponds to the denominator of the given fraction) break the domain of the function g into four intervals: $(-\infty, 0)$, $(0, 1]$, $[1, 2)$, and $(2, +\infty)$. Let us analyze the behavior of the function g in each of these intervals.

It is true for any x_1 and x_2 in the interval $(2, +\infty)$, where $x_1 < x_2$, that $f(x_1) < f(x_2)$, as proven in subsection part a of this problem. Also, $f(x_1) > 0$ and $f(x_2) > 0$. From this, according to the properties of inequalities, it follows that

$$\frac{1}{f(x_2)} < \frac{1}{f(x_1)}$$

or that $g(x_2) < g(x_1)$. This means that in the interval $(2, +\infty)$ the function is decreasing.

It is also true for any x_1 and x_2 in the interval $[1, 2)$, where $x_1 < x_2$, that $f(x_1) < f(x_2)$. In addition, $f(x_1) < 0$ and $f(x_2) < 0$. It is clear from this that

$$\frac{1}{f(x_2)} < \frac{1}{f(x_1)}$$

or that $g(x_2) < g(x_1)$. This means that in the interval $[1, 2)$ the function g is also decreasing.

Take care, however, to note that it is inaccurate to conclude that the function g is decreasing on the set consisting of the interval $[1, 2)$ and the interval $(2, +\infty)$. This is clearly untrue since, for example, the value of $g(1.5)$ is lower than the value of $g(3)$ even though $1.5 < 3$.

In an analogous fashion one can show that the function g increases in the interval $(-\infty, 0)$ and in the interval $(0, 1]$.

This solution represents the application of a more general method that reduces the study a function's monotony to the proof of inequalities. (For someone who knows this method the above assignment is an exercise rather than a problem, as defined in Chapter 3.) It is evident that one should not overuse this method. Calculus provides a more convenient and more general technique, but the solution of some problems, including whether the product or the sum of increasing (or decreasing) functions is also increasing (or decreasing), is useful as preparation for studying Calculus.

Example 4

Determine all the values of the parameter a, such that: a) the equation $x^2 - 6x = a$ has solutions and they all lie in the interval $[1, 4]$; b) the equation $x^2 + 2(a-4)x + a + 16 = 0$ has solutions and they are all greater than -2.

Discussion and Solution

a) This assignment can be completed with standard algebraic techniques: the given equation $x^2 - 6x - a = 0$ can be solved by using the formula for quadratic equations,

$$x = \frac{6 \pm \sqrt{36 + 4a}}{2}.$$

One can then write down the system of inequalities:

$$\begin{cases} \dfrac{6 + \sqrt{36 + 4a}}{2} \geq 1 \\[2mm] \dfrac{6 + \sqrt{36 + 4a}}{2} \leq 4 \\[2mm] \dfrac{6 - \sqrt{36 + 4a}}{2} \geq 1 \\[2mm] \dfrac{6 - \sqrt{36 + 4a}}{2} \leq 4 \end{cases}.$$

(In fact, by noting that one of the solutions of the quadratic equation is greater than the other, it is sufficient to write down only two inequalities: that the lower solution is greater than or equal to 1 while the higher does not go above 4.) This system of inequalities is equivalent to the inequality $\sqrt{36 + 4a} \leq 2$. By solving this inequality (and without forgetting to take into account that the discriminant of the equation, which equals $36 + 4a$, should not be negative), we shift to a system equivalent to it

$$\begin{cases} 36 + 4a \geq 0 \\ 36 + 4a \leq 4 \end{cases}$$

and we get the answer: $-9 \leq a \leq -8$.

From a technical point of view, such a solution is hardly simple. The problem-solving strategy of drawing a picture allows one to make this solution visually much clearer. As discussed above, the connection between equations, functions and graphs can be used extremely productively in such situations. We explore some of these connections in what follows.

Another Solution

Let us graph the function $y = x^2 - 6x$ and mark on it the points where the abscissas are $x = 1$ and $x = 4$ (Figure 9.3). Their ordinates are -5 and -8 respectively. The condition of the problem specifies that the horizontal straight lines $y = a$ intersects the graph in such a way that the abscissas of these points of intersection lie in the interval $[1, 4]$. Translating, or reformulating, the question from algebraic notation and inequalities into an analogous question about graphs takes practices; however, the benefit in this case is a much simpler solutions. The graph shows that the straight line $y = a$ will intersect the graph only for values of a above the minimum of the

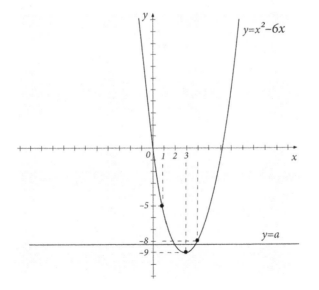

Figure 9.3

function, $a \geq -9$, while *both* the abscissas of the points of intersection lie in the interval $[1, 4]$ only if $a \leq -8$. From this we get the answer: $-9 \leq a \leq -8$.

b) The second problem, too, can be solved without the help of graphs but it would be even more technically complex than the previous problem. A graphic solution in the spirit of the previous one is also possible but it too is technically not as easy. Let us examine its key stages though.

First of all, one needs to transcribe the given equation in the form $f(x) = a$ (where f is some expression). To do this one must perform the appropriate transformations and move to one side all the terms containing a and to the other all the terms without a: $2ax + a = -x^2 + 8x - 16$. From this we get:

$$-\frac{x^2 - 8x + 16}{2x + 1} = a .$$

Let us now construct the graph of the function

$$f(x) = -\frac{x^2 - 8x + 16}{2x + 1}$$

(Figure 9.4a). To do this we must apply Calculus methods or else use a graphing calculator. By examining the graph, the given equation has solutions only for $a \leq 0$ and for $a \geq 9$, while for $a \geq 9$ at least one point of intersection of the graph and the straight line $y = a$ has the abscissa lower

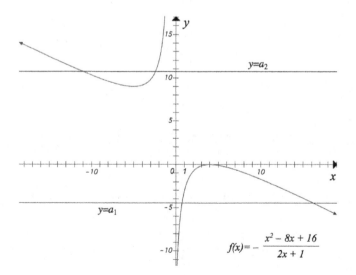

Figure 9.4a

than –2. For $a \leq 0$ the abscissas of all (two or one) points of intersection are greater than –2. The answer is: $a \leq 0$.

Another Graphic Solution

There is, however, another graphical solution that does not require the construction of such a complex graph. Let us first observe that the discriminant of the equation $x^2 + 2(a-4)x + a + 16 = 0$ equals $4(a-4)^2 - 4(a+16)$. By solving the inequality $4(a-4)^2 - 4(a+16) \geq 0$, we can determine that the given equation has solutions for $a \leq 0$ and for $a \geq 9$. Let us now take into account that the graph of the function $g(x) = x^2 + 2(a-4)x + a + 16$, which corresponds to the left-hand side of the given equation, is a parabola. The condition of the problem presumes that this parabola is positioned approximately as in Figure 9.4b; in particular, it is clear that the inequality $g(-2) > 0$ must be satisfied so that the solutions to the equation, the zeros of the function, have abscissa values greater than –2. This condition, however, does not necessarily guarantee the required position of the parabola, since the function being positive at $x = -2$ is also fulfilled if the parabola is positioned as in Figure 9.4c. Therefore, we also note that in the required position of the parabola the abscissa of its vertex needs to be greater than –2. It is easy to see that this condition, together with the condition $g(-2) > 0$, and the non-negative discriminant guarantee the required position of the parabola: it must intersect the abscissa axis (since the discriminant is non-negative), while the number –2 cannot lie between the solutions (since $g(-2) > 0$) and, finally, cannot lie to the right of the solutions (since it lies to the left of the abscissa of the vertex).

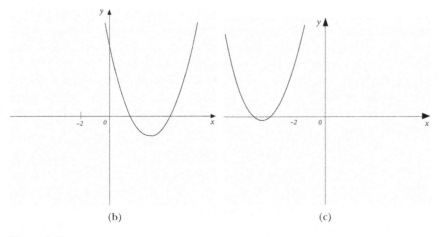

(b)   (c)

Figure 9.4b, c

All that remains to be done is to solve the inequalities obtained in this way. Since the abscissa of the vertex of the parabola is $x = -(a-4)$, and $g(-2) = 4 - 4(a-4) + a + 16$ we get the system of inequalities:

$$\begin{cases} a \le 0, \ a \ge 9 \\ -(a-4) > -2 \\ 4 - 4(a-4) + a + 16 > 0 \end{cases}.$$

By solving the inequalities we get a system equivalent to it

$$\begin{cases} a \le 0, \ a \ge 9 \\ a < 6 \\ a < 12 \end{cases}.$$

From this we get the answer: $a \le 0$.

Example 5

Find all functions f, such that for all numbers x, the following equation is fulfilled $f(x) + 2f(-x) = 2 - x$.

Discussion and Solution

This assignment is an example of a functional equation–an equation for which the solution is not a number but a function. The main difficulty of this assignment lies in the application of functional symbolism and the problem therefore contributes to developing the skill of using this symbolism. The strategy of examining a special case is of use here and can be utilized by looking at one special value of the variable x.

Since the given equation is satisfied for any value of the variable, then it ought to be satisfied also if one substitutes x with $-x$. Therefore, the equation becomes $f(-x) + 2f(-(-x)) = 2 - (-x)$ or $f(-x) + 2f(x) = 2 + x$. Let us now solve the system

$$\begin{cases} f(x) + 2f(-x) = 2 - x \\ f(-x) + 2f(x) = 2 + x \end{cases}$$

in relation to $f(x)$. To do so we must multiply the second equation by -2 and add the result to the first equation. We get: $-3f(x) = -2 - 3x$. From this we get that

$$f(x) = x + \frac{2}{3}.$$

Consequently, the equation $f(x) + 2f(-x) = 2 - x$ implies that

$$f(x) = x + \frac{2}{3}.$$

It is easy to see that this function satisfies the given condition since for any number x the equation

$$x + \frac{2}{3} + 2\left(-x + \frac{2}{3}\right) = 2 - x$$

is true. Thus, the only function that satisfies the condition is

$$f(x) = x + \frac{2}{3}.$$

Example 6

Calculate the sum $1 + 2 \cdot 2 + 3 \cdot 2^2 + \ldots + 49 \cdot 2^{48} + 50 \cdot 2^{49}$.

Discussion and Solution

In order to demonstrate the possibility of applying a variety of heuristic strategies, we solve this problem in several different ways.

Solution one.   An obvious solution method would be to look for a pattern. To do so let us examine several sums constructed by the same principle as the one above:

$$1 + 2 \cdot 2 = 1 + 4 = 5;$$

$$1 + 2 \cdot 2 + 3 \cdot 2^2 = 1 + 4 + 12 = 17;$$

$$1 + 2 \cdot 2 + 3 \cdot 2^2 + 4 \cdot 2^3 = 1 + 4 + 12 + 32 = 49.$$

By analyzing the first two sums, we find in both cases a result of one more than a power of two: $5 = 1 + 2^2$ and $17 = 1 + 2^4$. However, the number 49 cannot be expressed in this way because $49 - 1 = 48$, which is not a power of two. If we try to connect it in some way with a power of two (which is logical since the assignment contains powers of two) we can write down $48 = 3 \cdot 2^4$. The appearance of the number 3 alerts the solver to be on the lookout for a pattern, since the 3 appeared in relation to examining the third sum. In this way, the second sum can expressed similarly, as $17 = 1 + 2 \cdot 2^3$, while the first sum equals $1 + 1 \cdot 2^2$. Using this result, the fourth sum would be expected to be $1 + 4 \cdot 2^5 = 129$. It is easy to verify that this is the case:

$$1+2\cdot 2+3\cdot 2^2 +4\cdot 2^3+5\cdot 2^4 =1+4+12+32+80=129.$$

We can now formulate the assertion in a general form, as

$$1+2\cdot 2+3\cdot 2^2 +...+n\cdot 2^{n-1}+(n+1)\cdot 2^n =1+n\cdot 2^{n+1},$$

which can be proven using mathematical induction.

Since the assertion has already been proven for $n = 1$ (as well as $n = 2, 3$, and 4), what remains is to prove the inductive hypothesis: that the implication, if the statement is true for n then it also must be true for $n + 1$, is true. To do so, we assume the statement is true for n, and prove that it also must be true for $n + 1$. In other words, what remains to be proven is that

$$1+2\cdot 2+3\cdot 2^2 +...+n\cdot 2^{n-1}+(n+1)\cdot 2^n +(n+2)\cdot 2^{n+1} =1+(n+1)\cdot 2^{n+2},$$

by using the fact that

$$1+2\cdot 2+3\cdot 2^2 +...+n\cdot 2^{n-1}+(n+1)\cdot 2^n =1+n\cdot 2^{n+1}.$$

Now, by assuming the latter equation is true, we can assert that

$$1+2\cdot 2+3\cdot 2^2 +...+n\cdot 2^{n+1}+(n+1)\cdot 2^n +(n+2)\cdot 2^{n+1} =1+n\cdot 2^{n+1} +(n+2)\cdot 2^{n+1}$$

would also have to be true. By factoring, the following result is obtained:

$$1+n\cdot 2^{n+1}+(n+2)\cdot 2^{n+1} =1+(2n+2)\cdot 2^{n+1} =1+(n+1)\cdot 2^{n+2}.$$

This proves the required equality. In conclusion, we introduce $n = 49$ into the general formula and obtain the answer to the original question: the total sum equals $1+49\cdot 2^{50}$.

Solution two. Without guessing the possible answer, one can think of similar, but simpler, problems. One series in particular comes to mind, namely the sum of the geometrical progression with 2 as quotient (e.g., a sum of the type $1+2+2^2+2^3+...+2^n$), which is somewhat similar to the given sum yet can be calculated without too much trouble. By subtracting this easily obtainable sum $(1+2+2^2+2^3+...+2^{49})$ from the original one, we get $2+2\cdot 2^2+...+48\cdot 2^{48}+49\cdot 2^{49}$. Once again, by subtracting the sum $2+2^2+2^3+...+2^{49}$ from this, we obtain the remainder $2^2+...+47\cdot 2^{48}+48\cdot 2^{49}$.

If we continue in this fashion we can break the above sum into several smaller sums that can be calculated much more easily:

$$1 + 2 \cdot 2 + 3 \cdot 2^2 + \ldots + 49 \cdot 2^{48} + 50 \cdot 2^{49} =$$

$$= 1 + \quad 2 + \quad 2^2 + \ldots + \quad 2^{48} + \quad 2^{49} +$$

$$+ \quad 2 + \quad 2^2 + \ldots + \quad 2^{48} \quad 2^{49} +$$

$$+ \ldots\ldots\ldots\ldots\ldots\ldots\ldots\ldots\ldots\ldots\ldots\ldots\ldots\ldots\ldots\ldots +$$

$$+ \quad\quad\quad\quad\quad\quad\quad\quad\quad 2^{48} \quad 2^{49} +$$

$$+ \quad\quad\quad\quad\quad\quad\quad\quad\quad\quad\quad 2^{49}$$

For any whole k such that $0 \leq k \leq 48$, using the formula for the sum of the geometrical progression, we get that $2^k + 2^{k+1} + 2^{k+2} + \ldots + 2^{49} = 2^{50} - 2^k$. Let us now work out the sums in the above lines:

$$1 + 2 \cdot 2 + 3 \cdot 2^2 + \ldots + 49 \cdot 2^{48} + 50 \cdot 2^{49} = 2^{50} - 1 + 2^{50} - 2 + 2^{50} - 2^2 + \ldots 2^{50} - 2^{48} + 2^{49}$$

In conclusion let us again use the formula for the sum of the geometrical progression and the fact that we had 50 lines in the above notation.

$$1 + 2 \cdot 2 + 3 \cdot 2^2 + \ldots + 49 \cdot 2^{48} + 50 \cdot 2^{49} = 49 \cdot 2^{50} - (1 + 2 + 2^2 + \ldots + 2^{48}) + 2^{49}$$

$$= 49 \cdot 2^{50} - 2^{49} + 1 + 2^{49}$$

$$= 1 + 49 \cdot 2^{50}$$

Solution three. Lastly, yet another, more refined solution, is described, which could be used to reveal links between the most diverse parts of a mathematics course. Let us again examine a similar problem, but this time not a simpler one, but rather a more general one. Indeed, the number 2 (as the base) is not so important. We can examine almost exactly the same problem by replacing the number 2 with the variable x and then finding the sum, $1 + 2x + 3x^2 + \ldots + 49x^{48} + 50x^{49}$. Having experience solving problems in a Calculus course suggests yet another way of describing the regularity through which the terms in this sum are formed. One can say that the sum that is being sought is the derivative of the sum $1 + x + x^2 + x^3 + \ldots + x^{49} + x^{50}$. This sum can easily be found by again using the sum for geometrical progression: it equals

$$\frac{x^{51} - 1}{x - 1}.$$

Substituting this rational expression for the polynomial, we can now find the derivative of this function

$$y = \frac{x^{51}-1}{x-1}$$

(which would be precisely the desired sum). According to the rules of differentiation we get that

$$\left(\frac{x^{51}-1}{x-1}\right)' = \frac{51x^{50}\cdot(x-1)-(x^{51}-1)}{(x-1)^2} = \frac{50x^{51}-51x^{50}+1}{(x-1)^2}.$$

So, in order to solve the original problem all we need to do now is replace x by 2:

$$\frac{50\cdot 2^{51}-51\cdot 2^{50}+1}{(2-1)^2} = 100\cdot 2^{50}-51\cdot 2^{50}+1 = 1+49\cdot 2^{50},$$

which results in the answer: $1+49\cdot 2^{50}$.

Reflection
Assignments and Topics for Discussion

1. Give an example of a function for which the domain is the interval $[0,1]$, while its range consists: a) of two numbers, 0 and 2; b) of two intervals $(-1,1)$ and $(2,3)$; c) of the interval $[-1,1]$ and the number 2.
2. Determine the range of the following functions:

   a) $f(x) = x^2 + 6x$;

   b) $f(x) = \dfrac{x}{x^2-2x+2}$;

   c) $f(x) = x^4 + 2x^2 - 1$;

   d) $f(x) = 4^x - 2^{x+2}$.

3. Prove that if the functions $y = f(x)$ and $y = g(x)$ decrease in the interval X and, at the same time, have only negative values, then the function $y = f(x)g(x)$ is increasing in the interval X. Is it true that for any functions $y = f(x)$ and $y = g(x)$, which are decreasing in the interval X, the function $y = f(x)g(x)$ is increasing in the same interval?
4. Without using Calculus methods or the help of the graphing calculator, indicate the intervals for which the function,

$$y = \frac{1}{x^2+8x},$$

is increasing and decreasing.

5. How many solutions does the equation $f(x) = a$ have for each possible value of a: a) $f(x) = 2x^2 - 3x + 2$; b) $f(x) = 9^x - 6 \cdot 3^x$.
6. Find all values a such that: a) the equation $x^2 + 2(a+2)x + 5a + 4 = 0$ has solutions, all of which are less than –1; b) the equation $x^2 + (a-5)x + a^2 - a = 0$ has two solutions and the number 2 lies between them.
7. Find all functions f, defined along the entire number line (apart from zero) such that for all $x \neq 0$ the following equation is satisfied:

$$f(x) + 3f\left(\frac{1}{x}\right) = x + 2.$$

8. Establish whether a sequence can simultaneously be arithmetic and geometric. If so, find all such sequences.

PLANNING ASSESSMENT IN THE STUDY OF FUNCTIONS

This section describes how one student teacher, Ricardo, planned to assess the unit he was asked to teach in middle school. His plans reflect discussions that took place at the student teachers' seminar and incorporate observations and comments from his fellow student teachers.

Preliminary Information

As part of his student teaching experience, Ricardo had to teach the unit devoted to linear functions. This was by no means the first time Ricardo's students had come across linear functions and equations, but Ricardo's impression was that not all students remembered what they had learned before; additionally, the purpose of the lesson was to help students gain a more profound understanding of functional dependencies.

The Textbook
The textbook introduced the topic of linear functions by acquainting readers with the coordinate plane and by presenting solutions to example problems where the task was to identify particular points (x, y) on the plane. The textbook followed this section with a large number of word problems, all of which were solvable by means of linear functions. While many of these problems preceded the study of the "slope-intercept" algorithm for graphing linear functions, some also were discussed following the algorithm as a sort of application of what had been learned. The textbook only briefly mentioned that there were other, non-linear, kinds of dependencies. In

addition, a few assignments were devoted to the study of functional language (for example, the task was to find particular values of given functions, such as, $f(-3)$). At the same time, the textbook gave examples of how to determine the value of a slope, how to graph a linear function and how to analyze graphs (including piece-wise linear functions). The unit concluded with a section where linear equations were solved with the help of graphs.

Specifying Unit Objectives
Ricardo defined the following teaching objectives for the unit:

- Acquaint students with the simplest kinds of dependencies
- Teach students to use and understand different ways of expressing such dependencies
- Show them how what they have learned can be used to solve real-world problems
- Demonstrate how different parts of mathematics are mutually interrelated—in particular, how graphs are connected to solving equations

In preparing his assessment plan, Ricardo strove to specify these general objectives further by considering exactly what sorts of problems students should learn to solve and exactly how to judge the objectives that had been attained. Ricardo was well aware that the assessment plan needed to be flexible and that the information he would gain in the course of the lesson was likely to prompt changes both in the teaching itself and in the assessment of the unit. Nonetheless, he decided that planning assessment was actually one of the most important parts of planning the entire unit, because this helped him conceptualize exactly what he wanted to teach his students and how he should go about doing this. By thinking up assessment assignments he also worked on assignments that were to be done in the process of instruction itself.

At what point is it possible to conclude that students have mastered the topic "Linear functions"? Is it when they are able to recognize or graph a linear function, for instance? Or, perhaps when they can describe in words the properties of a linear function and provide examples of other (non-linear) functions that do not have these properties? Or, is it only when they can apply linear functions in solving problems where such functions are not explicitly mentioned?

Ricardo understood that the ability to solve each of these different types of assignments demonstrated a different level of mastery of the topic studied. By observing lessons in other classes, Ricardo also knew that students could, for example, correctly graph linear functions based on a given formula, but still fail to be able to "read" and interpret the graph, particularly ascertaining values of the function based on the graph. He had also witnessed situations where students were able to solve linear equations but could not interpret the answer's meaning in relation to the corresponding word problem; the ability to solve an applied problem, evidently, potentially meant little more than that the student had learned the appropriate algorithm well.

What Ricardo concluded from these observations was that assessment assignments needed to be varied—they needed to include both comparatively easy assignments that only involved recalling previously learned information (without which it would be difficult to proceed further) and also problems where students could demonstrate that they were able to apply what they had learned to new situations.

Planning Assessment

At the initial planning stage, Ricardo felt it was unnecessary to prepare his assessment instruments completely. He decided that he could do this later in the process of studying the material. For the initial planning, he limited himself to making broad sketches of assessment questions that he thought of using. Rather than thinking of assessment as a means to quantify students' learning, Ricardo believed that assessments needed to consist of all manners of collecting information, which could also be of help to students themselves in the actual study of the topic. As such, his desire was to use different forms and methods of assessment that would cater to more accurately capturing the aptitudes of all his students. Ricardo therefore decided on the following forms of assessment:

- Observation of student work.
- Written work to be done in class, including *analysis of regular class assignments, "one-minute papers", quizzes*, and *the final test*.
- Written work to be done at home, including *homework assignments, mini-essays*, and *a small-group project*.
- Interviews with some students.

This is how Ricardo planned to use these assessment forms.

Observation of Student Work

By observing how students worked in class, by noting what exactly it was that caused them difficulties, as well as stimulated their interests, Ricardo hoped to get a better understanding about their learning process and then to use this information to make improvements. At first, Ricardo wanted to create a written checklist where he would note the participation of each student; however, he later abandoned the idea, as it was difficult to do properly during the course of a lesson. Nonetheless, he still hoped to keep a mental checklist of this sort, focusing especially on those students whom he knew had problems with previous topics.

Analysis of Regular Class Assignments

What Ricardo had in mind for analyzing regular class assignments was an evaluation of the so-called "Do now" assignments that would be given to students in most lessons. Ricardo's idea was that he would always collect and check students' "Do now" papers, but would not give any formal points; instead he would limit himself to verbal commentaries. He thought that this would be of greater help in making both him and the students understand what caused them the most difficulties. As an additional benefit, he also thought that collecting "Do now" papers would make students take these assignments more seriously.

"One-Minute Papers"

So called "one-minute papers" (which in real situations actually take closer to two or three minutes) contain questions prompting students to reflect on the material studied, which allow the teacher, informally, to establish how well the students are coping with "qualitative" assignments.

Such assignments can test to what extent students have assimilated particular aspects of the concepts introduced in the course. For example, after defining slope, Ricardo planned to ask students to answer which of the following could be the slope of a linear function: a) –5, b) $\frac{2}{7}$, c) $2x$, d) π.

Such assignments can also precede and anticipate future class discussion, prompting students to find answers to certain key questions on their own. For example, after discussing the solution of the equation $2x = 6$, Ricardo planned to ask the class: "Can a linear equation of this type ($ax = b$) have no solution?"

Ricardo wanted to discuss the students' answers in class, believing that this should help motivate them and keep them involved. Such work was understood as part of formative assessment, for which awarding formal points was not planned. Ricardo thought of giving such assignments during lessons that were devoted to the study of new concepts and algorithms.

Quizzes

Ricardo planned to give one quiz after studying the coordinate plane and introducing linear functions for the first time; another one after studying the algorithm for graphing linear functions; and finally, yet another after working on solving linear equations and doing assignments about interpreting graphs. Each quiz was to last 10–15 minutes. Some of the questions that Ricardo thought he might use in the first quiz were:

- Mark on the coordinate plane the following points $(2, 4)$, $(-4, -2)$;
- Which of the following relationships are linear: a) $y = 2 + x^2$; b) $y = 3x + 5$; c) $y = x - 1$.
- Which of these graphs (Figure 9.5) is that of a linear function? Give the value of the function depicted on the third graph, for $x = 2$.
- Maria has $10. Her mother gives her $3 each day. Let us assume Maria does not spend any of her money. (a) How much money does Maria have after one day? And after two days? And after three? (b) Does the diagram (Figure 9.6) accurately show how much money Maria has each day? If not, correct it; (c) Express with a formula how much money (y) Maria has on each day x. Is this a linear rela-

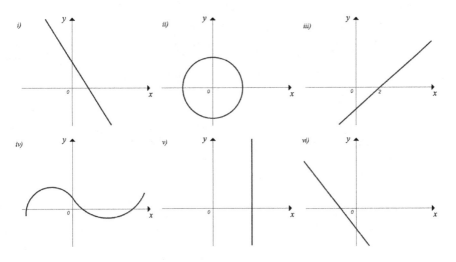

Figure 9.5

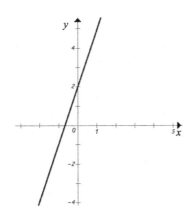

Figure 9.6

tionship? (d) Let us say that Maria does spend some of the money. Propose an amount of her daily expenditure so that the formula expressing the amount of money she has each day is still linear. Justify your answer; and (e) Propose some amount of her daily expenditure so that the amount of money she has each day cannot be described with a linear function.

Thus, among the quiz assignments, Ricardo included those that involved a direct reproduction of what had been learned, those where this knowledge needed to be applied, and finally, those where students were required to think independently and critically (while making use of the reasoning they already experienced in class). This first quiz (as well as the other two) contained questions that involved constructing and reading graphs, performing some calculations, manipulating variables, and also reasoning and exploring patterns.

In the last quiz Ricardo planned to make use of the graphing calculator. In his view, using the calculator would reduce purely technical difficulties that students might experience in constructing graphs, and enable him to diagnose more precisely what it was that students found difficult when solving equations and reading graphs. (On the final test, Ricardo planned to include problems where these skills would be combined with constructing graphs.)

His quiz included assignments of the following kind:

- Establish for which values x the function $y = 2x - 1$ has the value 5.
- Solve the equation $-\frac{1}{2}x + 1 = 2$.

Ricardo anticipated that, in completing such assignments with the aid of technology, students could use the calculator to help construct the necessary graph on the screen and then simply find the answer by using the graph. This way, even those who had not yet mastered the algorithm for constructing graphs—but who understood how to interpret graphs—would still be able to answer this type of assignment.

Final Test

Ricardo believed that the final test should be based on principles similar to those used on quizzes. At the same time, he did not think this test should be simply a larger collection of questions from all three parts of the unit. Ricardo wanted to include certain problems on the test that would require students to synthesize various aspects of what they had learned. To ensure this, Ricardo decided to use blocks of assignments on the exam, each consisting of several questions about a single situation. Answering these questions required students to view the situation from different perspectives.

For example, one of the problems that Ricardo planned to include looked like this:

A cyclist traveled at the speed of 10 miles per hour along a straight road connecting town A with town B. He traveled in the direction of town B and started his journey when he was 12 miles away from town A.

- How far away was he from town A after one hour?
- Write down the formula expressing the distance between town A and the cyclist depending on the length of time he had been traveling.
- Construct a graph of the dependency of the distance between town A and the cyclist from the time he had been traveling.
- When will the distance between the cyclist and town A equal 25 miles?
- Another cyclist started traveling along the same road at the same time as the first one. Figure 9.7 is the graph depicting the distance between the second cyclist and town A as a function of the time he had been traveling. How far was he from point A when he started his journey and how fast was he going?
- Construct a graph expressing the distance between the two cyclists as a function of time.

Ricardo did not imagine that students would have to complete all the assignments in the test successfully, but rather planned to define his exact evaluation criteria after the test had been completed. Of course, only students who demonstrated proficiency in answering the basic questions

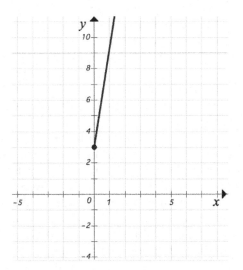

Figure 9.7

would pass the test, but delaying the specification of the evaluation criteria allowed him to factor in how the class as a whole coped with the work.

Homework Assignments

Ricardo planned to collect and grade each of the students' homework assignments. This grade was to be included as part of the final grade for the entire unit. Ricardo decided, however, to use a pass/fail grading scheme for each homework, rather than award detailed points. His argument was that homework was a means of studying a topic rather than its result. He did not want to punish students who could not do particular assignments at first but then learn how to do them through subsequent work in class and after additional consultation. Consequently, what Ricardo wanted to assess was whether the students had made maximal effort to solve the problem or not (and in particular, whether it was evident that work had been done, even if it did not produce the correct result).

Mini-Essays

Ricardo planned to ask students to write some slightly more elaborate answers to certain questions as homework. These would have the form of mini-essays that, in his view, allowed students to express their understanding of the issues tackled in the unit relatively open-endedly. One mini-essay topic concerned the practical application of linear functions. Students were asked to select any real life processes which could be modeled by a linear function or a piece-wise linear function, and to explain what sorts of questions could be answered by such modeling. Students were also asked to give an example of a process that could not be modeled by a linear function. (They were, of course, supposed to choose a problem that would differ from those already examined in class). Ricardo knew that not all students would take this assignment as seriously as others and that while some of them might use the internet or available literature, others were likely to limit themselves to only a slight modification of the standard school problems. Nonetheless, Ricardo still thought that this sort of assignment would be of use to students.

Ricardo also planned to give students a task that served both as a combination of a mini-essay and an experiment of sorts. The students were supposed to measure the temperature in their room at home three times during a day: before leaving for school, upon returning from school, and before going to bed. Then, they were to explain whether they thought the process of temperature change during the day was linear or not. They were also supposed to say why, even without any special experiments, one could immediately state that the change of outdoor temperature during the year is not a linear process. Ricardo believed that the verbal form of the assignment would help students develop their reasoning skills.

Group Project

Ricardo liked the work outlined in the article by Barnes (1999). The article discussed how students can work in groups on solving problems that are formulated as narratives. Here, students are meant to provide answers not in a purely mathematical form, but as a speech delivered in a court of law, for example, or as a movie script. Inspired by this example, Ricardo came up with the following assignment (giving different graphs and somewhat different stories to different groups).

Terrible things are happening in this world! Someone has broken into Rabbit's house and eaten all his jam! And this was not all: immediately afterwards, someone has taken all of Eeyore's honey from his house. Suspicion fell on Winnie-the-Pooh. But Winnie denied it all, saying that he had spent that evening at home, that he had perhaps exchanged a few words with Piglet who happened to be passing by, and that he had also been for a stroll to look at the clouds. Luckily, it turned out that Rabbit had enough foresight to install a mechanism in Winnie's house that constantly measured Winnie's distance from the house. Figure 9.8 is the graph depicting Winnie's movements. Write the speech of the prosecutor accusing Winnie of the above crime and also the speech of the lawyer defending him.

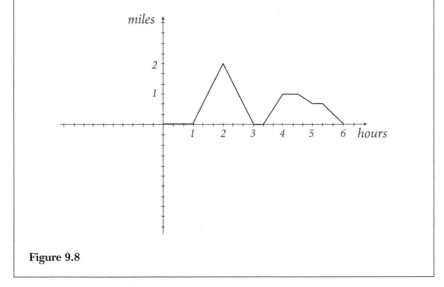

Figure 9.8

Some aspects of this assignment could be quite hard for students to deal with. For example, it may go unnoticed that no one ever claimed that Winnie was moving along a straight line (and hence that if, according to the graph, the distance appeared not to be changing, this did not necessarily mean that Winnie was not moving). Also, they might not consider whether the envisaged positioning of Rabbit's and Eeyore's houses was such that Winnie's movements could be deemed probable. Ricardo believed that a group discussion of how one should interpret the graph (discovering contradictions between the graph and Winnie-the-Pooh's testimony, and also thinking up different arguments either in Winnie's defense or as a justification of his indictment) would help students overcome these difficulties and learn how best to communicate their thoughts to others. However, the idea was to ask each student individually to write his or her own text on behalf of the prosecutor and the defense lawyer.

Interviews

Ricardo knew that he would not be able to interview each student during the lessons. However, he saw his office hours as an additional opportunity to speak to students who experienced particular problems and to discover from these conversations the likely cause of their difficulties. (Naturally, such interviews were not accompanied by any sort of formal grade.) In these conversations, Ricardo hoped to establish how interesting the topic was to the students, what they liked and disliked about it, and what sorts of difficulties they were experiencing in its study. In doing so, Ricardo carefully planned to observe each stage in the solution of particularly difficult problems, and, where necessary, then simplify the conditions during the discussion.

Grading Schema

Ricardo planned to give the final grade for the unit by using the following schema:

Class activity and homework—25%
Quizzes—20%
Mini-essays—10%
Group project—15%
Final test—30%

Discussion

One clear virtue of Ricardo's assessment plan is the variety of means of assessment, which include both oral and written work, both short and long assignments, both those testing the students' writing skills and those assuming the use of different forms of representation, both those that aim at reproducing acquired knowledge and those that require a further development and application of this knowledge. It is clear that Ricardo has understood and assimilated thoroughly the principles of the taxonomy of educational objectives (Bloom, 1956).

Ricardo's assessment questions also vary in terms of difficulty. For example, the last assignment in the final test above assumed both the independent derivation of the necessary formula in a comparatively unfamiliar situation and the construction of a graph, whereas the second assignment in the final test involved only the derivation of the formula, and this following a helpful recommendation—namely to calculate the distance between the cyclist and the town after one hour.

It is quite legitimate to claim that students who are capable of solving such a wide variety of assignments (including some that are quite new to them) have successfully mastered concepts and have acquired experience in making connections between different parts of mathematics as well as between mathematics and the real world. A teacher who has planned such assessment and bears it in mind when teaching the unit will also be successful in attaining the unit objectives that have been outlined above.

Of course, one must still accept that any approach to assessment has both its positive and negative aspects. For example, "one-minute papers" (the term was actually introduced by Bressoud (1999) to describe a type of work slightly different from the one outlined above) are very effective in getting students to reflect on a topic and in allowing the teacher to observe how they do this. At the same time, it is clear that this activity, let alone its analysis, can take up a substantial part of the lesson. As such, it may be counterproductive to overuse this form of assessment.

At the student teachers' seminar, debate revolved around Ricardo's scheme for calculating the final grade. Some expressed the view that "traditional" forms of assessment, such as tests and quizzes, should be given more weight, while others argued that more room should, on the contrary, be provided for homework and the student project. Here, as in so many other cases in teaching practice, it is hardly possible to give a general recommendation. Much still depends on the idiosyncrasies of the class as well as the tastes and inclinations of the teacher.

It is clear, however, that whatever means of assessment are applied, these need to be planned in advance and discussed with the students. The teacher can and must make students of the class conscious participants in the process of instruction. The aims and objectives of the unit need to be clear to students from the start. They must also understand fully the principles and methods of assessment. Only then will assessment fulfill its proper role as a motivational force and a support of learning.

Assignments and Topics for Discussion

1. Write about your impressions of Ricardo's assessment plan. What did you like about it and what would you have done differently?
2. Compile some assignments for Ricardo's second quiz (given after studying the algorithm for graphing linear functions).

3. Compile another block of assignments for the final test in the same unit.
4. Read the article by Barnes (1999). Come up with another assignment for a creative writing project.
5. The school principal has asked you to give an oral exam on functions and graphs. How would you organize it? What, in your view, are the pros and cons of this form of assessment?
6. Acquaint yourself with the book by Gold et al. (1999). Select from it an untraditional form of assessment and see if it can be used in the study of functions. If so, how exactly would you use it?
7. Pick any textbook in Algebra or Pre-Calculus and create an assessment plan for the unit devoted to quadratic functions in the textbook.

CHAPTER 10

SOLVING EQUATIONS
AND INEQUALITIES

This chapter continues the discussion of the study of algebra. Its aim is to outline the basic problems of teaching equations and inequalities at school. The chapter discusses:

- The role and significance of solving equations and inequalities in school mathematics and the treatment of these areas of mathematics in contemporary school textbooks.
- The main difficulties experienced by students and their typical errors in the study of linear and quadratic equations and inequalities.
- What research says about the causes of these difficulties and about ways of overcoming them.
- Some typical yet challenging problems on equations and inequalities.
- The planning of lessons devoted to the solving of word problems that can be reduced to linear equations, both in ordinary and advanced classes.

Mathematics in Middle and Secondary School, pages 269–307
Copyright © 2015 by Information Age Publishing
269

EQUATIONS AND INEQUALITIES: HOW THEY ARE STUDIED AND SOLVED

The very concepts of "equation" and "inequality," as well as of their "solutions," are far from straightforward. Algebraic methods of solving equations and inequalities also often cause students considerable difficulties. This is why we shall devote a separate chapter to this topic. However, it must be kept in mind that this topic is intimately linked to the study of patterns, functions and graphs. Equations describe patterns and can, as already mentioned, be solved with the help of graphs. Consequently, in this chapter we shall often mention functions, continuing the discussion started in the preceding chapters.

| **Examining** *an* **Example** | **From the Babylonians to Our Own Times: Three Solutions to One Problem** |

A person borrowed some money. The condition of the loan was for the money to be returned in a year's time, adding to it in interest a fifteenth of the amount borrowed. The value of the total amount the borrower had to return was 192 (in whichever currency). How much money was borrowed in the first place?

Such a problem can be found in almost any contemporary textbook. But similar problems already were being posed and solved thousands of years ago; they can be found on Ancient Egyptian papyruses and Babylonian clay tablets (Eves, 1990). It is easy to imagine situations where one would have to solve such problems. For example, a person knows that in a year's time he will have a certain amount of money (in our example, 192 of some currency), which he will be able to use towards the repayment of a loan, and he wants to know how much money he can borrow now.

A good student in a modern classroom would solve the problem using an algebraic expression and equation, akin to the following manner. Let us say that the money borrowed is x. The additional sum to be repaid in interest on top of this money is then $\frac{x}{15}$. This means that the total to be repaid is $x+\frac{x}{15}$, which, as specified, is 192. One therefore gets the equation $x+\frac{x}{15}=192$. Simplifying this, one gets $\frac{16x}{15}=192$. Multiply 192 by 15 and divide it by 16. The answer is: 180.

But here is another solution. Let us try out any number that one can easily find a fifteenth of (such as 30, for instance) and check if it fits. If one borrows 30 then one needs to return this plus 2 in interest, which makes 32. What one was supposed to get was 192, which is 6 times higher

(192 ÷ 32 = 6). This suggests that one ought to try out a number six times higher than 30: 30 · 6 = 180. The answer is therefore: 180. This is how Ancient Egyptians solved such problems, and how these problems were still being solved centuries later (Eves, 1990).

Nowadays, students who dislike algebra often approach the problem in a different way still. They try out a number slightly lower than 192—say, 170. The calculator tells them that the sum to be added to this as interest at the end of the year is 11.33. But the figure they then get—181.33—is too low. So they try out something slightly higher—say, 175. The repayment is then 186.66—i.e., still too low. Finally, they go for 180. The interest now is 180 ÷ 15 = 12 and the total is 192, i.e., exactly what was needed! The answer is therefore: 180. The efficiency of the modern day calculator makes this approach of "guess and check" not terribly inconvenient or time consuming.

Discussion

As we have seen, there are many different ways of solving this ancient problem. Yet students often think that to solve equations or inequalities all that is needed is to learn a rule (an algorithm), which will supposedly enable them to reach the correct answer without fail. In reality, however, solving equations and inequalities is by no means reducible to learning rules by heart. As we have seen above, several different algorithms could be utilized for solving one and the same kind of problem, which makes conceptual understanding of solutions and equations even more important. It would therefore be particularly good if classroom lessons encouraged students to come up with different possible ways of solving an equation independently and then to discuss the respective advantages and disadvantages of these methods.

For example, here are a few questions that naturally could arise for discussing the solutions carried out above.

- Is it appropriate to use the method of the Ancient Egyptians (which was later known in Europe as "the rule of false position")?
- Is it appropriate to use the method of the student who dislikes algebra?
- Finally, why is the first method outlined above considered to be the "best" one?

In order to answer these questions it is important to consider what is really being asked in the problem, or, in other words, to understand the very concept of "solving an equation."

The correct answer is clearly 180. But simply providing the right answer does not exhaust the solution. One could, in fact, have had two or three correct answers, and the solution of an equation actually presumes the discovery of all possible answers. In the above case, however, it was sufficient to indicate the one answer that fits because linear equations with a non-zero coefficient of the unknown can only have one solution. Thus, all three methods were able to lead to the correct solution. But would they all be as effective with other linear equations? And if so—why?

The justification of all three methods is given below as one of the assignments. Let us just emphasize once more that the standard school algorithm is by no means the only appropriate one (or indeed, for many students, the easiest one) that one should always automatically apply.

What Sorts of Equations and Inequalities are Studied at School?

Equations and inequalities are some of the essential tools of school algebra. It would probably be fair to say that most school assignments in mathematics are reducible to equations or inequalities. What is important is that equations and inequalities enable the solution of real life problems that arise before people in their everyday activities. They are not just special school exercises that teach students a particular abstract solution method, which seems (at least at first glance) to be of use only at school. For many years now mathematics educators have argued that the organization of the algebra course should center on the equation and its uses (Barber, 1932). Consequently, much attention today is accorded to constructing and solving equations and inequalities.

At first it might appear that the amount of mathematical material to be studied here is not all that large. Students need to learn about linear equations of the type $ax = b$ and $ax + b = cx + d$, about quadratic equations, and also (though usually not everyone) about more complex equations that are reducible to quadratic ones and those that are linked to the study of elementary functions, such as, for example, $2^x = 4$ or $\sin x = \frac{1}{2}$. Students are also likely to come across systems of equations (usually of the linear kind). The study of inequalities, on the other hand, is usually exhausted by learning how to solve linear and, sometimes, quadratic inequalities, whereas proving the solutions for inequalities is practically never done.

And yet not all students are likely to master all the required materials. Why is that? One of the reasons is that mistakes and difficulties mentioned in previous chapters are likely to manifest themselves in solving equations and inequalities. Yet many student errors are actually linked to an inadequate understanding of certain key concepts. This is why simple practice and repetition without proper explanations of why and for what purpose things are done the way they are often fails to bring about the desired results. Thus, learning in the classroom needs to focus on developing students' conceptual understanding of solving equations and inequalities.

Solving Linear Equations

Linear equations are the simplest and at the same time the most common type of equation in school practice. As already mentioned earlier, linear functions are used for modeling many different processes that can be observed in economics, physics, biology, and everyday life. Consequently, in all these spheres one has to examine equations of the type $ax = b$ or those reducible to them.

Despite the indubitable practicality of linear equations, students often perceive the common methods for solving them, which they learn at school, as something artificial. It seems far easier to them to reason numerically without the help of equations (and variables in general). The episode below records a dialogue that took place during an actual lesson.

Examining
an **Example**   **Episode from a Lesson**

> **Teacher:** (dictating the problem) "Three bagels and a cup of coffee cost \$2.95, while two bagels and a cup of coffee cost \$2.30. How much does a bagel cost and how much is a cup of coffee?"
>
> **Student:** A bagel is 65 cents, and a cup of coffee . . . , just a second, the cup of coffee is \$1.
>
> **Teacher:** Good job, but the answer itself is not enough. You need to show me how you got this. What sorts of equations did you construct?
>
> **Student:** None actually. For $2.95 - 2.30 = 0.65$, which means that a bagel costs 65 cents. Two bagels is then \$1.30, and the coffee is $\$2.30 - \$1.30 = \$1$.
>
> **Teacher:** This is not what you are supposed to do in the exam. For that sort of solution you won't get full credit. Let's look at what you actually need to do first. First you need to introduce a variable. What variable are we going to choose for the price of a bagel? . . .

From this point on things then carried on as one might have expected. With some effort the class formulated the equations $3x + y = 2.95$ and $2x + y = 2.30$, and then had even greater difficulty solving these.

The conclusion from this episode is simple: if you want to show students how useful it is to apply equations and to use the particular solving methods that you teach them, then you have to select the kind of tasks or assignments where equations are genuinely useful! Otherwise, despite the undisputed usefulness of linear equations, and the fact that the methods used to solve them are the most convenient and reliable, students may be persuaded that these methods are being studied simply for the purposes of completing an exam or (at the very best) for some special situations they are not familiar with.

Reflecting on Research: What research says about student difficulties associated with the lack of conceptual understanding
In Chapter 7 we already mentioned the difficulties experienced by students in connection with constructing equations and even understanding the equals sign itself. Research (Byers & Herscovisc, 1977) has already noted that students sometimes use the sign " = " simply as a divider and that they perform operations on each side without any care, yet in the end still reach the correct answer. For example, they might write down a solution in the following way.

Solve for x:

$$6x+3 = 4x+5$$

$$6x+3-3 = 4x+5$$

$$6x = 4x+5$$

$$6x = 4x+5-4x-3$$

$$6x-4x = 5-3$$

$$2x = 2$$

$$x = 1$$

Even before getting to the transformation of an equation during the solving process, the concept of the "solution" of an equation itself often causes problems. Difficulties experienced by many students (including those in high school) when solving equations of the type $5x-3x+2 = 2(x+1)$ demonstrate this well. It is clear that the equation should be reduced to the form $0 \cdot x = 0$. Students unfamiliar with this situation then give all manner of inappropriate answers such as: "the equation has disappeared," "there are no solutions (since there is no equation)" or "$x = 0$." They find it difficult to comprehend that the solution to this equation is, in fact, any number. And the reason for this probably lies not so much in the fact that they rarely encounter this kind of assignment in school practice, but also that they do not even consider what a "solution" of an equation actually means.

Wagner (1981) provided an interesting example of an assignment that tested students' understanding of the concept of the "solution of an equation." Students were given two equations, $7W + 22 = 109$ and $7N + 22 = 109$, and they were then asked to establish which would be greater, W or N. Experiments demonstrated that the majority of students either thought that they first needed to solve each equation separately and only then provide an answer, or else they gave altogether wrong answers.

Some Conclusions and Recommendations

Such findings yet again force us to consider how school practice relates mathematical procedures to mathematical content. So many students learn the algorithm but fail to understand what it is exactly they are doing. Likely, this can be explained by the fact that far more attention is devoted to algorithmic assignments (and assessments) than to work with concepts.

It is important to work on the concept of the "solution" of an equation, and to explain to students why it is necessary at each stage of the solution process to maintain an equation with the same solution set. This does not imply that teachers should even use the word "equivalence," or other special terminology, let alone the sign for equivalence, "⇔". A formal use of these or any other additional terms and symbols does not necessarily help students reach proper conceptual understanding. Only in the process of solving and discussing a variety of relevant problems can students grasp the essence and meaning of concepts, learning how to reason about a process and not just mechanically complete a procedure.

Here are some examples of problems that would allow students to work with the concept of the "solution of an equation."

- Is it true that 2 is the solution of the equation $3x + 2 = 5$?
- Give an example of any equation that would have the solution 2.
- Do equations $2x + 5 = 3$ and $2x - 3 = -5$ have the same solutions?

A more complex assignment would be the following: What should the coefficient "a" be for the equation $ax = 4$ to have the solution 1? Try to think of other problems of this type.

Reflecting on Research: On different methods for solving linear equations

Even the simplest of linear equations can, as we have seen, be solved by a whole variety of means. Kieran (1992) cites a range of different solving methods, in addition to those that are usually recommended in textbooks and the basic trial-and-error substitution method. Among them are the following:

A. Use of number facts (e.g., when solving, for instance, the equation $3 + x = 5$, students can simply recall that $3 + 2 = 5$ and can therefore give the correct answer—2—straightaway)

B. Use of counting techniques (e.g., when solving the same equation, $3 + x = 5$ students count, starting from 3, until they get to 5 (...4, 5) and note that there were two numbers after 3 and that 2 is therefore the solution)

C. Cover-up (e.g., when solving the equation $3x + 4 = 5x$ students note that 4 ought to equal $2x$ as they are simultaneously considering the equation $3x + 2x = 5x$, and from this they conclude that $x = 2$).

Kieran (1992) also noted that certain solving methods that are basically the same, such as, for example, the method of performing the same operations on both sides and the method of transposing (Change Side—Change Sign), are often perceived by beginning algebra students as completely different.

As already discussed, it would be wrong as a matter of principle to tell students that their method of solving the equation is incorrect simply because they happen to be using a method different from the one recommended by the teacher. The use of "one's own" method, in fact, demonstrates that the student is solving the problem with thought and understanding. Teachers should certainly not rush to dismiss the students' own ways of arriving at the solution. Even a method such as "the use of number facts" above, which appears like sheer guesswork, in reality, suggests that the student possesses a certain degree of number sense, based on their original and subsequent attempts. The fact that the teacher can provide situations where the student would recognize the limited nature of this method, however, is a totally different matter.

| **Examining** |
| **an Example** |

Moving from One Method to Another

While solving the equation $3 + x = 100$ by using the "counting technique" above will undoubtedly produce the correct solution, it is obvious that this is not a particularly convenient way of doing so since a significant amount of time is required to count from three to one hundred. It is possible, therefore, in the course of discussing different equations that the student would gradually move towards using more "common" methods. For instance, students could start by modifying their own method: in order to solve the equation $3 + x = 100$ they would need to count from 4 to 100, and they may realize that since they know that there are 100 whole numbers counting from 1 to 100, and that three of them are not higher than 3, that they would count 97 numbers. This would make students see that the problem can be solved by subtraction. This in itself would be an important step, which could then be developed further.

Using the Idea of Inverse Operation: On a Particular Classroom Technique

As already mentioned in Chapter 7, in order to be able to study algebra well, it is vital to have a solid foundation in arithmetic. Similarly, in order to solve equations it is very important to be able to apply arithmetic operations with understanding: especially to comprehend subtraction as the inverse of addition and division as the inverse of multiplication.

Swan (2002) proposes the use of assignments where the process of solving linear equations is understood as the reverse of constructing them. Consequently, students are first asked to create equations: they do so gradually, step by step, together with the teacher and they take note of each individual stage. Here is an example of how one could proceed:

Write down $x = 1$.
Multiply this by 3: $3x = 3$.
Subtract 2: $3x - 2 = 1$.
Divide by 5: $\dfrac{3x-2}{5} = \dfrac{1}{5}$.

Once the equation is created, students can start solving it. The process now moves in reverse, from the more complex equation to the original starting point $x = 1$, which becomes the solution. In doing so, students are asked to think what sorts of operations they would need to perform at each step in order to get to the line above. Students thereby note that in order to "cancel out" the division by 5, they need to multiply by 5 and in order to "cancel out" the subtraction by 2 they must add 2, and so forth. After such exercises students find it easier to solve equations that they themselves have not created. They now get into the habit of figuring out which operation was last used in order to obtain the equation and they consider which operation to use in order to cancel that one out. They follow this line of thinking until they reach the solution.

On the Use of Models

It is also appropriate to use models in order to make clearer to students the meaning of particular operations in solving linear equations. Kieran (1992) mentioned research, however, that argued that the application of models did not seem to have much influence on how students operated with symbols. It is true that students can often see models as something entirely separate from the symbolic notation of equations, and that models frequently have specific limitations associated with them. However, it seems that this is precisely why their interconnection should be emphasized and different ways of representing one and the same equation should be

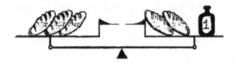

Figure 10.1

demonstrated, hopefully accomplishing an even richer understanding of a particular algorithmic path and its meaning.

Probably the most prevalent means of explaining to students how solving a linear equation works is by using a balance. Students can, for example, be shown a balance in equilibrium, where one side contains three loaves of bread and the other two loaves and a 1lb weight (one could also use an illustration of this situation (Figure 10.1)). Students can be asked to determine the weight on one loaf of bread. Once the students have proposed the obvious answer (1 lb) the teacher can remove two loaves from each side and show that the one remaining loaf does, indeed, weigh 1 lb. From the conceptual model, asking students to reflect on the symbolic notation of the equation $3x = 2x + 1$ and how it could be solved helps reinforce the algebraic process. This model, too, however, has particular limitations, as "negative objects" can be especially hard to depict.

Examples from geometry can also be used. In Figure 10.2, the two figures are known to have the same area. The first is made of three identical pieces of an unknown area, while the second is made of two such pieces and a rectangle whose area is 1. Students are asked to determine the area of the five identical figures. This is yet another model for the same equation $3x = 2x + 1$. By asking students to solve this problem, to write it down symbolically and to consider what equation has actually been solved, the teacher helps students broaden their understanding both of the concept of "equation" itself and of ways of solving equations.

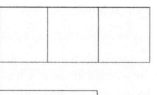

Figure 10.2

Manipulatives (including algebra tiles), both commercial ones and those that are self-created, can serve as another useful model for equations. The previous chapter discussed the use of graphs in studying and solving equations (especially linear ones). Pedagogical literature also dwells on the experience of using technology even in the early stages where students are only beginning to study linear equations (e.g., Klein & Kertay, 2002). The use of such aids is beneficial insofar as it allows students to recognize immediately that a process has a linear character. It thereby persuades them of the importance of solving linear equations.

Solving Quadratic Equations

Quadratic equations are one of the most traditional topics in school mathematics. In the previous chapter we discussed the modeling of real world processes with the help of quadratic functions. This means that when studying these processes it is also useful to solve quadratic equations.

There are two particularly good examples of the use of quadratic functions (and, therefore, quadratic equations). If the speed at which a point moves along a straight line at the moment t is given with the formula $V(t) = V_0 + at$ (where V_0 is the initial velocity and a is acceleration) then the distance covered is given with the formula

$$S = S_0 + V_0 t + \frac{at^2}{2}$$

(where S_0 is the distance covered at the initial moment).

The other example comes from geometry. Areas of polygons can often be expressed as values of quadratic functions. For example, the area of the figure bounded by the coordinate axes and the straight lines $y = 2x + 3$ and $x = a$ (Figure 10.3a) is given with the formula $a^2 + 3a$. A simpler example is the rectangle with the sides x and $x + 3$, whose area is then $x^2 + 3x$ (Figure 10.3b).

Quadratic equations are the simplest example of non-linear equations. The teacher's task is gradually to prepare students for the acquisition of broader concepts—students are first acquainted with specific equations, linear ones, but it then becomes desirable gradually to move on to solving equations more generally and the first step in this direction is toward quadratic equations.

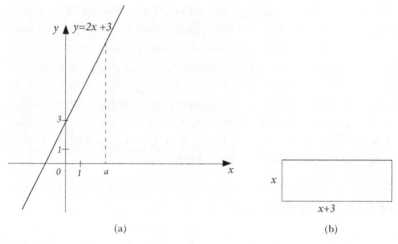

(a) (b)

Figure 10.3

Reflecting on Research: Moving from linear equations to quadratic equations

Difficulties that students have in solving quadratic equations are most often attributable to their fundamental difference from linear equations and to the problem of relying on old knowledge in a new situation (Matz, 1982; Zaslavsky, 1997). Seemingly meaningless actions (such as, for example, the following "solution" of the equation $x^2 = 4x - 3$: $x = \sqrt{4x - 3}$) are explicable by the uncritical use of previous experience acquired in the process of solving linear equations.

Linear equations always have solutions (apart from those, seemingly rare in school textbooks, that are reducible to the form $0 \cdot x = a$, where $a \neq 0$, such as, for instance, the equation $3x - x = 2(x - 1)$), whereas quadratic functions can be without real solutions or they can have one or two solutions. Linear equations are solved by a direct use of inverse operations, while quadratic functions, at first glance at least, require a fundamentally different approach. Finally, quadratic equations are technically more complex, and their solution requires procedures that are far more complicated than those used for linear equations. You must be prepared for the fact that every one of these differences can cause difficulties for students. We discuss below how to make the transition from linear equations to quadratic ones smoother.

Main Methods for Solving Quadratic Equations

One can cite three basic algebraic methods for solving quadratic equations. The first method involves factoring the equation and then applying the assertion that the product of polynomials equals zero if and only if at least one of these polynomials equals zero. The virtue of this method lies in the fact that it is relatively easy for students to apply. It is usually not difficult to guess the appropriate numbers, and one does not even need to perform complicated algebraic transformations or grasp some radically new concepts.

The drawback of this method is that its usefulness is limited to only a relatively small number of cases. One could even say without exaggeration that it is suitable only for specially selected problems that one finds in school textbooks. When it comes to quadratic equations found in the real world, solutions are usually not integers and are consequently not as easy to guess. Furthermore, the method of factoring the equation often leads students to the fundamentally mistaken view that if one cannot "guess" how to factor a trinomial, then this means that it does not have a solution (e.g., the equation $x^2 - 2x - 1 = 0$). Usiskin (1980) argues that solving quadratic equations by factoring quadratic trinomials ought, in fact, to be excluded from the school syllabus (this recommendation is also expressed in the National Council of Teachers of Mathematics Curriculum and the Evaluation Standards for School Mathematics (1989)).

The second method for solving quadratic equations is that of "completing the square" and then extracting its square root. This method can be applied in all cases but presumes a far greater skill of manipulating variables and therefore cannot be used as a basic method.

The third method is to use the formula for quadratic equations

$$(x = \frac{-b \pm \sqrt{b^2 - 4ac}}{2a} \text{ for the quadratic equation } ax^2 + bx + c = 0).$$

The formula itself can be derived by the method of "completing the square." Using it is, of course, easier than carrying out algebraic transformations, but similarly can cause difficulties.

On Mistakes in Using the Formula for Quadratic Equations.
Some Recommendations.

The most common conceptual mistakes in applying such a formula are associated with erroneous interpretations of the letters used in the formula. For example, students often think that the a in the formula is not the leading coefficient, but simply the first number that appears in a particular notation. Consequently, they assume that in the equation $3 - 4x + x^2 = 0$, $a = 3$, while $c = 1$.

In order to overcome such mistakes the teacher should give assignments where equations would be written down in different forms ($4x - x^2 - 3 = 0$ and $3 + x^2 - 4x = 0$) and where students would be asked to determine the values of the coefficients in the formula.

The source of many student errors is the mechanical application of formulas and a failure to see that the answers obtained are implausible. Situations where students are, for instance, solving the equation $x^2 - 8x + 9 = 0$, mistakenly put +36 instead of –36, and write

$$x = \frac{8 \pm \sqrt{64 + 36}}{2},$$

getting the results $x = 9$ and $x = -1$, is fairly common. In committing this error students fail to notice that this answer could not be obtained since the product of solutions must be 9 (as is clear from factoring). Roebuck (1997) points out that it is useful to combine the use of formulas with the factoring method. Indeed, spending extra time on checking solutions and examining their plausibility is particularly important today since the use of technology greatly reduces the time required for the calculation itself, while the value of knowing how to analyze results is surely going to increase over time.

One Possible Sequence for Studying Quadratic Equations

Some research (Movshovitz-Hadar, 1993) argues in favor of the creation of a transition from linear functions and equations to quadratic ones by first studying quadratic functions in the form $y = a(x-b)(x-c)$. Solving equations of the type $(x-b)(x-c) = 0$ and even $(ax+b)(cx+d) = 0$ is a natural sequel to the study of linear equations, while simultaneously providing students with an opportunity to broaden their understanding of what an equation is and what its solutions can be. In this context, a few examples of standard quadratic equations that can be solved by means of factoring can also be examined: $x^2 - 3x = 0$ or $x^2 - 4x + 3 = 0$. Here the teacher does not need to get all the students to solve such equations by means of factoring. On the contrary, the teacher can show the limitedness of this method and its uselessness in the majority of cases, demonstrating to students the need for a more reliable method. The study of the formula for solutions of quadratic equations (based on "completing the square") can still conclude with the discussion of how to use it to factor a trinomial and also of how to obtain and use the equalities

$$x_1 \cdot x_2 = \frac{c}{a} \text{ and } x_1 + x_2 = -\frac{b}{a},$$

where x_1 and x_2 are the solutions of the quadratic equation $ax^2 + bx + c = 0$ (Usiskin et al, 2003). In particular, these equations enable one to check the solutions obtained from the formula for quadratic equations (as discussed above). Time gained by abandoning a detailed study of factoring as the primary means of solving quadratic equations can no doubt be better spent on improving the students' conceptual understanding of the topic and on applying what has been learned.

Establishing Connections with the Study of Graphs

In conclusion, let us note that it is important for students to see the link between solving quadratic equations and studying the graph of a quadratic trinomial. Graphs and properties of functions were discussed in greater detail in previous chapters; here we simply reiterate the importance of studying these parts of mathematics in connection once more. Students can and should be given assignments where they would be asked to relate a graph and an equation. Here are some examples of such assignments specifically for quadratic equations:

Examining *an* Example

- The graph of the parabola $y = ax^2 + bx + c$ traverses points $(2, 0)$ and $(5, 0)$. Indicate the solutions of the equation $ax^2 + bx + c = 0$.
- The equation $ax^2 + bx + c = 0$ has solutions $x = 1$ and $x = 3$. What do you think the graph of the function $y = ax^2 + bx + c$ looks like? Draw it and compare your graph with that of your neighbor. Are they the same? Do they have to be the same?
- It is known that the abscissa (or x-coordinate) of the vertex of the parabola $y = ax^2 + bx + c$ equals 3. Is it possible that the solutions of the equation $ax^2 + bx + c = 0$ are: a) $x = -2$, $x = -5$; b) both negative; c) both positive; d) one positive and the other negative?

Zaslavsky (1997), basing her argument on Silver (1990), speaks of the importance of using in regular school practice such non-standard assignments about quadratic functions that are usually found only in pedagogical research on mathematics teaching. Such assignments can help the teacher diagnose conceptual obstacles faced by students and they can also contribute towards overcoming them. For example, Zaslavsky (1997) remarked that students often think that quadratic trinomials that have the same roots, such as $x^2 - 4x + 3$ and $2x^2 - 8x + 6$, could be considered effectively the same (which, on the model of equations, is true that they can genuinely be treated as if they are the same, providing they are equivalent, though on the model of functions, they may differ). The second of the above-quoted assignments could help tackle this fallacy.

Solving and Proving Inequalities

Solving inequalities is rightly considered to be one of the most difficult topics in the school syllabus. At the same time, inequalities could, in fact, be considered to be even more important as a means of modeling the real world than equations. In everyday practice one very frequently has to establish certain limitations and make certain evaluations, which basically amounts to working with inequalities. Situations for comparison and contrast, without which no conscious choice can be made, are also essentially reducible to inequalities. Consequently the ability to solve inequalities and represent their solution in different ways is of vital importance. Moreover, the study of inequalities broadens, generalizes and deepens the knowledge gained in working on equations.

Examining an Example

Example of a Real Life Problem Reducible to the Study of Inequalities

First, we look at a problem type that almost everyone is likely to tackle at some point.

A man is required to make regular phone calls to two different foreign countries. Table 10.1 represents prices for 1 minute of talk-time offered by two different companies (there are no connection charges).

TABLE 10.1

	First country	Second country
First company	10 cents	4 cents
Second company	16 cents	2 cents

In which case would it make sense to use the services of the second company?

Solution: Let us say that the man plans to spend x minutes talking with the first country and y minutes with the second country. In that case, if he plans to use the first company he will need to pay $10x + 4y$. If he uses the second company he will have to pay $16x + 2y$. It would be preferable to use the second company if the following inequality applied $10x + 4y > 16x + 2y$, or, in other words, if $2y > 6x$, i.e., if $y > 3x$. The answer is therefore that it is more profitable to use the services of the second company only if the man plans to make more than three times as many phone calls to the second country than to the first country.

Methods for Solving Inequalities in School Mathematics

Tsamir and Almog (2001) cite three basic methods used to solve in-equalities at school: algebraic manipulations, drawing a graph and using the number line.

The first method is used, for example, when solving inequalities such as $5x - 3 > 8x$. We add $-8x$ to both sides of the inequality and get $-3x - 3 > 0$. We then add 3 to both sides and get $-3x > 3$. Finally, by dividing both sides by -3 and by changing the inequality sign we get the answer $x < -1$. Tsamir and Almog (2001) see this method as also applicable to the solution of quadratic equations of the type $(x - a)(x - b) > 0$ where one uses the assertion that the product is positive only if both factors are positive or if both are negative, and then solves the systems

$$\begin{cases} x - a > 0 \\ x - b > 0 \end{cases} \text{ and } \begin{cases} x - a < 0 \\ x - b < 0 \end{cases}.$$

The second method is applied in the following way, when solving, for example, the inequality $x^2 - 4x + 3 > 0$. Let us graph the function $y = x^2 - 4x + 3$ and outline all its points that have a positive ordinate (Figure 10.4). We then see that the abscissas of all these points can be defined by the condition $x > 3$ or $x < 1$.

The third method is applied by first solving the equation $x^2 - 4x + 3 = 0$. Its solutions are $x = 1$ and $x = 3$. By placing these on the number-line, the line is now divided by these two points into three intervals (Figure 10.5). Let

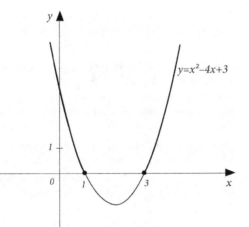

Figure 10.4

Figure 10.5

us now take any random number from each of these intervals (e.g., $x = 0$, $x = 2$ and $x = 5$) to check if the inequality applies to these values. It is clear that $0^2 - 4 \cdot 0 + 3 = 3 > 0$, $2^2 - 4 \cdot 2 + 3 = -1 < 0$ and $5^2 - 4 \cdot 5 + 3 = 8 > 0$. We conclude that the solution of the inequality are the intervals from which we selected the numbers to which the inequality applies (this follows from the Intermediate value theorem (Usiskin et al, 2003)). The answer is therefore: $x > 3$ or $x < 1$.

Students often use these three methods in combination. For example, one first does some algebraic transformations and then constructs a graph.

Reflecting on Research: On the most common mistakes in solving inequalities

Among errors committed by students in solving inequalities (Tsamir and Almog, 2001), the one that ought to be mentioned first is probably the mechanical application of the algorithm devised for the corresponding equation. For example, when solving the inequality $-4x > -8$, students get $x > 2$, because they simply divide both sides by -4 (which would indeed lead to the correct solution if this were the equation $-4x = -8$). When solving the inequality $x^2 > 4$, they sometimes write down the meaningless solution $x > \pm 2$, by analogy with $x = \pm 2$, which is the correct solution of the equation $x^2 = 4$. When solving a somewhat more complicated inequality $\frac{2}{x} < 1$, students multiply both sides by x, and get $2 < x$, which is clearly incorrect since it implies that the solution excludes all negative numbers (although for the equation $\frac{2}{x} = 1$ such a multiplication would indeed lead to the correct answer $x = 2$).

Another class of mistake encountered in solving inequalities consists of logical errors and the failure to take into account all possible cases. For example, when solving the inequality $(x - 1)(x - 4) < 0$ and when considering cases where the first factor is negative and the second positive, students sometimes examine the inequalities $x - 1 < 0$ and $x - 4 > 0$ separately and this is how they write down the answer: $x < 1$ and $x > 4$. At other times, students limit themselves to the examination of only one possible case—for example, for the above inequality $(x - 1)(x - 4) < 0$ they forget to examine the case

$$\begin{cases} x - 1 > 0 \\ x - 4 < 0 \end{cases}.$$

There are also usually errors concerning boundary values and their inclusion or exclusion in the answer. For example, in solving the inequality

$$\frac{x-3}{x-2} \leq 0$$

students sometimes fail to include 3 in the answer, or else mistakenly include 2.

How to Tackle These and Similar Mistakes?

These and similar errors committed in solving inequalities show that the solution is often carried out without thought, as if performing a ritual that is empty of meaning. Applying the different methods discussed above on a single problem can be a useful way of drawing the students' attention to the content and meaning of the algorithms they are using. Such a combination of different approaches, which allows the use of multiple representations of the same concept, is recommended in pedagogical literature (e.g., Piez & Voxman, 1997; Parish 1992; Edgecomb, 1987). In particular, the approach can be utilized in solving linear inequalities where graphing methods are usually applied much less frequently than in solving the more complex quadratic inequalities. In these contexts, the use of graphing calculators opens up many additional possibilities.

Examining *an* **Example**   **Episode from a Lesson**

The teacher gives students two assignments: 1) Solve the inequality $x > 2x - 3$; 2) Examine, using a graphic calculator, the functions $y = x$ and $y = 2x - 3$, and say when the former lies above the latter.

The class completes the assignments and then goes on to discuss them.

> **Joe:** So . . . We write $x - 2x > 2x - 3 - 2x$, then $-x > -3$. And now we divide $x > 3$.
> **Teacher:** And what about the other assignment?
> **Lisa:** This is the picture I got (Figure 10.6).
> **Joe:** Same here.
> **Teacher:** So when does the graph of the function $y = x$ lie above the graph for $y = 2x - 3$ then?
> **Joe:** . . . Well, at the start—here (he points).
> **Teacher:** So, for which x?
> **Joe:** Hmmm. Less than 3. . . . Whoops . . . I must have made a mistake.

The class then goes on to discuss Joe's mistake.

Clarifying the meaning of operations that are carried out.   We have already argued above that one must spend more time discussing with students the very concept of the solution of an inequality, and that one must give them

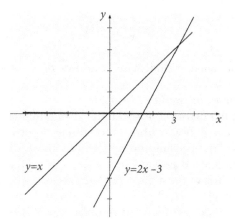

Figure 10.6

assignments that would foster checking the solutions they have reached. In particular, it is useful to give assignments where they would have to provide examples of numbers that would work as solutions (for example, questions like: "name a number that satisfies the inequality $x > \pm 2$" or "does 0 satisfy this inequality?" would help students realize the meaninglessness of the answer $x > \pm 2$). Equally useful is the examination of real-life situations that lead to a given inequality, or the formulation of various word problems that would be reducible to it.

Failure to perceive the content of problems and an over-reliance on learning algorithms, which lead to errors mentioned above, are often the result of studying these algorithms. If an algorithm is presented to students without its proof or any sort of explanation it is only to be expected that students will not see any sense in it. This, however, is precisely how algorithms for solving inequalities are sometimes presented to students: "How can you solve the one-step linear inequality $x - 2 < 4$? Add 2 and you will get the answer $x < 6$." This is often where the explanation ends.

The grounding of algorithms does not necessarily have to be mathematically rigorous. Using students' own everyday experiences can be sufficient reference. Students are normally very familiar with problems of the following type: "Sharon has less money than Tracy. The girls receive $10 each. Who has more money now?" Using these examples it is easy to formulate the general rule that if $a < b$, then $a + c < b + c$ for any numbers a, b and c. The above-mentioned algorithm derives from precisely this rule.

On Proofs of Inequalities

There are also numerous examples of real-life situations where we, in effect, prove rather than solve inequalities. One *proves* that there is not enough money for some expense, that this path is shorter than another, or that the soup can be poured from one saucepan into another. The proven inequalities can be quite simple, but they can also be extremely complex. Unfortunately, very little time at school is devoted to proving inequalities. And yet such assignments would be as useful in developing students' reasoning and proving skills as the more commonly used geometrical proofs. (For example, see assignment 13 below.)

The teacher usually does not have the opportunity to go into different proofs of inequalities (and this in fact is not necessary anyway). However, teaching students to solve inequalities ought to be done in combination with proofs and justification. This is the only way to achieve a conscious acquisition of the material studied.

Reflection

Assignments and Topics for Discussion

1. Demonstrate that every linear equation with a nonzero leading coefficient has only one solution. Provide a graphic interpretation of this assertion.

2. How would you justify the first method used to solve the loan problem described at the beginning of this chapter?

3. Justify the rule of false position. To do so, demonstrate that if $at + bt = k$, and $\frac{c}{k} = p$, then the number pt is the solution of the equation $ax + bx = c$.

4. Demonstrate that a linear equation which has a whole number solution can always be solved by the method of trial and error, as in solving the problem of the loan. Why can this method not be applied in other cases?

5. The equation $5x+2=3x+3$ has been solved by a student in the following manner: $7x = 6x, 7x - 6x = 0, x = 0$. Where exactly did the student make a mistake? How would you explain to the student the error of his strategy by using models?

6. Interview a few students (or observe their work in class): what do you see as the most typical mistakes they make in solving quadratic equations by factoring?

7. The following equation is examined: $x^2 + px + 5 = 0$. a) Can both its solutions be higher than 3? b) Can its solutions be one positive and one negative? c) Can both its solutions be irrational numbers? d) Can one of the solutions of this equation be a rational and the other an irrational number? e) Can both solutions of this equation be whole numbers if p is a fraction?

8. Think up a few more assignments, being modeled after the previous question, where the student is asked to establish what the equation's solutions can and cannot be.

9. Think up several assignments for which the solution requires students to correlate the quadratic equation $ax^2 + bx + c = 0$ and the graph of the function $y = ax^2 + bx + c$.

10. The following formula has been proposed as the solution of the quadratic equation

$$ax^2 + bx + c = 0 : x = \frac{2c}{-b \pm \sqrt{b^2 - 4ac}}.$$

Does it work for the equation $x^2 + 4x + 3 = 0$? Explain why it is unsuitable if $c = 0$. Explain why it is correct in all other cases.

11. Prepare a plan for studying the unit devoted to quadratic equations, in accordance with the plan that has been sketched out above (in the section "One possible sequence for studying quadratic equations").

12. How would you explain to students different ways of solving the inequality $2x < 14$ that use the three methods described in the last section of this unit?

13. Prove that the path from home to school in Figure 10.7 via Route A is shorter than via Route B.

14. Formulate any word problem, the solution of which would be reducible to the inequality: a) $2x + 3 < 15$; b) $x^2 - 4x > 12$.

15. How would you justify to students that $x > 3$ is the solution of the inequality $4x > 12$?

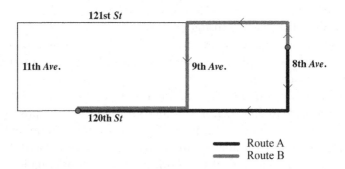

Figure 10.7

HOW TO SOLVE IT? A SELECTION OF PROBLEMS

This section will examine some relatively difficult equations and inequalities that intend to be representative of some particularly important types of assignments and methods of solution.

Example 1

Solve the equation $(x-1)x(x+1)(x+2) = 24$.

Discussion and Solution

The equation can be solved by several methods. Using a graphing calculator the student can visualize the function $y = (x-1)x(x+1)(x+2) - 24$ and see that it traverses the x-axis at two points: $x = 2$ and $x = -3$. Drawing a picture is a useful problem solving strategy. However, the solution that involves the use of a graphing calculator is not considered to be entirely rigorous. To test rigorously whether the numbers $x = 2$ and $x = -3$ are indeed solutions of the given equation is easy—it is sufficient to plug them into the equation and see that the equation is satisfied. However, to construct the graph of the function $y = (x-1)x(x+1)(x+2) - 24$ and to determine that this graph does not cross the x-axis on other places, one needs to use Calculus. Such a solution is certainly possible, but requires fairly advanced knowledge.

Once we have noticed that $x = 2$ and $x = -3$ are the solutions of the given equation, it is possible to reason in another way. By dividing the polynomial $(x-1)x(x+1)(x+2) - 24 = x^4 + 2x^3 - x^2 - 2x - 24$ first by $x-2$, and then by $x+3$, we get the polynomial $x^2 + x + 4$ (Usiskin et al., 2003). We now see that $(x-1)x(x+1)(x+2) - 24 = x^4 + 2x^3 - x^2 - 2x - 24 = (x-2)(x+3)(x^2 + x + 4)$. Since it is easy to see that the equation $x^2 + x + 4 = 0$ does not have real solutions, we come to the conclusion that the given equation has only two solutions $x = 2$ and $x = -3$.

There is still another approach; moreover, one that does not require either "guessing" the solutions or dividing polynomials. This approach requires a different representation of the given expression by means of chunking. By multiplying in pairs the internal and external factors in the expression we get $(x-1)x(x+1)(x+2) = (x^2 + x - 2)(x^2 + x)$. We now use chunking: we say that $x^2 + x = t$, and that $x^2 + x - 2 = t - 2$. Now instead of the original equation we have the equation $t(t-2) = 24$. By solving this quadratic equation we get the solutions $t = 6$ and $t = -4$. It now remains to solve the equations $x^2 + x = 6$ and $x^2 + x = -4$. The former has roots at $x = 2$ and $x = -3$, while the latter does not have any solutions.

Example 2

Solve the equation $x^3 + x^2 + x = -\frac{1}{3}$.

Discussion and Solution

The graphical method is not of much use here. It is easy to see from a graphing calculator that the function $y = x^3 + x^2 + x + \frac{1}{3}$ traverses the abscissa axis in one point only, but it is difficult to determine the abscissa of that point precisely. (While a calculator can provide an accurate decimal approximation of a root, this does not always help clarify the exact numerical solution.) What is needed here is to think of an analogous, yet simpler, problem. The solution of a quadratic equation is essentially performed by completing the square and then extracting the square root. Would it be possible in the above case to try and complete the cube and then extract the cubic root?

Let us transform the above equation. By multiplying its left and right sides by 3 and then transferring all the terms to one side we get the equation: $3x^3 + 3x^2 + 3x + 1 = 0$. Now we have to remember the equality $(a+b)^3 = a^3 + 3a^2b + 3ab^2 + b^3$. Once we have done that it easy to notice that $x^3 + 3x^2 + 3x + 1 = (x+1)^3$, which means that $3x^3 + 3x^2 + 3x + 1 = 2x^3 + (x+1)^3$. The equation can therefore be transcribed as $2x^3 + (x+1)^3 = 0$ or else as $(x+1)^3 = -2x^3$. We now have to extract the cubic root from both sides: $x+1 = -\sqrt[3]{2}x$. Finally, by solving this linear equation we get that

$$x = -\frac{1}{\sqrt[3]{2}+1}.$$

Example 3

Without solving the equation $x^2 + 2x - 1 = 0$, calculate the sum

$$\frac{1}{x_1} + \frac{1}{x_2},$$

where x_1 and x_2 are the solutions of this equation.

Discussion and Solution

With this problem it is useful to work backwards. Let us transform the sum we are trying to calculate:

$$\frac{1}{x_1} + \frac{1}{x_2} = \frac{x_1 + x_2}{x_1 x_2}.$$

We must now take into account that if x_1 and x_2 are the solutions of the quadratic equation $ax^2 + bx + c = 0$, then $x_1 \cdot x_2 = \frac{c}{a}$ and $x_1 + x_2 = -\frac{b}{a}$. Consequently, for the given equation we get that $x_1 + x_2 = -2$, and $x_1 \cdot x_2 = -1$. Finally,

$$\frac{1}{x_1} + \frac{1}{x_2} = 2.$$

Example 4

Solve the system of equations $\begin{cases} xy = 2 \\ xz = 3 \\ yz = 6 \end{cases}$.

Discussion and Solution

Systems of equations with three unknowns are rarely encountered in school. But the situation where one has to solve a system such as the one given above is easy to imagine. Let us examine a rectangular parallelepiped, the area of one face is 2 square inches, the area of another face is 3 square inches, and the area of the third is 6 square inches. Establishing the dimensions of this parallelepiped is reducible to solving the given system (for positive numbers). Indeed, it is not necessarily evident whether there is a unique parallelpiped with these properties or not.

Naturally, one can express x from the first equation, insert it into the second equation and then carry on as if solving a system of two equations with two unknowns. But there is also another way of solving the above system. First, we note the evident pattern on the left-hand side of the three equations, and we use this to multiply all three equations to arrive at $x^2y^2z^2 = 36$. It is now easy to conclude that $xyz = \pm 6$. After establishing this it becomes very simple to determine the three unknowns: in order to find x one simply divides this last equation by the third equation in the system; in order to find y one divides it by the second and in order to find z one divides it by the third. So $x = \pm 1$, $y = \pm 2$ and $z = \pm 3$. The answer is:

$$\begin{cases} x = 1 \\ y = 2 \\ z = 3 \end{cases} \text{ and } \begin{cases} x = -1 \\ y = -2 \\ z = -3 \end{cases}.$$

Example 5

Prove the inequalities:

a) $2a+c>5$, with the condition that the inequalities $a+b>2$ and $c-2b>1$ are satisfied

b) $2x^2+2y^2 \geq (x+y)^2$

c) $a^4+b^4 \geq a^3b+ab^3$

d) $a^2+b^2+c^2 \geq ab+bc+ac$

Discussion and Solution

a) Assignment A is based on two properties of inequalities: the fact that inequalities can by multiplied by positive numbers; and the fact that it is possible to add together inequalities with the same sign. Since $a+b>2$, then $2a+2b>4$. If we add to this the inequality $c-2b>1$, we get $(2a+2b)+(c-2b)>4+1$. This gives us precisely the required inequality $2a+c>5$.

b) Assignment B, along with many other inequalities, are proven by means of obtaining an inequality equivalent to the original one. It is effectively a form of working backwards. The inequality that needs to be proven is transformed into an inequality that can be proven and from which, in turn, one can then derive the desired inequality statement. The transformation process is effectively repeated until an obviously true inequality remains. The chain of equivalent inequalities demonstrates that by starting from an obviously true inequality one can eventually reach (and thereby prove) the given inequality.

By opening the parentheses of the inequality that needs to be proven, $2x^2+2y^2 \geq (x+y)^2$, we get $2x^2+2y^2 \geq x^2+2xy+y^2$. By subtracting x^2+y^2 from both sides we get $x^2+y^2 \geq 2xy$, i.e., $x^2+y^2-2xy \geq 0$, or in other words $(x-y)^2 \geq 0$. This inequality is clearly true since the square of any number is never negative. Since all the inequalities are equivalent to the original one, the proof is complete. In fact, all of the transformations can be done in reverse order: from the true inequality $(x-y)^2 \geq 0$ it follows that $x^2+y^2-2xy \geq 0$ or $x^2+y^2 \geq 2xy$, and from here it follows that $2x^2+2y^2 \geq x^2+2xy+y^2$ or $2x^2+2y^2 \geq (x+y)^2$.

c) Let us reason about part C in the same way as in the previous case. The inequality $a^4+b^4 \geq a^3b+ab^3$ is equivalent to the inequality $a^4+b^4-a^3b-ab^3 \geq 0$, i.e., to the inequality $(a^4-a^3b)+(b^4-ab^3) \geq 0$. By extracting the common factors we get $a^3(a-b)+b^3(b-a) \geq 0$. By extracting the factor $a-b$, we get $(a-b)(a^3-b^3) \geq 0$. What remains to be done is to prove this inequality. This can be done by accounting for all possibilities. If $a \geq b$, then $a^3 \geq b^3$, which means that the expression $(a-b)(a^3-b^3)$ is non-negative since it is the product of non-negatives. If $a<b$, then $a^3<b^3$,

which means that the expression $(a - b)(a^3 - b^3)$ is positive as a product of negatives.

It is also possible to reason in another way:

$$(a-b)(a^3-b^3) = (a-b)(a-b)(a^2+ab+b^2)$$

$$= (a-b)^2\left(a^2+2a\cdot\frac{b}{2}+\left(\frac{b}{2}\right)^2+\frac{3b^2}{4}\right)$$

$$= (a-b)^2\left(\left(a+\frac{b}{2}\right)^2+\frac{3b^2}{4}\right)$$

Since the square of any number is never negative, then this expression is also not negative as the product of non-negatives.

D. This inequality can be established by utilizing the simpler inequality $x^2 + y^2 \geq 2xy$, which we proved above. First, the following inequalities are justified: $a^2 + b^2 \geq 2ab$, $a^2 + c^2 \geq 2ac$, and $b^2 + c^2 \geq 2bc$. By adding together these three inequalities we get $2a^2 + 2b^2 + 2c^2 \geq 2ab + 2bc + 2ac$. Dividing this inequality by 2 results in the desired inequality $a^2 + b^2 + c^2 \geq ab + bc + ac$.

Example 6

Find all values a, for which the equation $\dfrac{2a}{x} = a - 1$ has no solution.

Discussion and Solution

This is an example of an assignment that does not require the solution of an equation, but rather its analysis. In such problems it is critical to thoroughly account for all possibilities.

It is clear that the given equation can be transcribed as:

$$\begin{cases} 2a = (a-1)x \\ x \neq 0 \end{cases}.$$

If $a = 1$, the equation $2 \cdot 1 = 0 \cdot x$ results, which does not have any solutions (and which means that the original equation has no solutions either). If, however, $a \neq 1$, then the equation $2a = (a - 1)x$ has a single solution

$$x = \frac{2a}{a-1}.$$

One must take into account, however, that the solution $x = 0$ of this equation is extraneous to the original equation. Thus it is necessary to establish for which values a the equation $2a = (a-1)x$ has the solution of 0. To do so it is sufficient to replace x with 0 in the equation: $2a = (a-1) \cdot 0$. It follows that $a = 0$. Thus, if $a = 0$ the equation $2a = (a-1)x$ has a single solution: $x = 0$, while the original equation will have no solutions. The answer is therefore: The equation

$$\frac{2a}{x} = a-1$$

has no solutions if $a = 0$ and $a = 1$.

Example 7

Prove that the equation $ax^2 - (a+2b)x + b = 0$ has at least one solution for all a and b.

Discussion and Solution

The given equation is a quadratic one if $a \neq 0$. The discriminant of this equation is $(a+2b)^2 - 4ab = a^2 + 4ab + 4b^2 - 4ab = a^2 + 4b^2$. It is evident that the sum of the squares is never negative, which means that the quadratic equation has a solution.

If, however, $a = 0$ the given equation takes the form $-2bx + b = 0$. If $b \neq 0$, its solution is $x = \frac{1}{2}$. If, however, $b = 0$, then the equation takes the form $0 \cdot x = 0$, which means that x can be any number. Consequently, in all the cases examined the equation has at least one solution.

Reflection   **Assignments and Topics for Discussion**

1. Solve these equations:
    a. $(2x-1)^6 - 9(2x-1)^3 + 8 = 0$,
    b. $(x^2 - 5x + 7)^2 - (x-2)(x-3) = 1$,
    c. $20x^4 - 28x^2(x^2+1) + 9(x^2+1)^2 = 0$.
2. Without solving the equation $x^2 + 2x - 1 = 0$, calculate the sum $x_1^3 + x_2^3$ where x_1 and x_2 are the solutions of this equation.
3. Solve the equation

$$\begin{cases} x + y = 3 \\ x + z = 4. \\ y + z = 5 \end{cases}$$

4. Prove these inequalities:
   a. $a^2 + 3b^2 + 5c^2 \leq 1$, with the condition that the inequalities $a \geq b \geq c \geq 0$ and $a + b + c \leq 1$ are satisfied;
   b. $(a^2 - b^2)^2 \geq 4ab(a - b)^2$;
   c. $a^2 + b^2 + 1 \geq ab + b + a$.

5. Prove that the equation $ax^2 - (a + b)x - (a - b) = 0$ has at least one solution for all a and b.

6. Using the equality $a^3 + b^3 + c^3 - 3abc = (a + b + c)(a^2 + b^2 + c^2 - ab - ac - bc)$, prove the inequality

$$\frac{x + y + z}{3} \geq \sqrt[3]{xyz}$$

   is true for all positive numbers x, y, z. (*Note:* this is the inequality between the arithmetic and geometric means.)

7. Prove the inequality

$$\frac{a + b + c + d}{4} \geq \sqrt[4]{abcd}$$

   for four positive numbers a, b, c, d (i.e., the inequality between the arithmetic and geometric means).

PLANNING A LESSON DEVOTED TO EQUATIONS

This section will discuss the preparation of two lessons by a student teacher, Phillip. His lesson plans were discussed at the student teachers' seminar and the remarks and observations of his fellow student teachers were then incorporated into his plan.

Preliminary Information

Phillip conducted lessons in two different classes, one honors and another ordinary, but the plan for both was (at least at first glance) more or less the same—a unit devoted to linear equations. In both classes Phillip started off with a discussion of one-step equations and then moved on to solving multistep equations and equations with variables on both sides. However, whereas in the honors class students remembered much from the year before and quickly grasped the new material, in the ordinary class Phillip had to explain everything from the very beginning. Students made mistakes with basic arithmetic operations and in the very application of algorithms, something that alarmed Phillip. In both classes Phillip was expected to conduct a lesson devoted to solving word problems with the help of linear equations. Word problems had already been used many times during the study of linear equations. In these lessons, by using word problems, Phillip wanted to demonstrate the importance of linear equations in general and to emphasize especially their role in solving real-life problems. The lessons were meant to be used for reviewing material already studied as well as for providing students the opportunity to improve their skill in solving word problems.

The Textbook

The same textbook was used in both classes. The book contained many different problems, but they were all of approximately the same level of difficulty. Only at the end of each section was there one problem that was supposed to be harder than the rest. The textbook also contained a section at the back specifically devoted to problem solving strategies, such as constructing a table or creating a drawing. Phillip, however, preferred to make use of material from this section from the start, while working on the main part of the unit. Students found it far easier to solve problems with the help of tables and drawings, so Phillip thought it was unreasonable to delay the explanation of these methods for later. For this reason, Phillip could not use the material from the textbook exactly as it appeared there, but had to assemble his own materials for each lesson or else combine materials from various parts of the textbook.

The Goal

In Phillip's mind, the main goal of the lesson was improving the students' mastery of solving word problems that are reducible to linear equations. The realization of this goal presupposed overcoming (wholly or partially) a number of difficulties that Phillip's students seemed to be experiencing. First of all, as already mentioned, many students had trouble solving linear equations in general, even without first having to extract the important information from word problems. Secondly, students did not find the translation of a word problem into mathematical language (i.e., the construction of an equation) straightforward by any means. Apart from that, Phillip was concerned that many students saw mathematics as something disconnected from real life and he was particularly keen to use this lesson to demonstrate how mathematics can be applied. Consequently, Phillip formulated the following lesson objectives:

- Students will be able to review material already studied.
- Students will be able to practice modeling and "translation" from verbal to mathematical language.

- Students will be able to realize that the methods for solving problems that they are learning in class are of genuine help in real life.

Defining Differences of Approach in Teaching Two Different Kinds of Classes
Phillip formulated the same objectives for both classes. At the same time, he also understood that the two lessons had to be different. Students from the more advanced class were certain to solve problems more quickly, given less arithmetic difficulties, which meant that there would be time left to spare. Furthermore, they were likely to find easier problems uninteresting since they had already worked on similar assignments before. They would therefore not be learning anything new and would not be developing their own thinking, if the classes were not differentiated in some way. Realizing these things, Phillip gave up his original idea of simply selecting more problems of essentially the same type for the advanced class.

Phillip even considered not using this lesson at all in the honors class, thinking that he could instead move on to the next lesson straightaway in order to finish the unit more quickly. However, his cooperating teacher objected to this: the better understanding of mathematics is determined not by the speed at which standard assignments are completed but by how profound an understanding of the material studied is developed. When teaching children that are talented and have a genuine interest in mathematics, it is important not to rush through the material and then simply depart from it. Instead, such students must be given the opportunity to acquire a deeper insight into the subject matter and thereby further develop their gifts and interests.

The differences between the two lessons needed to be determined by different performance objectives—one could expect that the more advanced class would be able to solve more complex equations and also form equations that had more complex conditions. Phillip's main task was to select just the right assignments for the two lessons.

Lesson Plan for the Ordinary Class

In the *ordinary class* Phillip decided to use comparatively simple word problems. In doing so he organized the lesson into three interconnected parts. In the first part students were supposed to work with the concepts "equation" and "solution of an equation," and to recall the algorithm for solving linear equations. The second part was a transitory one—here students were supposed to practice "translating," i.e., moving from a formula to ordinary, verbal language, and vice versa. Finally, in the third part they were supposed to actually solve word problems. As a result, the lesson plan was as follows.

Do Now (approximately 5 minutes)

Working on their own, students were supposed to answer the following questions:

Examine the equation $x + 3 = 2x + 1$.

a) Is 0 its solution? What about 1? b) Remove the number 3 from the equation and replace it by another number so that its solution would be 1. c) What can you say about the solutions of the equations $x + 3 = 2x + 1$ and $x - 1 = 2x - 3$ without actually finding these solutions? d) Solve the equation $x + 3 = 2x + 1$.

Discussion of Answers to These Questions (3–5 minutes)

According to Phillip's plan students were supposed to provide answers to the first three questions (with brief explanations) orally and from their seats, while the solution of the equation was to be done on the board.

Work in Pairs on "Translation" Followed by Discussion
(approximately 10 minutes)

Next, Phillip planned to give students three pictures (Figure 10.8) and ask them to use them to formulate word problems that could be expressed by the equation $x + 3 = 2x + 1$. For example, in the first case one could say that on one side of the balance there lies a weight of unknown mass (the unknown x) plus a 3 lb weight, while on the other side there are two such

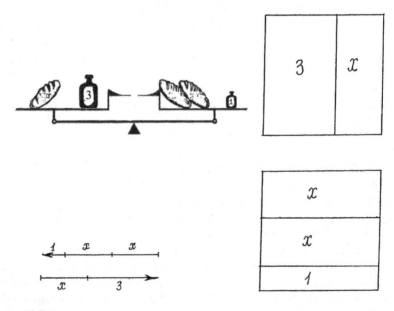

Figure 10.8

weights plus a 1 lb weight. In the second case one could say that the same figure can be made of either a rectangle with the area 3 and another with the area *x* or of one with the area 1 and two with the area *x*. Finally, in the third case one can say that the man went a certain unknown distance (*x*), rested and then went a further 3 miles. On his way back he went twice the distance before taking a break (*2x*) and then walked another 1 mile before reaching the original starting point. If different pairs had different word problems Phillip planned to hear them all out.

Solving Word Problems (20 minutes)
Phillip planned to give students the following two problems.

1. Jane is on a diet. She wants to eat some beef with vegetables for her lunchtime meal. The portion of vegetables is 80 calories, while 100g of beef is 160 calories. How much beef is Jane allowed to eat if, according to her calculations, she is allowed only 350 calories for this meal?
2. A travel agent offers a customer the choice of two vacation packages for the same price. The first was for 7 nights in a hotel and the airfare—roundtrip costing $250 dollars. The second was for only 5 nights in the same hotel but also with a two-day sea-cruise costing $490. How much did one night in the hotel cost and how much did each package cost in total?

Phillip decided to recommend to students the following work-plan:

A. Introduce variables.
B. Formulate equations.
C. Answer questions.
D. Check and discuss answers and solution.

Students were supposed to work in small groups, while the results were to be discussed by the class as a whole at the end. Phillip's plan prompted students to introduce unknowns. In addition to this, Phillip recognised that, generally speaking, these problems can also be solved arithmetically. If students came across such a solution Phillip planned to discuss with the class the advantages and disadvantages of each solution, assuming that the majority of the class would find the algebraic solution easier.

Closing Remarks
For his closing remarks Phillip wanted to emphasize the importance of checking the plausibility of the end-result and also to point out that linear equations are a particularly convenient tool for solving the most diverse problems.

Assessment

Phillip planned carefully to observe how students solved the problems in all three parts of the lesson in order to assess the errors and difficulties of each student. Work in pairs and small groups was supposed to ensure that students who were experiencing difficulties would be helped straightaway both by other members of the group and by the teacher.

Lesson Plan for the Honors Class

When planning the lesson for the *honors class* Phillip thought it necessary to select more difficult problems in the main part of the lesson. At the beginning of the lesson he, like with the other class, decided to give assignments that concerned the concept of the "solution of an equation" and the application of algorithms for solving equations. However, he also made these assignments harder, i.e., presupposing both more complex transformations and a higher level of reasoning skills.

Phillip decided that it was not necessary to give this class "translation" assignments, since these students had already worked with similar models before and had no trouble introducing unknowns or formulating equations in simple situations. Instead he decided to give them an assignment that would develop their critical thinking—to analyze whether an equation had been correctly formulated based on the conditions given in the problem. In his view, such an assignment was also supposed to remind students about the relationship between distance, speed and time, which would be of help to them in the third part of the lesson, which involved a much more difficult formulation of an equation on the basis of a word problem.

Phillip also decided to prepare yet another assignment on top of this basic plan, just in case all or some students dealt with the main problems quicker than he expected them to. In this extra assignment he wanted to present students with a situation where it would be essential and especially meaningful to analyze the end-result.

Consequently, the lesson plan was as follows.

Do Now (approximately 5 minutes)

Working on their own, students are asked to answer the following questions:

Examine the equation $x + 3 = 2x + 1$.

a) Is 1 its solution? b) What can you say about the solutions of the equations $x + 3 = 2x + 1$ and $0.5x + 1.5 - 0.5 = x$, without determining these solutions first? c) Solve the equation $x + 3 = 2x + 1$. d) Determine the number a so that the equation $x + 3 = 2x + a$ would have the solution $x = 1$. e) Give any number a so that the equation $x + 3 = 2x + a$ would have a negative solution.

Discussion of Answers to the Above Questions (5 minutes)
Students were supposed to give their answers orally from their seats, after which short notations were to be made on the board.

Work in Pairs on Establishing the Correctness of the Equation
Derived from a Problem and the Discussion of Results (5–7 minutes)
Students were to be given the description of a particular situation. In this situation the variable x was to be introduced in three different ways. Students would then be asked if it was possible to formulate the equation $x + 3 = 2x + 1$ in each case.

> Jim traveled from point A to point B in the following way. He first ran 3 miles then walked 1 hour. He returned the same way. He first walked 2 hours (at the same speed as before) and then ran 1 mile. (a) Let x be the speed at which Jim walked. (b) Let x be the time Jim spent running back. (c) Let x be the distance that Jim walked on his way back.

When discussing the solution Phillip was keen to point out that a drawing would make the situation much clearer and would be of great help in finding the solution.

Solving Word Problems (20–25 minutes)
Phillip planned to give students the following problems.

1. The water in a river is moving at 2 miles per hour. From point A to point B a boat traveled 3 hours and from point B to point A the trip took 4 hours. What is the distance between points A and B?
2. A cyclist leaves point A. When he is 3 miles from his starting point a motorcyclist sets off in pursuit of him along the same road. The motorcycle is 3 times faster than the bicycle. At what distance from point A will the motorcyclist catch up with the cyclist?

As with the weaker class, Phillip decided to propose to students the following work plan:

A. Introduce variables.
B. Formulate equations.
C. Answer questions.
D. Check and discuss answers and solution.

The plan was for students to work in small groups. Once they completed these assignments Phillip was going to give them the following problem and then discuss with them its solution and its conditions.

A father is 43 years old and his son is 7. In how many years will the father be 10 times older than his son?

While discussing the solutions Phillip planned to highlight the fact that a variable can be introduced in different ways and that the variable x does not necessarily need to correspond to the question being asked in the text of the problem. He also wanted to show that sometimes analyzing an equation and its solution helps to formulate the problem more accurately (as in this last assignment).

Closing Remarks

In his closing remarks Phillip also planned to reiterate that many simple as well as complex real-life situations can be reduced to linear equations.

Assessment

In this lesson as well Phillip did not want to give any formal marks but preferred instead to assess students' difficulties and achievements by observing their work during the course of the lesson. The lesson was supposed to generate several problem situations that students had not encountered previously. Phillip planned to pay particular attention to how students dealt with these situations and what sorts of problem-solving strategies they utilized.

Discussion

Although they share a common topic, it is clear that Phillip's two lessons are radically different. Firstly, there are differences in the way questions are formulated. For example, students normally find it more difficult to work with a second variable a (as in the equation $x + 3 = 2x + a$) than to answer the same question when formulated as "remove the given number and replace it by another." Secondly, there are also differences in the level of difficulty involved in forming equations from word problems. For example, if in the problem about the boat that travels upstream and downstream students introduce as a variable the distance S between A and B then the construction of the resulting equation,

$$\frac{S}{3} - \frac{S}{4} = 4,$$

though possible, is far harder than to construct an equation for the speed v of the boat $3(v+2) = 4(v-2)$ and then determine the distance from that solution. It is clear that students in a more advanced class will not find this material easy, as sometimes happens in review classes.

Phillip also made sure to incorporate a certain degree of flexibility in the way he planned the lessons. It is impossible to predict exactly how solving the problems will go, especially if problems are new to students and supposed to challenge them, so it is essential to have a back-up plan as well.

Some Suggestions for Changes to the Lesson Plan for the Honors Class

At the student teachers' seminar, someone expressed the view that in the main part of the lesson it would be sufficient to do only one problem—the one with the boat traveling upstream and downstream, whereas the one about the bicycle and motorcycle could be left as a reserve. Someone else also proposed to move the problem about the ages of the father and son into the main part of the lesson, and to confine the previous task to only constructing an equation for one of the two remaining word problems. This was justified by the fact that demonstrating to students the importance of analyzing and interpreting the result obtained was especially useful.

The equation $43 + x = 10(x + 7)$ constructed for this problem, where x is the number of years that need to pass for the father to be 10 times older than the son, has a negative solution. The father will become 10 times older than the son in -3 years! One could say that the answer to the question should be: in the years to come the father will never become 10 times older than the son. At the same time, the question itself could be reformulated as: When was the father or when will he be 10 times older than the son? The answer then would be three years ago. Indeed, in a sense the largest value for "how many times older is a father than his son" is at birth; the function, $(36 + t)/(t)$ only decreases over time.

The seminar participants found the discussion of the solution and the need to reformulate the problem important for the development of the students' ability to apply mathematics in real life, which made them keen on finding a place for this problem in the lesson.

It is hardly possible to give any general recommendations about this, though. Much depends on the abilities of the class (even advanced classes can differ among themselves considerably) and on what has been planned for the lessons to come. Any "unused" problems could still be given to students and discussed at some point in the future.

On Some Similarities Between the Two Lessons

Despite differences, Phillip's lessons also contained a considerable degree of similar features. In both cases the solution of word problems takes place against the background of revising the material already studied and, especially, of working with the concept of the "solution of an equation." Phillip strove to construct assignments in such a way that students would be prepared for them by other, easier assignments. For example, in the lesson designed for the advanced class, there was first a discussion of a problem in which students were reminded of the formula $d = vt$ that relates the distance covered d, the speed v and the duration t of a particular movement.

This formula was then used again in the problem that followed. In the lesson designed for the ordinary class, students first practiced forming equations (on familiar material) and only then started working on actually solving word problems.

Phillip strove to find a reasonable link between that which students already knew well and that which was completely new to them. For instance, students in the ordinary class had used modeling with weights many times already, but Philip's assignment was relatively new: previously they used modeling in the process of *solving* an equation; now they were asked to use it in order to *construct* an equation. The students in the advanced class had already been constructing equations based on the conditions of a problem; however, they had not been asked to *check* the equation they constructed quite as frequently. By successfully linking what is known and what is unknown a teacher facilitates genuine learning yet makes sure that this remains within the students' abilities.

Keeping a Balance Between Different Forms of Work in a Class

Phillip also did his best to balance different forms of work during a class period. Students worked on their own, in pairs, in small groups and as an entire class. This created opportunities for developing forms of mathematical communication among students and also catered to the different abilities and attitudes of each student. At the same time no part of the lesson dragged on for too long. The teacher was able to keep control over what happened in class and also make any adjustments to the original plan.

The skill of finding such a "golden mean" in both the content and form of study, is, as already mentioned, essential in order to achieve an effective lesson.

Reflection
Assignments and Topics for Discussion

1. Write down your impressions of Phillip's lessons. What did you like about them and what would you have done differently?
2. Think up some problems analogous to the ones used in Phillip's lesson plans.
3. Think up or select a few more challenging problems that would be reducible to linear equations.
4. Imagine that in the ordinary class for which Phillip had designed the first lesson there happened to be one particularly gifted student. What additions (if any) would you make to Phillip's lesson plan to cater to this child?

5. Prepare lesson plans devoted to the study of word problems reducible to quadratic equations both for an ordinary and an advanced class. Draw on Phillip's plans above.

PART IV

This part discusses the teaching of geometry. Its aim is to introduce the reader to the theoretical and practical aspects of teaching and studying geometry.

CHAPTER 11

GEOMETRY AS A SCIENCE
AND A SCHOOL SUBJECT

The chapter begins the discussion of the study of geometry at school. Its aim is to acquaint the reader with the results of research on the development of geometrical thinking in schoolchildren and to help future teachers prepare for the nurturing and further cultivation of such thinking.

In particular, the chapter discusses:

- The development of geometry as a school subject and the need for reform in the way it is taught.
- The principal tasks that stand before the teacher of geometry, and the reasons why school geometry is so important today.
- What research says about how schoolchildren study geometry and about what the teacher needs to accomplish at each stage of the students' development.
- How to develop students' geometrical imagination through "informal" geometry.
- How to teach proofs in the geometry course.
- Ways of using manipulatives and technology in geometry classes.

Mathematics in Middle and Secondary School, pages 311–346
Copyright © 2015 by Information Age Publishing
311

HOW GEOMETRY IS TAUGHT AND STUDIED

Debating Geometry

"The study of geometry in the secondary school has been one of the most controversial issues debated by mathematicians and educators during the entire twentieth century," noted Howard Fehr (1973) some years ago. It seems natural to expect that debates about school geometry are unlikely to cease in the twenty-first century either. What sort of geometry is needed in school? Do we need it at all? How should it be taught and to whom? For years there has been no consensus on these and many other related issues.

Teaching According to Euclid

And yet geometry was once considered the oasis of stability in school mathematics, the part of the curriculum that remained unchanged despite waves of reforms in education. Euclid's *Elements* served as the bible of geometry teachers for centuries. In the second half of the twentieth century the great French mathematician Dieudonné (cited in Fehr, 1973) still clamored "Euclid must go!"—which only confirmed Euclid's continuing presence in school mathematics, even then. This is unique among mathematical disciplines: algebra, analysis, not to speak of discrete mathematics, formed as parts of school mathematics only considerably later. So why have the content and approach of Euclid's *Elements* remained so influential in educating new generations?

Combining visual clarity with rigor. In large part, the visual presentation and rigor of Euclid's *Elements* demonstrate a high degree of pedagogical mastery. It was not in vain that the outstanding mathematician and historian of mathematics, van der Waerden (1961), called Euclid the greatest mathematics teacher of all times. Euclid's geometry has become the model of what mathematics is meant to stand for—rigor, logical orderliness and provability. Centuries after Euclid, the philosopher Spinoza (1997) called his book *Ethic: Demonstrated in Geometrical Order*. The expression might appear strange to the modern ear, but it conveys well that the term "geometrical" had once served as a virtual synonym for the term "logically proved."

Contrary to popular opinion, Euclid's book was not devoted to geometry *per se*, but to mathematics as a whole, insofar as the Ancient Greeks expressed both algebra and what we would today call analysis through the language of geometry. In modern times, it is much more common to use other forms of representation, but even today we understand geometry as the most "visual" of mathematical languages. What Euclid did was to show how to organize that which is visually self-evident in such a way that it can then be used to prove what is visually not as obvious. A drawing, image or sketch appear naturally in the study of Euclidean geometry, making it clearer and more accessible than other, more abstract, parts of mathematics.

Euclidean geometry—a treasure house of problems. Over the centuries Euclidean geometry has also been enriched by hundreds of extremely interesting and beautiful problems. It was not by accident that Polya (1981), discussing the general methods of problem solving, frequently used classical geometrical problems of constructions with a compass and a straightedge. The visual clarity of such problems is matched by the sophistication and elegance of their solution.

Reasons Behind Calls for Change

Yet many, following Dieudonné, still reckoned that "Euclid must go!" One of the reasons is that over the centuries the world has learned far more than what was known in Euclid's times. In Classical Antiquity algebra was absorbed by geometry, however, later on it was geometry, in fact that ended up, to a certain extent, just a part of algebra. The coordinate method, invented by Descartes, and certain other methods obtained in its subsequent development, permitted the study of geometrical objects to be reduced to the study of equations and inequalities. Such methods made it easier to make generalizations and to shift from planes and three-dimensional space to the study of multi-dimensional spaces, thus turning Euclidean geometry into only a particular case of a more general phenomenon.

Shift of attitude towards Euclidean geometry as a science. When Lobachevsky and Bolyai, around 1830, independently from one another, created a completely new, non-Euclidean, geometry, it became clear that Euclidean geometry was by no means the only one possible (Eves, 1990). A few decades later, Felix Klein proposed a general way of classifying geometry that used "transformations" as a key concept—a concept that played only a minimal role in Euclidean geometry. It thus became obvious that the older geometry needed to make room for a new one, which in turn, required something of a makeover of the study of geometry.

The emergence of new requirements in the teaching of geometry. It is not only from a purely mathematical perspective that the teaching of Euclidian geometry can be criticized, but also from a pedagogical one. The expansion and democratization of education in the twentieth century also created the need to make the study of geometry more accessible and relevant to the increasingly broader student base—education was no longer just for a select group but for the masses. Geometry was then taught not directly from Euclid, but from textbooks that actually contained far more assignments and explanations than were present in the *Elements* and that were adapted to the needs of mass education (Herbst, 2002a). But even these textbooks were often quite rightly criticized for excessive abstractness and for what appeared as an unnecessary and overly pedantic pursuit of extreme rigor.

The Era of Searching and Change

So how does one reconcile the need for incorporating new innovations in geometry, while at the same time making it accessible to the student masses? How does one find a place for geometrical transformations without renouncing classical problems? How does one teach logic and deduction without falling into unintelligible and excessive abstractness? This is precisely what has been at the center of the debate for decades (Henderson, 1973; Stanic & Kilpatrick, 2003). Courses in geometry were radically revised in the period of the so-called New Math reforms. This was followed by periodic returns to a "back to basics" approach, by searches for a compromise between the old and the new content, and by all manner of restructuring, additions and revisions. This work is far from complete and the mathematics teacher of the twenty-first century needs to take an active part in it.

Challenges for the Geometry Teacher of Today

Notably, the CCSS-M (2010) made a relatively large shift, along the lines of Klein's suggestion that develops the notion of geometrical congruence not based on ideas about length and angle, but on axioms of rigid transformations. Indeed, the High School Geometry standards (CCSS-M.HSG-CO.B.6—CCSS-M.HSG-CO.B.8) specify that students should "Understand congruence in terms of rigid motions," further describing that the more traditional means of establishing congruence (e.g, SSS, SAS, etc.) should be developed from these rigid motions. However, many of the NCTM (2000) standards still summarize some of the primary ideas in geometry.

In particular, the NCTM (2000) states that the teaching of geometry "should enable all students to:

- Analyze characteristics and properties of two- and three-dimensional geometric shapes and develop mathematical arguments about geometric relationships
- Specify locations and describe spatial relationships using coordinate geometry and other representational systems
- Apply transformations and use symmetry to analyze mathematical situations
- Use visualization, spatial reasoning, and geometric modeling to solve problems." (p. 41)

All of the above is no doubt important, but what seems to be crucial here is the reference made to *all* students. Traditionally, geometry has been understood as a subject that was really necessary only to those who went to college, and was therefore not always taught to everyone. Today, however, it is important to bring geometry to each and every schoolchild. The question inevitably arises: what for?

Why Should We Teach Geometry to Everyone?

Usiskin (1997) rightly observes that neither the answer "you need it for college," nor the claim that "you need it to survive," quite work. It goes without saying that not all schoolchildren will be going to college. At the same time, the parents of probably a third of today's students have never been taught geometry in their lives, yet have managed to survive perfectly well. So how exactly does geometry benefit those who study it?

Usiskin goes on to liken the situation of a person who has not studied geometry to that of a person who arrives in a foreign country without speaking its language: "you can get along but you will never appreciate the richness of the culture." To demonstrate the importance of studying geometry, he describes it in the following way:

- Geometry is the branch of mathematics that connects mathematics to the real, physical world.
- Geometry is the branch of mathematics that studies visual patterns.
- Geometry is a vehicle for representing phenomena whose origin is neither visual nor physical.

More on these key aspects of geometry. We live in a world of geometrical bodies. Without speaking the language of geometry it is difficult to appreciate the culture of the world around us. For sure, even without studying geometry, it is evident, for instance, that round things can roll. However, for someone living in a technological world that is becoming ever more complex, it is impossible to do much without properly understanding geometrical concepts.

When observing architecture or painting, when watching something at the cinema or the theatre, while at work or when going for a walk, the person who has experience in analyzing visual patterns will see far more than someone who lacks it. And it is Geometry that teaches us how to analyze these patterns.

Geometry is also a way of clarifying something unintelligible, an important means of representation. Geometry teaches one to draw, to sketch and, generally speaking, to make things visible. This is precisely how geometry is used in lessons devoted to algebra—algebraic equations and properties

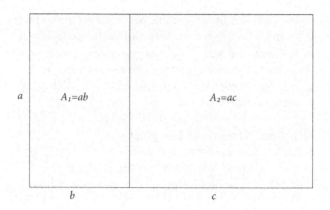

a $A_1 = ab$ $A_2 = ac$

b c

Figure 11.1

are explained with the help of drawings, for example, the concept of 'area' can help illustrate the distributive property: $a(b + c) = ab + ac$ (Figure 11.1).

Let us also not forget the logical orderliness and beauty of geometry—they too are just as important. But for all of this to be of genuine use to each and every student, the teacher must be ready to face many challenges when teaching geometry.

Examples of the Variety of Approaches That the Teacher Must Be Prepared to Use

Mathematics teachers need to be able to show students how geometry pervades everyday life and how it can help them discover novel aspects of the real world. At the same time, the teacher must help schoolchildren develop their own thinking, including the culture of working with scientific concepts, without which even the everyday use of geometry would remain deficient (Vygotsky, 1986). The teacher must be able to show, for example, how the concept of "transformation" helps explain what happens to the size of the image while Xeroxing, or why one building might appear more "regular" than another (e.g., see Figure 11.2). The teacher must also be able to explain to students the actual concept of "transformation" and show them which families of isometries exist in the Euclidean plane (translations, rotations, reflections and glide reflections). The teacher has to develop the students' geometrical intuition, while simultaneously showing them that problems cannot be solved without rigorous mathematical reasoning.

All these tasks cannot, of course, be realized all at once. The study of geometry needs to develop over the entire period of schooling. Depending on the level and context, the study of geometry can be both mathematically rigorous, and so-called "informal." How geometry is taught must depend on the exact stage of development reached by the students.

How Students Understand Geometry

What did you do in math today?

The teacher first drew on the board some congruent triangles and then spent half an hour proving what was already evident.

This exchange between parent and child conveys the feeling that students often experience in geometry lessons: all appears to be so straightforward at the start, so why does it have to be muddled, as if on purpose.

Reflecting on Research

Psychological and educational research has shown that the problem lies neither in children's laziness nor their lack of attention nor in the fact that the teacher has poorly explained the proof. Geometrical thinking passes through several successive developmental stages and one cannot simply leap from one level to another arbitrarily.

Levels in the Development of Geometrical Thinking

Dina and Pierre van Hiele (1959, 1986) have distinguished the following levels in the development of thinking in students.

Level 1. Visual. At this level students can differentiate geometric configurations and they can operate with them by noticing, for example, that they are similar to certain familiar objects in the surrounding world. They are not, however, able to specify and describe the properties of these geometrical objects.

Level 2. Descriptive or analytic. Once they have reached this level students can recognize and characterize geometric configurations by their properties. Schoolchildren are able not simply to distinguish the rectangle from the trapezoid, but also to observe that a rectangle is a rectangle because all its angles are right. However, at this stage, the ability to establish a correspondence between different classes of objects (for example, to characterize the rectangle as a parallelogram) or to comprehend geometrical proofs is still not developed.

Level 3. Abstract. At this level students become able to comprehend the subordination of objects to particular classes. They can work with formal definitions and use equivalent assertions. They can conduct short proofs, establishing, for instance, the immediate consequences of this or that assertion. However, they still fail to see geometry as a single deductive system.

Level 4. Formal deduction. At this level students are fluent in understanding and logically deducing assertions within a single axiomatic system. It is at this level that proof becomes for the student the principal means of establishing truth in geometry.

Level 5. Rigor.   Those who reach this level are able to think of geometrical objects as formal constructions described within the framework of an axiomatic theory without relying on visual representations. They understand the possibility of using different axiomatic foundations in geometry.

According to the van Hiele theory these stages are sequential and hierarchical—it is impossible to reach a level without first passing through the ones below it. The process of learning itself, however, is discontinuous—the shift from one level to the next takes the form of a leap.

Debates about the van Hiele theory.   Some aspects of this theory have provoked debate (Clements & Battista, 1992; Nickson, 2000). One contentious issue is the number of levels that should be distinguished. Suggestions have been made to group the three highest levels into a single one, which would be dubbed "theoretical," and to add an extra Level 0 that would precede the level of visual recognition. Another controversial issue is the theory of discontinuous learning, as well as the notion of strictly hierarchical levels. Nonetheless, the principal ideas of the van Hiele research remain highly influential and pertinent.

Some Practical Conclusions

Summing up the conclusions of this research in a consciously simplified form, if your student John has only learned visually to differentiate between triangles and quadrilaterals (Level 1), but cannot, for example, describe essential characteristic differences between these objects, then there is simply no point in trying to explain to him the deficiencies of the axiomatic system used in a textbook as compared to some other axiomatic foundation (Level 5). The first task is to get to the stage where the student is able to explain that the triangle is different from a quadrilateral by virtue of the fact that it has a different number of sides (Level 2). Next, the student must become able to conclude that both triangles and quadrilaterals are polygons and also that every polygon with fewer than 5 sides is either a triangle or a quadrilateral (Level 3). After this the student must learn to derive properties of triangles and quadrilaterals by using axioms and theorems studied in class (Level 4).

It is important, however, not to subsequently believe that the teacher's job is simply to wait for the student to reach the required level spontaneously. Quite the opposite: progress from one level to the next is achieved less by virtue of biological maturation and more through the process of instruction. A person could remain at Level 1 even at the age of 25 yet also could reach Level 5 at the age of 16. Senk (1989) emphasized the importance of the curriculum in developing students' geometrical thinking, expressing extreme concern at how little attention is paid to geometry in middle school: "Of what little is taught, not much is learned." Students might be ready for new, more demanding assignments, but if these are not given to them, the breakthrough in their developments simply will not happen. The teacher's task is precisely to create classroom situations in which the students' thinking would be given an opportunity to develop.

Clements and Battista (1992) remark that, according to the van Hiele theory, the higher levels of geometrical thinking are reached not via a teacher directly telling students but rather in the process of problem solving. Here they distinguish the following five phases in student development, indicating the role the teacher plays in each of them.

Stages of student development and the teacher's role in each of them.

- *Information.* At this stage students are acquainted with geometry for the first time, and the teacher's role is to provide them with appropriate material.
- *Guided orientation.* At this stage the teacher's task is to engage students in the active study of geometrical objects.
- *Explicitation.* Here the teacher's role is to help students express in explicit terms their intuitive understanding of a maturing geometric idea.
- *Free orientation.* At this stage the teacher selects assignments that allow students to develop and enrich their understanding, highlighting new aspects.
- *Integration.* At this stage the teacher encourages students to grasp what they have learned and to reorganize it structurally (in the way customary in formal and rigorous mathematics).

On the role of middle school. Children come to school with some very basic geometrical understanding, which is then to a certain degree developed in elementary school. Traditionally, though, it is only in high school that children start systematically carrying out geometric proofs. The role of the middle school, however, is no less important, since it is precisely here that the transition to the theoretical levels of geometrical thinking takes place. The teacher's ability to organize suitable problem-solving activities on geometrical material accessible to students is no doubt crucial to their development at this stage.

Reflection

Assignments and Topics for Discussion

1. Select a geometrical theorem from a school textbook. Is it proved in the textbook? If so, how? Check if this theorem exists in Euclid's *Elements.* If so, how is it proved there? Are the two proofs, in Euclid and

(a)   (b)

Figure 11.2 (a) Lincoln Memorial. [Photograph]. In Encyclopædia Britannica. Retrieved from http://www.britannica.com/EBchecked/media/75343/The-Lincoln-Memorial-Washington-DC; (b) Walt Disney Concert Hall. [Photograph]. In Encyclopædia Britannica. Retrieved from http://www.britannica.com/EBchecked/media/94486/Walt-Disney-Concert-Hall-Los-Angeles-designed-by-Frank-O

the modern textbook, the same? Could you propose another proof of the same theorem?

2. Give examples of interesting geometrical constructions in the world around us. Why did you find these constructions interesting? Could they be used as examples in a lesson? If so, how?

3. How would you explain to students that one of the buildings depicted in Figure 11.2 seems more "regular" to you than the other? What is more "regular" a circle or a square? Why?

4. Give examples of situations from real life where one has to provide definitions and check if a particular object corresponds to it or not.

5. Give some examples of assignments that would correspond to each of the five levels in the van Hiele schema.

6. You have been asked to design a unit on Area. What might it look like to align you instruction about Area to the first 3 Van Hiele levels? Provide a sequence of 3 instructional tasks you might develop (one aligned to each level) that could help students learn the concept of Area at that level.

USING A VARIETY OF APPROACHES

Geometry Is Not Just Proofs

Ms. Cho began the lesson by explaining a game that she used to play with her friends when she was little. One player would draw the head of a person on a piece of paper, fold it, and then pass it on to the next player. The second player would draw the neck and shoulders, again fold the paper, pass it on to the next, and so forth. In the end the paper would be unfolded to everyone's amusement, as the outcome was usually funny, along the lines of the one depicted in Figure 11.3.

Figure 11.3

"Now, would it be possible," asked the teacher, "to explain *in words* what is drawn on the piece of paper without actually unfolding it and showing it to everyone?"

Ms.Cho then drew a figure on the board (Figure 11.4 a), and asked the class to examine it closely and commit it to memory. She then concealed the drawing and asked: "Tell me, what should I draw in order to get exactly the same figure."

"A rectangle," said someone.

"And how does one draw a rectangle?" Ms. Cho feigned ignorance, "Like this?" (Figure 11.4.b)

"Noooo," cried the class, "all the angles need to be right!"

"Oh, all right then," the teacher nodded seemingly getting it, "Like this you mean?" (Figure 11.4c)

"No!" Some rushed up to draw it themselves, but the teacher reminded them that, according to the rules of the game, they could only explain to her in words what should be drawn and could not do the drawing themselves. After a while someone suggested first to draw a segment, then to drop perpendiculars from both its ends in the same direction, and then from the other end of one of the two perpendiculars to draw another perpendicular up to the point where it transects the other perpendicular coming from the original segment (Figure 11.4 d). In the process it became clear that the lengths of the segment and the perpendiculars were also important. After measuring the original figure the class was able to formulate and test the algorithm for constructing the figure in question.

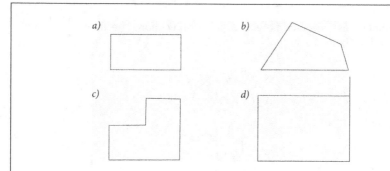

Figure 11.4

When the discussion was finished Ms. Cho divided the class into groups. Each group was given a different figure (e.g., Figure 11.5) and asked to describe it (i.e., to work out and formulate the algorithm for its construction). Each description was then passed on to the next group which discussed it and whose representative was then asked to construct the figure on the board. In the end the entire class compared the original figure and the one obtained in this way and discussed how the assignment was performed.

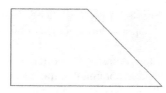

Figure 11.5

In the course of this activity students did not carry out any proofs. And yet they did genuine geometry. There is no doubt that they were developing the skills of distinguishing the properties of geometrical figures and of describing them. The teacher never asked whether a particular description of the figure was what actually defined it. Nevertheless, the students were, in effect, already answering this question, though in an informal way, and they were therefore being prepared for the next stage of geometrical development.

Informal Geometry: Working on Concept Formation

Van Dormolen and Arcavi (2000) note that: "Definitions are usually not starting points of a new idea, but rather the end point." Students must not simply learn by heart what a circle is, but must, under the teacher's supervision, form a mental image of the concept and realize the necessity for its exact description (i.e., definition). In the end they ought to be able to reach a verbal definition of the circle themselves. Work on concept-formation is a vital component of geometry in middle school. This geometry could be called "informal" insofar as it does not presume an acquaintance with axioms and rigorous proofs or with any sort of sophisticated use of mathematical symbolism. This does not mean, however, that it lacks substance and variety or that it fails to challenge students.

Today one rarely sees lessons in middle school where the teacher would simply be dictating to the class the properties of geometrical figures. Usually the lesson is constructed as a sequence of activities. However, all too often these activities are based on students simply recognizing particular objects or measuring some of their magnitudes. By contrast, assignments that prompt students to define and describe geometrical figures independently are given extremely rarely. And yet student can and should be involved in a whole range of fundamentally different assignments, all of which would be developing various aspects of their geometrical thinking. Here are some suggestions for how this can be achieved.

"Find Common Features. Divide into Groups"

Even seemingly simple problems based on recognizing objects are not quite so straightforward to schoolchildren. One of the difficulties lies in the fact that schoolchildren often link some additional, irrelevant feature to the analyzed concept (Clements & Battista, 1992). For instance, the problem "Indicate all right triangles represented in Figure 11.6" has been known occasionally to cause difficulties because students sometimes think that the right angle cannot be situated "on top." As already mentioned, it is important to encourage students to express their thinking and to explain how they have reached the solution and why particular objects belong to a particular group, while others do not.

This can be achieved through slightly more complex problems in which students are asked to determine the common features of particular objects

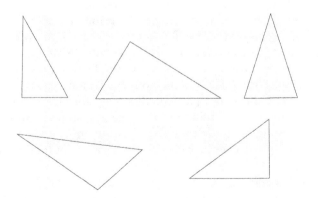

Figure 11.6

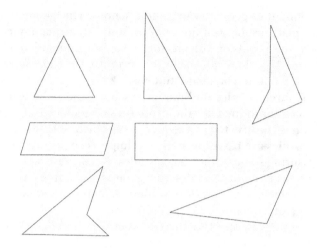

Figure 11.7

and/or reclassify them in one way or another. Such problems are to a large degree open-ended. For example, asking students to divide the figures represented in Figure 11.7 into two groups will likely produce very different answers. They could, for example, be divided into quadrilateral and triangles, or into figures that have a right angle and those that do not, or even those that are convex and those that are not. The teacher must emphasize from the beginning that the problem can be solved in different ways and that any solution is acceptable so long as it is properly justified.

Why are such assignments important? What is important is not the answer itself but rather the process of searching for common properties of objects, which inevitably requires some analysis, and also the process of searching for the appropriate verbal means to express any differences. The mathematical language used by students can be rather imperfect initially, but it should become increasingly more precise through discussion with peers and the teacher. One of the virtues of this type of assignment is that it prompts students to look for new and more accurate ways of expressing themselves.

Another virtue of such problems lies in the fact that they help develop logical thinking. The students' ability to relate various classes of objects has been highlighted above as a particularly important factor in determining their level of geometrical thinking. By engaging students in this kind of work, by prompting them to deal with such problems, and by helping them find a solution, the teacher actively aids the progress of their thought.

"Cut and Re-Assemble"

There is a whole variety of traditional assignments in cutting up and reassembling geometrical objects. We have already mentioned some useful

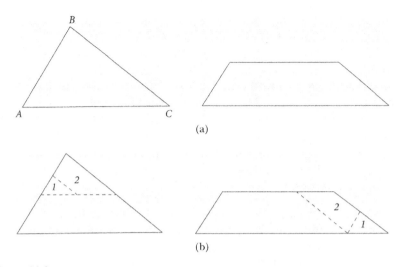

(a)

(b)

Figure 11.8

classical problems where this method helps establish the equality of the areas of different figures. Here is one example of such a problem:

"Cut the given trapezoid into pieces and use these pieces to assemble the given triangle ABC (Figure 11.8a)." The solution is represented in Figure 11.8b.

Similar problems can be particularly useful for deriving geometrical formulas. In this way derivation becomes provable and at the same time visually clear. Students can also be asked to discuss whether this can be done in all cases, i.e., whether figures with equal areas can always be made up of the same set of pieces. In the general case, the answer is negative. For example, the figures represented in Figure 11.9 have equal areas but the rectangle cannot be assembled out of a finite range of pieces that make up the circle. However, for polygons the answer is affirmative (Eves, 1963). Naturally, having students prove this assertion in middle school is undesirable, but the analysis of a few concrete figures is still useful as a way of developing students' geometrical intuition.

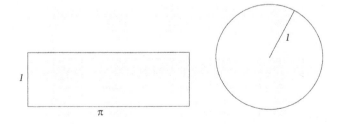

Figure 11.9

The ability to recognize congruent figures mentally is also developed in answering simple-sounding questions such as:

"Cut a square into 4 congruent parts. Do this in all ways possible that you can think of." Some answers are provided in Figure 11.10.

Sobel and Maletsky (1999) suggest a similar problem: "Cut some 4×4 squares from graph paper. Then find how many different ways you can cut them into congruent halves along the grid lines." Some possibilities are provided in Figure 11.11.

A step in the direction of proof. There are also other examples of cutting assignments, such as the following:

"A figure is represented in Figure 11.12a.

A. Assemble any larger figure out of a number of these figures
B. Show that the figure in Figure 11.12b, can be assembled out of such smaller figures
C. Determine whether the figure in Figure 11.12c can be assembled out of such figures."

The last question entails a step in the direction of geometrical proof. When students see that they are not getting anywhere with assembling the figure

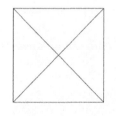 

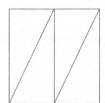 

Figure 11.10

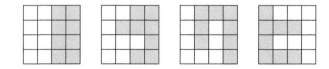

Figure 11.11

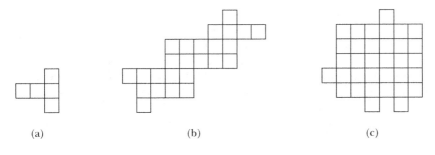

(a) (b) (c)

Figure 11.12

in Figure 11.12c, they can be asked whether it is possible to demonstrate that it is not just they who are having trouble with it, but that the figure itself cannot be constructed as such. A short proof would consist in showing that the number of cells that the figure in Figure 11.12c is made up of is not divisible by 5, while the number of cells of the smaller figure is made up of 5 cells. This means that the latter can be used to only build figures with the number of cells that are multiples of 5. Students, however, usually reason differently, namely by examining various possible cases ("If a figure is positioned in this way, then the next one must be put that way, . . ." and so forth). What is important, though, is the very experience of reasoning, and especially the realization that it is necessary to justify the impossibility of constructing the figure, rather than being content to say: "it does not seem possible."

"Imagine and Draw"

A lot has already been said about problems that require giving examples. In geometry such examples can be created as drawings, thereby instantly uniting the description with a visual image. Here are some assignments that bring this out.

- Is it possible for the diagonal of a quadrilateral to lie outside it?
- Can two parallelograms be non congruent if their sides are mutually parallel?
- A circle is given. Is it possible to construct another four circles with the same radius that would be tangent to this circle and would not intersect each other? What about five circles? And six?

There can be a great variety of such questions. Depending on their stage of development, students can answer them with different degrees of understanding. At first, methods of trial and error prevail ("let us try drawing it; it might just work"); gradually, however, students learn to plan their drawings and start off by forming a mental image of what is required.

On the role of such assignments in the development of spatial abilities. Let us dwell some more on the role that such assignments (where one is asked to imagine something, then describe and draw it) may play in developing students' spatial abilities. Indeed, spatial abilities can be substantially enhanced through instruction (Bishop, 1980), especially with the help of this kind of assignment. When assigning such problems, it is desirable for students later to have the ability to check their conclusions on a model. Some examples of this type of assignment have already been given in Chapter 4. Here are a few more:

- A cube is being examined. Is it possible for a plane to intersect a cube in such a way that the section would be a triangle? A rectangle? A pentagon? A hexagon? A heptagon?
- Imagine, describe and draw two different polyhedrons with five vertices.
- The right triangle ABC, with right angle ABC, is revolving around the straight line $\overleftrightarrow{AC}$. Describe the 3-D solid obtained in this way. And if the triangle is revolving around the straight line $\overleftrightarrow{AB}$, what does the solid look like?
- Which 2-D figure needs to be revolved in order to obtain the figure in Figure 11.13?
- Which of the nets in Figure 11.14 can be used to construct a cube?

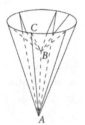

Figure 11.13

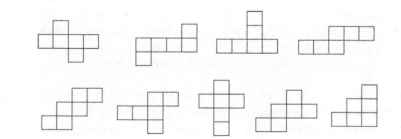

Figure 11.14

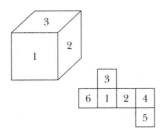

Figure 11.15

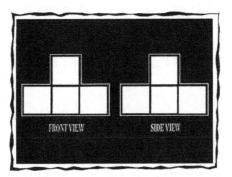

Figure 11.16

- Figure 11.15 shows a cube, the faces of which are numbered 1 to 6, and also a net of this cube. What numbers are on the back and side faces of the cube?
- An object is made up of small cubes. Figure 11.16 shows the view of the object from the front and the left side. What is the maximum and minimum number of small cubes that could be used to create this object?

When giving such assignments, the teacher needs to find time for a certain amount of preparatory work, as well as subsequent discussion of the solution. It is particularly useful to analyze drawings of spatial figures, to compare them with models and to discuss how they were obtained. Asking students to construct models themselves could also be helpful. Students can, for example, discuss what sort of net is needed in order to obtain a tetrahedron, for instance. They can then draw this net, cut it out and glue it together.

Such assignments should appear regularly in lessons. Students' spatial reasoning will progress only through consistent and systematic work. The use of manipulatives and technology also play an important role (as will be discussed below).

"Explain Why the Drawing Proves the Formula"

Geometry can also be used to make assertions from other parts of mathematics in a visual way. Algebraic assertions can, for example, be translated into a geometrical language for this purpose. Students are likely to find it difficult to perform such "translations" (i.e., to know what exactly to draw) all on their own. However, they should be able to reason adequately on a ready-made drawing. Here are three examples of such assignments.

Analyze Figure 11.17 and use it to reach an assertion about the sum $1 + 2 + \ldots + n$.

Analyze Figure 11.18 and use it to reach an assertion about the sum $1 + 3 + \ldots + (2n + 1)$.

Analyze Figure 11.19 and use it to reach an assertion about the infinite geometric sum $1 + x + x^2 + \ldots$. (What constraints are there on the value of x?)

"Investigate"

Theorems and assertions otherwise studied in high school also can be used as something that middle school students can investigate. This idea is hardly new. Teachers have traditionally asked students to measure the angles of triangles and find their sum, for example. Another common assignment is to ask students to construct the three medians of a triangle, whereby they reach the conclusion that the medians intersect in a single point. The modern, broader understanding of geometry, together with the availability of computerized technology, such as dynamic geometry software, now permits teachers to easily organize other types of investigation as well.

Figure 11.17

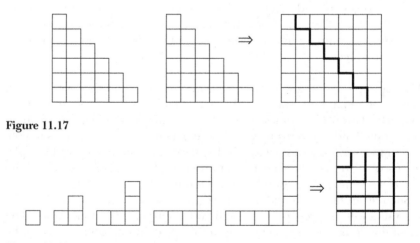

Figure 11.18

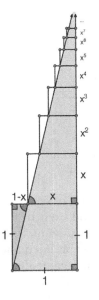

Figure 11.19

In modern geometry plenty of attention is devoted to problems that were not even considered in Euclid's time—problems that have to do with ascertaining certain geometrical magnitudes and defining the position of particular groups of points (Boltyanski et al., 1997). Naturally, such problems usually cannot be studied rigorously by schoolchildren, but they can provide material that students can experiment on. This opens up a whole new perspective on geometry.

| Examining *an* Example | **Examples of Problems Requiring Investigation** |

Examine the following problem:

Three towns are situated at the vertices of the isosceles right triangle MNK (Figure 11.20a). Determine the location of the airport A so that the total dis-

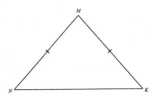

Figure 11.20a

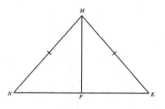

Figure 11.20b

tance of straight roads leading to it from each of the towns (i.e., the sum AM + AN + AK) would be minimal.

This problem is a particular case of Fermat's problem (Coxeter, 1961). Its solution in a general form, and even in the given case, is far from easy. However, today's middle school student, working in the computer environment, can move on quickly to experimentation. It is relatively easy to come up with the hypothesis that the sought-after point A will lie somewhere on the altitude $\overline{MP}$ of the triangle (Figure 11.20b), otherwise there would be more than one such point, since the triangle is symmetrical in relation to the straight line $\overleftrightarrow{MP}$, which does not look very plausible. Students can confirm this hypothesis by considering a few examples. They can then compare the sums of distances for different points lying on the altitude. Once they have found point A they can study its properties, notably the angle NAK (which turns out to be 120°).

Such assignments, among others, help students see the need for proofs, thereby aiding the transition to the next stage of studying geometry—the level of deduction. Let us stress again that the process of developing the students' thinking does not happen all on its own, or even simply by virtue of giving students particular problems. Teachers should continuously aid students by drawing their attention to the most significant aspects of what they are studying, by asking why-questions and by encouraging students to ask such questions themselves.

Continuing with the Informal Approach

The above problems do not exhaust all the different ways of working with students in informal geometry. Indeed, classical problems of constructing figures with a limited range of drawing instruments (a compass and a straightedge, a compass only, or just a right-angled set square, etc.), which have not been discussed here, remain extremely useful. What is important, though, is not to pose these problems as ready-made algorithms that are derived from no-one-knows-where, but rather as exercises in applying certain heuristic problem-solving strategies.

While completing such exercises, students will be able to "precisely describe, classify, and understand relationships among types of two-and three-dimensional objects using their defining properties" (NCTM, 2000). This is important, especially if one wants to achieve the appropriate transition to a more rigorous and abstract geometry course. And yet this does not imply once a particular stage is reached that informal geometry "disappears" and simply gives way to rigorous deductive geometry. The habits developed in the informal approach, the skill of experimentation, of formulating hypotheses, and finally, of working with a drawing or a model, will remain useful here too, as will the types of assignments outlined above.

Teaching Proofs

> The teacher, Mr. Brown spent the lesson meticulously proving a theorem. The next day a girl who had not attended the class asked him: "So there is nothing for me to catch up on for the next lesson? I've been told that nothing new was done."

The teacher was somewhat offended by this comment for, in his view, the lesson had, in fact, been extremely important. Children, however, often perceive things differently—what they find important is learning how to act rather than how to justify the fact that their actions are correct. Analyzing this sort of miscommunication between teachers and students (when students are asking themselves: "what is he after here?"), Herbst (2002b) describes it as an unwitting parting from the didactic contract—of the tacit agreement about what goes on in the process of instruction (Brousseau, 1984).

Proofs in the History of Mathematics and Mathematics Education

History demonstrates that humanity did not understand or appreciate the role of proof immediately. Ancient Egyptians built pyramids, but it appears that they did not consider why the methods they were using were correct (Eves, 1990). Only with Ancient Greek mathematics did proofs acquire such a vital role.

On the other hand, teaching students proofs, asking them to learn them by heart and to reproduce them (rather than conduct them independently), has been considered an essential part of school mathematics for centuries. The more contemporary motto "Not to learn proofs, but to prove, must be the task" (cited in Herbst, 2002a) has emerged only comparatively recently. Indeed, the two-column system of proof appeared in American schools specifically as a way to show students what they must do in order to carry out proof independently. This quite progressive step was made only at the beginning of the twentieth century (Herbst, 2002a).

It is worth noting that today the role of proofs in geometry varies across different curricula. Hoyles et al. (2003) remark on the "enormous variation in the approach taken to proof." While in some countries proofs as such are hardly mentioned, in others formal proofs run throughout the entire geometry course. And yet, more or less everywhere, geometry is the mathematics course in which proofs are used the most. In other courses (e.g., algebra) proofs are accorded far less attention. This is especially the case in the United States.

Why Are Proofs Essential to the Geometry Course?

The CCSS-M (2010) SMPs indicate that students should regularly engage in constructing viable arguments and critiquing the reasoning of others, as a frequent way of engaging in and practicing mathematics. So why are proofs so essential to the geometry course?

Moore (1994) rightly observes that even in lower-level university courses only very few proofs are required of students. For this reason the experience that students gain with geometrical proofs is probably their only encounter with proofs before embarking on upper-level mathematics courses, where full proofs are required everywhere. From this situation, students who emerge from a geometry course having not learned to construct proofs are unable to do mathematics seriously at all.

Geometry proofs are a guide to mathematical proofs in general. Without knowing anything about mathematics of the kind studied in upper-level courses, which includes rigorous proof, it is impossible for students to know whether they actually want and are able to take such courses in the first place. This means that by reducing proof in mathematics, access to serious mathematics is simply barred for the majority, and especially, in fact, to educationally disadvantaged groups of the population.

Moreover, proofs are important not just as a way of preparing students for further mathematical study. Traditionally, it has been considered that "geometrical demonstration is to be chiefly prized as a discipline in complete, exact and logical statement" (Eliot et al, cited in Herbst, 2002a). Experience carrying out proofs helps develop logical thinking.

In the modern world, we frequently have to test certain propositions by deriving their consequences, by examining particular cases, or by checking the veracity of some general assumption. Of course, simple and direct transfer of all the theorems developed in a proof to other spheres should not be expected. However, Vygotsky (1986) highlighted the mutual interaction of processes (taking place in school) where scientific concepts are formed and where the understanding of concepts encountered in everyday life is gradually perfected. Consequently, it can be expected that the experience of logical analysis in proving theorems will be relevant not just for the study of geometry.

This still does not exhaust the significance of proofs. Herbst (2002a) rightly stresses the role of proofs "as the internal mechanism by which mathematical concepts and properties are shaped—in particular, as the search for the conditions under which certain assertions are true." Only by carrying out proofs can students fully comprehend what exactly a particular property provides and, in general, how truth is established in mathematical assertions. Proof thus serves as a tool for understanding the discipline of mathematics as such. However, for them to truly serve this purpose, much needs to be changed in the way proofs are usually carried out and taught in school.

Reflecting on Research: Student difficulties in understanding the role of proofs

Schoenfeld (1985) has remarked that schoolchildren often see proofs as just a formal procedure, for some reason customary in geometry, and with no obvious relation to problem solving. The formal side of the proof—the meticulous noting down of statements and reasons often conceals its substantive side—i.e., the reason why the proof is being carried out.

Fishbein and Kedem (1982) conducted an experiment where students were asked to prove that by joining the four midpoints of an arbitrary quadrilateral a parallelogram is formed. Afterwards, they asked the students whether it would be useful to check this assertion again on various examples to make sure it is indeed correct. A large number of students thought that checking would be useful, thereby demonstrating clearly that they had failed to understand why they had carried out the proof in the first place. In fact, students often perceive three or four examples as more convincing evidence than a proof, since in their mind a proof is just a single example (Balacheff, 1988; Chazan, 1993).

Combining "Formal" and "Informal" Approaches

These and other studies (Clements & Battista, 1992; Hershkowitz, 1990) are evidence of the rift that seems to exist between informal (empirical) and formal geometry. Generally speaking, proofs come up rarely and, most importantly, are often used without proper motivation. All too often, proofs appear disconnected from what is actually dealt with during the lesson, but rather in the form of an educative problem that stands in isolation and exists simply to give students an idea of how the deductive method works. Yet, the deductive method itself is here compromised by the fact that it is used to reach some quite obvious assertions, using postulates that students tend to perceive as artificial (Usiskin, 1997).

Proofs need to *grow out* of the empirical approach. Schoolchildren should be asked to work on situations where hypotheses that first come to mind actually turn out to be false and where trying to generalize from only a few examples ultimately leads to erroneous results. For schoolchildren, the fact that one or even a few cases do not confirm an assertion in a general way is not as obvious as it is to a professional mathematician. Students need to be asked to consider how many confirming cases are necessary before one can be persuaded of the veracity of an assertion (sometimes it is indeed possible to check all the possibilities, but more often this proves to be impossible). The question of how, in principle, one can become fully convinced of the truth of a theorem should be accorded as much attention as its formulation and its formal proof.

Choosing a reasonable level of mathematical rigor.   On the other hand, proof is not just formal notation organized in two columns. Even in the context of scholarly mathematics, different levels of rigor of exposition depend on the context in question (Usiskin, 1987). In school proofs one should certainly not attempt to emulate courses in the foundations of geometry and meticulously list all the axioms used. If the professional mathematician, in devising such a course, chooses the minimal (the most concise) system of axioms, the mathematics educator ought to choose the system that is the most effective from a pedagogical point of view—i.e., the one that is visually clearest, the most natural and also the most convenient for students to use themselves when carrying out proofs (which means that the system of axioms could include some "redundant" ones; i.e., those that could be proven on the basis of others and that are therefore not strictly necessary). What is more, the grounding of the school course in geometry should not necessarily entail the explicit listing of axioms. One can simply discuss "obvious" assertions and use these in the process of proving assertions that are "not obvious."

Others have characterized varying taxonomies of students' proof and proving schemes. Harel and Sowder (1998), for example, characterized three broad categories of increasing sophistication: external conviction proof schemes, empirical proof schemes, and analytical proof schemes. Overall, external conviction schemes rely on external authority of some form, whereas empirical schemes rely on examples and inductive arguments, and analytical schemes rely of definitions, properties and deductive arguments. They further distinguish some of these schemes according to inductive, perceptual, transformational, and axiomatic ways of engaging in reasoning.

Proof Can Be "Informal"!   Usiskin (1987) suggests that the term "informal geometry" is in actuality not entirely appropriate, insofar as it is usually difficult to answer the question: "where does informality stop and formality begin?" Students should certainly be taught proofs, but these proofs can remain "informal." For instance, one can prove the fact that the two base angles of an isosceles triangle are congruent, by folding across the bisectors of the angle at the vertex (Usiskin, 1987). Both giving up all attempt at proof and trying immediately to explain to students in detail the full system of axioms used are unjustifiably extreme. Proof, experiment, visual representation and intuitive thinking must all be interconnected. Furthermore, the teacher must always take into account the specific difficulties experienced by the class in question and the exact level that the students have attained.

Reflecting on Research: Student difficulties in carrying out proofs

Research discusses some of the difficulties students experience in carrying out proofs. Students often fail to remember the required assertions (Brumfield, 1973) and they do not make enough use of the necessary schemas and mental models. In other words they fail to organize adequately what they know (Chinnappan, 1998; Lawson & Chinnappan, 2000). Usiskin (1997) lists several causes of difficulties experienced by students. Among them is the fact that students actually have poorly developed writing skills and also that the study of proofs takes place in isolation from the rest of the course. Students are not exposed to the kind of ideas used in proofs (if-then statements, justification, etc.) prior to starting the geometry course, and these ideas are not developed or applied further in subsequent study.

NCTM (2000) cites the development of reasoning and communication skills as one of the principal tasks of school mathematics. The CCSS-M (2010) Standards for Mathematical Practice similarly emphasize these two ideas, specifying that students should "Reason abstractly and quantitatively" as well as "Construct viable arguments and critique the reasoning of others." Such work should take place for the entire duration of schooling. In regard to improving students' written proofs, one of the keys to success lies in ensuring that proofs do not appear only in geometry.

Developing Proof Skills: Different Age Groups

This, however, does not eliminate the need for constantly developing proof skills in geometry. Clements and Battista (1992) distinguish three age groups in the development of proof skills. At the first level (7–8 years of age) children's thinking is unsystematic and not always entirely logical. At the next level (between the ages of 7–8 and 11–12) the students' thinking becomes logical but remains empirical in character. Only at the third stage (from the age of 11–12) do students become capable of mathematical deduction.

NCTM (2000) notes that "early efforts at justification by young children will involve trial-and-error strategies or the unsystematic trying of many cases" (p. 59). However, by the time they reach the upper classes of elementary school, gradually, working under the teachers' supervision, students learn to become more systematic, which includes being more capable of carrying out meaningful lines of reasoning and proofs. Similar to the development of communication skills, students' reasoning and proof starts off by using pictures and signs. Later, they start adding detail to the text. After that students start to provide justifications, using ordinary language. Finally, they acquire the ability to carry out proofs using mathematical symbolism (NCTM, 2000, p. 62).

Middle and secondary teachers usually work with children who have been through the first stages of the lengthy and systematic process that prepare them for understanding and independently carrying out proofs. However, the subsequent stages of this process are no less important as plenty still depends on how the teacher scaffolds the students' work. Students are often still unable to operate within the framework of an entire axiomatic system or to carry out a proof entirely on their own. However, they can do the whole or at least part of the proof with the support of the teacher, and they can reason deductively, while remaining within the limits of a relatively narrow range of assertions.

Examples of Assignments for Developing Proof Skills

An example of such work would be exercises with "if–then statements" or "because statements," when the teacher asks students to choose from a set of propositions the one that completes an assertion (giving an explanation of their choice). For example, such an assignment may look something like this:

In Figure 11.21 is a triangle. Choose the phrases that can be used to complete the sentence and explain your choice.
The angle ACB is 60° because...

1. All angles in triangles are 60°
2. ...the length of the base of an isosceles triangle should be smaller than the sum of the lengths of its legs
3. ...in isosceles triangles the base angles are congruent and sum of angles in a triangle equal to 180°

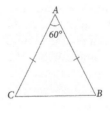

Figure 11.21

Filling out the blanks in proofs. It is also possible to give students exercises where they must fill out spaces left blank in a proof. Here is an example of such an assignment based on the proof of a comparatively complex assertion:

In Figure 11.22 is an isosceles triangle ABC. $\overrightarrow{BK}$ is the bisector of the angle DBC. Fill in the gaps of the proof that the straight lines $\overleftrightarrow{BK}$ and $\overleftrightarrow{AC}$ are parallel.

1. $m\angle DBC = 180° - m\angle ABC$, because...
2. $m\angle ABC = 180° - m\angle BAC - m\angle BCA$, because...
3. From these two assertions it follows that...
4. Since AB = BC, then...
5. From points 3 and 4 it follows that $m\angle DBC = 2m\angle BCA$.
6. This equality can be rewritten as $m\angle BCA = ...$
7. Since $\overrightarrow{BK}$ is the bisector of the angle DBC, then $m\angle KBC = ...$
8. From points 6 and 7, it follows that...
9. From point 8 it follows that the straight lines $\overleftrightarrow{BK}$ and $\overleftrightarrow{AC}$ are parallel, because...

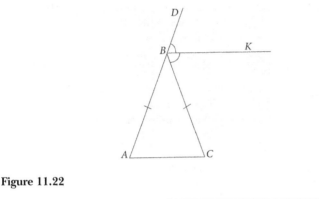

Figure 11.22

Filling out blanks in this example involves a whole variety of assignments: namely, finding *reasons*, including the citing of theorems already studied, and also formulating *statements*, both very simple ones (transformation of equalities) and those that assume a certain level of knowledge and logical development. Of course, the basic difficulty of the proof is removed by the fact that the entire reasoning sequence is provided in advance. Nevertheless, such work performs a useful transition from simply understanding somebody else's proof to carrying out proof independently. It is also possible to use proof analysis in this way, especially when students are asked to locate faults within a proof sequence and to propose ways of amending it.

Organizing a collective "recollection" of useful facts. Doing proofs independently is more successful if it is preceded by a collective "recollection" of facts used in proving other facts. In organizing this sort of "recollecting," it is better not to formulate explicitly even the facts that require proving, but instead to leave it to students to discover these for themselves.

Examine the following problem.

In Figure 11.23 is a rhombus ABCD. $m\angle CAD = 30°$. Prove that $m\angle ABC = 120°$.

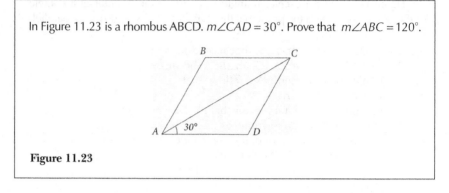

Figure 11.23

It is useful to do preparatory work for this proof by discussing with students what they know about rhombuses. One can also reformulate the assignment and make it more open-ended by saying: "Discover as much new information about this rhombus as possible. Explain how you have obtained this information."

Such an approach helps connect the "mathematics of proof" with the "mathematics of discovery." Proof here emerges as part of problem solving, clarifying what exactly is obtained from the information provided and how this information can be used.

Encouraging Students to Use a Variety of Approaches

As students are developing the skill of carrying out proofs, the teacher can begin to involve them in discussing other approaches to the same proof or of critiquing the arguments of another proof. The CCSS-M (2010) standards specify that students should regularly engage in "construct[ing] viable arguments and critique[ing] the reasoning of others." NCTM (2000) calls on teachers to "select and use various types of reasoning and methods of proof." The next chapter contains one example that demonstrates a range of possible ways of proving the same fact. The teacher must always be open to different approaches to proof that students themselves might take. Students should feel the pleasure not just of discovering a new fact but also of discovering a new proof.

Making Abstractions Visual

From time immemorial people have used physical objects to facilitate mathematical operations (Eves, 1990). The use of concrete objects and physical actions makes it easier to work with abstract mathematical concepts.

In studying geometry, which by its nature deals with the visual, the role of manipulatives is particularly significant. Educational research (Fuys et al., 1988) provides convincing evidence of their pedagogical utility. Indeed, many geometrical models and other teaching aids for performing geometrical experiments exist (starting with simple blocks and the geoboard); alternately, many can be created from scratch or found in the immediate surroundings. And yet such manipulatives are still not used nearly enough.

Different Aspects of Using Manipulatives

Mistretta (2003) states that 75% of the schoolchildren that she surveyed had no experience in working with manipulatives, while only 5% responded that they used them systematically. Other studies confirm this data (Cook-Bax, 1996). Literature also notes that textbooks often fail to recommend the use of manipulatives to a sufficient degree (Clements & Battista, 1992).

At the same time, the use of manipulatives in itself does not guarantee success. Students can experience difficulties in transferring to other situations what they have grasped in their work with manipulatives. In particular, they can continue to associate certain properties with the prototype, failing to generalize them (Nickson, 2000).

The problem therefore lies in how to use manipulatives in the most effective way and how to prepare meaningful activities with them. Here, the teacher's role is vital, on the one hand engaging students in problem solving, and on the other asking very precise questions, helping them make the necessary generalizations.

Using Models of Geometrical Objects

Models of different geometrical objects enable students to see and actually "feel" the objects in question. The ability to recognize geometrical objects (corresponding to the first level in the van Hiele schema) is formed precisely through contact with concrete objects. It is important for the teacher to draw the students' attention to the fact that, for example, the classroom usually has the shape of a rectangular parallelepiped, and indicating its vertices, edges and faces. It is then desirable to ask further questions, such as, "can you point to other objects with the same form," or "can you identify polyhedrons that are not parallelepipeds." Comparison between different models is the first step towards generalization and abstraction.

Comparing models to other forms of geometrical representation helps in the further development of abstract thought. Kelly et al. (2002) discuss the use of blocks as a way to develop students' understanding of projection and perspective. Assignments asking students to draw an object from a model, or, on the contrary, to select a model that would correspond to a drawing, or else to imagine an object and then test one's image on a model, have already been mentioned above.

Strutchens et al. (2001) discuss the use of manipulatives as a way of evaluating the development of the students' understanding of geometrical concepts. In one study students were given different triangles and asked to compare their perimeters without using a straightedge. To complete the assignment it was sufficient to directly compare the sides of the triangles. This, however, proved too hard for many students since the operation went beyond their understanding of the concept of perimeter.

Work with manipulatives as a multi-stage activity. Teachers can also give students assignments where the analysis of concrete objects leads to formulating certain generalizations, which can in turn be tested on other concrete models. For instance, students can be asked to calculate the number of vertices (v), edges (e) and faces (f) of different polyhedrons and then to study the connection between these numbers. By examining the models, students can reach the hypothesis that $v - e + f = 2$. They can then be asked to test the hypothesis on other polyhedrons (by doing a drawing or by using a different model). Such testing can include, for example, *proof* that for all pyramids the formula $v - e + f = 2$ is true (since the number of side faces is the same as the number of base vertices and the number of base edges is the same as the number of side edges and base vertices). The teacher can then also propose to students to work with a polyhedron with a "hole" (Figure 11.24), thus prompting them to make further observations and generalizations.

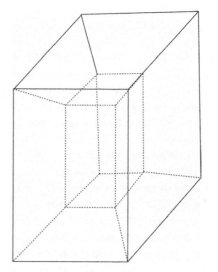

Figure 11.24

Perham et al. (1997) describe how in working with models of triangles—by cutting them out and weighing them—the students reached the hypothesis that the point of intersection of the medians is the triangle's center of gravity. In the process they were involved in answering the question of why different triangles may weigh the same amount. By working with real materials that could be cut up, the students were able to see clearly that the change in shape did not necessarily change either the weight or the area of the triangle, and this helped them resolve any difficulties.

Summing up: Manipulatives as part of the problem-solving oriented classroom. The role of manipulatives was significant in each of the above cases, but what was particularly important was that they were not used in isolation but as part of a unified process that included exploration, reasoning and, at times, proof. Technology can also provide a wealth of resources for work of this kind.

Using Virtual Manipulatives

In the process of instruction one can use not only real but also virtual manipulatives, defined as interactive Web-based representations of objects (Moyer et al., 2002). The advantages of virtual manipulatives over concrete ones lies in their greater availability—students can use them at any time, including at home (providing one has Internet access, of course). Students can also modify virtual manipulatives far more freely than real ones. Finally, middle school students are generally more interested in working with computers than blocks, for example, which they perceive as "baby stuff" (Moyer et al., 2002). Some websites containing relevant material are cited in the appendices.

Using Dynamic Geometry Software

Pedagogical literature has discussed in considerable detail various aspects of the possible use of software in the process of instruction (Clements & Battista, 1992; Hoyles and Noss, 2003; Lagrange et al, 2003). Research indicates considerable improvements in teaching thanks to the use of technology. Some problems have also been noted, however, many of them similar to the ones occurring in the use of concrete manipulatives (e.g., the difficulty students have in performing generalizations and transferring what they have learned from one set of examples to another, and also the students' over-reliance on visual cues, etc.).

Exciting new possibilities are opened by the use of dynamic geometry software, such as Geometer's Sketchpad, GeoGebra, Cabri, or Sketch-Up. (Wasserman, 2014b, for example, discusses how the dynamic features of SketchUp may help students learn spatial reasoning and three-dimensional geometry, as connected to the Common Core State Standards in Mathematics.) They are especially useful in conducting mathematical experiments (an example of such experimentation with the use of technology has been given above, in the section discussing problems based on investigation). New drawings appear instantly and, most importantly, students can observe the actual *process* of a transformation. The "dragging" action, which enables the transformation of one object into another by simply moving the computer mouse, is more persuasive to students then the examination of a series of isolated cases—though, in fact, the dynamic manipulation simply serves to facilitate examining a large quantity of cases. Crucially, students are here exploring different situations themselves. The assertions reached in the process consequently appear far less abstract to them than those that they encounter in school textbooks. They have a feeling of "ownership" of the hypothesis they come up with, and the proof seems more natural and necessary to them than if it had been presented to them ready-made (Clements & Battista, 1992). Though deVilliers (2006) also describes the difficulties that can occur transitioning from the infinitely many inductive examples in a dynamic geometry environment to explanation through deductive reasoning, as students do not always see the need for further proof.

 Examples of Working with Problems in a Computer Environment

Galindo (1998) describes how the following problem can be used in class:

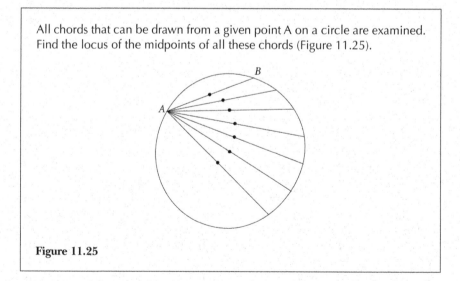

All chords that can be drawn from a given point A on a circle are examined. Find the locus of the midpoints of all these chords (Figure 11.25).

Figure 11.25

With the help of the dynamic geometry software students can move the other end B of the chord $\overline{AB}$ around the circle, and then trace or follow the path traversed by the middle of the chord. They can see that this locus of points is a circle. Only then can the teacher ask the question of actually proving this assertion, which is far from simple. The crucial step of formulating the hypothesis that needs to be proven is, however, made by the students themselves. Studying the situation with the help of a computer gives students a more convincing justification of the assertion in question.

Recently, with NCTM's *Focus in High School Mathematics* series, Dick & Hollebrands' (2011) edited volume also discusses in detail many other similar examples where technology can be used to support reasoning and sense making in the secondary classroom.

Aiming for the most productive use of technology: New challenges for teachers. In practice, the organization of students' creative work using dynamic geometry software can be extremely varied (e.g., Contreras, 2003; Zheng, 2002). What is important to note, however, is that such software in itself does not produce educational results. Lange (2002) describes, for instance, the failure of a teacher who wanted to lead his students to the independent discovery of the fact that the perpendicular bisector of the segment $\overline{AB}$ is the locus of the points equidistant from the endpoints A and B of this segment. Successful computer demonstrations did little to enable students to answer the question: "And what have you noticed?" Students gave a whole variety of answers (e.g., "however much you move the point the original segment remains the same" or "the distances between the point and the endpoints change when you move the point," etc.) but never the correct one.

Depending on the class, different strategies can be recommended in such situations. The teacher could, for example, render the question a bit more precise: "What have you noticed about the position of point D when it is equidistant from A and B?" It would also be possible to prepare the ground for the main assignment by giving students a selection of simpler problems that would point them in the desired direction. The problem could also be formulated more generally from the start (e.g., "how can one construct a perpendicular in relation to the given segment?" or "how can one find the point that would be equidistant from three other points?"), with subsequent activities being a function of solving this main problem, something that would allow students to structure their observations better. Either way, the role of the teacher as an organizer of the students' activities remains decisive.

What computers can do is improving by the day, and educational software is becoming more and more diverse. Geometry is at the cutting edge of IT research and development in this context. You need to follow the progress of technology and the new possibilities it affords in order to make its use in teaching as effective as possible.

Reflection

Assignments and Topics for Discussion

1. How could one define a square? What assignments would you give to students to prepare them for defining it and for their subsequent work with this concept?

2. Prepare some assignments based on those provided in the section "Geometry is not just proofs." For what school age students do you think they would be appropriate?

3. During the lesson a student says to the teacher: "What do I need the proof for? You tell me that what we are trying to prove is true and I fully believe you. Your word is enough for me." What would you answer if you were the teacher?

4. Give some examples of possible exercises with proofs from the algebra or the pre-calculus course.

5. Prepare some exercises on the model provided in the subsection "*Examples of assignments for developing proof skills*" where one is asked to choose between different endings for "because" or "if-then" statements.

6. Select a proof and prepare on its basis an assignment for filling in the blanks, using the model provided in the subsection "*Examples of assignments for developing proof skills*".

7. Imagine that you are asked to prepare a lesson designed to begin study of the topic of "Proof." How would you structure it?

8. Select or invent examples of some middle school and some high school assignments where you think the use of manipulatives would be particularly useful.

9. Analyze a virtual manipulative of your choice. In which situations could you use it effectively?

10. The following problem is examined: Determine locus of points for C, the right-angled vertex in the right triangle ABC with the given hypotenuse AB. How would you structure the lesson devoted to the solution of this problem using a dynamic geometry environment?

CHAPTER 12

GEOMETRY

Problem Solving and Lesson Planning

This chapter continues the discussion of the study of Geometry (started in the previous chapter). Its aim is to help the reader make the most of practical work with students on this topic.
This chapter discusses:

- Some challenging assignments that demonstrate the diversity of topics, devices and methods of use in the study of geometry.
- Some examples of geometry lessons in middle and high school.

HOW TO SOLVE IT? A SELECTION OF PROBLEMS

This section will examine some particularly interesting geometry problems. In particular, they demonstrate the diversity of questions studied in geometry and the plurality of approaches and methods that can be used to tackle them.

Mathematics in Middle and Secondary School, pages 347–380
Copyright © 2015 by Information Age Publishing
All rights of reproduction in any form reserved.

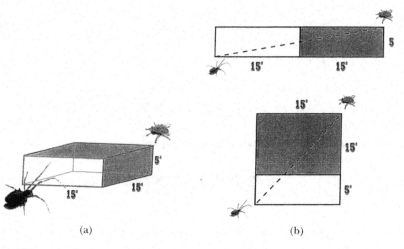

(a)   (b)

Figure 12.1

Example 1

A fly and a spider are sitting at the opposite ends of a box (Figure 12.1a). The fly is unable to move. The spider cannot decide which would be the quickest way to get to the fly—across the two side faces or first across the side face and then the top face. What would you advise the spider to do?

Discussion and Solution

This problem is useful for developing both spatial reasoning and proving skills. At the same time it can be seen as part of "informal" geometry, since everything here is very concrete and there is little need for abstract thinking. In order to determine the shortest way across the faces of the box we need to move from a three dimensional image to a flat one. Let us then draw the faces along which the spider can crawl (Figure 12.1b). We now see that the shortest path corresponds to the segment of a straight line. All that one needs to do now is to calculate—in the second case the path is evidently shorter, it is 25 feet.

Example 2

Is it possible to position 4 points on a plane in such a way that no 3 points would lie along a single straight line and no triangles formed have angles smaller than 45°? Is it possible to position 4 points on a plane in such a way that no 3 points lie along a single straight line and all triangles formed have angles larger than 45°?

Discussion and Solution

This example differs from the kind of geometry problems usually posed at school. This type of problem is usually found in combinatorial geometry where one studies different possible positions of figures under certain conditions and tries to establish the number of such positions. Problems in combinatorial geometry can be very complex, but it is desirable to find at least some room for them in school geometry. They emerge quite naturally in the process of geometrical experimentation—in the drawing and examination of models. At the same time, the discussion of why this or that construction can or cannot be obtained is useful for the development of reasoning skills.

In the above problem it is natural to start off by doing a drawing of the required position of the four points. In the first case it is actually not that hard to come up with the desired construction—one example is depicted on Figure 12.2a. Indeed, if the points occupy the vertices of a square, then in all the triangles there would be one right angle and two angles of 45°. None of the triangles have angles smaller than 45°. In the second case, however, any attempt to draw the construction in which all the angles would be larger than 45° fails. Let us prove this.

Four points can be distributed on a plane in two possible ways: either one of the points would lie inside the triangle formed by the other three (Figure 12.2b), or else the four points would form a convex quadrilateral (Figure 12.2c). In the first case, after marking all the points and connecting the inner point with the outer three, and after taking into consideration that the sum of all angles in a triangle equals 180° (see Figure 12.2d), we can write down that:

$$m\angle BAD + m\angle DAC + m\angle ACD + m\angle BCD + m\angle CBD + m\angle ABD = 180°.$$

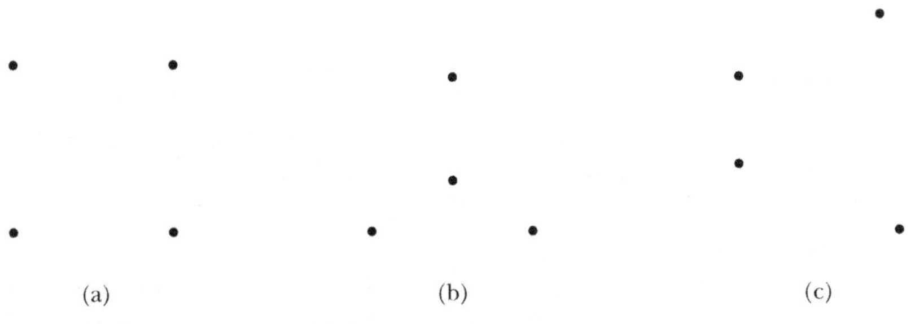

(a)   (b)   (c)

Figure 12.2a,b,c

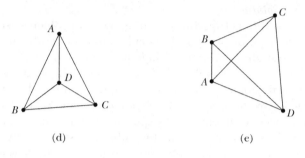

(d)   (e)

Figure 12.2d,e

Since one is adding up six angles, the smallest of them cannot be larger than

$$\frac{180°}{6} = 30°,$$

which means that it is evidently smaller than 45°.

We can reason in an analogous way in the second case and write that (Figure 12.2e):

$$m\angle ABD + m\angle DBC + m\angle ACB + m\angle ACD + m\angle BDC + m\angle ADB$$

$$+ m\angle BAC + m\angle CAD = 360°$$

Since the sum of eight angles equals 360°, this means that the smallest of them cannot be greater than

$$\frac{360°}{8} = 45°.$$

In this case too, at least one of the angles will not be larger than 45°.

Example 3

In Figure 12.3a are two ponds and point M. Mike said that when he walked in a straight line from the first pond to the second pond, point M was exactly midway. Mark out the path that Mike took.

Discussion and Solution

Using a more rigorous language, the problem can be formulated in the following way: indicate point A, lying on the curve U and point B lying on the curve V, such that point M would be the midpoint of the segment

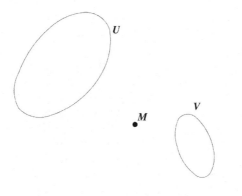

Figure 12.3a

$\overline{AB}$. Nothing is said here about the curves themselves. This is therefore a generalization of certain more concrete assignments in which one is given specific figures U and V. For instance, the following problem could be formulated: "The angle AOB is given and inside it is point M. Construct a segment, one end of which will lie on the side $\overrightarrow{OA}$ and the other on the side $\overrightarrow{OB}$ in such a way that M is its midpoint (Figure 12.3b). Here for set U one takes ray $\overrightarrow{OA}$, and for set V, ray $\overrightarrow{OB}$.

The above problem with the angle is comparatively easy. For instance, the fact that the diagonals of the parallelogram bisect each other can be used. Draw segment $\overline{OM}$, and extend it with the segment $\overline{MK}$ having the same length as $\overline{OM}$. Through point K one can then construct straight lines that would be parallel to the sides of the given angle. Let their points of intersection with these sides be N and L (Figure 12.3c). NKLO is a parallelogram, $\overline{OK}$ is its diagonal and M its center. Consequently, the diagonal $\overline{NL}$ will pass through point M and will be divided in half by it. In other words, the segment $\overline{NL}$ is precisely what is being sought.

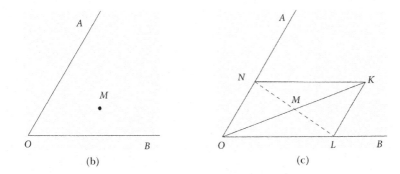

(b)   (c)

Figure 12.3b,c

However, such a solution is not possible for curves since one cannot construct any parallel lines or parallelograms here. So the problem needs to be examined anew.

Point M should be in the middle of the segment that we are looking for. This idea can be expressed in a different, at first glance more complex, way, by saying that point M should represent the center of the segment's symmetry. Such a formulation suggests that one needs to use transformations. In the case of point symmetry with the center M (or, using another wording, in the case of the rotation by 180° around point M), point A must pass into point B situated on the curve V. This gives us the means of construction.

Let us first construct curve W, by rotating curve U 180° around point M. We now situate point B at the intersection of the curves W and V (we assume that the curves are positioned in such a way that the problem has a solution). To construct point A let us rotate point B 180° around point M. Clearly, A must lie on the curve U since point B was situated on the curve W. The segment $\overline{AB}$ is the one we are looking for (Figure 12.3d). Naturally, there can be several solutions.

It could be observed that the solution of the problem with the angle was, in effect, quite close to the general solution insofar as the constructed rays $\overrightarrow{KN}$ and $\overrightarrow{KL}$ were symmetrical to the sides of the angle. In that case, however, one could have done without such terminology. The more complex problem has made its use inevitable and has revealed the essence of the method.

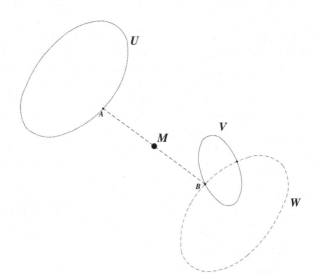

Figure 12.3d

Example 4

Prove that the medians of a triangle are concurrent and that their point of intersection divides each median into a ratio of $\frac{2}{1}$, counting from the vertex.

Discussion and Solution

This is a classical theorem from the common school course, which can be used to examine a whole variety of effective approaches to school geometry. Essentially, what we shall do below is use in different ways the heuristic strategy of examining a similar problem. The assertion about the medians is "similar" to many others, which means that the strategy used here can also be used in other cases.

Let us look at a triangle ABC, with $\overline{AM}$ and $\overline{BK}$ as its medians and O their point of intersection (Figure 12.4a). In order to prove the given assertion, it is sufficient to prove that

$$\frac{AO}{OM} = \frac{BO}{OK} = \frac{2}{1}.$$

In fact, then in a perfectly analogous way one can prove that if $\overline{CN}$ is the third median, and P the point of intersection of $\overline{CN}$ and $\overline{AM}$, then

$$\frac{AP}{PM} = \frac{CP}{PN} = \frac{2}{1}.$$

However, in that case we would get that points P and O are one and the same point, since they are both supposed to divide the segment $\overline{AM}$ into the ratio $\frac{2}{1}$, counting from point A. This will, indeed, mean that all three medians have a common point which divides each into the ratio $\frac{2}{1}$, counting from the vertex.

The proof that

$$\frac{AO}{OM} = \frac{BO}{OK} = \frac{2}{1}$$

can be obtained by different means.

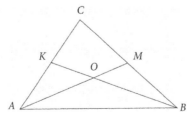

Figure 12.4a

Solution 1

In which geometrical assertions does one come across the ratio of the length of segments? One important example is the following theorem (sometimes called the side-splitting theorem).

If segment $\overline{XY}$ is parallel to side $\overline{AB}$ of triangle ABC, and points X and Y lie on sides $\overline{AC}$ and $\overline{BC}$, forming a similar triangle, then

$$\frac{CX}{AX} = \frac{CY}{BY}$$

(Figure 12.4b).

Let us use this assertion. To make things visually clearer, in Figure 12.4c the triangle ABC is positioned somewhat differently than before and we have also drawn the segment $\overline{KL}$, parallel to the segment $\overline{AM}$. Let us now examine the triangle AMC. From the side-splitting theorem we get that

$$\frac{CL}{LM} = \frac{CK}{AK}.$$

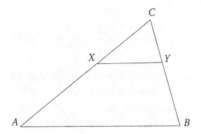

Figure 12.4b

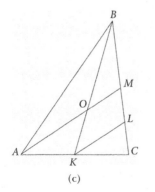

(c)

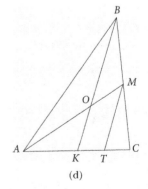

(d)

Figure 12.4c,d

Since K is the midpoint of the segment $\overline{AC}$, then $AK = KC$ and $ML = LC$. One can also write that

$$ML = LC = \frac{MC}{2}.$$

Since M is the midpoint of the segment $\overline{BC}$, it is also true that

$$ML = LC = \frac{BM}{2}.$$

Let us now apply the side-splitting theorem to the triangle BKL. We get that

$$\frac{BO}{OK} = \frac{BM}{ML}.$$

Since

$$ML = \frac{BM}{2},$$

we can conclude that

$$\frac{BO}{OK} = \frac{BM}{ML} = \frac{BM}{\frac{BM}{2}} = \frac{2}{1}.$$

By drawing the segment $\overline{MT}$ parallel to the segment $\overline{BK}$ (Figure 12.4d), and by repeating the above reasoning practically word for word, we get that

$$\frac{AO}{OM} = \frac{2}{1},$$

which completes the proof.

Solution 2

Let us examine the equalities that we need to prove from a slightly different perspective. That fact that

$$\frac{AO}{OM} = \frac{BO}{OK} = \frac{2}{1}$$

means that half of AO equals OM, and half of BO equals OK. Let us divide in half the segment $\overline{AO}$ with point F, and the segment $\overline{BO}$ with point G

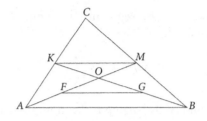

Figure 12.4e

(Figure 12.4e). It is now sufficient to prove that $OF = OM$, and that $OG = OK$ and the original assertion will also be proven. A good drawing helps us see how to reason further. Visually, the segments $\overline{FG}$ and $\overline{KM}$ appear to be congruent and parallel, with quadrilateral FKMG apparently being a parallelogram. From this would immediately follow precisely what we need to prove. Probably the best-known fact about the ratio of the length of segments is the fact that the diagonals of a parallelogram bisect each other. It would follow from this that $OF = OM$ and that $OG = OK$.

What remains to be done is to prove that FKMG is indeed a parallelogram, without appealing to the fact that this is simply visible. This follows from two assertions (given below as exercises but which can usually be found in standard geometry courses). The first is that a midsegment, which connects the midpoints of two sides of a triangle, is parallel to the third side and half its length. The segment $\overline{FG}$ is a midsegment in triangle AOB, while the segment $\overline{KM}$ is a midsegment in triangle ACB. Consequently, by using the above assertion we get that the segments $\overline{FG}$ and $\overline{KM}$ are parallel to $\overline{AB}$ and, therefore, to each other. Furthermore, $FG = \frac{1}{2} AB = KM$.

The second assertion is that a quadrilateral, two opposite sides of which are congruent and parallel, is a parallelogram. Since, as shown above, the segments $\overline{FG}$ and $\overline{KM}$ are parallel, and since $FG = KM$, this means that FKMG is a parallelogram, which completes the proof.

Solution 3

The solution can be supported by yet another assertion about the ratio of the lengths of segments—utilizing the similarity of triangles. As observed above, the straight lines $\overleftrightarrow{KM}$ and $\overleftrightarrow{AB}$ are parallel (Figure 12.4f), which

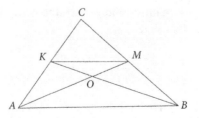

Figure 12.4f

means that $m\angle BKM = m\angle KBA$, and $m\angle AMK = m\angle MAB$ (since corresponding angles, formed by parallel lines and a transversal, are congruent). It follows from this that the triangle KOM is similar to the triangle AOB. This, in turn, entails that

$$\frac{AO}{OM} = \frac{BO}{OK} = \frac{AB}{KM}.$$

However, as already observed earlier

$$KM = \frac{AB}{2},$$

which means that in the end we get

$$\frac{AO}{OM} = \frac{BO}{OK} = \frac{2}{1}.$$

Solution 4

A fundamentally different approach to the solution is also possible—that makes use of coordinate geometry. First, we introduce a coordinate system in such a way that point A is the origin while point B lies on the abscissa axis (Figure 12.4g). Let its abscissa equal b. Let vertex C have the coordinates (c, d). In that case, we get that the coordinates of point M are

$$\left(\frac{b+c}{2}, \frac{d}{2}\right),$$

while the coordinates of point K are

$$\left(\frac{c}{2}, \frac{d}{2}\right).$$

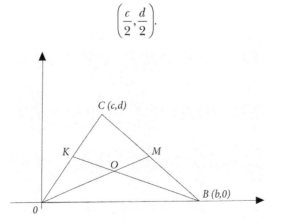

Figure 12.4g

We can now write the equation of the straight line that passes through points A and M:

$$y = \frac{d}{b+c} x.$$

The equation of the straight line that passes through points B and K is

$$y = \frac{d}{c-2b} x - \frac{db}{c-2b}.$$

Let us now solve the system of equations that we have obtained in this way in order to determine the coordinates of the point of intersection of the two straight lines. By equating the right-hand sides of the equations we get that

$$\frac{d}{b+c} x = \frac{d}{c-2b} x - \frac{db}{c-2b}.$$

This means that

$$\frac{d}{b+c} x - \frac{d}{c-2b} x = -\frac{db}{c-2b}$$

and that

$$\frac{d(c-2b-b-c)}{(b+c)(c-2b)} x = -\frac{db}{c-2b}, \text{ i.e., that } \frac{-3db}{(b+c)(c-2b)} x = -\frac{db}{c-2b}.$$

Hence, in the end,

$$x = \frac{b+c}{3}.$$

By now inserting the value of x into the equation

$$y = \frac{d}{b+c} x,$$

we get that

$$y = \frac{d}{3}.$$

Thus, the coordinates of point O are

$$\left(\frac{b+c}{3}, \frac{d}{3} \right).$$

It now remains to express through b, c, and d the lengths of the segments that are being examined. We have:

$$BO = \sqrt{\left(b-\frac{b+c}{3}\right)^2 + \left(0-\frac{d}{3}\right)^2} = \frac{1}{3}\sqrt{(2b-c)^2 + d^2},$$

$$OK = \sqrt{\left(\frac{c}{2}-\frac{b+c}{3}\right)^2 + \left(\frac{d}{2}-\frac{d}{3}\right)^2} = \sqrt{\frac{(3c-2b-2c)^2 + d^2}{6^2}} = \frac{1}{6}\sqrt{(2b-c)^2 + d^2},$$

$$AO = \sqrt{\left(0-\frac{b+c}{3}\right)^2 + \left(0-\frac{d}{3}\right)^2} = \frac{1}{3}\sqrt{(b+c)^2 + d^2},$$

$$OM = \sqrt{\left(\frac{b+c}{2}-\frac{b+c}{3}\right)^2 + \left(\frac{d}{2}-\frac{d}{3}\right)^2} = \sqrt{\frac{(b+c)^2 + d^2}{6}} = \frac{1}{6}\sqrt{(b+c)^2 + d^2}.$$

From this we instantly get that

$$\frac{AO}{OM} = \frac{BO}{OK} = \frac{2}{1}.$$

The coordinate method can also be applied in another way (assignments are proposed at the end of this section).

Solution 5

In this method, we use the heuristic strategy of examining a simpler problem. Let us say that the triangle ABC is equilateral (Figure 12.4h). In that case its medians are also its bisectors and its altitudes. The proof that the point of intersection O of its medians $\overline{AM}$ and $\overline{BK}$ divides them into the ratio $\frac{2}{1}$ is easier than in the general case. For instance, from the right triangle AMB with the angle of 60°, one gets that

$$AM = \frac{AB\sqrt{3}}{2},$$

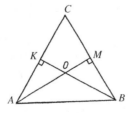

Figure 12.4h

while from the right triangle BOM with the angle of 60°, one gets that

$$OM = \frac{BM}{\sqrt{3}}.$$

Since

$$BM = \frac{AB}{2},$$

it means that

$$OM = \frac{AB}{2\sqrt{3}} = \frac{AM}{3}.$$

Consequently,

$$\frac{AO}{OM} = \frac{2}{1}$$

(the second equality can be obtained in a similar way).

Now that the assertion is proven for equilateral triangles, let us examine an arbitrary triangle ABC (Figure 12.4i). Let ABP be an equilateral triangle, with the vertex P situated outside the plane ABC. Let us examine the parallel projection onto the plane ABC in the direction of the ray $\overrightarrow{PC}$. In the case of a parallel projection, the ratios of the lengths of the segments lying on the same straight line or on parallel straight lines do not change. This

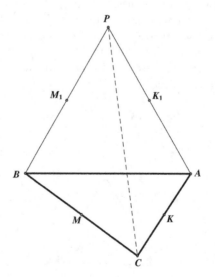

Figure 12.4i

Figure 12.4j

property can easily be noticed when one observes shadows: the shadow of an adult can become very short or very long, but if this adult is, say, one and half times the size of a child, his shadow will also be one and a half times the size of the child's shadow (Figure 12.4j).

By making use of this property we get that, insofar as vertex P is projected onto vertex C, then the midpoint of the segment $\overline{AP}$ will also be projected onto the midpoint of the segment $\overline{AC}$, while the midpoint of the vertex $\overline{BP}$ is projected onto the midpoint of the segment $\overline{BC}$. This way the medians of the equilateral triangle ABP are projected onto the medians of the triangle ABC, and the point of intersection of the medians of the equilateral triangle is projected onto the point of intersection of the medians of the triangle ABC. Finally, the ratio of the segments by which this point divides the median, should be the same as for the projected segments of the median of the equilateral triangle. As has been proven above, this ratio is $\frac{2}{1}$.

Solution 6

Let us try and introduce a little bit of physics here. If X is the center of gravity of one body and Y of another, then the center of gravity of the body that would be made up of these two bodies would lie on the segment $\overline{XY}$, and would divide it into the ratio inversely proportional to the respective weights of these bodies. In other words, if the weight of the first body equals m and the second n, then the center of gravity of the composite body Z would be situated in such a way that the following equality applies

$$\frac{XZ}{ZY} = \frac{n}{m}$$

(this is essentially the principle of the lever).

Let us now imagine that on each of the vertices of the triangle ABC hang equal weights. Where is the center of gravity of the segment $\overline{BC}$? Obviously in its midpoint, i.e., point M. Where is then the center of gravity of the entire triangle? Since the center of gravity of point A is the point itself, then the center of gravity of the whole triangle should be situated on the segment connecting point A and point M, i.e., on the median $\overline{AM}$. In what way will it divide this segment? Again, as is clear from physics, into the ratio $\frac{2}{1}$, since the segment $\overline{BC}$ weighs twice as much as point A.

One can reason in exactly the same way about the segment $\overline{AC}$ and vertex B, and about the segment $\overline{AB}$ and vertex C. The center of gravity should be on all three medians and divides each of them into the ratio $\frac{2}{1}$. This completes the proof.

It could be said that the latter proof is not really mathematical. However, it is possible to translate the above "physical" formulation into the language of vectors and then prove the assertion quite rigorously. What the language of "physics" has done is to make the proof visually clear and natural.

Example 5

Three segments with the lengths m_a, h_a and l_a are given (Figure 12.5a). Using a compass and a straightedge construct the triangle ABC, such that its median, its altitude and its bisector from vertex A have the given lengths.

Discussion and Solution

This is a classical construction problem. The full solution should include determining when, i.e., for which lengths m_a, h_a and l_a, the problem has a solution. It is clear, for instance, that there are no solutions if $m_a < h_a$, since there are no such triangles where the altitude is longer than the median drawn from the same vertex. Let us confine ourselves, however, to working out a plan of construction in cases where there are solutions.

As often happens with construction problems, it is useful to use the heuristic strategy of working backwards. Let us assume that the triangle is constructed and that $\overline{AH}$ is its altitude, $\overline{AM}$ its median and $\overline{AL}$ its bisector (Figure 12.5b).

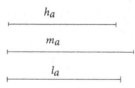

Figure 12.5a

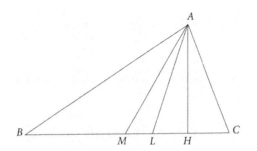

Figure 12.5b

What can be seen by looking at the drawing? It is immediately obvious that for the right triangles AHL and AHM the hypotenuses and the legs are known. These triangles can be constructed. For instance, one can construct the right angle with the vertex in point H, mark out on one of its sides the length AH = h_a, and then, using A as center, draw with the compass a circle with the radius m_a which will intersect the other side of the angle in point M. After this one can construct another circle with the center in point A, this time with the radius l_a, obtaining point L where this circle intersects the segment $\overline{HM}$ (Figure 12.5c).

What should be done next? In the triangle ABC point M ought to be in the middle of the segment $\overline{BC}$. However, one cannot simply mark out the equal segments $\overline{MB}$ and $\overline{MC}$ (Figure 12.5d). The equality $m\angle BAL = m\angle CAL$ would not necessarily be fulfilled.

To make the situation clearer let us do an additional construction (as before, assuming that the triangle ABC is constructed). The measure of the angle of the triangle is defined by the measure of the corresponding arc of the circumscribed circle. This suggests that examining this circle could be useful (Figure 12.5e). The ray $\overline{AL}$ intersects the arc BC at the point K, which divides the arc in half (since $\angle BAL \cong \angle CAL$). Let us note now that the perpendicular bisector of the segment $\overline{BC}$ should also divide this arc

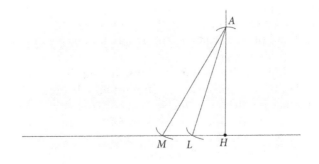

Figure 12.5c

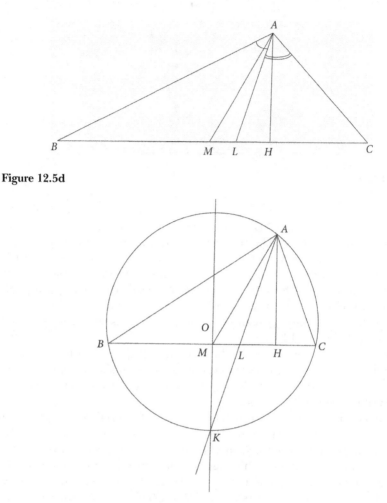

Figure 12.5d

Figure 12.5e

in half. This perpendicular bisector can be constructed—it ought to go through point M. We therefore see that point K lies on two straight lines, both of which can be constructed. This makes it clear how to proceed with the rest of the construction.

As suggested above, let us start by constructing the triangle AMH and the point L. Let us now construct the straight line that goes through point M and that is perpendicular to the segment $\overline{MH}$. Let us then extend the segment $\overline{AL}$ up to its point of intersection (K) with this straight line (Figure 12.5f). Let us now find the center of the circle circumscribing the triangle ABC. It should obviously lie on the perpendicular bisector $\overleftrightarrow{MK}$ of the segment $\overline{BC}$ that we have constructed. At the same time it should lie on the

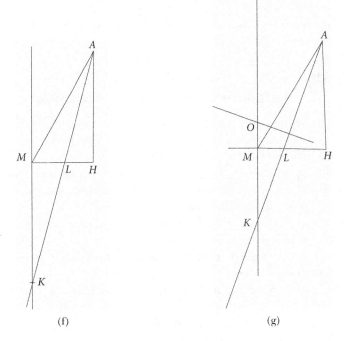

(f)   (g)

Figure 12.5f,g

perpendicular bisector of the segment $\overline{AK}$. Let us construct this perpendicular (this procedure is described in practically all geometry textbooks). Let
us mark its point of intersection with the perpendicular bisector $\overleftrightarrow{MK}$, point
O (Figure 12.5g). Now let us construct the circle with center O, so that

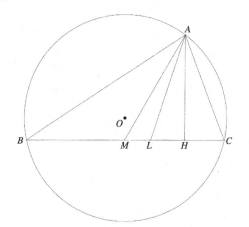

Figure 12.5h

it goes through point A. Let us, finally, extend the segment $\overline{MH}$ on both sides, up to its intersection with the circle in points B and C (Figure 12.5h). This is the triangle ABC that we were after.

Assignments and Topics for Discussion

1. Examine the cube $ABCDA_1B_1C_1D_1$, the edges of which are 1. Mark all points for which the distance between it and point A along the surface of the cube is less than $\sqrt{2}$.

2. Think up a problem that involves measuring the distance between points along the surface of a regular tetrahedron. Did you require a "net" to reach the solution?

3. There are 5 points on a plane, positioned in such a way that no 3 are lying on a single straight line. Prove that out of them one can always select three points that would serve as vertices of a triangle one angle of which would never be greater than 36°.

4. There are 4 points on a plane, such that no 3 are lying on a single straight line. Prove that out of them one can always select three that would serve as vertices of a right or an obtuse triangle.

5. In Figure 12.6 are two circles and point M. The task is to construct an isosceles right triangle with the vertex of the right angle at point M, and with the other two vertices (at the base) lying on each of the two circles respectively. Explain how to solve this problem with the

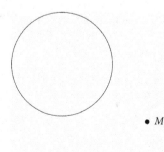

• M

Figure 12.6

Figure 12.7

help of a rotation. Think up an analogous problem that could be solved with the help of a rotation by 60°.

6. Two villages, A and B, are situated on the opposite sides of a river (Figure 12.7). Where should one construct a bridge, perpendicular to the riverbanks, for the path leading from village A, then across the bridge and then to village B, to be the shortest possible?

7. Prove that if in the quadrilateral ABCD the opposite sides $\overline{AB}$ and $\overline{CD}$ are parallel and congruent, then the quadrilateral is a parallelogram.

8. In Figure 12.8 is a triangle ABC. M is the midpoint of the side $\overline{AB}$ and N is the midpoint of the side $\overline{BC}$. K is a point on the straight line $\overleftrightarrow{MN}$ such that KN = MN. Prove: a) that the triangles CNK and MBN are congruent; b) that AMKC is a parallelogram; c) that the segment $\overline{MN}$ is parallel to $\overline{AC}$ and is half its length.

9. Let the coordinates of point M be (a, b), and of point K (c, d). Prove that the coordinates of point N that divides the segment $\overline{MK}$ into a ratio of $\frac{2}{1}$, counting from point M, are

$$\left(\frac{a+2c}{3}, \frac{b+2d}{3} \right).$$

Using this, prove the theorem about the point of intersection of the medians.

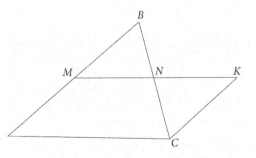

Figure 12.8

10. Give examples (either your own or from existing literature) of different proofs that the straight lines containing the altitudes of a triangle always intersect at a single point.
11. Referring to available literature, analyze several construction problems that use non-standard instruments—a compass only, a straightedge only, or a set square only.

PLANNING A LESSON DEVOTED TO GEOMETRY

This section will discuss how two student teachers, Erika and Marylyn, prepared lessons in geometry. They discussed their lesson plans at the student teachers' seminar and took into account all the comments made there.

Preliminary Information

Erika and Marylyn were supposed to teach lessons on related topics: Erika was to give a lesson on triangles in general, but especially isosceles triangles, while Marylyn's was to teach specifically the isosceles triangle and its properties. The key difference was that Erika taught in middle school and Marylyn in high school.

The lesson planned by Erika was part of a unit devoted to geometrical figures and the calculation of their areas. Most students were already acquainted with many geometrical concepts and facts from elementary school but they now needed to review and reorganize this knowledge in a new way.

The lesson planned by Marylyn, on the other hand, opened the unit devoted to polygons. It was assumed that students had already come across the concept of an isosceles triangle in a number of situations and that they could probably recall some of its properties, but that they had never conducted any rigorous proofs to establish these properties. The class had, however, done proofs in the study of other parts of geometry, though not all students were able to cope with such assignments particularly well.

The Middle School Textbook

The relevant part of the middle school textbook provided definitions for different types of triangles (right, acute, equilateral, etc). This section also contained the assertion that the sum of the angles of any triangle equals 180°, demonstrated by the following procedure: the "corners" of the triangles were cut off and students were asked to link them up and thereby get a straight line (Figure 12.9). Next, the textbook provided some assignments, most of which were devoted to working out the unknown angle in a triangle with the other two angles given. Erika especially liked the following

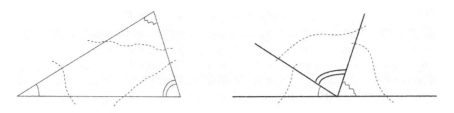

Figure 12.9

question from the textbook: "Can an isosceles triangle also be a right triangle? If so, what are its angles?" To answer this question, students needed to bring together all the disparate facts that they had learned up to that point. In other words, they were required to restructure all the geometrical information that they had accumulated up to that point. Erika reckoned that it was important to devote more attention to this kind of assignment.

The High School Textbook

The high school textbook contained proofs of the theorems which stated that, in an isosceles triangle, the line containing the bisector of the vertex angle is a line of symmetry for the triangle, that the angles opposite congruent sides are congruent, and that the bisector of the vertex angle coincides with the altitude and the median to the base. The range of problems attached to this section was sufficiently broad and varied. Among them were assignments devoted to recognizing and applying appropriate terms, assignments where theorems needed to be applied, and assignments where one was asked to carry out some relatively simple proofs independently. Marylyn was happy with the material from the textbook, though the question of how best to organize this material for her class was a different matter altogether.

Defining the Goals of the Lessons

Erika and Marylyn defined the main goal of their lessons in a similar way: students needed to recognize certain properties of geometrical figures and to learn how to use them. Erika formulated her goal in the following manner:

> students should familiarize themselves with the principal types of triangles and with the general property of the sum of the internal angles in all triangles, and they should also learn to apply this knowledge in problem solving.

Marylyn saw the goal of her lesson in the following way:

> students should learn the main properties of the isosceles triangle and they should learn how to apply them in solving problems.

However, upon closer inspection some differences emerged. In middle school, the learning entailed primarily becoming acquainted with a fact and forming a visual understanding of it. In high school, it assumed the ability to carry out rigorous proofs. In middle school, students were supposed to learn how to recognize objects that possessed a particular property, to construct them, to connect different properties, and to indicate their presence or absence using only very simple mathematical terminology. In high school, students were supposed to learn to construct a whole chain of logical consequences that would include the application of the properties that they had learned, the use of various methods of reasoning demonstrated in class, and the use of acceptable mathematical language and symbolism.

Erika wanted to construct her lesson in a way that would engage students in solving problems that developed their geometrical intuition and their skills of classification. Marylyn assumed that her students were at a higher level of abstract thought. She too, of course, considered it essential to develop their skills of geometrical observation, but she also wanted them to practice using observation and deductive logic together. In particular, she wanted students to see how previously studied properties of a reflection over a straight line can be used in carrying out certain proofs.

Lesson Objectives

Consequently, while remaining close in the formulation of their main goals, Ericka and Marylyn differed in the way they articulated their specific lesson objectives. For the middle school lesson, the objectives were as follows:

- Students will be able to practice analyzing properties of triangles.
- Students will be able to acquaint themselves with generally accepted terminology used in describing different triangles.
- Students will be able to acquaint themselves with the assertion about the sum of the angles in a triangle and with the reasoning through which it is confirmed.
- Students will be able to practice applying the above assertion in finding unknown values of angles and in defining the type of triangle according to the appropriate classification.

In high school the lesson objectives were:

- Students will be able to review the properties of reflection that they have already studied.
- Students will be able to familiarize themselves with generally accepted terminology used to describe isosceles triangles.

- Students will be able to acquaint themselves with the properties of the isosceles triangle and to take part in proving them as far as possible.
- Students will be able to practice identifying properties of triangles by applying the theorems that they have studied.
- Students will be able to practice reasoning and also to critically analyze some samples of proofs.

The Middle School Lesson Plan

Erika wanted to introduce as much material as possible through the students' own exploration. At the same time she knew that, in a single lesson and entirely on their own, students could not complete the activity with the angles of the triangle, the classification of triangles *and* solve a few problems. In elementary school, a significant amount of time is commonly devoted to measuring angles and finding the sum of the angles in a triangle. For this reason she decided that for independent work students should only be asked to classify triangles. She felt students should be able to do this assignment on their own since in previous lessons they measured different angles and segments and noted that angles could be acute, right and obtuse, which meant that they also ought to find it natural to classify triangles based on this sort of information. The activity with gluing angles together Erika decided to demonstrate herself, thereby saving some time for problems in which students were meant to bring together all that they had learned in the lesson.

As a result, the lesson was planned in the following manner:

Main Assignment (10 minutes)
Students were divided into small groups, each of which was given a selection of triangles that included those represented in Figure 12.10. The assignment was as follows: what is common to all these figures and what is different about them? What groups do you think these figures can be divided into?

Discussion of Answers (10 minutes)
The plan was to give the floor to a chosen representative of each group. Erika's expectation was that there would be different approaches to describing the differences between the triangles, including those unconnected to the size of the angles or the sides (although Erika strove to make all triangles approximately equal in terms of area, and although nothing had been said about the area thus far, students could have looked for differences in areas, since they were aware of this concept from everyday life). At the same time,

Figure 12.10

she also assumed that at least some students would mention that one of the triangles had all acute angles, while in others there were also right and obtuse angles, and also that some triangles had all different angles (or sides), while in others they were the same. It was assumed that students would notice the similarity between all the figures: that they were all triangles, had three angles, three vertices and three sides. In addition, Erika thought it was possible that someone might mention the fact that the sum of all the angles was 180°, since this property was discussed in elementary school.

Summing Up the Discussion (5–10 minutes)

The teacher's plan was to sum up the discussion by presenting two diagrams (Figure 12.11). Erika thought of suggesting that this was the best way to classify all triangles (without wishing to criticize other classifications offered by students, she planned to explain why such grouping was particularly important). In the process she planned to draw the students' attention to the fact that all triangles with two equal sides also had two equal angles, while equilateral triangles were simultaneously equiangular. (Her intention was to emphasize that, as would emerge in subsequent study, all the triangles have such properties and not just the models on which the students were working.) She also planned to tell (i.e., to remind) students about the general property of all triangles that the sum of its angles equals 180°. Erika planned to demonstrate herself the reasoning that confirms this, as derived from the textbook.

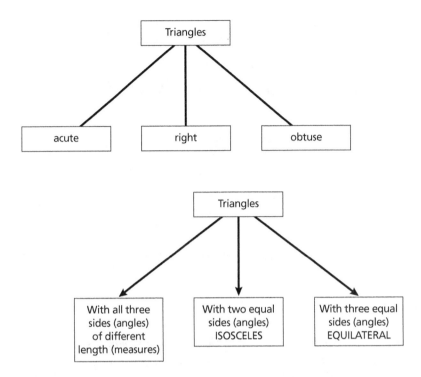

Figure 12.11

Problem Solving (10 minutes)

The plan was to give students the following series of assignments.

- Draw any acute, obtuse and right triangle.
- Find the measure of the angle *x* in the triangles represented in Figure 12.12. What sort of triangles are they?
- The values of two angles in a triangle are 15° and 45°. Is it true that this is an acute triangle?
- In an isosceles triangle an angle at the base equals 50°. Is this triangle acute?
- Can an isosceles triangle have a right angle at its base?
- Can a right triangle be isosceles? If so, what are its angles?
- Can an isosceles triangle be obtuse?

The assignments were to be done individually, and this was to be followed by group discussion.

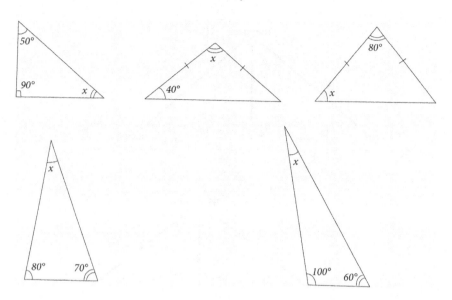

Figure 12.12

Discussion of the Solutions. Summing Up the Lesson (5 minutes)

The plan was briefly to comment on the answers given by the students (Erika would find out what particular students had come up with during the activity itself) and to summarize what had been done in the lesson.

The High School Lesson Plan

Marylyn felt that the key moment in the high school lesson was discussing the proof of the properties of an isosceles triangle. She did not think that students were capable of carrying out the proof themselves. At the same time, she was concerned that simply reading the proof from the textbook would be both too hard and uninteresting to students. Consequently, she sought a way of breaking the proof into parts that would be more suitable for students to work on independently. She also believed it was important to prepare students for understanding the proof and its implications, especially to review the properties of triangles and of reflection that were to be used in the proof. She wanted to leave at least some time for solving problems, where students could apply the theorem in new situations and where they could practice carrying out the type of reasoning required in proofs.

As a result, the lesson was planned in the following manner:

Do now (5 minutes)

The plan was to give students the following assignment:

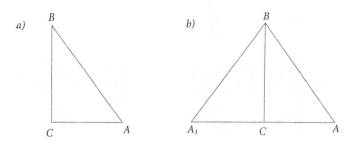

Figure 12.13

A right triangle ABC is given (Figure 12.13a). Draw a figure that would be obtained as a reflection image of this triangle over the line $\overleftrightarrow{BC}$. What sort of figure do the two figures make up together? Justify your view.

Discussion of Answers (5 minutes)

It was expected that students would draw Figure 12.13b and conclude that the original triangle and the one obtained as a reflection image together form an isosceles triangle. In this context, the teacher planned to note that the reflection image of a segment is a segment of the same length, while the reflection image of an angle is an angle of the same size.

Posing the Main Question (5 minutes)

The plan was:

- To remind students of the terminology used to describe an isosceles triangle (vertex angle, base angles, base)
- Give examples of isosceles triangles from real life
- Ask about the congruence of the base angles in an isosceles triangle

In particular, her idea was to draw the students' attention to the fact that at first sight the base angles might indeed seem equal, but that one needed to be persuaded that this will always be the case, and then to discuss with them how such a conclusion can be accomplished.

The Proof of the Main Theorem (15 minutes)

Marylyn planned to start the proof by demonstrating on a model how the isosceles triangle ABC folds over the straight line containing the bisector $\overline{AM}$ of the vertex angle A. She then planned to ask the class to explain what would then happen to point B. With students acting as advisors, Marylyn planned to write briefly on the board that after the reflection over the straight line containing the bisector of the vertex angle A, the image of point B is point C, while the image of point C is point B, and then to

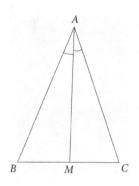

Figure 12.14

provide a justification for this. The plan was then to conclude that line $\overleftrightarrow{AM}$ is a line of symmetry for triangle ABC (Figure 12.14).

After this, the idea was to ask the class to name some segments and angles in the triangle that would be the reflection images of others. The assumption was that the students would on their own (or in response to the teacher's leading questions) indicate that $\angle ACB$ is the reflection image of $\angle ABC$, that the segment $\overline{CM}$ is the reflection image of $\overline{BM}$, and finally, that $\angle AMC$ is the reflection image of $\angle AMB$. One could then draw the conclusion from this, again with the participation of the class, that $\angle ACB \cong \angle ABC$, that CM = BM (which meant that the bisector $\overline{AM}$ was also the median), and finally, that $\angle AMC \cong \angle AMB$, and that, because these angles are right, the segment $\overline{AM}$ was also the triangle's altitude. The plan was also to formulate all these conclusions verbally without using formal notation.

Problem Solving (15 minutes)

At this point in the lesson, Marylyn planned first to give the class a few problems to work on together. The assignments would be given on a Smartboard (or an overhead transparency) so that those wishing to provide answers could make notes on the triangles themselves and could explain their answers. The following problems were to be used:

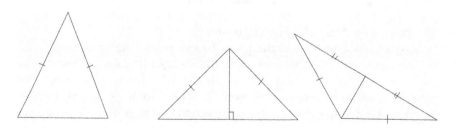

Figure 12.15a

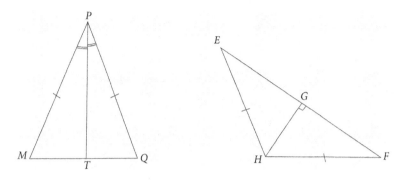

Figure 12.15b

- Several triangles are given (Figure 12.15a). Mark the congruent angles and explain why they are congruent.
- Two triangles are given (Figure 12.15b). a) Mark the pairs of congruent segments (in addition to those already given in the figure). b) Is it true that the triangle PTQ is right? c) If FE = 10, find the length of the segment $\overline{FG}$.

Next the plan was to give the following assignment (it too was to be presented on a transparency, accompanied by an oral explanation).

"Examine the following assertion that the base angles of any triangle are congruent. Analyze its proof (Figure 12.16). Is everything there true?"

Triangle ABC is given. Let $\overline{AM}$ be its bisector. Let us examine the reflection over the straight line $\overleftrightarrow{AM}$. Since the straight line containing the bisector of the angle is the symmetry line of the angle, the reflection image of the ray $\overrightarrow{AB}$

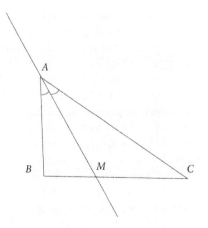

Figure 12.16

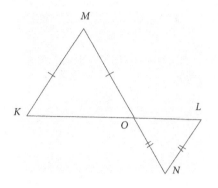

Figure 12.17

is the ray $\overrightarrow{AC}$. This means that the reflection image of point B is point C and of point C is point B. Consequently, the reflection image of the angle ∠ABC is the angle ∠ACB. Thus, ∠ACB ≅ ∠ABC.

In conclusion, the following proof problem was to be presented (for discussion and solution in pairs).

On Figure 12.17 the segments $\overline{MN}$ and $\overline{KL}$ intersect in point O. MK = MO, ON = NL. Prove that ∠MKO ≅ ∠OLN.

The lesson was to finish with a brief discussion of the solution to this problem and a general summing up.

Discussion

The topics studied in these two lessons were very similar. However, a teacher needs to be prepared for different styles of exposition depending on the audience. Using the terminology introduced in the first section of this chapter, Erika's task was to help students develop from the second to the third van Hiele level, while Marylyn's was to help them progress from the third to the fourth. Lessons that incorporate tangible materials ought to be present much more in middle school than in high school. On the other hand, in high school, and, in particular, in the lesson examined above, more attention must be devoted to proof (rather than just plausible reasoning and an accumulation of evidence). In Erika's lesson, the fact that the base angles of the isosceles triangle were congruent was accepted as the outcome of the observation conducted on concrete triangles (even though it was mentioned that this would be proven for all cases in the future). In Marylyn's lesson the key moment was precisely the proof itself.

One of the virtues of Marylyn's lesson was the fact that she did not make the proofs too formal, and, in particular, that she did not refrain from using a model that allowed students to visualize what happens by reflecting "half" of a triangle. Indeed, it is helpful for the students' understanding to use informal geometry at every stage of their development (and especially at the beginning of the study of proofs).

Debatable Aspects of the Lessons

One could, of course, approach Marylyn's lesson from the opposite perspective and reproach her for not including practically any exercises in writing down proofs. The plan was for students to discuss proofs, to "advise" the teacher on how to continue the proof, and finally, to read the finished proof. Yet no attention was given to the full exposition of proofs in students' notebooks, and this part was confined merely to a brief sketching out of the principal stages of the proof.

Here, as is usually the case, a teacher's judgment should be based on the realities of school practice. It was hardly possible to include exercises in writing proofs using proper symbolism in a lesson that was already packed with other material. This is something that can only be done in the course of many lessons. Practicing writing proofs must, in fact, include a whole variety of exercises, some of which were mentioned above, including the reading of different proofs. Trying to teach students everything at once is hardly likely to succeed.

In her own attempt to save time, Erika too made a decision that could be considered debatable: instead of asking students independently to do the activity confirming that the sum of angles in a triangle equals $180°$, she resolved to demonstrate this to the class herself. No doubt, it would have been possible to have students do this activity on their own, while leaving the classification of triangles to the teacher. Planning lessons requires constantly making decisions of this sort. The teacher should be aware of all the options that are at one's disposal and should make conscious decisions, depending on what seems particularly important in teaching a given class.

On Assignments Given in the Lessons

It is worth noting the variety and thoughtfulness of assignments in both lessons. The high school lesson included problems that involved recognizing what had already been learned, a critical analysis of an erroneous proof and, finally, independently carrying out a proof. In the middle school lesson there were problems that required students to draw objects, to use a particular fact that had been learned (both with the help of the drawing and without it), and, finally, assignments where one had to combine various disparate facts (e.g., that the sum of angles in a triangle is $180°$ and that the base angles of an isosceles triangle are congruent). The students' understanding, what they find hard or easy, changes with age. However, it is important at every level and in every class to know how to select a suitable variety of assignments and present them in an appropriate sequence.

Assignments and Topics for Discussion

1. Write down your impressions of Erika's and Marylyn's lessons. What did you like about them and what would you have done differently?
2. Compile some problems similar to those used in their lesson plans.
3. What would you give as homework after each of the above-described lessons?
4. Imagine that Marylyn's lesson was taught in middle school. What, in your view, would cause difficulties?
5. Create one lesson plan devoted to the properties of quadrilaterals for middle school students and another for high school students.

PART V

This part deals with the teaching and learning of Discrete mathematics. Its aim is to introduce the reader to the theoretical and practical aspects of teaching basic topics in Discrete mathematics.

CHAPTER 13

THE STUDY OF DISCRETE MATHEMATICS

This chapter is devoted to the study of Discrete Mathematics. Its aim is to acquaint the reader with the principal results of research into the teaching of this branch of mathematics and to provide recommendations for those who are about to start teaching it in schools.

The chapter discusses:

- Mathematical topics usually included in discrete mathematics and why schoolchildren need to be acquainted with them.
- Some psychological difficulties and misconceptions encountered while solving problems in probability and combinatorics.
- Different ways in which teachers can overcome these difficulties.
- The NCTM requirements for the teaching of discrete mathematics, including differences between middle and high school.
- How discrete mathematics can be incorporated into the teaching of other parts of mathematics, with some practical recommendations to novice teachers.
- Some problems in discrete mathematics that demonstrate the diversity of approaches and methods in this area, and that can be used when working with students who show a particular interest in the subject.
- Examples of how to construct lessons devoted to discrete mathematics in middle and high school.

Mathematics in Middle and Secondary School, pages 383–424
Copyright © 2015 by Information Age Publishing
All rights of reproduction in any form reserved.

FINDING A PLACE FOR THE NEW COURSE

The "Apparent" and the Calculated

D'Artagnan threw the dice with a trembling hand, and turned up the number three; his paleness terrified Athos, who, however, contented himself with saying, "That's a sad throw, comrade; you will have the horses fully equipped, monsieur."

The Englishman, quite triumphant, did not even give himself the trouble to shake the dice. He threw them on the table without looking at them, so sure was he of victory; D'Artagnan turned aside to conceal his ill humor.

"Hold, hold, hold!" said Athos, with his quiet tone; "that throw of the dice is extraordinary. I have not seen such a one four times in my life. Two aces!"

The Englishman looked, and was seized with astonishment. D'Artagnan looked, and was seized with pleasure (Dumas, 1999).

Thousands if not millions of readers have read this dramatic part of Dumas' classical adventure novel *The Three Musketeers* rejoicing at the good luck of their favorite hero D'Artagnan in the above, apparently hopeless, situation; and they probably carried on reading without giving the passage much thought, looking for further, yet more exciting adventures. It is likely that Dumas himself saw nothing unusual in what his heroes were saying here. For, indeed, a total of "two" does seem to come up quite rarely.

What Calculations Tell Us

It is not difficult to calculate, though, that if two dice are thrown, there are only 36 equally likely possible outcomes. A total of "two," on the other hand, can be obtained in only one way—as a double one. This means that the probability of a "two" turning up equals $\frac{1}{36}$. It is true that this is fairly low probability. Yet Athos surely threw dice literally thousands of times in his life. Is it likely that he saw a double one come up no more than three times up to that point? It is actually possible to calculate what the probability would be for a double one to come up only three times in a thousand throws (this is an assignment at the end of the section). The probability of this happening is, in fact, extremely low. Consequently, Athos' statement is rather surprising.

Acting Without Calculation: A Little Bit of History

However, only a person who actually tries to work out the above probabilities and who performs appropriate calculations in one form or another is likely to realize this. This is not something everyone does automatically even today, while hundreds and thousands of years ago, the very idea that one could perform any sort of exact calculation in situations of chance was unheard of. In those days people tried to predict the future by a variety of means—by interpreting omens or by hoping for miracles. Yet, the idea of mathematically calculating likelihood through probabilities arrived only relatively recently. Probability theory and combinatorics emerged as scientific disciplines many centuries after geometry, for instance. The reason for this has partly to do with the fact that the calculation of probabilities is psychologically harder to grasp than, say, the calculation of areas. The Italian mathematician Cardano (1501–1576), who is considered to be one of the founders of probability theory, himself wrote in his autobiography (1930) how certain omens and special sensations helped him when he played dice. Even he, therefore, found it difficult to separate emotions from rigorous reasoning.

On Similar Difficulties Today

Mathematics teachers are certain to encounter similar difficulties with their students. Greer (2001) observed that, "it is a major cognitive achievement to understand that rational decisions are possible in relation to chance phenomena" (p. 21). Today, of course, students are hardly likely to think that the way the coin drops will depend on the position of the stars or on whether they have crossed paths with a man dressed in black. Yet they still make assumptions based on impressions that form under the influence of some emotion, or by virtue of experiences that have little to do with the concrete problem at hand. They are likely to proceed simply on the basis that a certain answer seems natural and plausible to them, rather than on the basis of rigorous thinking and calculations. They can also fail to see the difference between certain key terms. (For example, outside school, in everyday life or in newspapers, one can often come across statements that some event or other is "statistically impossible," whereas what is really meant is that it is only "statistically unlikely"). A teacher must be ready for this sort of difficulty. What one is dealing with here is not students' lack of attention, but a fundamental difficulty with the area of mathematics being studied. To overcome it, teachers should work on it patiently and consistently over an extended period of time.

What is Discrete Mathematics and Why Should It Be Studied?

The very term *discrete mathematics* suggests its difference from its counterpart—continuous mathematics; hence the novelty of this part of mathematics. A fundamental area of mathematics, studied for decades and centuries in colleges, has been the Calculus course; then came yet more complex areas such as ordinary differential equations or partial differential equations, for instance. In these and many other fields of mathematics one studied problems that concerned limits of functions, continuous functions, their derivatives, and so forth. The description of the real world and of processes that went on in it was seen as linked primarily with this sort of mathematics. Processes were modeled with the help of continuous functions. Their changes were described by means of derivatives. One then formulated differential equations, which were, however, often not that easy to solve.

Some Famous Problems in Discrete Mathematics

Of course, other types of problems that concerned the study of objects of a different nature (finite sets, in particular) were also being posed and solved. Already by the thirteenth century the Italian mathematician Fibonacci studied sequences, finding ways of expressing subsequent terms through those that preceded them. Blaise Pascal (1623–1662) solved many problems in determining the probability of events. Leonard Euler (1707–1783) solved the famous problem of the bridges of Konigsberg, namely the question of whether it was possible to go over all of the bridges, crossing each of them only once (Eves, 1990). Many other problems of this kind were created and solved centuries before that. These "finite" problems were not solved merely out of a theoretical interest or for entertainment. The study of statistics, for instance, has turned out to be vital to the insurance business and its methods have been developing ever since the seventeenth century.

Growing Interest in Discrete Mathematics in Recent Decades

And yet the interest in such problems has grown remarkably in the second half of the twentieth century, when changes in society and technology have compelled us to deal with a vastly expanded quantity of information on a regular basis. Graham et al. (1994) called their course in the mathematical bases of computer science *Concrete mathematics*, thereby highlighting the fact that the reader is dealing with a mixture of continuous and discrete mathematics, and also that what is being studied cannot be considered abstract and purely theoretical.

What sort of conclusions can one draw on the basis of collected data? *When* should one make this or that decision? *How many* objects are required in this or that situation? *How* should one choose the required option out of so many being offered? Such questions come up all the time in everyday life. Many can, in fact, be answered with the help of discrete mathematics, for which new applications are constantly being discovered (*For All Practical Purposes*, 2001).

Discrete Mathematics in School

It is sometimes the case that certain classical parts of school mathematics need to be reduced in order to make room for new concepts and methods, some of which might only have just appeared in scholarly mathematics itself. Discrete mathematics, in contrast to geometry, for instance, does not have a centuries-old tradition that helps (though sometimes also hinders) its teaching. Discrete mathematics as a school subject is being established and shaped literally before our eyes. Any teacher, including the one who is only just embarking on this career, is capable of enriching it.

Today, discrete mathematics is commonly said to comprise Set theory, Combinatorics, Probability and Statistics, Graph theory, Basic logic, Matrix algebra, and sometimes a few other parts as well (Bogart, 1991). Approaching this question from a somewhat different perspective, Dossey (1991) distinguishes three types of problems pertaining to discrete mathematics: In the first group are existence problems, where one needs to establish whether or not a particular problem has solutions, and if so whether it is possible to work out some general algorithm for determining them. The second group represents counting problems, where one needs to determine the number of possible variants and, in particular, the number of possible solutions. Finally, the third group consists of optimization problems, where one is required to determine the best solution to a possible problem. Problems of all the above three types mutually overlap.

Examining an Example | **Queue Reduction: Example of a Real Life Problem**

When we rather quickly pay for our shopping in a supermarket, we usually do not realize that organizing the checkout registers, for example, actually requires quite a bit of mathematics. The problem of eliminating (or at least reducing) long queues is rarely perceived as mathematical in nature. Still it is a good example of a real-life problem involving all three types of tasks mentioned above. The first step is to consider if there is *an algorithm* for its solution, and this step is, as already mentioned above, not straightforward at all. Then one needs to solve a considerable number of *counting problems to optimize* the number of checkouts open to ensure that there are no long queues, yet that there are also no cashiers sitting idle (Takacs, 1962).

Why it is Important to Study Discrete Mathematics

The school must acquaint students with problems of discrete mathematics because practically every schoolchild is likely to encounter such problems in the future. Understanding how one makes decisions in particular situations is clearly vital to any intelligent citizen. The study of discrete mathematics fulfills yet another role as well. Kenney (1991, pp. vii–viii) lists the following uses of discrete mathematics:

- Discrete mathematics promotes the making of mathematical connections.
- Discrete mathematics provides a setting for problem solving with real-world applications.
- Discrete mathematics capitalizes on technological settings.
- Discrete mathematics fosters critical thinking and mathematical reasoning.

Problems in discrete mathematics arise naturally in the daily life of a school-child. This is truly *concrete* mathematics. Such problems are perhaps the easiest for students to pose themselves (with the appropriate support and assistance from the teacher). Their solution is usually not easy, but the first steps towards it are usually quite natural to students since they often involve a trial and error strategy. All this makes discrete mathematics an ideal tool for developing mathematical thinking, and a strong argument in favor of expanding its presence in school mathematics. School courses in discrete mathematics can also serve to help students see the variety in mathematics, beyond just algebra and geometry.

Of course, not all areas and approaches from cutting-edge discrete mathematics need to be reflected in the school course. In what follows, we shall discuss mainly probability and combinatorics. (Notably, we do not address the teaching and learning of statistics and statistics education in this chapter on discrete mathematics, though it, too, is becoming increasingly important; see, for example, the American Statistical Association's GAISE (2007) Report). The NCTM (2000) distinguishes as a separate content standard only data analysis and probability. The CCSS-M (2010) similarly describes Statistics and Probability content, though only one standard (HSS-CP.B.9) specifies learning about combinatorics. The study of several other areas of discrete mathematics should be integrated in the study of certain other, more traditional, parts of the mathematics course. This would enable teachers to acquaint students with a number of ideas and results from discrete mathematics, while simultaneously looking at traditional mathematics in a new light.

Overcoming Misconceptions and Difficulties Experienced in the Study of Discrete Mathematics

We have mentioned above certain psychological difficulties that school-children are likely to experience in the study of discrete mathematics. It is not surprising therefore that the way children reflect on problems of probability, the way they form ideas and conceptions in this sphere of mathematics, the way this type of thinking develops with age, and the way intuition in this area forms and functions—that all these questions have been the object of extensive study by cognitive psychologists (Nickson, 2000; Shaughnessy, 1992). Shaughnessy (1992) rightly observed that in these contexts psychologists mostly assume the role of observers and describers. Mathematics educators, on the other hand, need to be interveners—they must strive actually to modify and develop students' conceptions and beliefs. Of course, in order to perform intervention of this sort in an appropriate way, it is necessary to be familiar with what has so far been established about the specific difficulties experienced by students in this domain and about the way children's understanding of probability and combinatorics develops.

Reflecting on Research: Phases in the development of children's understanding of probability and combinatorics according to Piaget and Inhelder: Discussion

According to Piaget and Inhelder (1975), student development consists of three phases. During the first phase (usually up to the age of 7) the child fails to see the difference between necessary events and possible events. If one event takes place less frequently than another, children of this age are then likely to conclude that this event then ought to happen soon, regardless of its actual probability. They also do not realize, for example, that the probability of picking a white ball out of a box that contains one white and four black balls is the same as for a box that contains two white balls and eight black ones. They lack sufficient proportional reasoning inherent in problems of probability.

During the second phase (up to the age of 14) students become able to complete relatively simple assignments of the kind described above and they also acquire the necessary conceptual understanding of probability. However, they are unable to carry out rather more complex combinatorial reasoning required to work out theoretical probabilities. According to Piaget, they acquire this ability only later (after the age of 14), once they have reached the third and final phase of development.

Piaget's conclusions were part of his general theory of children's cognitive development, according to which a child passes through several stages, eventually reaching that of formal operations (usually between the ages of 11 and 15). Only at this stage, and even here not all at once, does a schoolchild become able to comprehend probability and combinatorics properly.

Not all scholars agree with these conclusions, though. Fischbein (1975), for example, has emphasized the role of instruction, noting, firstly, that even at the ultimate stage of formal operations combinatorial technique does not come spontaneously but only through appropriate instruction; and secondly, that with such instruction, the technique can actually be acquired even by children who are still at the lower stage of development—that of concrete operations.

And yet, regardless of the child's stage of development, instruction often seems to be harder in the case of probability and combinatorics than in the case of most other areas of mathematics.

Reflecting on Research: Intuition does not always lead to the correct answer: Some examples

Engel (1970) has argued that "we possess a natural geometric intuition but no probability intuition." It might, perhaps, be more accurate to say that our intuition, in fact, often deceives us when it comes to solving probability problems. Let us analyze a series of erroneous but quite typical answers that researchers have come across in studying the way people deal with probability problems (Kahneman & Tversky, 1972, 1973; Kahneman, Slovic, & Tversky, 1982; Shaughnessy, 1992).

> What is more probable—for a random man that one comes across to have a heart problem or for such a random man to be older than 70 and have a heart problem?

It is clear that the first case is more probable since by adding the age requirement in the second case we are inevitably reducing the number of favorable variants. Yet a considerable number of people answer this question incorrectly. Since it is well-established that the likelihood of having a heart-problem is greater for people who are over 70, solvers assume that the second event is more likely, failing to see how the question is actually structured. This is known as the *conjunction fallacy.*

> Which of the two sequences is more likely to occur when tossing a coin—HHHHHT or HTHTHT (H = heads, T = tails)?

Both these events are equally probable, and their probability is $\frac{1}{64}$. Yet many think that the probability of the latter event is greater since it seems to them that it corresponds better to the idea that both heads and tails ought to come up equally frequently, since there is generally a fifty-fifty chance that it would be one or the other. This is known as *representativeness*. In addition to a perception about frequency, people often associate randomness with probability, believing that a seemingly more random event (like a sequence of HHTHTTHHTTH) is more likely to occur than a seemingly less random event (like a sequence of HHHHHHTTTTT), despite both being equally likely. (While it is the case that there are more "random" appearing sequences of six heads and tails, when comparing two specific sequences this has no effect.)

> What is more probable—for heads to come up twice in three tosses or for it to come up twenty times in thirty tosses?

The exact calculation using Bernoulli's formula shows that the probability of the first event is $\frac{3}{8}$, while the probability of the second is

$$\binom{30}{20}\cdot\left(\frac{1}{2}\right)^{20}\left(\frac{1}{2}\right)^{10}.$$

It is easy to work out that the latter is less than 0.03, which means that the probability of the latter event is much smaller. This is quite natural: the probability of the number of heads deviating from exactly half the cases ought to decrease as the number of trials increases. Yet a considerable number of people assume that the probability in the above two instances is the same—by analogy with the equality

$$\frac{2}{3}=\frac{20}{30}.$$

One can cite many other similar examples and misconceptions (including positive and negative recency, the time-axis fallacy, and the availability and equiprobability biases). It could be said that in a number of cases the solvers simply do not seem to have grasped the condition properly, while in others (e.g., in the last of the above examples), they erroneously introduce their experience from a different part of mathematics. There are other possible explanations of the errors committed here (Kaheman & Tversky, 1972, 1973, 1982). In all such cases, however, the teacher is required to show students that their intuition has actually led them to an incorrect answer.

Using Errors in Developing Exploration Skills

We have already argued that it is actually very useful to use student errors as a stimulus for exploring the given situation and as a source of problems that then need to be solved. This seems to be especially important in the teaching of probability and combinatorics. A teacher should, in fact, not be afraid to use assignments packed with potential difficulties (studying "counterintuitive" problems of the kind outlined above is particularly useful). Such assignments should be given to students precisely in order to test their intuition. Fischbein (1987) stresses that it is important to show students as early as possible that it is common in mathematics to refute what at first appeared "obvious." Students themselves should be placed in the position of investigators testing their own intuition.

Examining *an* **Example**

Let us examine the following typical problem.

> A coin was tossed twice and both times it came up heads. What is more likely to occur if the coin is tossed for the third time—heads or tails?

A typical answer is that tails is now more likely, since both heads and tails should come up an equal number of times, yet heads has already come up twice. You can then propose to the class to discuss how best to test this answer. For example, one possibility would be to try and carry out an experiment: by doing, say, 50 series of three tosses (counting only those where heads comes up the first two times), and by analyzing the outcomes of the third toss, the students would be persuaded that their initial assumption that the third toss is more likely to be tails when the first two are heads is not confirmed by the experiment. This is known as *negative recency*, as well as by another common name, the *gambler's fallacy*.

At this point a teacher could move on to a series of "mental experiments": "Do you think that the probability of tails occurring in the third toss will change if we were to use a different coin? And what about if we replace the person tossing the coin? Do you think that the probability of heads or tails coming up will be influenced not only by what has happened with this coin beforehand, but also by what happens to another coin being tossed in the classroom next door?" Such discussion would help students realize that the outcome of the third toss does not depend on the outcome of the first two tosses. In what follows it can be clarified that the probability of heads coming up three times in a row is indeed lower than for this not to happen. It can then be pointed out that this assertion is actually quite different from the original assertion about the likelihood of heads turning up on the third toss.

Engaging students in this type of active investigation of concrete situations enables them to accumulate experience in working with probabilistic concepts and to develop certain schemata for dealing with them. This aids in the formation of an efficient probabilistic intuition, which in turn facilitates problem solving in the future (Fischbein & Gazit, 1984; Fischbein & Grossman, 1997).

Using Combinatorics

The difficulty of studying probabilistic material is increased by the fact that such study relies on knowledge and skills acquired in the study of other areas, starting with basic calculation skills. Most important is the students' acquaintance with combinatorics.

The ability to solve combinatorial problems, which arise naturally in many spheres of human activity, is important in and of itself. The way schoolchildren solve such problems has been researched from a variety of perspectives (Batanero et al., 1997; Fischbein & Grossman, 1997; English,

1991), though a practicing teacher usually can observe some common difficulties straightaway.

Episode from a lesson. "Four friends, Alex, Bill, Colin and David, are about to set off on a hiking trip. They have decided, however, that on the first day two of them should remain at the camp in order to set it up properly. How many combinations are there for choosing who will stay?"

The teacher has barely formulated the problem when students start shouting out answers: "eight", "No, four factorial", "No, four factorial times two factorial". Many different answers are given and even among them is the correct one, but this is hardly cause for joy, for it was obtained by the same kind of reasoning (or rather a lack of reasoning) as the other, incorrect solutions.

Where does this wild guessing come from? Combinatorial problems given in school are usually of the following kind—there are problems where one is asked to find the number of pairs made up of elements from two given sets, then there are problems in permutations, arrangements and combinations, and then finally, there are a few slightly more complex problems. Commonly, students are first given a range of general formulas and they then examine numerous examples of how these formulas can be applied. As a result, students regularly adopt the following strategy (even if no one is actually teaching it to them explicitly): "Figure out exactly what sort of problem it is and then apply the appropriate formula."

In the above problem two numbers are given: 4 and 2. Now, there are a number of combinatorial problems that are solved by means of multiplication, which would produce an answer of 8. The use of the factorial is also not infrequent in combinatorial problems, so students are often inclined to use it, without really considering what relation it bears to the problem itself. Similar to other areas of mathematics, where reliance on formulas does not generally produce good opportunities to learn mathematics, the teaching of combinatorics can be particularly prone to this sort of instruction given the power of these general formulas for solving problems.

Some typical errors. Such wild guessing is, of course, not the only cause of the students' errors. There are many other rather serious problems as well. Here is a list of some of the most typical ones (Batanero et al., 1997):

- Poor understanding of the condition of the problem and of what is actually being asked (for example, if the problem asks how many ways there are of distributing three different toys to three children, the student can reply that each child gets one toy).
- Misjudgment about whether the order of the objects is important to the solution or not (for example, in solving the problem of how many ways there are of choosing two children out of five, one of which

would get an orange and the other a pear, students can mistakenly decide that the problem requires them to determine the number of combinations, rather than the number of arrangements).

- Errors in counting objects, where certain elements are not being included (undercounting) or, on the contrary (overcounting), are included several times (for example, in solving the above problem about the four friends, a student can reason in the following way: "Let's say Alex is chosen first. Then one can select the second person in three different ways. The same is true for all the four friends. Hence the answer is: $4 \cdot 3 = 12$").

In addition, Wasserman (2013) discussed students' tendency toward a preferred vantage point on some problems, which can often lead students toward erroneous or much more difficult solutions.

Useful Tip!

Some Recommendations

These and other mistakes demonstrate the kinds of difficulties that are encountered in combinatorial reasoning. You should offset them by creating suitable conditions where students can practice and develop this sort of reasoning. Here are some recommendations:

- What needs to be addressed first and foremost is not the question of determining the final answer or of learning the appropriate rule, but of how to reason and what solution path to follow (it is especially important not to rush to impart to students general formulas for combinatorial problems).

- Types of reasoning required must be quite varied. Giving students ten more or less identical problems (e.g., in determining the number of permutations) in a row is hardly likely to develop their combinatorial thinking. Even if one then asks them to justify their reasoning, many of them are likely simply to repeat the reasoning from the previous problem without really considering if it is correct in that case as well. Slight changes in the formulation or context can help "refresh" the students' thought process.

- It is useful to give combinatorial problems as a series, where the same question is asked for sets that contain a different number of elements. The problem with only a few elements can then be solved simply by writing down all the possible variants, even without developing any sort of sophisticated strategy for calculating them. This, however, helps students understand better the condition of the problem and provides material and experience, which they can later refer to when solving similar, yet more complex, problems with a greater number of elements.

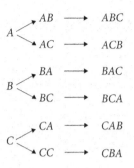

Figure 13.1

- When solving combinatorial problems it is good to make use of manipulatives that allow students to concretize their reasoning. Regardless of age, students generally find it easier, at least as a first step, to reason about a problem by examining the conditions on physical objects that can be arranged and re-arranged. Particularly important here is to teach students strategies for counting objects. For example, the use of tree diagrams where one systematically observes all the different variants that arise in a problem. (Figure 13.1 shows the tree for sorting out the different variants in the problem about how many ways there are of arranging three boys, A, B and C, in a sequence.)
- When solving combinatorial problems (and any other problems, of course) it is good to develop in students the necessary habit of self-control. Questions such as "Are all the objects (variants) accounted for?" or "Have some been counted several times, perhaps?" or "Would I consider these situations to be the same or different?" can at first be asked by the teacher, but eventually, they ought to become habitual to the students themselves.

Let us also further reiterate a key point already made above: work on overcoming difficulties and errors in the study of combinatorics and probability must be carried out systematically, patiently and over a lengthy period of time (one cannot hope for any quick-fixes here). The key to success lies in involving students in genuine problem solving—in investigation and discussion rather than in blind guesswork and the cramming of abstract formulas.

Discrete Mathematics from One School Year to the Next: Advice to Teachers

The NCTM (2000) formulates the Data analysis and Probability standard in the following way:

Instructional programs from prekindergarten through grade 12 should enable all students to:

- Formulate questions that can be addressed with data and collect, organize and display relevant data to answer them
- Select and use appropriate statistical methods to analyze data
- Develop and evaluate inferences and predictions that are based on data
- Understand and apply basic concepts of probability. (2000, p. 48)

In our modern world, we are constantly required to work with enormous quantities of data. This modern reality makes it important to develop in students the skills necessary to do such work. The range of methods available also gradually expand and some of these are accessible to students only in the final years of their school education; however, middle school students are already prepared to engage in a general discussion of the importance of collecting empirical data and representing it in particular ways.

Examining an Example | Examples of Assignments for Middle School

Encouraged by the teacher, students are perfectly capable of carrying out mini-investigations of, say, the daily schedule of their fellow students or their peers' views on certain issues. A teacher can begin such class activity by asking: "Someone has claimed that students your age spend a third of their day watching TV. Do you think this is true? Does this apply to your class? How can we check this?" The teacher can then discuss with students the design of such an investigation and its various limitations. Working in groups students can then carry it out and discuss the results they obtain in class. Next time, they should be able to conduct a similar investigation all on their own. The actual collection of data (as opposed to using already collected data) has been discussed as an important component of learning about data analysis and probability.

Opportunities for establishing connections. Problems in discrete mathematics often provide excellent opportunities for establishing connections between different areas of mathematics. For example, in order to represent some data obtained students might use a whole range of methods. They may use histograms and pie-charts, box-plots, two- and one-dimensional graphs, and so forth. On the one hand, using different means of representing results will permit students to see the usefulness of each of them. Next time they can take a more active position, i.e., not just use a method proposed to them, but actually select the one that appears to be the most persuasive and the most visually clear to them. On the other hand, it allows them to review areas of mathematics that they have already studied and to examine these from a different perspective.

| **Examining** *an* **Example** | **One More Sample Assignment** |

Table 13.1 depicts the scores of ten students on two different tests. (The maximum score on each test is 100 points).

Students can be asked to reflect on how this data can be represented graphically. For example, they could draw a graph, one coordinate of which would contain the results from the first test and the other from the second, and where the result of each student would correspond to a single point on the graph (Figure 13.2a). They could also draw a number line that would represent the differences between the results from the first and the second test for each student (Figure 13.2b). Alternately, students could construct

TABLE 13.1

Students in sequence	Score	
	Test #1	Test #2
1	80	95
2	90	100
3	100	100
4	60	80
5	40	50
6	75	60
7	85	90
8	30	50
9	100	95
10	95	95

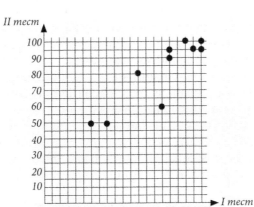

Figure 13.2a

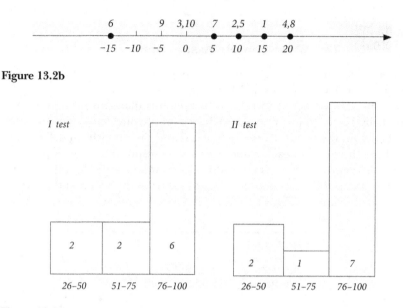

Figure 13.2b

Figure 13.2c

a histogram that would represent the share of students who have obtained a certain number of points (from 0 to 25, from 26 to 50, from 51 to 75 and from 76 to 100; Figure 13.2c). Many other options are possible as well.

Developing the Assignments for the High School Course

While not specifically about statistics, the context of working with statistical data can be used for discussing discrete mathematics. In particular, statistics and data analysis continues in high school where compiling surveys and conducting experiments reach a higher stage. Discussing how it is possible, for example, to determine the opinion of a group on some issue without interrogating all its members, but merely by selecting a representative sample, can demonstrate to students many aspects of discrete mathematics. Here arise questions of combinatorics (e.g., about the number of possible samples) as well as of probability (e.g., when can one consider the sample to be representative of the population as a whole).

The techniques for processing and inferring results can also be brought to a new level here. Students can, for example, be acquainted with statistical concepts such as the least-squares regression line and the correlation coefficient. Technology allows one to carry out comparatively simple calculations in such cases.

In high school, students' understanding of probability can also be developed further. Here students learn many more facts from the theory of probability, they utilize appropriate new terminology, and become able to use a variety of techniques with greater sophistication. If in middle school students are acquainted with the concept of probability itself, and learn how to determine the probability in comparatively simple cases and to carry out simulations of particular phenomena (with the use of technology, for example), then in high school students get to study some more complex theoretical concepts (e.g., conditional probability) and learn how to solve some much harder problems.

Helping Students Attain Maturity in the Understanding of Probabilistic Phenomena

Even more important, however, is the fact that in high school students are expected to reach a higher level of maturity in the understanding of probabilistic phenomena, ceasing to be affected by subjective beliefs and "emotions." Jones et al. (1997) have distinguished four levels in understanding the basic concepts of probabilistic theory. At the first level, the child predicts the most/least likely event based on subjective judgments, while at the fourth level the student systematically uses quantitative judgments and expresses probabilities numerically. Both in middle and high school the same class can include children who have reached different levels in their probabilistic understanding. A teacher can rarely afford to treat a class as a uniform body and not make any distinction in his/her approach toward different students. Both in middle and high school there are likely to be students who are still situated at the lower, more "subjective" levels. If the teacher's approach is carefully thought through, though, their progress can be quite rapid. However, if these students are not accorded sufficient attention, this development will simply not take place.

The practical conclusion one can draw from this is that when solving probabilistic problems, it is most important to devote enough attention to the initial stages that involve properly grasping the conditions of the problem and discussing a plan for solving it. This allows key difficulties experienced by students to manifest themselves early and it enables the teacher to tackle them in good time.

Applying Ideas of Discrete Mathematics in Different Parts of the Course: Some Examples

As has already been remarked, many parts of discrete mathematics are integrated into other areas of mathematics. Questions of probability, of combinatorics and of graph theory are interlinked and arise naturally in solving many different problems. The discussion of such questions substantially enriches the students' understanding by showing them how to apply discrete mathematics in a variety of areas and by requiring them always to keep this part of mathematics in mind, and not just deal with it in one or two chapters of the textbook and then forget about it. Here are some examples that illustrate ways to incorporate discrete mathematics across a variety of other topics:

How probable is...? Students frequently make errors when applying the properties of logarithms. For example, they mistakenly assume that the following equality is true: $\log_2(x+y)=\log_2 x+\log_2 y$. The cause of this error is understandable: the logarithm of the product of positive numbers equals the sum of their logarithms; also, a misconception of the "distributive" property may lead students to this conclusion. This mistake can, however, be used as a basis for an interesting and useful discussion. The discussion can be introduced by the following set of assignments.

- Give some numbers x and y, for which the equality $\log_2(x + y) = \log_2 x + \log_2 y$ would not be true.
- Can you give any two numbers x and y for which this equality would be true?

It is quite easy to provide answers to these questions. For example, numbers $x = y = 1$ are evidently the ones required in the first case, while the numbers $x = y = 2$ fit the second. However, one can then ask a harder question: what is the probability of one choosing positive integers x and y at random (such that neither is higher than 10) for the above equality to apply? It is not difficult to conclude that out of a hundred possible pairs, the only one for which the given equality applies is the pair $(2, 2)$, which means that the answer is $\frac{1}{100}$.

If there is enough time, even harder questions can be posed: what is the probability of choosing real numbers x and y at random (such that neither is higher than 10) for the above equality to apply? The answer to this question can include:

- A discussion of how one can determine probability where there is an infinite number of outcomes;
- A discussion of problems that incorporate geometrical probability and their solution (e.g., when selecting a point from a square, what the probability is of choosing a point from its upper half);
- A reformulation of the above problem as one that concerns the equation $x + y = xy$ where $0 < x \le 10$ and $0 < y \le 10$;
- A construction of a geometrical model—a square with a side length of 10 and a curve $y = \frac{x}{x-1}$ (Figure 13.3);
- Finding the answer that the probability, despite their being solutions that make it true, equals 0.

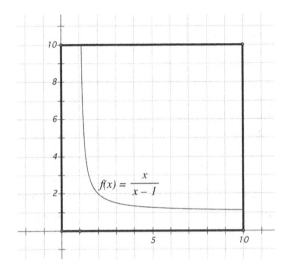

Figure 13.3

This problem is a good example of how a probability question can help tie together a number of different parts of the course, although the problem is clearly rather complex.

It is possible, however, to ask probability questions on far simpler material and not only in high school but also in middle school (Joyner et al., 2002). It is possible, in fact, to use literally any step in a lesson for this purpose ("We decided to examine this angle of the triangle, but we could also have examined this one. Which angle is more likely to be chosen if the selection is made at random? And in the case of an obtuse triangle, is it more likely that one would choose an obtuse or an acute angle?") Apart from being useful for the development of the students understanding of probability, such "spontaneous" questions also help form their understanding of mathematics as an area open to investigation.

Let's count, how many such objects are there... Questions in combinatorics also arise naturally while examining almost any sort of mathematical material. For example, in constructing the diagonal of some polygon, it is natural to show that a different diagonal could also be drawn. This in turn prompts one to ask the question of how many diagonals there are in a polygon. In fact, whenever pairs of elements are being compiled it is natural to ask about the number of such pairs. When writing down solutions in a sequence, it is natural to ask in how many different ways this can be done, and so forth. This sort of question can be put to students well before one starts with the "official" study of combinatorics.

Using graphs to make the subject matter clearer. Tree-graphs can also be used well before they are formally studied. Students can, for instance, be shown their application as a means of illustrating the notation of a particular algorithm. For example, Figure 13.4a depicts the algorithm for the solution of inequalities of the type $ax < 0$. We have already mentioned the use of tree-graphs in solving combinatorial problems. Graphs are also useful in working with certain terms and concepts. For example, Figure 13.4b represents a graph that may help students understand how different classes of parallelograms relate to one another. Sketches of this sort are frequently used since they are genuinely helpful to students' understanding. By introducing the term "graph," the teacher enables students to get accustomed to the concept and thereby prepares them for its future in-depth study.

Games—A profound concept that helps raise student interest. Some problems in discrete mathematics can be given as supplementary material to the main material studied, as a kind of workout for when students feel a little exhausted from the current lesson's work. Many interesting problems in discrete mathematics are commonly given as a form of entertainment,

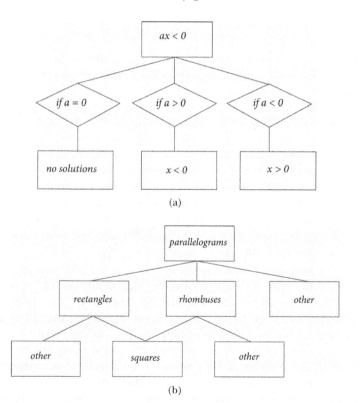

(a)

(b)

Figure 13.4

but they can also be used for serious study in mathematics. One example is certain types of games (concrete examples are given in the next section). Students can be asked to play the game and then discuss what would be the best strategy—i.e., what would be the algorithm for winning the game. The mathematical study of games is very important in today's world and a place ought to be found for it at school (if only in its most basic form).

Some Recommendations

To sum up, here are some recommendations for teachers:

Useful Tip!

- It is useful to understand discrete mathematics not so much as a distinct area that ought to be imparted to students simply in itself, but more as an opportunity to tie together various different parts of mathematics.
- Discrete mathematics gives plenty of opportunity for the students' own investigative work. Here there are plenty of situations where one is asked to generalize about or elaborate on what has been observed, backing this up by concrete experience. This area of mathematics also presents exceptional problem-posing opportunities for students (Sriraman & English, 2004). A teacher should try to use it in this way as much as possible, creating a suitable environment in class for this purpose, with his/her own conduct serving as a model of problem-posing activity.
- When studying discrete mathematics, genuine real-life situations should be used as frequently as possible (which is not that difficult at all! For example, how many different burgers could you order at Wendy's, given that burgers could have any of seven possible toppings?). At all levels, but particularly in middle school, one must avoid formalism, routine and the cramming of formulas. The framework of the "game" is far more appropriate. The study of discrete mathematics can and should be entertaining!
- When assessing students' work, the focus must not just (or not at all) be on someone's ability to obtain the correct numerical answer, but rather on their ability to carry out the appropriate reasoning and to select an adequate strategy. This approach to assessment should also be made clear to students.
- When studying discrete mathematics it is beneficial to use technology both to simulate processes and to process data. A teacher should therefore plan lessons in a way that incorporates the application of technology. Special attention should be paid to the types of student work, such as individual and group projects.

Reflection

Assignments and Topics for Discussion

1. Determine the probability of a "two" (double one) coming up three times if two dice are thrown a thousand times. Is it higher or lower than 0.00001?

2. How would you explain to a schoolchild that the expression "statistically impossible" is inappropriate?

3. Using the book *For All Practical Purposes* (2001), prepare a story that would involve some modern application of discrete mathematics. Could this material be used in high school? What about middle school? If so, how exactly?

4. Name some applications of discrete mathematics in your own daily life? What parts of discrete mathematics do you happen to use most often?

5. Using assignments found in the section "*Intuition does not always lead to the correct answer: some examples*" as a model, formulate some more questions that would "provoke" the kind of typical student misconceptions discussed there.

6. In a lottery, 6 numbers from 1 to 40 are drawn at random. Compare the probability of the following two series of numbers being drawn: 1, 2, 3, 4, 5, 6 and 2, 8, 19, 24, 31, 39. What do you think is the answer commonly given to this question and why?

7. Solve the following sequel to the problem about the four boys going on a hiking trip (discussed above in the analysis of how problems in combinatorics are solved): How many variants are there of selecting two boys remaining in camp in such a way that Alex and David are never together? Using this question as a model, formulate a few other such problems that would act as sequels to the original one.

8. Compile a series of combinatorial problems starting with a problem that students could solve simply by writing down all the possible variants.

9. Give an example of a combinatorial and a probabilistic problem that one could naturally give in the context of some typical school activity (e.g., the collection of homework assignments).

10. Give an example of an assignment in discrete mathematics in which it would be desirable to use technology. Give an example of another situation where technology can be used to demonstrate a phenomenon.

HOW TO SOLVE IT? A SELECTION OF PROBLEMS

Problems in discrete mathematics are often of an investigative nature and can be quite hard. In this section we shall limit ourselves to problems that demonstrate some important methods used in discrete mathematics, but that nonetheless may be accessible to middle and high school students of a higher level who are especially interested in the topic.

Example 1

A box contains pencils of different colors: 11 red ones, 9 blue and 8 green. Pencils are being taken out of the box in complete darkness. What is the minimum number of pencils that need to be taken out in order to ensure that: a) among those taken out there are four pencils of the same color; b) among those taken out there is at least one pencil of each color; and c) no less than 7 red pencils have been taken out?

Discussion and Solution

Problems like this (which can be of varying degrees of complexity) are useful as a way of developing students' skills for taking into account all the possible variants, and more generally, of creating a culture of reasoning (especially the strategy of working backwards).

a) Let us first examine the "wrong" situation (i.e., the one that we do not want to happen); namely, the situation where there are not four pencils of the same color. This is when there is a maximum of three pencils of each of the three colors (i.e., 9 in total). This means that if we were to take out 10 pencils there would inevitably be four pencils of at least one color. A rigorous proof of this assertion practically repeats the above reasoning. Let us assume the contrary—that it is possible to take 10 pencils, yet for there not to be four pencils of a single color. In that case there would have to be no more than 3 red, green and blue pencils each (i.e., 9 in total); which is a contradiction. This solution is an example of the so-called pigeonhole principle, according to which if there are n holes and $n + 1$ pigeons, then there is at least one hole that will contain at least two pigeons (cf. assignment 1 below).

b) Let us again start with the "wrong" variants. If we take out, say, 11 pencils, then it is not impossible that they could all be red. Even if we take out 20 pencils, it is still not impossible that there would be no green ones, because 11 of them could be red and 9 could be blue. Consequently, one must take out 21 pencils to be certain that there are pencils of all three colors (this is again easily proven by examining the contrary assumption).

c) Using the same line of reasoning as above, the answer is 24. Let us prove that by taking out 24 pencils we can be certain that there are 7 red ones among them. Let us assume that this is not the case, i.e., that there are no more than 6 red pencils. However, since there are no more than 9 blue and 8 green pencils, if there were only 6 red ones, we would have only 23 pencils. Since 24 pencils have been taken out we end up with a contradiction. (Note that in most cases it is unnecessary to demand this sort of rigorous proof from students.)

Example 2

At a party, there were 6 girls and an unknown number of boys. First, each girl gave a candy to each of the boys she knew. Then, each boy gave a candy to each girl he did not know. It is known that in this way 30 candies in total were given out. How many boys were there at the party?

Discussion and Solution

This playful problem could be given in middle or even in elementary school, yet even high school students might not find it that easy. The key is to understand what is being expressed by the number 30. (One could say that the solution to the problem is an example of using the heuristic strategy of adopting a different point of view.)

Let us examine any pair involving a boy and a girl. If the boy and the girl do not know each other then the boy gives the girl a candy, but if they do know each other then the girl gives the boy a candy. Either way, each pair corresponds to a single candy. This means that 30 is the number of pairs that can be formed in this way. Now, if there were n boys and 6 girls the number of pairs is $6n$. By solving the equation, $6n = 30$, we get the answer: there were 5 boys at the party.

Example 3

   A. There are 26 students in a class. Is it possible that 10 of them are friends with 3 other people in the class, 11 of them with 5 other people, and 5 of them with 4 other people?

   B. A state has 26 cities. Is it possible that that 10 of them are linked by airplane routes with 3 other cities, 11 of them with 5 other cities and 5 of them with 4 other cities?

Discussion and Solution

These two questions actually amount to the same problem. One could use the following reformulation: Is it possible to construct a graph with 26 vertices in such a way that 10 of them are connected by an edge with 3 others, 11 of them with 5 others and 5 of them with 4 others? What we are doing here is applying the heuristic strategy of drawing a picture. However, to draw such a graph is hardly a simple matter, for there are rather a lot of vertices to account for. It is perhaps rather more useful to adopt a different point of view instead and to try, without doing any sort of drawing, first to establish some of the properties of this kind of graph. For instance, how many edges is this graph meant to contain? From the first type of vertex there should come out three edges, from the second five and from the third four. It is clear that each edge links up two vertices. This means that the number $10 \cdot 3 + 11 \cdot 5 + 5 \cdot 4 = 105$ should be double the number of edges. However, this is impossible since a doubled whole number has to be even. We therefore reach the conclusion that it is impossible to draw such a graph. The answer to both questions in the above problem is therefore negative.

Example 4

How many five-digit numbers are there which contain the digits: 1, 1, 2, 3, 4?

Discussion and Solution
This is a typical multi-step combinatorial problem. It is essential to account for all the possibilities thoroughly. The construction of the five-digit number in question can be imagined in the following way. First, establish the two places that would contain the ones, then, in the remaining places one insert a 2, 3 and 4 in whichever order. It is clear that the number of ways to select two places from the five available is

$$\binom{5}{2} = \frac{5!}{2! \cdot 3!} = \frac{4 \cdot 5}{2} = 10.$$

On the other hand, there are $3! = 6$ different ways to position 2, 3 and 4 in sequence. It is clear that for each of the 10 ways of selecting the position of the ones there correspond 6 ways of filling the remaining places. Consequently, the number of possible five-digit numbers of this kind is $10 \cdot 6 = 60$. The answer is: 60. Notably, the solution to this problem about ordered digits involved both combinations (unordered) and permutations (ordered); in particular, it is important to reason about what is unordered in the selection of the two places for the ones digits, and ordered for the others.

Example 5

A teacher has 12 students in the class. She is going to split the students into four groups of 3 students. In how many different ways can she group the students?

Discussion and Solution

This question, too, is a multi-step combinatorial problem. In this problem it is essential to distinguish when the order of the objects is important—particularly, because the multiplication principle is based on counting *ordered* pairs. For being placed into groups, the order of the students does not matter. Therefore, the natural solution involves first selecting the three students in one group, (which can be done in

$$\binom{12}{3}$$

ways), then selecting the three students in another group—

$$\binom{9}{3} \text{ ways}$$

etc.—which leads to a solution of:

$$\binom{12}{3}\binom{9}{3}\binom{6}{3}\binom{3}{3}.$$

However, in this solution, while each group has been unordered, the multiplication of these combinations naturally creates an ordered quadruple, where group 1 is meaningfully different from group 2, etc. This would, in fact, not be the case in this classroom context (unless, say, every group was going to complete a different problem). Therefore, the complete solution needs to account for this overcounting; namely, the solution is:

$$\frac{\binom{12}{3}\binom{9}{3}\binom{6}{3}\binom{3}{3}}{4!}.$$

Example 6

The numbers from 1 to 15 are written out in a line. Two players take turns placing pluses and minuses between them. Once all the signs are inserted the sum total is calculated. If the total is even the first player wins, if it is odd the second wins. Who will win if both players play correctly and how should one play?

Discussion and Solution

This is a trick question. Middle school students can first be asked to play the game, and then to formulate their observations and justify their conclusions. Although it might at first glance appear that there are a vast number of possibilities here, it is actually not that difficult to account for all of them. The game is always won by the first player regardless of the way the game is played. There are eight odd numbers between 1 and 15. Since there is an even number of odd numbers they can be written with any sign in front of them yet the result will always be an even number. As for the even numbers the result will always be even regardless of how many there are or what sign is in front. The final result will therefore always be even.

Example 7

There are three cards in a bag. One of the cards has both sides green, another has both sides blue, and the third card has one green side and one blue side. Bob pulls a card out, and sees that the side is blue. What is the probability that the other side is also blue?

Discussion and Solution

This is an example of a problem that helps reveal some typical student misconceptions. Students often reason in the following way: "Since one has pulled out a card with a blue side then this must be either the card with two blue sides or the card with one blue and one green side. The first instance is favorable, while the second is not. The answer ought to be $\frac{1}{2}$."

This sort of reasoning is not much better than the humorous proof that the probability of coming across a dragon in the street is $\frac{1}{2}$, because the dragon will either be there or not: we have two outcomes, one of which is favorable. It is quite obvious, though, that this sort of reasoning is wrong –although there are two outcomes, they are not equally likely.

The above reasoning about the cards is just as problematic. Whether one has pulled out a card with two blue sides or with one blue and one green side is not equally probable. The former could actually have happened in two cases (because one could have pulled it out with either blue side as up). The second, however, could only have happened in one case. This means that the probability that one has pulled out the card with two blue sides is actually twice as great. This means that in the above case, out of all possible outcomes, actually $\frac{2}{3}$ are favorable ones. The answer is: $\frac{2}{3}$. Another way to reason is not about cards at all, but rather about blue sides. There are three (equally likely) possibilities for blue sides that Bob could be looking at, two of which have blue on the other side.

Example 8

Anna and Barbara are tourists. Anna is planning to get to a particular monument between 12:00 noon and 1:00 p.m. and to spend 10 minutes there. Barbara also wants to get to the monument sometimes between 12:00 noon and 1:00 p.m., but hopes to spend 20 minutes there. What is the likelihood that Anna and Barbara will meet at the monument?

Discussion and Solution

The heuristic strategy of drawing a picture is of use in solving this problem. It is a classical example of a problem that can be solved with the help of so-called geometrical probability. In order to draw a picture let us introduce the variables. Let us say that Anna reaches the monument at x minutes after noon and Barbara at y minutes after noon. It is clear that the inequalities $0 \le x \le 60$ and $0 \le y \le 60$ are true. Each pair of numbers x and y corresponds to a point in the square represented in Figure 13.5a. The time Anna leaves is then $x + 10$ minutes after noon; while the time Barbara leaves is $y + 20$ minutes after noon. One can now say that Anna and Barbara will meet at the monument if the numerical segments $[x, x + 10]$ and $[y, y + 20]$ have at least one common point. This is, of course, possible only if either the inequality $x \le y \le x + 10$ or $y \le x \le y + 20$ is fulfilled. Let us depict in Figure 13.5b the set of points of the given square with the coordinates x and y that satisfy these inequalities. It now remains to be observed that the probability that Anna and Barbara will meet can be defined as the probability of selecting at random a point from the shadowed region of the square in Figure 13.5b when a point from the square as a whole is being selected at

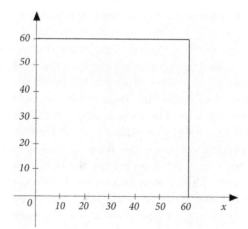

Figure 13.5a

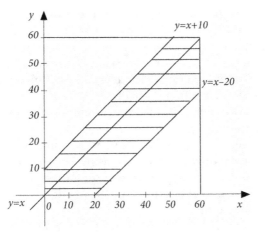

Figure 13.5b

random. This probability equals the ratio of the areas of the section in question and the square as a whole. Since the region that has not been selected comprises two triangles, with respective areas

$$\frac{50 \cdot 50}{2} = 1250 \text{ and } \frac{40 \cdot 40}{2} = 800,$$

then the area of the shadowed region equals $3600 - 1250 - 800 = 1550$, while the probability we were trying to establish equals

$$\frac{1550}{3600} = \frac{31}{72}.$$

The answer is: the probability that Anna and Barbara will meet at the monument is

$$\frac{31}{72}.$$

Assignments and Topics for Discussion

1. Prove the following general pigeonhole principle: if there are n holes and $kn + 1$ pigeons, then there is at least one hole which will have at least k pigeons. What exactly plays the role of the holes and the pigeons in example 1a on page 405?

2. Let a plane be painted in two colors. Prove that on it there will be two points of the same color 1 inch apart. Explain why the solution of this problem is an example of the pigeonhole principle.

3. The numbers 1, 2, 3, 4, 5, 6, 7, 8, 9 are divided into three groups. Prove that for at least one of these groups of numbers the product of its digits will not be lower than 72.

4. Think up a problem for which one would need to apply the pigeonhole principle.

5. Compile a few more problems of the type found in example 3 in the section "How to solve it". How arbitrarily can one select numbers for the above solution to apply? Generalizing these problems formulate a general assertion about the numbers of edges that come out of the vertices of a graph.

6. In a city there are five islands connected by bridges (in Figure 13.6. the islands are represented by circles and bridges by lines). Can one go round all the islands crossing each bridge only once? (The problem of this type for the Konigsberg bridges was first solved by Leonard Euler.)

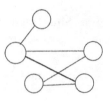

Figure 13.6

7. How many nine-digit numbers are there in the notation of which there would be three ones, two twos and one 3, 4, 5 and 6, respectively?

8. How many numbers greater than 3,000,000 can be formed by arranging the digits 1, 2, 2, 3, 6, 6, 6?

9. How many ways can you distribute amongst eight friends the following five gift cards, a $1, $2, $5, $10, and $20 gift card?

10. A Pizza store has 6 toppings to choose from (pepperoni, olives, sausage, ham, mushrooms, and anchovies). (a) How many ways are there to make a pizza with three different toppings? (b) How many ways are there to make a pizza with three toppings if double and triple toppings are allowed?

11. On the board there are 15 ones and 15 twos. A player's move consists of wiping out two numbers and then, if they were the same, writing down a two, and if they were different, writing down a one. If in the end a one remains, then the first player wins, if a two remains the

second player wins. Who will win if the game is played correctly and how should one play in order to win?

12. A student says that the probability of the total of "three" (a one and a two) coming up when two dice are thrown is $\frac{1}{11}$ because there are altogether 11 outcomes (2, 3, 4, ... and 12). Is this reasoning correct? Why? How would you explain the situation to the student? Another student says the probability of the total of "three" coming up when two dice are thrown is $1/21$ because there are altogether 21 outcomes $\{(1,1)\,(1,2)\,(1,3)\,(1,4)\,(1,5)\,(1,6)\,(2,2)\,(2,3)\,(2,4)\,(2,5)\,(2,6)$ $(3,3)\,(3,4)\,(3,5)\,(3,6)\,(4,4)\,(4,5)\,(4,6)\,(5,5)\,(5,6)\,(6,6)\}$, and only one results in a "three." Is this reasoning correct? Why? How would you explain the situation to the student?

13. The coefficients p and q of the equation $x^2 + px + q = 0$, where $|p| \le 10, |q| \le 10$, are selected at random. What is the probability that the equation will: (a) have solutions with different signs? (b) have real solutions?

14. You propose the following game. One takes a piece of paper and divides it into rows of congruent squares. A coin is then randomly dropped on it. If it touches or crosses any of the lines you lose. If it falls clear of any lines, you win. What should the relation be between the side of the square and the radius of the coin for you to be likely to win such a game?

15. Think up a problem that can be solved by the method used in example 7 in the section "How to solve it".

16. Monty Hall presents you with three doors, behind one of which is a prize. You choose one of the doors. No matter which door you choose, Monty will always open one of the other doors to reveal a goat. You, then, have the option to stick with your original choice or to switch to the unopened door. What should you do?

PLANNING A LESSON DEVOTED TO DISCRETE MATHEMATICS

This section will show how a student teacher, Sharon, planned lessons in combinatorics for middle and high school. Her plans reflect the discussion that took place at the student teachers' seminar and incorporated the observations and criticisms made by her fellow student teachers.

Preliminary Information

Sharon first taught in high school, then in middle school. It so happened that in both cases she was asked to teach units devoted to closely linked topics. In high school she taught the course entitled *Precalculus and Discrete mathematics*. She was allocated the unit devoted to combinatorics. Later on, in middle school, she was asked to teach the unit devoted to various concepts of discrete mathematics, including the introduction to combinatorics. Although the topics in both settings were evidently similar, the students were radically different. In high school the class consisted of 16–17-year-olds with high levels of motivation and interest in the subject. In middle school the students were 12–13 years of age and the class was in no way selective.

The High School Textbook

The high school textbook (which Sharon examined to start with) contained complex material, expounded in a rigorous and generalizing fashion. There was an entire chapter devoted to combinatorics, which included a systematic exposition of the counting principle, permutations, combinations and their properties, the binomial theorem and the Pascal triangle, and then, finally, combinations with repetitions and multinomial coefficients.

For some parts of the textbook, Sharon actually wanted to find some slightly more challenging problems than those given in the textbook. This was especially the case with the section devoted to the counting principle. The issue was not that the problems in the textbook were too simple, but that they were obviously merely illustrative. The dominant part of the textbook was theoretical. A certain method or rule would be explained and then only a few problems were given where this would be applied. Sharon thought that her class would be able to do much more, and also to get more out of it, if students engaged in independent investigations, one which would, of course, be based on the facts studied in class, but which at the same time would require more initiative from the students themselves. She also wanted to find problems where the solution would be more interesting and unusual than that of standard questions (e.g., how many ways there are to compile a restaurant menu out of three different dishes), which she thought were too familiar to students and which they tend to solve in a purely mechanical way (e.g., a few numbers are given, let's just multiply them).

Defining the Goal of the Lesson in High School

Sharon planned to teach a lesson that followed a study of the counting principle and that would be devoted to solving problems based on this topic. The main goal of the lesson was clear to her: *to engage students in the solving of meaningful problems, the solution of which would involve, but would not be exhausted by, the use of the counting principle.* Sharon wanted the problems to be interesting not just from the point of view of studying combinatorics, but also as a way of establishing connections between different parts of mathematics. She hoped to find a single problem, the solution of which would incorporate several stages, and where the students would be able to generalize themselves what has been studied and to formulate new questions.

Choosing the Main Problem to be Solved

Having examined different collections of problems, Sharon decided to use the following one.

> A circle is divided into p equal sectors (where p is a prime number). There are n different colors. The circle is to be painted (each sector in one color only) and can then be rotated. How many different color-patterns are there?

Accounting for all possibilities in this problem involves a number of difficulties. First of all one must distinguish between single-colored patterns and multi-colored (minimum two-colored) ones. It is obvious that there are n single-colored patterns in total and that it does not matter here whether the circle can be rotated or not. However, with multi-colored patterns there is a difference. If the circle is colored in a particular way, and then twisted by angles that are multiples of $\frac{2\pi}{p}$, a new pattern will be generated each time if the circle is understood as fixed. (Figure 13.7a represents a pattern where $n = 2$ and $p = 3$. Figure 13.7b shows patterns obtained when the original pattern is twisted.) If however the circle is said to be rotatable then such patterns are actually indistinguishable. In other words for each pattern of the rotatable circle there are p patterns of the fixed one. By using the counting principle one can then calculate that there are in total n^p patterns of the fixed circle. Out of these there are $n^p - n$ that are not single-colored. For a rotatable circle, on the other hand, there are p times fewer such patterns, i.e.,

$$\frac{n^p - n}{p}.$$

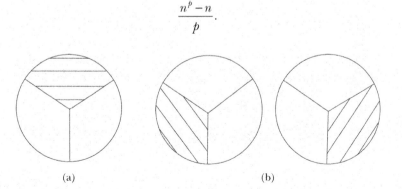

(a)   (b)

Figure 13.7

Consequently, in total the number of patterns of the rotatable circle is:

$$\frac{n^p - n}{p} + n.$$

This problem seemed interesting to Sharon because of the connections it has with other parts of mathematics, such as geometry and number theory (obtaining, in fact, in the same "sweep" that $n^p - n$ is always a multiple of p, which in number theory is called Fermat's Little Theorem).

Analyzing Difficulties Posed by a Problem and Reflecting on How to Simplify It

At the same time Sharon knew that the problem was extremely hard, even for her otherwise quite advanced class. A rigorous proof that by turning the circle by angles that are multiples of $\frac{2\pi}{p}$ there arise different patterns was clearly something her students were not able to deal with. There was also the danger that the students would actually completely ignore this possibility and would not attribute any significance to the fact that p is a prime number. There were many other potential difficulties as well.

Sharon therefore faced a typical pedagogical problem for a creative teacher—how to adapt an interesting but overly difficult problem so that the class would be able to both deal with it and benefit from it. Sharon went down the path of breaking the problem up into a series of simpler problems.

Formulating the Lesson's Objectives.

Sharon then formulated the following objectives.

- Students will be able to compile lists of possible variants of complex cases where the coincidence and the difference of variants is not obvious
- Students will be able to discuss possible generalizations of the problems they solve and also to pose further problems
- Students will be able to investigate a variety of geometrical objects
- Students will be able to see the connection between combinatorial reasoning and other areas of mathematics (in particular, number theory)

The High School Lesson Plan

As a result Sharon constructed the following plan.

Do Now (5 minutes)

The class would be given the following problem to work on individually: "In how many different ways can one color each of the pictures in

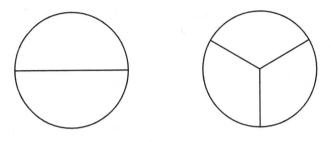

Figure 13.8

Figure 13.8. (each sector in one color only) using only two colors (not necessarily both of them)."

Discussion of the Solution and the Formulation of the Next Problem (5–7 minutes)

While discussing student answers Sharon hoped at some point to refer to the counting principle. Next she planned to ask how many different patterns there can be if the circles can be rotated. (Sharon anticipated that this question would actually be asked by the students themselves in the course of the discussion.) Finally, the intention was to discuss the solution for the case where the circle could be rotated, and where two colors and two sectors were used. The discussion was to be conducted simply by drawing all the possible variants on the board.

Group Work on a Variation of the Above Problem for Three Sectors and First Two and Then Three Colors (5 minutes)

This modified question (about rotatable circles with three sectors, using two and then three colors) was to be given to students working in small groups. Once they came up with the answer for two colors, the problem was to be made more complex by introducing the third color.

Discussion of the Solutions (3–5 minutes)

It was assumed that students would propose different ways of calculating the possible variants (for example, the problem with three colors could have been solved by first examining the cases where all three colors are used; and then simply referring to the already solved problem for two colors only).

Problem Posing (10 minutes)

Next, Sharon would ask students to formulate a few problems themselves based on what had already been done. She anticipated that students might develop the problem in the following directions:

- By increasing the number of colors $(4, 5, 6, \ldots n)$
- By increasing the number of sectors into which the circle is divided $(4, 5, 6, \ldots p)$
- By replacing the circle by another figure (e.g., square)
- By changing the nature of the geometrical transformation (e.g., the figure is not being rotated but reflected over an axis of symmetry)

Sharon expected that students would easily come up with the former two questions, while the latter two were likely to be harder to formulate.

Studying the Color-Patterns Involving Four Sectors and Two Colors (5 minutes)

The plan was to ask the question that would emerge from the solution of the case with three sectors: "Is it true that for four sectors one can reason in the same way—that there are $4^2 - 4$ multi-colored patterns for a fixed circle and 4 times fewer patterns for a circle that can be rotated?" Working in groups, students were to investigate this situation, reaching the conclusion that the given assertion is not true. (For example, there are not 4 rotational variants if the circle sectors are colored by alternating the two colors; i.e., Red, Green, Red, and Green.)

Studying the Color-Patterns Involving Five Sectors and First Two, Then Three Colors (5 minutes)

It was assumed that students would be persuaded (not particularly rigorously in the case of three colors) that the reasoning that turned out to be incorrect in the case of four sectors remains true in this case.

Teacher's Conclusion (5 minutes)

The plan was to sum up the discussion by writing out a general formula for p sectors where p is a prime number. The idea was then to draw the students' attention to the significance of this formula in number theory, which can be justified by combinatorial reasoning. The homework was to include problems involving the coloring of a rotating circle divided into six sectors using two colors, and also the coloring using two colors of a square divided into four quadrants, where color-patterns are considered different only if they do not coincide when reflected over a chosen axis $\overline{MN}$ (Figure 13.9).

The Difference of Middle School

When Sharon later had to teach in middle school, she saw immediately that the above material would be of little use. For instance, the general formula

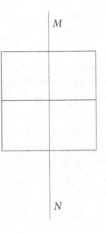

Figure 13.9

$$\frac{n^p - n}{p} + n,$$

which is perfectly understandable to high school students, means very little to students in middle school. The examination of different variants that high school students were likely to accomplish quickly, yet still with care, was likely to cause difficulties to middle school students, who would do it much more slowly and would probably commit errors by losing sight of some of the variants. The difference, of course, here was not so much in the students' knowledge and technical abilities but in their readiness to reason.

The Middle School Textbook

The textbook used in middle school contained a lot of different material. It included an introduction to histograms, pie charts and other means of graphing data; it discussed the concepts of mean, median and mode; it introduced the combinatorial counting principle; it discussed how to determine the probability of an event for a finite number of possible outcomes and also the solution of some probabilistic problems based on simple combinatorial reasoning. It was clear that the authors of the textbook saw its purpose not in getting students to assimilate specific knowledge, but in providing them with an opportunity to learn how to reason.

Defining the Goal of the Lesson in Middle School

Sharon planned a lesson that was to be devoted to solving problems using the counting principle. In the previous lesson students had learned about it and solved a few problems based on it. Despite all the differences between middle and high school, there actually was some similarity between Sharon's two plans. In middle school Sharon also thought that it was important to give students a variety of problems so that they could practice reasoning rather than just formally multiply a few numbers. The principal goal of the lesson could therefore be formulated in the following way: *to engage students in solving meaningful problems that require a conscious and thoughtful use of the counting principle.* How can one make the use of the counting principle consciously and thoughtfully? To achieve this Sharon felt that it was important to give students a wide range of situations and contexts, whereby it would be hard for students simply to repeat mechanically what they had already done earlier. In particular, Sharon thought it would be useful to use geometrical assignments resembling those she gave to high school students (though, what in one case was the first stage of the lesson, in the other was its outcome). Apart from that she planned to give problems that would require more than just applying the counting principle. Generally speaking, what she considered most important was not so much the use of the counting principle itself, but more the systematic and purposeful examination of all the possible variants.

Objectives of the Lesson

The accomplishment of the main goal of the lesson assumed the realization of the following concrete objectives:

- Students will be able to determine the number of possible variants in a variety of situations by using the counting principle and by rejecting some variants (e.g., by finding which variants coincide).
- Students will be able to see the connection between combinatorial reasoning and other parts of mathematics (geometry, in particular).
- Students will be able to get involved in discussing possible generalizations of the problems that they solve, and also in further problem posing.

The Middle School Lesson Plan

Sharon then constructed the following lesson plan.

Do Now (5 minutes).

Students were given the following problems.

- Your friend has a good collection of books at home. You decide to borrow one book on a historical topic and one adventure novel.

How many different choices do you have if your friend has 20 history books and 15 adventure novels?

- A box contains a lot of red, blue and green pencils. Nick and Peggy each take a pencil. How many possible ways of doing this are there?

Discussion of the Solution (7–10 minutes)

In the course of the discussion, Sharon planned to review the counting principle and to discuss its application in solving these problems. The intention was also to answer the following questions (as part of class discussion):

- How many ways are there of choosing the pencils in the above situation if it is known that Nick will not take a green pencil?
- How about if three people take a pencil from the box—how many ways are there then? And what if there are four people?

Group Work on the Assignment (10 minutes)

The plan was then to divide students into groups and give each group the following assignments.

Figure 13.10 depicts a rectangle made up of two cells.

Figure 13.10

- How many ways are there of inscribing a two-digit number in the rectangle (one digit in each cell) if one can only use the digits 3, 4 and 5 (though not necessarily only once)?
- How many ways are there of doing this so that one would not get a number divisible by 5?
- How many ways are there of coloring this rectangle using pencils of two different colors (so that each cell is colored in one color entirely, but where you do not necessarily have to use both colors)?
- The rectangle is cut out so that it can be rotated. How many different ways of coloring it are there now?

Each group is given a piece of paper containing a large number of pictures of such rectangles so that the students can write numbers in them or color them accordingly. The plan here was to make the questions clearer by letting students use pictorial examples.

Discussion and the Posing of New Problems (10 minutes)

After discussing the solutions, the last of which was to be accompanied by a demonstration using the pictures provided, Sharon planned to propose to students to ask some questions themselves, which would develop further what had been discussed up to that point. She anticipated that students are likely to develop the above problem in the following directions:

- By changing the dimensions of the rectangle (1×3, 1×4, 2×3)
- By enlarging the number of colors or by adding more digits
- By changing the conditions (e.g., so that the numbers would not be divisible by 3; or so that the numbers would not contain all the same digits, etc.)
- By replacing the rectangle with another geometrical figure

Sharon wanted this problem-posing exercise to take place in a relatively free way, allowing students to discuss their questions in groups beforehand, if they so wished. She also thought that it might even be possible to start discussing ways of solving some of these problems, stressing the role of the counting principle, though without necessarily reaching the solution itself. The idea was, however, to assign some of the proposed problems as part of their homework.

Group Work on the Assignment (10 minutes)

To finish off the lesson Sharon planned to ask students (divided into groups) to determine how many ways there are of coloring a circle that can be rotated, if the circle is divided into three equal sectors and if only two colors are used. Each group was to be given about 12–15 blank circles to experiment on.

Conclusion of the Lesson (5 minutes)

The plan was then to discuss the latter problem and again to draw the students' attention to the need for a systematic approach to accounting for all the variants. This was also the time to give and explain the homework assignment.

Discussion

The topics of the two lessons above were obviously related and the questions that, in Sharon's view, students were able to formulate themselves, were evidently similar. However, the search for an answer to these questions was not as easy for middle as for high school students. This is why the primary difference in the lessons was in the difficulty of the problems given in class. Furthermore, Sharon planned her lessons so that middle school students would have more time to study each problem through a direct, visual examination of specific examples (something that, of course, was not disallowed in high school either).

Yet, similar teaching methods were used in both lessons: they were built as a series of interconnected activities, starting off with assignments similar to the ones done in the previous lessons and then gradually moving on to new and more complex materials. As already mentioned, this aids the students' comprehension of the problem, teaches them to make generalizations and, finally, to ask new questions. Both lessons used material from different parts of mathematics, and in both cases the teacher used the device of "slightly" modifying the problem in order to undermine the automatism of simply applying a pre-learned rule.

Both lessons were to a large degree "open-ended," in the sense that they could have been developed in a variety of directions. For example, it is easy to imagine a situation where there would simply not have been enough time to solve the assignment at the end of the middle school lesson. At the same time, it is also easy to imagine the situation where the section devoted to formulating new problems would have been completed quicker than expected. As has already been argued, one should not be afraid of such open-endedness in lesson planning—it is simply unavoidable in lessons based on problem solving.

Sharon's high school lesson is also especially interesting as an example of the "simplification" of a complex problem. It is great if a teacher is able to use in class problems of the kind found in the second section of this chapter. But this is clearly not always possible. Nonetheless, the teacher can still consider making such difficult problems accessible to students. By examining the case with three and four sectors in the above lesson, students were able to understand the underlying idea of the problem and its principal difficulty, namely the coincidence of some of the color-patterns. The resulting formula was not, of course, proven in any sort of rigorous fashion, but it was sufficiently grounded. Demonstrating beautiful and interesting mathematics to students should be valued no less than teaching them some important rule.

In both middle and high school, when teaching both students who are genuinely keen on mathematics and those whose interest in the subject has still not been properly awakened, one can and should always seek out attractive and meaningful problems. It is precisely in the skill of finding such problems and presenting them to students in an adequate manner, engaging them in the proper process of reflection, where the mastery of the teacher truly lies.

Assignments and Topics for Discussion

1. Carry out a rigorous proof of the fact that when a circle divided into p (where p is a prime number) equal sectors painted in different colors is being rotated by angles that are multiples of $\frac{2\pi}{p}$, one gets exactly p different patterns of the fixed circle.
2. Write down your impressions of Sharon's two lessons. What did you like about them? What do you think ought to be done differently?
3. Compile some problems analogous to the ones used in the above lesson plans. In particular think up a problem that requires using the counting principle, the answer to which would be: (a) 3^7, (b) $3^7 - 1$.
4. How would you judge the effectiveness of Sharon's lessons?
5. Prepare one lesson plan for middle and one for high school devoted to the topic of permutations.

APPENDIX

RECOMMENDED WEB SITES

Sites Containing Useful References

ERIC
  www.eduref.org
Mathematics Education Directory
  http://dir.yahoo.com/Science/Mathematics/Education/
Mathematics Virtual Library
  http://www.math.fsu.edu/science/

*Sites of Professional Organizations of Mathematics Educators
and Non-Profit Mathematics Education Organizations*

Association of Mathematics Teacher Educators
  http://www.amte.net
International Group for the Psychology of Mathematics Education
  http://igpme.org
Mathematical Association of America
  www.maa.org
National Consortium for Specialized Schools of Math, Science
    and Technology
  www.ncsssmst.org

Mathematics in Middle and Secondary School, pages 425–427
Copyright © 2015 by Information Age Publishing

National Council of Mathematics Supervisors
www.ncsmonline.org
National Council of Teachers of Mathematics
www.nctm.org
The Consortium for Mathematics and Its Applications
http://www.comap.com

Sites Containing Mathematical Problems and Other Resources

Art of problem solving
http://www.artofproblemsolving.com/
Aunty Math: Fun Challenges for Kids (K–5)
http://www.aunty.math.com/
Cool Math (ages 13–adult)
http://www.coolmath.com/
Interactive Mathematics Miscellany and Puzzles (K–12)
http://www.cut-the-knot.com
Math Brain Teasers (Grades 38)
http://www.eduplace.com/math/brain/
Math Forum (K–12)
http://mathforum.org/
Math Word Problems for Children
http://www.mathstories.com/
MathsNet (UK)
http://www.MathsNet.net/
Mathwire
http://www.mathwire.com

Sites of Mathematics Competitions

American Mathematics Competitions
http://maa.org/math-competitions
American Regions Mathematics League (HS)
http://www.arml.com
High School Mathematical Contest in Modeling (HiMCM)
http://www.comap.com/highschool/contents/
The Mandelbrot Competition (HS)
http://www.mandelbrot.org/
MATHCOUNTS, National Society of Professional Engineers Information
Center (middle grades math competition)
http://www.mathcounts.org/

Math League (HS)
  http://www.mathleague.com/
Mathematical Olympiads for Elementary and Middle schools
  http://www.moems.org/

REFERENCES

American Statistical Association. (2007). Guidelines for assessment and instruction in statistics education (GAISE) PreK-12 Report. Alexandria, VA: Author.

Arnold, L.W., & Clifford, J. C. (1999). Characteristics of effective middle level teachers. *Education.* Chula Vista, *119*(4),734–736.

Arnol'd, V. I. (1998). Preface. In R. Graham, D. Knuth, & O. M. Patashnik. (Eds.), *Concrete Mathematics.* Mir.

Baker, D. P. (1997). Surviving TIMMS or everything you blissfully forgot about international comparisons. *Phi Delta Kappan, 79,* 295–300.

Balacheff, N. (1988). Aspects of proof in pupils' practice of school mathematics. In D. Pimm (Ed.), *Mathematics, teachers, and children* (pp. 216–238). London: Hodder and Stoughton.

Ball, D. L., & Thames, M. H., & Phelps, G. (2008). Content knowledge for teaching: What makes it special? *Journal of Teacher Education, 59*(5), 389–407.

Barber, H. (1932). Present opportunities in junior high school algebra. In *The teaching of algebra. The seventh yearbook of the national council of teachers of mathematics.* New York, NY: Teachers College, Columbia University.

Barnes, J. (1999). Creative writing in trigonometry. *Mathematics Teacher, 92*(60), 498–503.

Batanero, C., Nabarro-Plavo, V., & Godino, J. (1997). Effect of the implicit combinatorial model on combinatorial reasoning in secondary school pupils. *Educational Studies in Mathematics, 32,* 181–199.

Becker, J. P., & Jacob, B. (2000). The politics of California school mathematics: The anti-reform of 1997–99, *Phi Delta Kappan,* 529–537.

Mathematics in Middle and Secondary School, pages 429–443
Copyright © 2015 by Information Age Publishing
429

Becker J., & Shimada, S. (Eds.) (1997). *The open ended approach: A new proposal for teaching mathematics.* Reston, VA: National Council of Teachers of Mathematics.

Beckmann, C. E., Thompson, D. R., & Senk, S. L. (1999). Assessing students' understanding of functions in a graphing calculator environment. *School Science and Mathematics.* Bowling Green. *99*(8), 451–456.

Begle, E. (1979). *Critical variables in mathematics education.* Washington, DC: Mathematical Association of America and National Council of Teachers of Mathematics.

Bell, A., Swan, M., & Taylor, G. (1981). Choice of operation in verbal problems with decimal numbers. *Educational Studies in Mathematics, 12,* 399–420.

Bishop, A. J. (1980). Spatial abilities and mathematics achievements—A review. *Educational Studies in Mathematics, 11,* 257–269.

Bishop, A., Seah, W. T., & Chin, C. (2003). Values in mathematics teaching—The hidden persuaders? In A. J. Bishop, M. A. Clements, C. Keitel, J. Kilpatrick, F. K. S. Leung (Eds.), *Second international handbook of mathematics education* (pp. 717–766). Dordrecht/Boston/London: Kluwer Academic Publishers.

Black, P., Harrison, C., Lee, C., Marshall, B., & William, D. (2004). Working inside the black box: Assessment for learning in the classroom. *Phi Delta Kappan, 86,* 9–22.

Bloom, B (Ed.) (1956). *Taxonomy of educational objectives: The classification of educational goals.* New York, NY: D. McKay Co., Inc.

Bogart, K. (1991). The roles of finite and discrete mathematics in college and high school mathematics. In M. J. Kenney & C. R. Hirsch (Eds.), *Discrete mathematics across the curriculum, K-12. 1991 yearbook.* Reston: VA: NCTM, 78–86.

Boltyanski, V., Martini, H., & Soltan, P. (1997). *Excursions into combinatorial geometry.* New York : Springer.

Booth, L. R. (1988). Children's difficulties in beginning algebra. In *The ideas of algebra, K-12, 1988 yearbook of the national council of teachers of mathematics.* Reston, Virginia: NCTM.

Borasi, R. (1992). Algebraic explorations of the error $\frac{16}{64} = \frac{1}{4}$. In S. Brown, & M. Walter, (Eds.), *Problem posing: Reflections and applications* (pp. 159–163). Hillsdale, NJ: Hove and London: Lawrence Erlbaum Associates, Publishers.

Boulton-Lewis, G. M., Cooper, T. J., Atweh, B. Pillay, H., Wilss, H., & Mutch, S. (1997). The transition from arithmetic to algebra: A cognitive perspective. *Proceedings of the 21st conference of the international group for the psychology of mathematics education, 2,* 185–192.

Boyer, C. B. (1989). *A history of mathematics.* New York, NY: Wiley.

Bradis, V. M., Minkovskii, V. L., & Kharcheva, A. K. (1999). *Lapses in mathematical reasoning.* Mineola, NY: Dover.

Bressoud, D. M. (1999). The one-minute paper. In B. Gold, S. Z. Keith, & W. A. Marion (Eds.), *Assessment practices in undergraduate mathematics.* MAA, 87–88.

Brooks, J. G., & Brooks, M. G. (1993). *In search of understanding: The case for constructivist classroom.* Alexandria, VA: Association for Supervision and Curriculum Development.

Brousseau, G. (1984). The critical role of the didactical contract in the analysis and construction of situations in teaching and learning mathematics. In H.-G.

Steiner (Ed.) , *Theory of mathematics education* (pp. 110–119). Occasional paper 54. Bielefeld, Germany; IDM.

Brown, S. I. (2001). *Reconstructing school mathematics.* New York, NY: Peter Lang.

Brown, S. I., & Walter, M. I. (1990). *The art of problem posing.* Hillsdale, New Jersey, Hove and London: Lawrence Erlbaum Associates, Publishers.

Brumfield, C. (1973). Conventional approaches using synthetic Euclidean geometry. In K. Henderson (Ed.). *Geometry in the mathematics curriculum. Thirty-sixth yearbook* (pp. 369–380). Reston, VA: National Council of Teachers of Mathematics.

Bruner, J. S. (1966). *Toward a theory of instruction.* New York, NY: W.W. Norton.

Bulgakov, M. A. (1968). *Black snow: A theatrical novel.* New York, NY: Simon & Schuster.

Butt, T (1980). Posing problems properly. In S. Krulik & R. E. Reys (Eds.), *Problem solving in school mathematics. 1980 Yearbook* (pp. 23–33). Reston, VA: National Council of Teachers of Mathematics.

Byers, V., & Herscovisc, N. (1977). Understanding school mathematics. *Mathematics Teaching, 81,* 24–27.

Cangelosi, J. (1984). Increasing student engagement during questioning strategy sessions. *Mathematics Teacher,* 470–472.

Cardano, G. (1930). *The book of my life.* Translated from the Latin by Jean Stoner. New York, NY: E.P. Dutton & Co., Inc.

Carman, R. A. (1971). Mathematical mistakes. *Mathematics Teacher, 54,* 109–115.

Carpenter, T. P., Corbitt M. K., Kepner, H. S., Jr., Lindquist, M. M., & Reys, R. E. (1981). *Results from the second mathematics assessment of the National Assessment of the Educational Progress.* Reston, VA: National Council of Teachers of Mathematics.

Carpenter, T. P., Franke, M. L., & Levi, L. (2003). *Thinking mathematically: Integrating arithmetic and algebra in elementary school.* Portsmouth, NH: Heinemann.

Carroll, W. (1996). Mental computation of students in a reform-based mathematics curriculum. *School Science and Mathematics;* Bowling Green, *96*(6), 305–311.

Chazan, D. (1993). High school geometry students' justification for their views of empirical evidence and mathematical proof. *Educational Studies in Mathematics, 24,* 359–387.

Chazan, D., & Yerushalmy, M. (2003). On appreciating the cognitive complexity of school algebra research on algebra learning and directions of curricular change. In J. Kilpatrick, W. G. Martin, & D. Schifter (Eds.), *A research companion to companion to principles and standards for school mathematics* (pp. 123–135). Reston, Virginia: NCTM.

Chinnappan, M (1998). Schemas and mental models in geometry problem solving. *Educational Studies in Mathematics, 36,* 201–217.

Civil, M. (2000) Parents as learners and teachers of masthematics: towards a two-way dialogue. In. M. J. Schmidt & K. Safford-Ramus (Eds.), *Adults learning mathematics: A conversation between researchers and practitioners. Proceedings of ALM-7,* 173–177. Medford, MA, Tufts University.

Clarke, D. (2003a). *The structure of mathematics lessons in Australia.* Paper Presented at the symposium "Mathematics Lessons in Germany, Japan, the USA and

Australia: Structure in Diversity and Diversity in Structure". At the Annual Meeting of AERA.

Clarke, D. (2003b). International comparative research in mathematics education. In A. J. Bishop, M. A. Clements, C. Keitel, J. Kilpatrick, & F. K. S. Leung (Eds.), *Second international handbook of mathematics education* (pp. 141– 184). Dordrecht/Boston/London: Kluwer Academic Publishers.

Clements, D. H., & Battista, M. T. (1992). Geometry and spatial reasoning. In D. A. Grouws (Ed.), *Handbook of research on mathematics teaching and learning* (pp. 420–464). New York, NY: Macmillan.

Clement, J., Lochhead, J., & Monk G. (1981). Translation difficulties in learning mathematics. *American Mathematical Monthly, 88*, 286–290.

Conan Doyle, A. (1893). The adventure of the Musgrave ritual. London: *The Strand Magazine.* volume V,479–489.

Contreras, J. N. (2003) A problem-posing approach to specializing, generalizing, and extending problems with interactive geometry software. *Mathematics Teacher, 96*(4), 270–276.

Cook-Bax, J. E. (1996). *An investigation of the differential effects of Mira manipulative use on secondary students' development of geometric proofs involving perpendicular bisectors in polygons.* Unpublished doctoral dissertation. University of New Orleans.

Cooney, T. (1985). A beginning teacher's view of problem solving. *Journal for Research in Mathematics Education, 16*, 324–336.

Cooney, T., & Wiegel, H. (2003). Examining mathematics in mathematics teacher education. In J. Bishop, M. A. Clements, C. Keitel, J. Kilpatrick, & F. K. S. Leung (Eds.), *Second international handbook of mathematics education* (pp. 795– 822). Dordrecht/Boston/London: Kluwer Academic Publishers.

Coxeter, H. S. M. (1961). *Introduction to geometry.* New York, NY: Wiley.

Courant, R., & Robbins, H. (1996). *What is mathematics? An elementary approach to ideas and methods.* Oxford University Press.

De Bruxelles, S. (2001). Pupils sum up maths teachers as fat nerds. *Christian Science Monitor,* January 12.

Descartes, R. (1952). Rules for the direction of the mind. In *Great books of the western world* (Vol. 31). Chicago, IL: Encyclopedia Britannica, Inc.

deVilliers, M. (2006). Some pitfalls of dynamic geometry software. *Learning and Teaching Mathematics, 4*, 46–52.

Dewey, J. (1933). *How we think.* Boston, MA: D.C. Heath and company.

Dick, T. P., & Hollebrands, K. F. (Eds.) .(2011). *Focus in high school mathematics: Technology to support reasoning and sense making.* Reston, VA: NCTM.

Donoghue, E. (2003). Algebra and geometry textbooks in twentieth-century America. In G. M. A. Stanic & J. Kilpatrick, (Eds.), *A history of school mathematics* (pp. 329–398). Reston, VA: NCTM.

Dossey, J., McCrone, S., Giordano, F., & Weir, M. (2002). *Mathematics methods and modeling for today's mathematics classroom. A contemporary approach to teaching grades 7–12.* Brooks/Cole. Thompson Learning.

Dossey, J. A. (1991). Discrete mathematics: The math for our time. In M. J. Kenney, & C. R. Hirsch (Eds.), *Discrete mathematics across the curriculum, K-12. 1991 yearbook.* /Reston: VA: NCTM, 1–9.

Dubinsky, E (1993). Computers in teaching and learning discrete mathematics. In D. L. Ferguson (Ed.), *Advanced educational technologies for mathematics and science.* Berlin-New York, NY: Springer-Verlag.

Dumas, A. (1999). *The three musketeers.* New York, NY: Random House Inc.

Duncker, K. (1945). *On problem solving.* Psychological Monographs 58, No 5 (Whole # 270) Washington, DC: American Psychological Association.

Edgecomb, K. M. (1987). Graphing quadratic functions and inequalities. *Mathematics An Introduction to the History of Mathematics.Teacher, 80*(10), 545–546.

Engel, A. (1970). Teaching probability in intermediate grades. In L. Rade (Ed.), *The teaching of probability and statistics* (pp. 87–150). Stockholm: Almqvist and Wiksell.

English, L. (1991). Young children's combinatoric strategies. *Educational Studies in Mathematics, 22,* 451–474.

English, L., Cudmore, D., & Tilley, D. (1998). Problem posing and critiquing: How it can happen in your classroom. *Mathematics Teaching in the Middle School.* Reston, VA., *4*(2), 124–129.

Even, R. (1993). Subject-matter knowledge and pedagogical content knowledge: Prospective secondary teachers and the function concept. *Journal for Research in Mathematics Education, 24,* 94–116.

Eves, H. W. (1990). *An introduction to the history of Mathematics. With cultural connections by J. H. Eves.* Philadelphia: Saunders College Pub.

Eves, H. (1963). *A survey of geometry* (Vol. 1). Boston: Allyn and Bacon, Inc.

Fehr, H. F. (1973). Geometry as a secondary school subject. In K. Henderson (Ed.), *Geometry in the mathematics Curriculum. Thirty-sixth yearbook* (pp. 369–380). Reston, VA: National Council of Teachers of Mathematics.

Fernandez, C., Yoshida, M., & Stigler, J. W. (1992). Learning mathematics from classroom instruction: On relating lessons to pupil's interpretations. *Journal of the Learning Sciences, 2*(4), 333–365.

Fernandez, C., & Chokshi, S. (2002). A practical guide to translating lesson study for a U.S. setting. *Phi Delta Kappan, 84*(2), 128–134.

Ferrini-Mundy, J., Lappan, G., & Phillips, E. (1997). Experiences with patterning. *Teaching Children Mathematics.*

Fischbein, E. (1975). *The intuitive sources of probabilistic thinking in children.* Dordrecht, The Netherlands: Reidel.

Fischbein, E. (1987). *Intuition in science and mathematics.* Dordrecht, The Netherlands: Reidel.

Fischbein, E., & Gazit, A. (1984). Does the teaching of probability improve probabilistic intuitions? *Educational Studies in Mathematics, 15,* 1–24.

Fischbein, E., & Grossman, A. (1997). Schemata and intuitions in combinatorial reasoning. *Educational Studies in Mathematics, 34,* 27–47.

Fischbein, E., & Kedem, I. (1982). Proof and certitude in the development of mathematical thinking. In A. Vermandel (Ed.), *Proceedings of the sixth international conference for the psychology of mathematics education* (pp. 128–131). Antwerp, Belgium: Universitaire Instelling Antwerpen.

For All Practical Purposes. Mathematical Literacy in Today's World. (2001) / by CO-MAP. W.H. Freeman and Company.

Freudenthal, H (1982). Variables and functions. In G. Van Barneveld & H. Krabbendam (Eds.), *Proceedings of conference on functions* (pp. 7–20). Enshede, The Netherlands National Institute for Curriculum Development.

Fuys, D., Geddes, D., & Tischler. R. (1988). The van Hiele model of thinking in geometry among adolescents. *Journal for Research in Mathematics Education Monograph no. 3*. Reston, VA: National Council of Teachers of Mathematics.

Gage, J. (2002). Using the graphic calculator to form a learning environment for the early teaching of algebra. *The International Journal of Computer Algebra in Mathematics Education.* Hemel Hempstead, *9*(1), 3–27.

Galindo, E. (1998). Assessing justification and proof in geometry classes taught using dynamic software. *Mathematics Teacher, 91*(1), 76–82.

Garofalo, J., & Lester, F. (1985). Metacognition, cognitive monitoring, and mathematical performance. *Journal for Research in Mathematics Education, 16,* 163–176.

Gold, B., Keith, S., & Marion, W. (Eds.) (1999). *Assessment practices in undergraduate mathematics.* MAA.

Gough, P. B. (1997). Call off the horse race. *Phi Delta Kappan, 79,* 178.

Graham, R. L., Knuth, D. E., & Patashnik. O. (1994). *Concrete mathematics: A foundation for computer science.* Reading, Mass.: Addison-Wesley.

Greenes, C., & Rigol, G. (1992). The use of calculators on college board standardized tests. In J. T. Fey (Ed.), *Calculators in mathematics education, 1992 yearbook* (pp. 186–194). Reston, VA: National Council of Teachers of Mathematics.

Greer, B. (2001). Understanding probabilistic thinking: The legacy of Efraim Fischbein. *Educational Studies in Mathematics, 45,* 15–33.

Hadamard, J. (1945). *An essay on the psychology of invention in the mathematical field.* Princeton, NJ: Princeton University Press.

Hamley, H. R. (1934). *Relations and functional thinking in mathematics. The ninth yearbook of the national council of teachers of mathematics.* New York, NY: Teachers College, Columbia University.

Hansen, W. (1994). Using graphical misrepresentations to stimulate student interest. *Mathematics Teacher,* Reston, *87*(3), 202–205.

Harel, G., & Sowder, L. (1998). Students' proof schemes: Results from exploratory studies. In A. Schoenfeld, J. Kaput, & E. Dubinsky (Eds.), *Research in collegiate mathematics education III* (pp. 234–283). Providence, RI: American Mathematical Society.

Harvey, J. (1992). Mathematics testing with calculators: Ransoming the hostages. In T. A. Romberg (Ed.), *Mathematics assessment and evaluation: Imperatives for mathematics educators* (pp. 139–168). Albany: State University of New York Press.

Henderson, K. (1973). *Geometry in the mathematics curriculum. Thirty-sixth yearbook.* Reston, VA: National Council of Teachers of Mathematics.

Herbst, P. G. (2002a). Establishing a custom of proving in American school geometry: Evolution of the two-column proof in the early twentieth century. *Educational Studies in Mathematics, 49,* 283–312.

Herbst, P. G. (2002b). Engaging students in proving: A double bind on the teacher. *Journal for Research in Mathematics Education, 33*(3), 176–203.

Hershkowitz, R. (1990). Psychological aspects of learning geometry. In P. Nesher & J. Kilpatrick (Eds.), *Mathematics and cognition. A research synthesis by the international group for the psychology of mathematics education* (pp. 70–95). Cambridge: Cambridge University Press.

Holmes, A. (2000). Graphical determination of the behavior of wild and crazy functions. *Mathematics Teacher,* Reston, *93*(4), 328–329.

Hoyles, C., & Noss, R. (2003). What can digital technologies take from and bring to research in mathematics education? In A. Bishop, M. Clements, C. Keitel, J. Kilpatrick, & F. Leung, F. (Eds.), *Second international handbook of mathematics education* (pp. 323–350). Dordrecht/Boston/London: Kluwer Academic Publishers.

Hoyles, C., Küchemann, D., & Foxman, D. (2003). The role of proof in different geometry curricula. *Mathematics in School, 32*(4), 36–40.

Howson, G. (2005). "Meaning" and school mathematics. In J. Kilpatrick, C. Hoyles, O. Skovsmose, & P. Valero (Eds.), *Meaning in mathematics education* (pp. 17–38). Springer.

Jones, G. A., Langrall, C. W., Thornton, C. A., & Mogill, A. T. (1997). A framework for assessing and nurturing young children's thinking in probability. *Educational Studies in Mathematics, 32*, 101–125.

Joyner, J., & Reys, B. (2002). Providing opportunities to learn probability concepts. *Teaching Children Mathematics. 8*(8), 482–487.

Kahneman, D., & Tversky, A. (1972). Subjective probability: A judgment of representativeness. *Cognitive Psychology, 3*, 430–454.

Kahneman, D., & Tversky, A. (1973). Availability: A heuristic for judging frequency and probability. *Cognitive Psychology, 5*, 207–232.

Kahneman, D., Slovic, P., & Tversky, A. (1982). *Judgment under uncertainty: Heuristics and biases.* Cambridge: Cambridge University Press.

Kantowski, M. G. (1980). Some thoughts on teaching for problem solving. In S. Krulik & R. E. Reys (Eds.), *Problem solving in school mathematics* (pp. 195–203). *1980 yearbook.* Reston, VA: National Council of Teachers of Mathematics.

Karp, A. (2006). And now put aside your pens and calculators...: On mental problem solving in the high school mathematics lesson. *Focus on Learning Problems in Mathematics, 28*(1), 23–36.

Karp, A. (2007). "Once more about the quadratic trinomial...": On the formation of methodological skills. *Journal of Mathematics Teacher Education, 10*(4–6), 405–414.

Karp, A. (2008). Which problems do teachers consider beautiful? A comparative study. *For the Learning of Mathematics, 28*(1), 36–43.

Karp, A. (2010). Analyzing and attempting to overcome prospective teachers' difficulties during problem-solving instruction. *Journal of Mathematics Teacher Education, 13*(2), 121–139.

Karp, A., & Vogeli, B. R. (2002). Beautiful minds need able beholders. *NCSM Journal.*

Keitel, C., & Kilpatrick J. (1999). The rationality and irrationality of international comparative studies. chapter 16. In G. Kaiser, E. Luna, & I. Huntley (Eds.), *International comparisions in mathematics education* (pp. 241–256). London: Falmer Press.

Kelly, K. (2002). Lesson study: Can Japanese methods translate to U.S. schools? *Harvard Education Letter, 18*(3), 4–7.

Kenney, M. J. (1991). Preface. In M. J. Kenney & C. R. Hirsch (Eds.), *Discrete mathematics across the Curriculum, K–12. 1991 yearbook* (pp. VII–VIII). Reston: VA: NCTM.

Kieran, C. (1992). The learning and teaching of school algebra. In D. A. Grouws (Ed.), *Handbook of research on mathematics teaching and learning* (pp. 390–419). New York, NY: Macmillan.

Kilpatrick, J. (1978). Variables and methodologies in research on problem solving. In L. Hatfield (Ed.), *Mathematical problem solving*. Columbus, OH: ERIC, 7–20.

Kilpatrick, J. (1985) A retrospective account of the past twenty-five years of research on teaching mathematical problem solving. In E. A. Silver (Ed.), *Teaching and learning mathematical problem solving: Multiple research perspectives* (1–16). Hillsdale, NJ: Lawrence Erlbaum.

Klein, R., & Kertay, P. (2002). An introduction to simple linear equations: CASs with the TI-89. *Mathematics Teacher, 95*(8), 646–649.

Kogelman, S., & Warren, J. (1978). *Mind over math*. New York, NY: McGraw-Hill.

Kolb, D. (1984). *Experiential learning: Experience as the source of learning and development*. Englewood Cliffs, NJ: Prentice-Hall.

Korithoski, T. (1996). Finding quadratic equations for real-life situations *Mathematics Teacher, 89*(2), 154–157.

Krutetskii, V. A. (1976). *The psychology of mathematical abilities in schoolchildren* (J. Kilpatrick & I. Wirszup, Eds.; J. Teller, Trans.). Chicago: University of Chicago Press.

Kurchak, J., & Hajys, G. (1963). *Hungarian problem book* v.1. New York, NY: Random House.

Lagrange, J-B., Artigue, M., Laborde, C., & Trouche, L. (2003). Technology and mathematics education: A multidimensional overview of recent research and innovation. In A. Bishop, M. Clements, C. Keitel, J. Kilpatrick, & F. Leung (Eds.), *Second international handbook of mathematics education* (pp. 237–270). Dordrecht/Boston/London: Kluwer Academic Publishers.

Lange, G. (2002). An experience with interactive geometry software and conjecture writing. *Mathematics Teacher, 95*(5), 336–337.

Lawson, M. J., & Chinnappan, M. (2000). Knowledge connectedness in geometry problem solving. *Journal for Research in Mathematics Education, 31*(1), 26–43.

Leder, G., Pehkonen, E., & Törner, G. (Eds.) (2002). *Beliefs: A hidden variable in mathematics education?* Dordrecht/Boston/London: Kluwer Academic Publishers.

Lennes, N. J. (1932). The function concept in elementary algebra. In *The teaching of algebra. the seventh yearbook of the national council of teachers of mathematics* (pp. 52–73). New York, NY: Teachers College, Columbia University.

Lewis, C. (2002). *Lesson study: A handbook of teacher-led instructional change*. Philadelphia: Research for Better Schools.

Linchevski, L., & Livneh, D. (1999). Structure sense: The relationship between algebraic and numerical contexts. *Educational Studies in Mathematics, 40*, 173–196.

Lovinelli, R. (2000). Animating graphs. *Mathematics Teacher,* Reston, *93*(5), 408–411.

Lum, L. (1995). Precalculus explorations of function composition with a graphing calculator. *Mathematics Teacher,* Reston, *88*(9), 734.

Ma, L. (1999). *Knowing and teaching elementary mathematics: Teachers' understanding of fundamental mathematics in China and the United States.* Mahwah, NJ: Lawrence Erlbaum Associates.

Malone, T. W., & Lepper, M. R. (1987). Making learning fun: A taxonomy of intrinsic motivations for learning. In R. Snow & M. Farr (Eds.), *Aptitude, learning and Instruction. Vol. 3: Cognitive and affective process analyses,* (pp. 223–253). Mahwah, NJ: Lawrence Erlbaum Associates.

Manouchehri, A. (2001). A four-point instructional model. *Teaching children mathematics.* Reston, VA, *8*(3), 180–186.

Markovits, Z., Eylon, B.-S., & Bruckheimer, M. (1986). Functions today and yesterday. *For the Learning of Mathematics, 6*(2), 18–24.

Mathematical Models with Applications (2002). /COMAP. W.H. Freeman and Company.

Matz, M. (1982). Towards a process model for high school algebra errors. In D. Sleeman & J. S. Brown (Eds.), *Intelligent tutoring systems* (pp. 25–50). London: Academic Press.

McCoy, L. P. (1997). Algebra: Real-life investigations in a lab setting. *Mathematics Teaching in the Middle School.*

Merriam-Webster (2006). [electronic resource]. Springfield, Mass.: Merriam-Webster. http://www.m-w.com/

Merseth, K. (2003). *Windows on teaching math: Cases of middle and secondary classrooms.* New York, NY: Teachers College Press.

Meyerson, L. (1992). Mathematical mistakes. In S. Brown, & M. Walter. (Eds.), *Problem posing: Reflections and applications* (pp. 153–158). Hillsdale, New Jersey, Hove and London: Lawrence Erlbaum Associates, Publishers.

Mistretta, R. M. (2003). Intersecting and perpendicular lines: Activities to prevent misconceptions. *Mathematics Teaching in the Middle School,* 9(2), 84–91.

Moore, R. C. (1994). Making the transition to formal proof. *Educational Studies in Mathematics, 27,* 249–266.

Moritz, R. E. (1942). *Memorabilia mathematica: The philomath's quotation-book; 1140 anecdotes, aphorisms and passages by famous mathematicians, scientists & writers.* Washington, DC: Mathematical Association of America.

Movshovitz-Hadar, N. (1993). A constructive transition from linear to quadratic functions. *School Science and Mathematics, 93*(6), 288–298.

Moyer, P. S., & Bolyard, J. J. (2002). What are virtual manipulatives? *Teaching Children Mathematics, 8*(6), 372–377.

National Council of Teachers of Mathematics (2000). *Principles and Standards for School Mathematics.* Reston, VA: Author.

National Council of Teachers of Mathematics (1989). *Curriculum and Evaluation Standards for School Mathematics.* Reston, VA: Author.

Nemirovsky, R. (1993) *Symbolizing motion, flow, and contours: The experience of continuous change.* Unpublished doctoral dissertation. Harvard University.

Newell, A., & Simon, H. (1972). *Human problem solving.* Englewood Cliffs, NJ: Prentice Hall.

Nickson, M. (2000) *Teaching and learning mathematics. A teacher's guide to recent research.* London; New York, NY: Cassell.

Panasuk, R., Stone, W., & Todd, J. (2002). Lesson planning strategy for effective mathematics teaching. *Education.* Chula Vista. *122*(4), 808–829.

Parish, C. (1992). Inequalities, absolute values and logical connectives *Mathematics Teacher, 85*(9), 756–757.

Peck, D., & Jencks, S. (1988). Reality, arithmetic, algebra. *Journal of Mathematical Behavior, 7,* 85–91.

Perham, A. E., Perham, B. H., & Perham, F. L. (1997). Creating a learning environment for geometric reasoning. *Mathematics Teacher, 90*(7), 521–526, 542.

Piaget, J., & Inhelder, B. (1975). *The origin of the idea of chance in children* (L. Leake, Jr., P. Burrell, & H. D. Fishbein, trans.) New York, NY: Norton.

Piaget, J. (1952) *The origins of intelligence in children.* New York, NY: International Universities Press.

Piez, C. M., & Voxman, M. H. (1997). Multiple representations—Using different perspectives to form a clearer picture. *Mathematics Teacher, 90*(2), 164–166.

Pimm, D. (1987). *Speaking mathematically. Communication in mathematics classrooms.* London and New York, NY: Routledge.

Pollak H. O. (1970). Applications of mathematics. In Edward G. Begle (Ed.) *Mathematics education, The Sixty-Ninth Yearbook of the National Society for the Study of Education* (pp. 311–334). Chicago, IL: National Society for the Study of Education.

Pollak, H. O. (2003). Word problems: Bad, good, and whimsical—Activation through real world situation. In B. Vogeli & A. Karp (Eds.), *Activating mathematical talent* (pp. 57–65). Boston, MA: Houghton Mifflin and National Council of Supervisors of Mathematics.

Polya, G. (1973). *How to solve it.* Princeton, NJ: Princeton University Press.

Polya, G. (1981). *Mathematical discovery.* New York, NY: John Wiley & Sons.

Polya, G. (1954). *Mathematics and plausible reasoning; Vol. 1. Introduction and analogy in mathematics; Vol. 2. Patterns of plausible inference.* Princeton, NJ: Princeton University Press.

Polya, G., & Szego, G. (1976). *Problems and theorems in analysis.* Berlin, New York, NY: Springer.

Posamentier, A. S., & Krulik, S. (1998). *Problem solving strategies for efficient and elegant solutions: A resource for the mathematics teacher.* Thousand Oaks, CA: Corwin Press.

Posamentier, A., Smith, B., & Stepelman, J. (2006). *Teaching secondary mathematics: Techniques and enrichment units.* Upper Saddle River, NJ: Pearson Merrill Prentice Hall.

Price, J., & Ball, D. (1997). 'There's always another agenda': Marshalling resources for mathematics reform. *Journal of Curriculum Studies, 29*(6), 637–666.

Report on Applied Mathematics in the Undergraduate Curriculum (1972). In *A Compendium of CUPM Recommendations,* Washington, DC: Mathematical Association of America, vol. 2.

Resnick, L. B., & Glaser, R. (1976). Problem solving and intelligence. In L. B. Resnick (Ed.), *The nature of intelligence* (pp. 205–230). Hillsdale, NJ: Lawrence Erlbaum.

Reys, R. E. (2001). Curricular controversy in the math wars: A battle without winners. *Phi Delta Kappan, 83*(3), 255–258.

Reys, B., Reys, R., & Hope, J. (1993). Mental computation: A snapshot of second, fifth and seventh grade student performance. *School Science and Mathematics, 93*(6), 306–315.

Roebuck, K. (1997). A formula for factoring. *Mathematics Teacher, 90*(3), 206–207.

Romberg T. A., Fennema, E., & Carpenter, T. P. (1993). *Integrating research on the graphical representation of functions.* Hillsdale, N.J.: Lawrence Erlbaum Associates.

Rubinstein, R. (2001). Mental mathematics beyond the middle school: Why? What? How? *Mathematics Teacher, 94*(6), 442–446.

Russell, B. (1903). *Principles of mathematics.* Cambridge: University Press.

Saul, M. (2001). Algebra: What are we teaching? In A. Cuoco (Ed.), *Roles of representation in school mathematics. NCTM 63rd yearbook* (pp. 35–43). Reston, VA: National Council of Teachers of Mathematics.

Schmidt, W. H., McKnight, C. C., & Raizen, S. A. (1997). *A splintered vision: An investigation of U.S. science and mathematics education.* Dordrecht: Kluwer.

Schmidt, W. H. (1999). *Facing the consequences: Using TIMSS for a closer look at United States mathematics education* Dordrecht, Boston: Kluwer Academic Publishers.

Schoenfeld, A. (1985). *Mathematical problem solving.* New York, NY: Academic Press.

Schoenfeld, A. (1987). What's all the fuss about metacognition. In A. Schoenfeld (Ed.), *Cognitive science and mathematics education.* Mahwah, NJ: Lawrence Erlbaum Associates.

Schoenfeld, A. (1992). Learning to think mathematically: Problem solving, metacognition, and sense making in mathematics. In D. A. Grouws (Ed.), *Handbook of research on mathematics teaching and learning* (pp. 334–370). New York, NY: Macmillan.

Schoenfeld A., & Arcavi, A. (1988). On the meaning of variable. *Mathematics Teacher, 81*(6), 420–427.

Schneider, L. J. (2000). *The contest problem book VI: American high school mathematics examination.* Washington, DC: Mathematical Association of America.

Schoen, H. L., Fey, J. T., Hirsch, C. R., & Coxford, A. F. (1999). Issues and options in the math wars. *Phi Delta Kappan, 80*(6), 444–453.

Sharygin, I. F., & Ergangieva, L. N. (1995). Visible geometry [Nagliadnaya geometriya]. Moscow: MIROS.

Shaughnessy, M. (1992). Research in probability and statistics: Reflections and directions. In D. A. Grouws (Ed.), *Handbook of research on mathematics teaching and learning* (pp. 465–494). New York, NY: Macmillan.

Senk, S. (1989). Van Hiele levels and achievment in writing geometry proofs. *Journal for Research in Mathematics Education, 20*(3), 309–321.

Sfard, A. (1991). On the dual nature of mathematical conceptions: Reflections on processes and objects as different sides of the same coin. *Educational Studies in Mathematics, 22,* 1–36.

Shulman, L. S. (1986). Those who understand: Knowledge growth in teaching. *Educational Researcher, 15*(2), 4–14.

Silman, J. (1997). *Complete book of chess strategy: Grandmaster techniques from A to Z.* Siles Press.

Silver, E. (1990). Contributions of research to practice: Applying findings, methods and perspectives. In T. J. Cooney (Ed.), *Mathematics teaching and learning in the*

1990s: 1990 Yearbook of the NCTM. Reston, VA: National Council of Teachers of Mathematics, 1–11.

Silver, E., Kilpatrick, J., & Schlesinger, B. (1995). *Thinking through mathematics.* New York, NY: College Entrance Examination Board.

Silver, E., Mamona-Downs, J., Leung; S., & Kenney, P. (1996). Posing mathematical problems: An exploratory study. *Journal for Research in Mathematics Education, 27*(3), 293–309.

Sleep, L. (2012). The work of steering instruction toward the mathematical point: A decomposition of teaching practice. *American Educational Research Journal, 49*(5), 935–970.

Smith, J. P. (1973). *The effect of general versus specific heuristics in mathematical problem solving tasks.* Unpublished doctoral dissertation. Teachers College, Columbia University.

Sobel, M. A., & Maletsky, E. M. (1999). *Teaching mathematics. A sourcebook of aids, activities, and strategies.* Boston, MA: Allyn and Bacon.

Sowder, J. T. (1990). Mental computation and number sense. *Arithmetic Teacher, 37*(7), 18–20.

Spinoza, B. (1997). *Ethic: Demonstrated in geometrical order and divided into five parts.* Montana, US: Kessinger Pub. Co.

Sriraman, B., & English, L. (2004). Combinatorial mathematics: Research into practice. *Mathematics Teacher, 98*(3), 182–191.

Stanic, G., & Kilpatrick, J. (1989). Historical perspectives on problem solving in the mathematics curriculum. In R. Charles & E. Silver (Eds.), *The teaching and assessing of mathematical problem solving* (pp. 1–22). Reston, VA: National Council of Teachers of Mathematics.

Stanic, G. M. A., & Kilpatrick, J. (Eds.) (2003). *A history of school mathematics.* Reston, VA: NCTM.

Stanislavsky, K. (1976). *An Actor Prepares.* (E. R. Hapgood, trans). Intro. by John Gielgud. New York, NY: Theatre Arts Books.

Stein, M. K., Smith, M. S., Henningsen, M. A., & Silver, E. A. (2009). *Implementing standards-based mathematics instruction: A casebook for professional development* (2nd ed.). New York, NY: Teachers College Press.

Stiegler, J. W., Gonzales, P., Kawanaka, T., Knoll, S., & Serrano, A. (1999). *The TIMSS Videotape Classroom Study: Methods and Findings from an Exploratory Research Project on Eighth-Grade Mathematics Instruction in Germany, Japan, and the United States.* Washington, DC: National Center for Education Statistics.

Stigler, J. W., & Hiebert, J. (1999). *The teaching gap: best ideas from the world's teachers for improving education in the classroom.* New York, NY: The Free Press.

Stigler, J. W., & Stevenson, H. (1992). *The learning gap: Why our schools are failing and what we can learn from Japanese and Chinese education.* New York, NY: Summit Books.

Strutchens, M. E., Harris, K. A., & Martin, W. G. (2001). Assessing geometric and measurement understanding using manipulatives. *Mathematics Teaching in the Middle School, 6*(7), 402–405.

Swan, M. (2002). *Learning mathematics through discussion and reflection. Algebra at GCSE.* School of Education. The University of Nottingham.

Takacis, L. (1962). *Introduction to the theory of queues.* New York, NY: Oxford University Press.

Tall, (1992). The transition to advanced mathematical thinking: Functions, limits, infinity and proof. In D. A. Grouws (Ed.), *Handbook of research on mathematics teaching and learning* (pp. 495–511). New York, NY: Macmillan.

Thorndike, E. L. (1921) *The new methods in arithmetic.* New York, NY: Rand McNally & Company.

Tsamir, P., & Almog, N. (2001). Students' strategies and difficulties: The case of algebraic inequalities. *International Journal of Mathematical Education in Science and Technology, 32*(4), 513–524.

Twain, Mark (1991). *The adventures of Tom Sawyer.* Philadephia: Courage Books.

Twain, Mark (1992). *The celebrated jumping frog, and other stories.* Pleasantville, NY: Reader's Digest Association.

Usiskin, Z. (1987). Resolving the Continuing Dilemmas in School Geometry. In M. M. Lindquist, & A. P. Shutle (Eds.), *Learning and teaching geometry, K–12. 1987 yearbook* (pp. 17–31). Reston, VA: National Council of Teachers of Mathematics.

Usiskin, Z. (1988). Conceptions of school algebra and uses of variables. In *The ideas of algebra, K–12, 1988 Yearbook of the National Council of Teachers of Mathematics.*

Usiskin, Z. (1995). What should *not* be in the algebra and geometry curriculum of average college-bound students. *Mathematics Teacher, 88,* 156–164.

Usiskin, Z. (1997). The implications of "geometry for all". *NCSM Journal,* October.

Usiskin, Z., Peressini, A., Marchiotto, E. A., & Stanley, D. (2003). *Mathematics for high school teachers.* An Advanced Perspective. Upper Saddle River, NJ: Prentice Hall.

Young, S., & Shaw, D. G. (1999). Profiles of effective college and university teachers. *The Journal of Higher Education.* Columbus, *70*(6), 670–686.

Yoshida, M., Fernandez, C., & Stigler, J. W. (1993). Japanese and American students' differential recognition memory for teachers' statements during a mathematics lesson. *Journal of Educational Psychology, 85,* 610–617.

van der Waerden, B. L. (1950). *Modern algebra.* New York, NY: F. Ungar.

van der Waerden, B. L. (1961). *Science awakening.* New York, NY: Oxford University Press.

Van Doren, C. (1965). *Benjamin Franklin.* New York, NY: The Viking Press.

Van Dormolen, J., & Arcavi, A. (2000). What is a circle? *Mathematics in School,* November, 15–19.

Van Dyke, F. (2003). Using graphs to introduce functions. *Mathematics Teacher, 96*(2), 126–137.

van Hiele, P. M. (1959). Development and learning process. *Acta Paedagogica Utrajecthina,* 17.

van Hiele, P. M. (1986). *Structure and insight.* Orlando: Academic Press.

Verstappen, P. (1982). Some reflections on the introduction of relations and functions. In G. Van Barneveld & H. Krabbendam (Eds.), *Proceedings of conference on functions* (pp. 166–184). Enshede, The Netherlands National Institute for Curriculum Development.

Vogeli, B. R. (1997). *Special secondary schools for the mathematically and scientifically talented. An international panorama.* New York, NY: Teachers College Columbia University.

Vygotsky, L. S. (1971). *The psychology of art.* Cambridge, Mass., M.I.T. Press.

Vygotsky, L. S. (1982). *Collected works,* volume 2. (In Russian) Moscow: Pedagogika.

Vygotsky, L. (1986). *Thought and language.* Cambridge, Mass.: MIT Press.

Wagner, S. (1981). Conservation of equation and function under transformation of variable. *Journal for Research in Mathematics Education, 12,* 107–118.

Wasserman, N. (2013). Exploring teachers' categorizations for and conceptions of combinatorial problems. In S. Reeder & G. Matney (Eds.), *Research council on learning mathematics (RCML) conference proceedings* (pp. 145–154). Tulsa, OK: RCML.

Wasserman, N. (2014a). Introducing algebraic structures through solving equations: Vertical content knowledge for K–12 mathematics teachers. *PRIMUS, 24*(3), 191–214.

Wasserman, N. (2014b). Bringing dynamic geometry to three dimensions: The use of SketchUp in mathematics education. In D. Polly (Ed.), *Cases on technology and common core mathematics standards* (pp. 68–99). Hershey, PA: IGI-Global.

Wasserman, N., & Arkan, I. (2011). Technology tips: An Archimedean walk. *Mathematics Teacher, 104*(9), pp. 710–715.

Watson, A., & Mason, J. (2005). *Mathematics as a constructive activity. Learners Generating examples.* Mahwah, NJ—London: Lawrence Erlbaum Associates, Publishers.

Webb, L., & Carry, L. (1975). Interaction of spatial visualization and general reasoning abilities with instructional treatment in quadratic inequalities: A follow-up study. *Journal for Research in Mathematics Education, 6*(3), 132–141.

Webster's (1979). *New universal unabridged dictionary.* (2nd ed.) New York, NY: Simon & Schuster.

Wertheimer, M. (1959). *Productive thinking.* New York, NY: Harper and Row.

Wickelgren, W. (1974). *How to solve problems.* San Francisco, CA: W.H. Freeman and Company.

Wilien, W. (1986). *Questioning skills, for teachers.* Washington, DC: National Education Association.

Willoughby, S. (1997). Functions from Kindergarten through Sixth Grade *Teaching Children Mathematics, 3,* 314–318.

Wilson, L., Andrew, C., & Sourikova, S. (2001). Lesson shape and structure in Primary Mathematics lessons: A comparative study in the North East of England and St. Petersburg, Russia: some implications for the daily mathematics lesson. *British Educational Research Journal, 27*(1), 29–58.

Wong, M. P. H. (1997). Numbers versus letters in algebraic manipulations: which is more difficult? *Proceedings of the 21st Conference of the International Group for the Psychology of Mathematics Education, 4,* 285–290.

Woods, P. (1996). *Researching the art of teaching. Etnography for educational use.* London and New York, NY: Routledge.

Wu, H. (1997). The mathematics education reform: Why you should be concerned and what you can do. *American Mathematical Monthly, 104*(10), 946–954.

Zaslavsky, O. (1997). Conceptual obstacles in the learning of quadratic functions. *Focus on Learning Problems in Mathematics, 19*(1), 20–44.

Zheng, T. (2002). Do mathematics with interactive geometry software. *Mathematics Teacher, 95*(7), 492–497.

CPSIA information can be obtained at www.ICGtesting.com
Printed in the USA
LVOW04s2024100415

434169LV00005B/14/P

4843020